June 22–24, 2016
Chicago, Il, USA

I0053635

Association for Computing Machinery

Advancing Computing as a Science & Profession

TVX'16
Proceedings of the ACM International Conference on
Interactive Experiences for TV and Online Video

Sponsored by:
ACM SIGCHI

In Cooperation with:
ACM SIGMM and ACM SIGWEB

Supported by:
SAMSUNG, proto.10, LUSO-AMERICAM DEVELOPMENT foundation, FX PAL, IIT, and Georgia Tech

**Association for
Computing Machinery**

Advancing Computing as a Science & Profession

The Association for Computing Machinery
2 Penn Plaza, Suite 701
New York, New York 10121-0701

Copyright © 2016 by the Association for Computing Machinery, Inc. (ACM). Permission to make digital or hard copies of portions of this work for personal or classroom use is granted without fee provided that copies are not made or distributed for profit or commercial advantage and that copies bear this notice and the full citation on the first page. Copyright for components of this work owned by others than ACM must be honored. Abstracting with credit is permitted. To copy otherwise, to republish, to post on servers or to redistribute to lists, requires prior specific permission and/or a fee. Request permission to republish from: permissions@acm.org or Fax +1 (212) 869-0481.

For other copying of articles that carry a code at the bottom of the first or last page, copying is permitted provided that the per-copy fee indicated in the code is paid through www.copyright.com.

Notice to Past Authors of ACM-Published Articles
ACM intends to create a complete electronic archive of all articles and/or other material previously published by ACM. If you have written a work that has been previously published by ACM in any journal or conference proceedings prior to 1978, or any SIG Newsletter at any time, and you do NOT want this work to appear in the ACM Digital Library, please inform permissions@acm.org, stating the title of the work, the author(s), and where and when published.

ISBN: 978-1-4503-4067-0 (Digital)

ISBN: 978-1-4503-4603-0 (Print)

Additional copies may be ordered prepaid from:

ACM Order Department
PO Box 30777
New York, NY 10087-0777, USA

Phone: 1-800-342-6626 (USA and Canada)
+1-212-626-0500 (Global)
Fax: +1-212-944-1318
E-mail: acmhelp@acm.org
Hours of Operation: 8:30 am – 4:30 pm ET

Printed in the USA

Welcome from the General Chairs

At IIT Institute of Design (ID), we are excited to bring the International Conference on Interactive TV and Online Video (ACM TVX2016) to Chicago, USA. We love this opportunity to connect the great academic and industry institutions of our region with world-class researchers in multi-disciplinary aspects of Interactive Media Systems. We believe that a number of companies and academic institutions of USA would benefit from exposure to this collection of research papers and industry talks. In this era of curved televisions, large screen smartphones, the Internet of Things, and data in "the cloud," there are many new opportunities for interactions and immersion in rich media and social life around it.

IIT Institute of Design's (ID's) role as a pioneer is to constantly usher in new opportunities. Our school has been an advocate in the development and dissemination of modern design right from its founding in 1937 as the New Bauhaus. In the 1960s, ID became a center of the first design methods movement, developing tools for structured planning—among the first applications of computers to design. In the early 1990s, ID helped pioneer the human-centered approach to design, applying ethnography and other social science research methods to the design process. In the early 2000s, ID helped launch the design thinking movement, linking design more closely to business innovation. Our school also has a long history and interest in Photography, and Design of rich media experiences for people.

This year's conference is the 3rd annual gathering of researchers and industry people and first ever to be held in USA. This conference builds on the success of previous conferences held in Brussels and Newcastle on Tyne. During the past decade, this conference has been known as EuroiTV and has been held in various European cities including Berlin, Leuven, Lisbon, Tampere, Salzburg etc. The iTV research community has conducted rigorous inquiries into the roles of various disciplines including design, psychology, sociology, and technology to create iTV and online video systems that support meaningful engagement and immersion in media. This year the conference continues to maintains its high-quality by using double blind peer reviews.

This conference would not be possible without the practical and financial support from different supporters. First of all, we would like to thank you for registering for and attending the conference, as you are an important part of our community and make these events possible. We would also like to thank all members of the organizing committee, who have been working very hard during more than a year to prepare the conference. Finally, we want to thank our sponsors, **ACM SIGCHI, ACM SIGWEB** and **ACM SIGMM** and our generous corporate supporter **SAMSUNG** who provided the much welcomed support for making this conference an enjoyable experience. Additionally, we also would like to thank our associate event presenters who helped bring this conference to you: Proto.io, Luso-American Foundation and FX PAL.

We wish you have a great conference and hope that you will enjoy your stay in Chicago!

Santosh Basapur
ACM TVX2016 General Chair
IIT Institute of Design
Chicago USA

Patrick Whitney
ACM TVX2016 General Chair
IIT Institute of Design
Chicago USA

Janet Murray
ACM TVX2016 General Chair
Ivan Allen College of Liberal Arts
Georgia Institute of Technology
Atlanta USA

Welcome from the Program Chairs

We are very pleased to present an exciting program for ACM TVX 2016, which has been put together based on many submissions from all over the world.

As the leading international conference for presentation and discussion of research into interactive experiences for online video and TV, the conference brings together international researchers and practitioners from a wide range of disciplines, ranging from human-computer interaction, multimedia engineering and design to media studies, media psychology and sociology, to present and discuss the latest insights in the field. ACM TVX 2016 presents research on new interaction technologies and techniques, experience design and evaluation, connected living rooms, and second screen interactions.

The call for papers attracted submissions from Asia, Europe, and the United States. Thirty eight full and short papers were submitted and subjected to a thorough double-blind review process. Each paper was assigned to an Associate Chair (AC) who recruited at least three reviewers per paper and wrote a meta-review summarizing the main points of each review. During the Program Committee meeting on March 21 - 22, 2016, in Chicago, IL, USA, each paper was discussed in depth and the final decision of which papers to accept was made, resulting in a high-quality program of 12 accepted full and short papers and an acceptance rate of 33%. Work in Progress papers were also reviewed by at least 2 reviewers per paper, of which 8 were accepted and will be presented as a poster during the conference. Full papers, short papers and Works in Progress are part of the main proceedings and will be included in the ACM Digital Library.

In addition to these submissions, there were several other categories that received submissions, resulting in 4 workshops, 3 courses, 5 Doctoral Consortium papers, 6 TVX in Industry presentations, and 6 demos, which are all made available in the adjunct proceedings.

Finally, we also encourage attendees to attend the keynote: *"We are the [virtual] 99%": Bringing the Promise of Live Digital Interaction to All the Peoples*, presented by Tawny Schlieski of Intel Corporation.

Putting together the program of ACM TVX2016 was a team effort. We would therefore like to thank the authors for providing the content of the program, the reviewers who worked very hard in reviewing papers and providing feedback for authors, and the ACs who managed the whole review process for each paper.

We hope that you will find this program interesting and thought-provoking and that the conference will provide you with a valuable opportunity to share ideas with other researchers and practitioners from institutions around the world.

Noor Ali-Hasan
ACM TVX2016 Program Chair,
Google (USA)

Jochen Huber
ACM TVX2016 Program Chair,
Synaptics Inc. (Switzerland)

Table of Contents

TVX 2016 Organization..vii

TVX 2016 Sponsors & Supporters...ix

Keynote

- "We are the [virtual] 99%": Bringing the Promise of Live Digital Interaction
  to All the Peoples..1
  Tawny Schlieski *(Oregon Story Board & Intel Corporation)*

Session I: Smart TVs and Input

- Uncovering the Underlying Factors of Smart TV UX over Time: A Multi-study,
  Mixed-method Approach..3
  Jincheul Jang, Dapeng Zhao, Woneui Hong, Youkyoung Park, Mun Yong Yi
  (Korea Advanced Institute of Science and Technology)

- Design Guidelines for Notifications on Smart TVs..13
  Dominik Weber, Sven Mayer, Alexandra Voit, Rodrigo Ventura Fierro, Niels Henze *(University of Stuttgart)*

- Who Has the Force? Solving Conflicts for Multi User Mid-Air Gestures for TVs 25
  Katrin Plaumann, David Lehr, Enrico Rukzio *(Ulm University)*

Session II. Live Events and Connected Living Rooms

- Rivulet: Exploring Participation in Live Events through Multi-Stream Experiences 31
  William A. Hamilton *(Microsoft Research & Texas A&M University)*,
  John C. Tang, Gina Venolia, Kori Inkpen *(Microsoft Research)*,
  Jakob Zillner *(Microsoft Research & VR Vis Research Center)*, Derek Huang *(Microsoft Research)*

- Analysis of User Behavior with a Multicamera HbbTV App in a Live Sports Event..............43
  Marc Aguilar, Sergi Fernández, David Cassany *(I2CAT Foundation)*

- Connecting Living Rooms: An Experiment in Orchestrated
  Social Video Communication..49
  Manolis Falelakis *(Aristotle University of Thessaloniki)*, Marian F. Ursu *(University of York)*,
  Erik Geelhoed *(Falmouth University)*, Rene Kaiser *(JOANNEUM RESEARCH)*,
  Michael Frantzis *(Goldsmiths, University of London)*

Session III. Understanding Users

- Confessions of a 'Guilty' Couch Potato Understanding and Using Context
  to Optimize Binge-watching Behavior...59
  Dimph de Feijter *(Breda University of Applied Sciences)*,
  Vassilis-Javed Khan *(Eindhoven University of Technology)*,
  Marnix S. van Gisbergen *(Breda University of Applied Sciences)*

- Understanding Video Rewatching Experiences..69
  Frank Bentley *(Yahoo)*, Janet Murray *(Georgia Institute of Technology)*

- "I Kind of Had an Avatar Switch": The Role of the Self in Engagement
  with an Interactive TV Drama 77
  Allie Johns, Adam Galpin, Joanne Meredith *(University of Salford)*,
  Maxine Glancy *(BBC Research & Development)*

Session IV. Second Screen and Gaming

- Enabling Frame-Accurate Synchronised Companion Screen Experiences...........83
  Vinoba Vinayagamoorthy, Rajiv Ramdhany, Matt Hammond *(BBC R&D)*

- Mining Subtitles for Real-Time Content Generation
  for Second-Screen Applications 93
  Johannes Knittel, Tilman Dingler *(University of Stuttgart)*

- *GameBridge*: Converging Toward a Transmedia Storytelling Experience through Gameplay 105
  Rachel Miles, Arielle Cason, Larry Chan *(Georgia Institute of Technology)*,
  Jing Li *(State Administration of Press, Publication, Radio, Film and Television)*,
  Ryan McDonnell, Janet Murray, Zixuan Wang *(Georgia Institute of Technology)*

Course Overviews

- **Practical UX Research Methodologies** 113
  Sarah E. Garcia *(UEGroup)*

- **Incorporating Kids and Teens into UX Research** 115
  Sarah E. Garcia *(UEGroup)*

- **Interactive Television Experience in Convergent Environment: Models, Reception and Business** 119
  Valdecir Becker *(UFPB - Federal University of Paraíba)*

Works-in-Progress

- **Region-of-Interest-Based Subtitle Placement Using Eye-Tracking Data of Multiple Viewers** 123
  Wataru Akahori *(Waseda University)*, Tatsunori Hirai *(Komazawa University)*,
  Shunya Kawamura *(Waseda University)*,
  Shigeo Morishima *(Waseda Research Institute for Science and Engineering)*

- **Semi-Automatic Camera and Switcher Control for Live Broadcast** 129
  Jeff Daemen, Jens Herder, Cornelius Koch, Philipp Ladwig, Roman Wiche, Kai Wilgen
  (Hochschule Düsseldorf, University of Applied Sciences)

- **Multi-Platform Application Toolkit** 135
  Miggi Zwicklbauer *(Fraunhofer FOKUS)*, Matthew Broadbent *(Lancaster University)*,
  Jean-Claude Dufourd *(Telecom ParisTech)*, Christian Fuhrhop *(Fraunhofer FOKUS)*, Stefano Miccoli *(Fincons)*,
  Fabian Schiller *(Institut für Rundfunktechnik)*, Ville Tuominen *(Leadin)*

- **Automated News Generation for TV Program Ratings** 141
  Soomin Kim, JongHwan Oh, Joonhwan Lee *(Seoul National University)*

- **A System Designed to Collect Users' TV-Watching Data Using a Smart TV, Smartphones, and Smart Watches** 147
  Jehwan Seo *(Samsung Electronics)*, Hyunchul Lim, Changhoon Oh *(Seoul National University)*,
  Hyun-Kyu Yun *(Samsung Electronics)*, Bongwon Suh, Joongseek Lee *(Seoul National University)*

- **Towards Biometric Assessment of Audience Affect** 155
  Jacob L. Wieland *(The Danish Broadcasting Corporation)*,
  Lars B. Larsen, Jeanette K. Laursen, Lotte I. Jørgensen, Anne Mette K. Jessen, Charlotte T. Jensen *(Aalborg University)*

- **REFLEX: Face Micro-Expression Recognition System for TV Content Curation** 163
  Paula Falco, Christina Noonan, Ge Cao *(IIT Institute of Design)*

- **Towards Media for Wellbeing** 171
  Carla Bernardino, Hugo Alexandre Ferreira, Teresa Chambel *(Universidade de Lisboa)*

Workshop Summaries

- **4th International Workshop on Interactive Content Consumption at ACM TVX'16** 179
  Britta Meixner *(FX Palo Alto Laboratory, Inc.)*, Werner Bailer *(JOANNEUM RESEARCH)*,
  Maarten Wijnants *(Hasselt University - tUL - iMinds)*, Rene Kaiser *(JOANNEUM RESEARCH)*,
  Joscha Jäger *(Merz Akademie)*, Rik Bauwens *(Vlaamse Radio- en Televisieomroeporganisatie)*,
  Frank Bentley *(Yahoo)*

- **Design Methods for Persuasive Media Experiences** 185
  Tom MacTavish, Santosh Basapur *(Illinois Institute of Technology)*

- **Design Strategies for Interactive Digital Narratives** 189
  Hartmut Koenitz *(University of Georgia)*

Author Index 193

ACM TVX 2016 Conference Organization

General Chairs: Patrick Whitney *(IIT Institute of Design, USA)*
Janet Murray *(Ivan Allen College of Liberal Arts, Georgia Institute of Technology, USA)*
Santosh Basapur *(IIT Institute of Design, USA)*

Program Chairs: Noor Ali Hasan *(Google Inc., USA)*
Jochen Huber *(Synaptics Inc., Switzerland)*

Program Coordination Chair: Tom Bartindale *(University of Newcastle, UK)*

Local Arrangements Chairs: Margo Schwartz *(IIT Institute of Design, USA)*
Lisa Snider *(IIT Institute of Design, USA)*

Courses Chairs: Jorge Abreu *(University of Aveiro, Portugal)*
Tom MacTavish *(IIT Institute of Design, USA)*

Workshops Chairs: Tom Bartindale *(University of Newcastle, UK)*
Hokyoung Blake Ryu *(Hanyang University, South Korea)*

iTV in Industry Chairs: Michael Darnell *(Samsung Research America, USA)*
Mike Evans *(BBC Research, UK)*

Demonstrations Chairs: Omar Niamut *(TNO, The Netherlands)*
Marty Thaler *(IIT Institute of Design, USA)*

Doctoral Consortium: Teresa Chambel *(University of Lisbon, Portugal)*
Sharon Strover *(University of Texas at Austin, USA)*

Work in Progress Chairs: Hartmut Koenitz *(University of Georgia, USA)*
Venu Vasudevan *(Arris Inc. USA)*

Media Chairs: David Green *(University of Newcastle, UK)*
Gustavo Cascio *(IIT Institute of Design, USA)*

Steering Committee: Pablo Cesar, Chair *(CWI, The Netherlands)*
David Geerts *(CUO/iMinds/KU Leuven, Belgium)*
Artur Lugmayr *(Tampere University of Technology, Finland)*
Konstantinos Chorianopoulos *(Ionian University, Greece)*
George Lekakos *(Athens University of Economics and Business, Greece)*
Marianna Obrist *(University of Sussex, UK)*
Hendrik Knoche *(Aalborg University, DK)*
David A. Shamma *(Yahoo! Research, USA)*
Santosh Basapur *(IIT Institute of Design, USA)*

Associate Chairs: Ingrid Trollope *(Google Inc., USA)*

Bianca Soto *(Google Inc., USA)*

Isha Dandavate *(Google/Youtube Inc., USA)*

Sarah Walter *(Google Inc., USA)*

Paula Barraza *(Sonos Inc., USA)*

Stacie Hibino *(Samsung Electronics, USA)*

Beth Harrington *(Verizon, USA)*

Libby Hemphill *(Illinois Institute of Technology, USA)*

Rene Kaiser *(Joanneum Research, Austria)*

Radu-Daniel Vatavu *(University Stefan cel Mare of Suceava, Romania)*

Michael Evans *(BBC, UK)*

Pablo Cesar *(CWI, The Netherlands)*

David Geerts *(KU Leuven, Belgium)*

Marie Jose Montpetit (*MIT, USA)*

Tanja Doering *(Universität Bremen,)*

Judith Redi *(TU Delft, The Netherlands)*

Ben Falchuk *(Ericsson, USA)*

David Green *(University of Newcastle, UK)*

Rodrigo Laiola Guimarães *(IBM, Brazil)*

Donny McMillan *(University of Stockholm, Sweden)*

Britta Meixner *(FXPAL, USA)*

Frank Nack *(University of Amsterdam, The Netherlands)*

Omar Niamut *(TNO, The Netherlands)*

Mark Rice *(Institute for Infocomm Research, Singapore)*

Teresa Romao *(Universidade Nova de Lisboa, Portugal)*

Alan Said *(Recorded Future, Sweden)*

Wendy Van den Broeck *(Vrije Universiteit Brussel, Belgium)*

Gretchen Gelke *(Samsung, USA)*

Jean-Claude Dufourd *(Telecom ParisTech, France)*

Alexander Raake *(TU Ilmenau, Germany)*

TVX 2016 Sponsor & Supporters

Sponsor:

In cooperation with:

Supporters:

"We are the [virtual] 99%"

Bringing the Promise of Live Digital Interaction to All the Peoples

Tawny Schlieski

President of Oregon Story Board

Director of Desktop Research at Intel Corporation

We are approaching the dawn of a communications revolution, where interactive digital information enables entertainment, education, and industry in ways that we have only imagined in science fiction. Investors have dropped more than a billion dollars into the industry in the first two months of 2016. The first wave of interface technologies are beginning to reach developers. And a handful of new experiences are making their way to consumers. So who benefits from this revolution? Virtual and Augmented Reality are the interfaces into a digital universe: a live, interactive computational space. This new space is not relevant only to the tech elite. This is a shift in how we communicate with computers and digital information that will give voice to many people, and empower companies and entrepreneurs from many disciplines to create a future, rich with opportunity.

The German philosopher Hegel described history as a running river: as a massive force, flowing down through known terrain, influenced not just by the rocks and the clay at a particular place, but also by everything that has come before. We can look upriver at the history of the live digital interaction revolution and see the formations that lead us here. The apocalyptic science fiction that fears the loss of our humanity, the gaming engines we use to build our new experiences, the virtual production and design capabilities that drove initial experimentation, and the billions of dollars that large corporations are spending to *own the interface* between the digital and human world.

But for all the power of those legacies, we are in fact still far up river. We are still at the beginning, perhaps not of history, but certainly of a new tributary, of the moment when a part of the running rivers of computation and narrative begin to divert, and to flow in a different direction. And being in the headwaters matters.

The first reason it matters is that the formation is complicated, and many of the small streams that divert

from the river, will dissipate and disappear [Virtual Boy, Google Glass, Disney Infinity...]. It is hard to be a first mover. There is intense risk for financial ruin, but also the real possibility of being mocked by the easy cynicism of the jaded critics who have seen it all before, who will gleefully predict its failure [again]. This is an unforgiving time, when good things will fail for bad reasons: corporations will lose faith in projects, ambitious companies' funding will dry up weeks before their critical breakthrough, and amazing, revolutionary content will [for reasons none of us grok] fail to ignite the audience's imagination. But those who survive, whether by luck or by skill, will sit at the beginning of this revolution. And those few, are important for another reason.

Those survivors [lucky or otherwise] will determine the future of this market in surprising and persistent ways. The things they value, the people they rely on, will set the path of this new river. We have seen this before, we only have to look at the industries of film, computers, and games, to see how persistent the values [and the complexion] of early pioneers remains. Those industries, as they grow, expend extraordinary efforts to diversify: not just because they seek some abstract notion of social justice, but because, ultimately, an industry built on a narrow definition of human experience will reach the limits of its market when it exhausts the supply of humans who share that experience.

The world is a bigger place than imagined by the founders of these legacy industries. We have the opportunity, as much as the obligation, to build this new industry, with a bigger foundation. With a broader foundation, which will grow based on the talents of more people, and will draw economic sustenance from the networks of that talent base.

We are standing at the headwaters of a new river, moving the rocks and the clay that will set the direction of this new river for generations to come. We, the individual practitioners of this new art, are the ones setting the course of this future. We are building this revolution. We are creating new things: bringing those things to audiences; and turning those audiences into markets. We can [must] look inward, to find partners we can trust and lean on during the hard years ahead, but we can also open our minds and our doors, and look outward, for new

Permission to make digital or hard copies of part or all of this work for personal or classroom use is granted without fee provided that copies are not made or distributed for profit or commercial advantage and that copies bear this notice and the full citation on the first page. Copyrights for third-party components of this work must be honored. For all other uses, contact the Owner/Author.

Copyright is held by the owner/author(s).
TVX'16, June 22-24, 2016, Chicago, IL, USA
ACM 978-1-4503-4067-0/16/06.
http://dx.doi.org/10.1145/2932206.2932220

voices, and new partners who we might never have sought before.

Yes, the very successful industries of film, computers, and games were formed in [relatively] closed circles. By people who thought, and looked, surprisingly like one another. But if we look back a bit further, to the American Gold Rush, we have a different model. One where many different people, both the favored sons of a healing nation, and the disenfranchised from foreign and domestic soils, ventured into an unknown territory together. As will happen to many of us, many of the worthiest of those adventurers failed, for reasons both good and bad, but those that survived did not all look the same. They did not think the same. And they gifted the western United States with a particular kind of economic vibrancy and diversity.

So the question is: what legacy will our revolution leave behind?

Uncovering the Underlying Factors of Smart TV UX over Time: A Multi-study, Mixed-method Approach

Jincheul Jang, Dapeng Zhao, Woneui Hong, Youkyoung Park, Mun Yong Yi
Graduate School of Knowledge Service Engineering, KAIST
Daejeon, South Korea
{jcjang, dapeng, woneui.hong, park60, munyi}@kaist.ac.kr

ABSTRACT

The objective of this research is to explore and identify Smart TV user experience (UX) factors over different time periods employing multiple methods so as to overcome the weakness of a single study approach. To identify the effect of contextual dimensions on the Smart TV UX, we conducted empirical studies exploiting different methods of think-aloud and diary method under two usage conditions: laboratory and real-life in the participants' residence. The factors identified through each study were integrated into a single set and further refined through peer review resulting in a final set of 19 UX factors. Metrics for these 19 UX factors were generated and used in an online survey, in which over 300 Smart TV users participated. The empirical evidences from each study suggest that the UX factors vary with respect to product temporality. The findings indicate practical implications for Smart TV manufacturers, marketing managers, application developers, and service providers.

Author Keywords

User Experience; Smart TV; Laboratory Experiment; Diary Study; Survey; Temporality

ACM Classification Keywords

H.5.2. User Interfaces

INTRODUCTION

As one of the major sources of entertainment, television plays a central role in home environment. People can enhance their relationship with family members by watching movies and shows together. According to the American Time Use Survey produced by the United States Department of Labor, watching TV as a leisure activity occupies the most time (2.8 hours per day), accounting for more than half of leisure time on average for those aged 15 and over.

Currently launched electronic devices including home appliances are now able to connect to Internet, set up an operating

Permission to make digital or hard copies of all or part of this work for personal or classroom use is granted without fee provided that copies are not made or distributed for profit or commercial advantage and that copies bear this notice and the full citation on the first page. Copyrights for components of this work owned by others than ACM must be honored. Abstracting with credit is permitted. To copy otherwise, or republish, to post on servers or to redistribute to lists, requires prior specific permission and/or a fee. Request permissions from Permissions@acm.org.
TVX 2016, June 22–24, 2016, Chicago, IL, USA.
Copyright © 2016 ISBN 978-1-4503-4067-0/16/06...$15.00.
DOI: http://dx.doi.org/10.1145/2932206.2932207

system, and support various online functions for convenience. The smartphone, for example, has become a primary device for communication and computing activities and continuously permeates every corner of our daily lives. A smartphone is now equipped with various smart functions, including web browsing, advanced sensors to capture contextual factors, high-speed wireless network, and new application installations, differentiating them from traditional mobile devices (called feature phones). Similarly to the mobile phone, television has rapidly evolved to become much smarter through advanced connectivity and sophisticated functionality. Smart TV, a television set with integrated Internet accessibility and online interactive media capacities with operating systems, has started to attract considerable attention from TV manufactures and consumers worldwide. According to Gartner Inc., all televisions produced in 2016 will belong to a category of smart products [27]. Given the development of the latest Smart TVs functions (e.g., games, three-dimensional (3D) movies, and fitness), maintaining a balance between complexity and diversity has emerged as an important challenge for television designers. In the past, traditional television designers highlighted viewers' relaxation and passivity as important factors in their viewing enjoyment [10, 31]. However, when designing Smart TVs, designers should consider various usability factors of complex entertainment environments such as network connection functions, picture resolution and quality, and the various content sources, such as broadcasting, movies, user created contents, and applications.

User experience (UX) has been studied in diverse fields such as human-computer interaction (HCI), marketing, and product design. Although UX is important, it has been difficult to define or capture its nature and scope effectively, as it involves understanding the human experience in its entirety [24]. In particular, the underlying factors of UX with regard to Smart TV are almost unknown rather than other products or services [4].

A comprehensive set of UX evaluation methods has been developed. Each research method has both positive and negative attributes, and thus, a single-method approach is unlikely to successfully capture the full spectrum of UXs [24]. In this research, we applied three different methods: the think-aloud method under laboratory conditions, the diary method under real-life conditions, and an online survey. The advantage of the think-aloud method is that it captures the UX factors expressed at the moment the user is first introduced to the product. However, it is limited because of the difficulty of extending it to a large number of experimental subjects. Further, it inherently suffers from the problems of unnatural user responses and an isolated setting in contrast to a real environment. The diary method can collect various UX factors related to the use of the real product in the home environment. However, it is difficult to conduct a long-term experiment because of the cognitive effort that is required from the subjects. In an online survey, the respondents' memory may be distorted by the time delay; however, a survey can collect the quantitative opinions of diverse users about UX factors. Moreover, UX for the Smart TV, an emerging product, has not been sufficiently studied because of the complex nature of the interactions between users and the various functions of the TV sets. Thus, the nature of Smart TV UX cannot be completely captured if only one of these research methods is applied. In order to gain a comprehensive picture of the Smart TV UX, we believe that various methods to analyze user reactions and behaviors should be employed.

The lifecycle of new electronic products has significantly changed because of the rapid change in consumer usage patterns. Manufacturers should now provide a number of functions on a user-friendly interface while also continuously updating these applications and firmware. In the UX research field, several studies that observe the patterns of user reactions to traditional devices over different time scales have been conducted [20, 21]. However, studies on the new Smart TV UXs using different research methods to observe users during various stage of the technology lifecycle are almost non-existent. Thus, in this study, we focused on determining the Smart TV UX factors over various temporalities using different research methods.

USER EXPERIENCE
For decades, HCI researchers and practitioners have contemplated the concept of UX and its underlying components. For example, McCarthy and Wright [26] defined UX quality as an evaluation of the use of technological artifacts in human life. They stated that UX has four sub-components: compositional, emotional, sensual, and spatio-temporal. Hassenzahl and Tractinsky [15] showed that UX is the outcome of a user's internal state, the system characteristics, and the usage context. Law et al. [24] conducted a literature survey to examine the scope and definition of UX, collecting the views of 275 researchers and practitioners on UX. Their study found a large number of definition statements for UX in various fields, and they concluded that UX is a dynamic, context-dependent, and subjective concept. Alben [3] and other researchers (e.g., [13, 24]), has noted that "experience" means all aspects of interactive use of an end-user product. Specifically, most researchers highlight UX elements as having both hedonic and pregnant aspects [15, 20]. Following the trends of previous UX research, we define UX factors that significantly influence user experience and cover all usage aspects in this study.

UX studies contribute to a theoretical background for the development and design of products and analysis of user behavior. UX research has been applied to various products including mobile applications, smartphones, and websites [4]. However, their analyses of UX factors indicate that certain products have been insufficiently studied. Bargas-Avila and Hornbæk mentioned that the products most frequently addressed in UX studies are art-based applications (such as interactive software and products) and mobile device applications. The forecasting report of Gartner Inc. stated that the Smart TV, an emerging product, will be a market-leading product in the near future [27]. However, an insufficient amount of research on its UX has been conducted because such research is more expensive than research on mobile devices, which are popular objects of UX research. Traditional TVs did not emphasize user experiences because those experiences were focused on simply watching broadcasting. For example, Csikszentmihalyi and Kubey [10] applied experience sampling methods to study the fluctuation of individuals' mood when watching traditional television. Hess et al. [17] conducted a study using the diary method and interviews to discover the interconnection traits between social TV (not Smart TV) and other devices. Our study conducts research on the new Smart TV user experience, utilizing various features based on previous user experience studies for other products.

At the same time, UX researchers also have been interested in the changes in UX and users' reactions with respect to temporality. On the first use, novice users who have little knowledge of the target product judge its perceived ease of use according to general or abstract criteria, whereas experienced users judge it according to specific or concrete attributes using their increased knowledge accumulated through their own experiences [7]. Research conducted by Karapanos et al. [20] suggested that UX moves through three phases: orientation, incorporation, and identification. These phases occur after the anticipation stage, which occurs when the user has expectations before being introduced to the product. In the orientation stage, users encounter the novel features with their learnability flow. Moreover, users may feel excited by these new features as well as frustrated from the target product. Next, the incorporation stage is the process of identifying the meaning of the product in real life. In this stage, the long-term usability of the product's functionality and usefulness become clear to users with increasing familiarity as they continue using the product. Finally, there is the identification stage, during which users' emotional attachment through socialization and personalization of their product interaction occur. Based on these stages, studies have verified the temporality of UX from real user narratives [21, 22]. However, these studies were applied using a single method, and they did not make full use of its advantages and disadvantages. In addition, the User Experience White Paper [32] defines four phases of UX: anticipated UX, which includes prior expectations and experiences; momentary UX, which is the user's feeling on the product as the user interacts with the target object; episodic UX, which consists of the user's feelings during a specific usage episode, and cumulative UX, which consists of the user's feelings over time. As for the temporal aspects of UX, Bargas-Avila and Hornbæk [4] showed that 70% of them were based on an analysis of the user's feelings after using the product, and studies that targeted all phases of UX temporality comprised only 17%. In sum, no previous research study has comprehensively captured the Smart TV UX over the entire temporality of the product since they focused either on user interactions with the technology or the users' intrinsic state. Traditional televisions have fewer interactive factors than other devices, thus their appearance is the most important factor affecting user satisfaction [10]. Different from conventional TVs, one UX issue of Smart TVs is related to its operating system, such as the effective control of the TV using a remote control device or voice commands or the customization of the user interface to meet user requirements [33].

In the absence of knowledge about the influence of temporality on Smart TV UXs, we combined multiple research methods to explore the complete spectrum of Smart TV UXs without being constrained by the limitations of a single-method approach. In this study, we observed the differences in UX between early and late usage stages in different Smart TV usage contexts through experiments in controlled lab and real-life usage environments, as well as an online survey.

RESEARCH FRAMEWORK

The overall framework of our study is shown in Figure 1. One objective of our study was to empirically identify UX factors while users were experiencing the Smart TV. Another objective was to determine the correlation between different periods in the Smart TV usage stage and the positive or negative UX factors identified by users. Thus, we experimentally targeted Smart TV users to elicit the UX factors of which they were conscious. First, we extracted keywords for the user expectations of Smart TVs from responses to a pre-test survey (Study 1) conducted prior to the laboratory and real-life condition experiments. We performed a laboratory condition experiment using the think-aloud method (Study 2) to extract the UX of first impressions. We next set up Smart TVs in the living rooms of real homes (Study 3). The subjects living in these homes kept a daily diary, and from their diary entries, we extracted keywords for the UX factors. Finally, targeting Smart TV users who had used the product within one year, we conducted an online survey (Study 4) to score the importance of the Smart TV UX factors, which were obtained from the results of the think-aloud and diary methods. Thus, we were able to observe the changes in the UX factors over time, including those UX factors collected prior to actual contact with the product. In Studies 2 and 3, popular Smart TV products produced by two major electronic companies were evaluated. We measured three indices of user consequence (perceived usefulness, satisfaction, and continuous intention to use) to check whether the consequences were different between the two manufacturers.

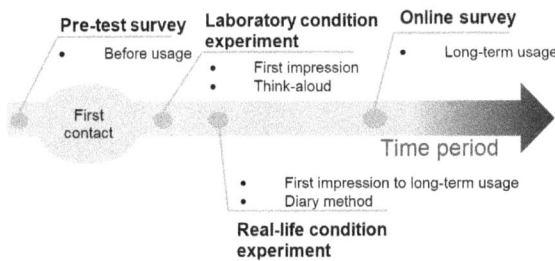

Figure 1. Research framework

Contents	First Coding	Second Coding
Unnecessary buttons	Inconvenience	Perceived helpfulness
Good to excellent picture quality for watching TV	Perceived picture quality	Perceived picture quality
Loading speed is too slow	Responsiveness	Perceived responsiveness

Table 1. Coding examples

We coded the user-mentioned think-aloud and diary data into abstracted keywords. An example of the coding analysis is shown in Table 1. We recruited four coders, two doctoral students and two master students, who had coding analysis experience and a deep understanding of a Smart TV's functionality. The analysis was conducted as follows. First, we transcribed the recorded think-aloud data and converted the written diaries and pre-test responses into a uniform text form. Second, we initially categorized similar codes into groups. Finally, we named each group based on the codes in the group. In the first round, after a detailed explanation of the coding procedure, the four coders independently coded the extracted statements. The correlation among the coders was 75%-a substantial agreement. After the initial coding activities, the coders examined the codes, discussed their discrepancies, and arrived at a consensus. In the case of Study 2, after reviewing sentence of their responses, the coder input users' feelings as positive, neutral, and negative condition. Then, all coders reaffirmed the feelings of all the elements through the discussions. In the case of Study 3, experimental participants responded the feelings as positive, neutral, and negative condition. After the codes were extracted by the coders, a panel comprising four of the authors further categorized the codes into groups such that similar codes were located together in a group. Word frequency is the most important variable in research on human memory and word processing; therefore, the frequency of keywords considered as the importance in each study.

STUDY 1: PRE-TEST SURVEY

Objective and Method

UX is often influenced by user expectations formed from prior knowledge of related products or others' opinions before the first use [32]. We requested users for their expectations of the Smart TV when the participants began the experiments in Study 2 and Study 3.

The survey was completed by a total of 23 participants who took part in one of the 2 user experiments: 15 participants from the laboratory condition experiment and 8 household representatives from the real-life condition experiment.

Results

As shown in Table 2, we extracted keywords from 21 user responses because 2 user responses did not include any keywords. In total, 35 keywords were extracted. Content diversity appeared with the highest frequency. For example, participants mentioned: "I would like to see the program without any payment, not even as pay-per-view," "I think Smart TV should

UX Factors	Frequency	
Content diversity	11	30.6%
Perceived picture quality	6	16.7%
Connectivity	6	16.7%
Real-life applicability	5	13.9%
Relative salience	4	11.1%
Others	2	5.6%
No response	2	5.6%

Table 2. Summary of Study 1 Results

recommend an appropriate program to me," and "TV should provide rich video content." In addition, perceived picture quality and connectivity were also frequently included in their expressed expectations. Thus, Smart TV users expected to watch various broadcast and Internet content on a television with a high quality screen connected to a network or other device [18]. In addition, the ability to schedule or replay contents were derived.

STUDY 2: LABORATORY CONDITION EXPERIMENT

Objective

The full UX spectrum includes a user's daily thoughts and feelings. However, user surveys or other methods can only collect responses after a time interval, and they are therefore based on the responder's selective and delayed recall of his/her experiences [9]. Thus, we naturally required a research method to collect user responses that reflect their feelings during the actual use of the product.

In the laboratory experiment in which the think-aloud method was applied, direct observation was performed in a controlled environment to study the behavior of users on the first contact with a product. The objective of this study was to derive new UX factors from freely voiced comments [29]. We set up an environment similar to an actual living room, simulating the environment of home setting. Based on the guidelines given to the subjects, we asked the participants to mention their thoughts and emotions naturally while using the Smart TV. The conversations were recorded and transcribed to text-based data that were later used to derive the UX factors.

Method

Laboratory Design
We took the real usage environment into consideration and set up a laboratory that allowed a relatively natural behavioral observation and data collection process [17]. As shown in Figure 2, we set up a private space with furniture, for example, a sofa with decorations, so that the participants could express their feelings and thoughts in a relatively relaxed and natural manner. Also, two popular Smart TV models produced by different manufacturers were used in this experiment.

Recruiting
A total of 15 participants (7 male and 8 female), undergraduate or graduate students in South Korea, were recruited by advertising on an online community board. The ages of the participants ranged from 20 to 29 years with a mean of 23.67 years. All the participants had smart device usage experience

Figure 2. Laboratory design

(e.g., a smartphone or smart tablet), but no experience using a Smart TV. Participants were given a monetary incentives of 15,000 Korean Won (approximately $13 USD).

Procedures
The participants took part in the think-aloud method experiment, in which they voiced their thoughts and emotions about the Smart TV. They used two Smart TVs sequentially and were provided with step-by-step manuals explaining the functions required for the given tasks. The participants performed the pre-test before they participated in the experiment and the post-test after the experiment. The pre-test consisted of a demographics questionnaire. To determine the effects of the different TVs, the post-test included the items of perceived usefulness, satisfaction, and continuous intention to use.

The participants were required to conduct the eleven most commonly used functions of the Smart TVs: controlling the screen using the remote controller, executing the YouTube application to watch a YouTube video, using the recommended programs menu, controlling the Smart TV by voice, switching external inputs, connecting with smartphones through a wireless network, using social network applications, recording video, surfing the Internet, gaming, and watching 3D movies. It was required to perform the same task for limited time to the experiment participants. Participants should mention the feelings within limited time. It was an average of 20 minutes for a response. The average number of sentence that participant mentioned was 45.6.

Text coding from records to text
The detailed procedures of coding and labeling UX factors mentioned in the previous 'Research Framework' session. The participants' audio response on their thoughts and feelings about the Smart TV were all recorded in the laboratory. The recorded data were transcribed to text and coded into single phrases using the following schema: action, specific features or factors of the Smart TV, and the emotional reaction of the user. Statements that were irrelevant in terms of deriving UX factors (e.g., comments about the manuals, meaningless dialogue, and repeated interjections) were excluded.

UX Factors	POS	NEU	NEG	SUM	
Controllability of the remote control	32	3	107	142	20.8%
Cognitive ease	18	2	92	112	16.4%
Perceived usability of the voice command	23	0	61	84	12.3%
Relative salience	44	4	16	64	9.4%
Perceived responsiveness	8	1	44	53	7.7%
Real-life applicability	24	0	18	42	6.1%
Perceived picture quality	19	0	17	36	5.3%
Perceived helpfulness	6	1	24	31	4.5%
Customized flexibility	1	4	21	26	3.8%
Stability	1	0	22	23	3.4%
Content diversity	6	0	7	13	1.9%
Perceived quality of 3D viewing	3	1	8	12	1.8%
Perceived aesthetics	7	0	3	10	1.5%
Appearance appropriate	3	1	6	10	1.5%
Connectivity	1	0	9	10	1.5%
Ease of adaptation	0	0	3	3	0.4%
Perceived playfulness	0	0	2	2	0.3%
Perceived security	0	0	2	2	0.3%
Perceived sound quality	0	0	1	1	0.1%
Others (price, services..)	4	1	3	8	1.2%

Table 3. Summary of Study 2 Results

Labeling UX factors
We summarized unified UX keywords into a single phrase. Four coders participated in this operation. The purpose was to express the user's feelings about the Smart TV in terms of UX in a form that the user could understand. For inter-coder consistency, the code consistency between statements was derived by discussing each UX factor. As a result, a total of 684 keywords were derived from the voiced sentiments, which were used as the base material for the final derived UX factors.

Results
As shown in Table 3, the most frequently mentioned factor was the controllability of the remote control, which accounted for 20.8% of the factors mentioned. The comments for the controllability of the remote control factor included several negative opinions, such as "using the remote control to click on menus was a little time consuming because of it was not sensitive" or "difficult to manually access the menu." The top three factors, Controllability of the remote control, cognitive ease, and perceived usability of voice command, were mostly mentioned negatively. This reflects the fact that during their first contact with the Smart TV, the participants found the control of its functions inconvenient. In addition, relative salience and perceived responsiveness, which are related to the first impression of the Smart TV, were highly ranked.

A paired samples t-test was performed to examine the effects of usage consequence for two brands of Smart TV. Perceived usefulness ($t = .22$, $p = .82$), satisfaction ($t = .08$, $p = .93$), and continuous intention to use ($t = .47$, $p = .64$) did not differ between the two manufacturers.

Figure 3. Real-life condition experiment

STUDY 3: REAL-LIFE CONDITION EXPERIMENT

Objective and Method
The diaries were directly written by the participants, describing their feelings about the product [19]. The participants were required to participate in a three- or six-week study so that their real feelings about Smart TV usage in their living room could be well captured, as shown in Figure 3. We provided TV which was randomly selected from two popular Smart TV models, the same as Study 2. After recruiting all the participants, the Smart TV was set up in his/her home; the pre-test was also conducted before this experiment and instructions were given to the participants. During the following three or six weeks, the participants were required to use the television for more than one hour per day and write at least three semi-structured diary entries each day. They were instructed that every diary entry should include the date and time of usage, the number of peer viewers, the types of Smart TV function they used, the motivation for using the function, their reactions, and their sentiments regarding the usage [17]. For example, a participant submitted the following report:

- Date: Nov. 30 (Sun)

- Time: 2PM – 3PM

- Number of peer viewers: 3

- Types of Smart TV function: YouTube app.

- Motivation for function usage: After lunch, we wanted to find and watch a "dinosaur" documentary.

- Reactions: I love comfortably watching YouTube content using a wide-screen Smart TV.

- Sentiment of usage: Positive

After keeping diaries using the workbook we provided, participants submitted the workbook to us every week. They also responded to the weekly survey that asked about the UX results, perceived usefulness (USEF), satisfaction (SATF), continued intention to use (CINT) the television [12], and any additional subjective comments. They responded to the survey on a seven-point Likert scale ("Strongly disagree" to "Strongly agree") for each construct.

Participants

We recruited participants who lived with at least two other people in a family. All families had no experience of using a Smart TV, but all the members had experience using smartphones. Six of the recruited families participated in the experiments for three weeks and two for six weeks. The researchers visited the family's home and installed the Smart TV with explaining the instructions for the experiment. In the real-life condition experiment, twenty-six participants (excepting young people under 10 years old) from eight households participated. The average age of the participants was 38.5 years. Four households included children whose ages ranged from 1 to 10 years. Two households included senior people over 60 years old. Participants were given monetary incentives of 100,000 Korean Won for each week (approximately $86 USD).

Results

We collected 689 semi-structured diaries from the participants written during the three- to six-week experimental period. The average duration of television usage was 68 minutes per day, and the major activities participants conducted using the Smart TV included: watching videos, surfing the Internet, connecting with other devices (e.g., smartphones and PCs), and watching live broadcasting. We also examined the differences in UX during different times of day: morning (05:00 – 12:00), afternoon (12:00 – 17:00), evening (17:00 – 21:00), and night (21:00 – 05:00). The most usage occurred at night (n = 230), followed by evening (n = 156), morning (n = 108), and afternoon (n = 76). No response was given in 119 cases (n = 119). Of all the responses, 61.0% (n = 417) were written about unique features of the Smart TV (not conventional TVs) such as video search, payment for content, smart application use, and the ability to view users' smartphone screens.

In the 689 texts that contained UX information gathered from the participants' reports, and Three-week participants were mentioned an average of 71.83 sentences (Max.: 84, Min.: 62). Six-week participants noted an average 107 sentences. Twenty UX factors were found, as shown in Table 4. Similar with Study 2, the most frequently mentioned factor was the most frequently mentioned factor was controllability of the remote control, which accounted for 26.3% of the factors mentioned. The comments on the controllability of the remote control factor included several negative opinions, such as "difficult to focus the cursor of the remote control" and "not easy to control the wheel on the remote control". In addition, real-life applicability and content diversity, which are related to a user's continuous impression of the television, were ranked relatively high.

We also performed a paired samples t-test to test the effects of the two brands of Smart TV. The results showed that the perceived usefulness ($t = 1.06$, $p = .30$), satisfaction ($t = 1.26$, $p = .22$), and continuous intention to use ($t = .69$, $p = .49$) did not differ between the two manufacturers.

The results of the weekly survey showed that the average of scores improved from the first to the last week, as shown in Figure 4. Similar to the quantitative results, the qualitative responses changed from abstract usability to long-term concrete opinions. For example, in the first week of the experiment,

UX Factors	POS	NEU	NEG	SUM	
Controllability of the remote control	49	8	124	181	26.3%
Real-life applicability	42	11	24	77	11.2%
Perceived picture quality	40	15	19	74	10.7%
Content diversity	14	4	44	62	9.0%
Perceived helpfulness	14	2	36	52	7.5%
Perceived responsiveness	14	1	26	41	6.0%
Connectivity	18	2	21	41	6.0%
Cognitive ease	5	2	21	28	4.1%
Perceived quality of 3D viewing	13	2	9	24	3.5%
Perceived usability of the voice command	14	2	4	20	2.9%
Perceived sound quality	3	3	7	13	1.9%
Ease of adaptation	6	2	4	12	1.7%
Customized flexibility	1	2	7	10	1.5%
Perceived playfulness	5	0	4	9	1.3%
Perceived security	0	0	5	5	0.7%
Stability	0	0	5	5	0.7%
Relative salience	2	1	0	3	0.4%
Perceived aesthetics	0	1	1	2	0.3%
Others (Price, service..)	5	2	23	30	4.4%

Table 4. Summary of Study 3 Results

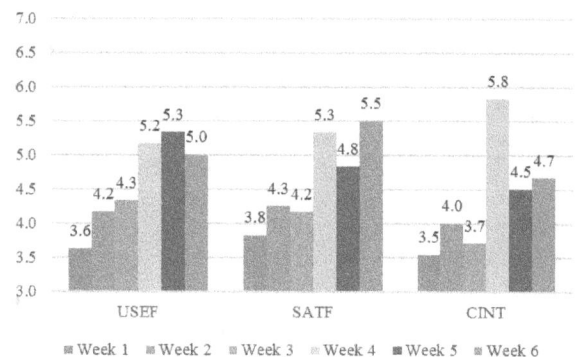

Figure 4. Results of the weekly survey in Study 3

there were responses about the difficulties of initial use such as "I think the television had excellent picture quality, but it was difficult to operate the remote controller," or "While there were convenient features in the television, there were some difficult-to-use features. A description is needed." In the second week, there were opinions such as "Now I am a little more familiar with the television," "Overall, I could distinctly recognize the difference from regular TV," and "I used television with functions available in a simple operation." Over the third week, there were opinions about overall satisfaction such as "There were points of the Smart TV that were convenient for me," "I am generally satisfied and appreciate the TV picture and sound quality." However, negative opinions also remained, such as, "The remote control was still uncomfortable, even after using it for six weeks."

REVIEWING SESSION AND DEFINING UX FACTORS

A validation of the results of the three experiments was performed. The validation was performed by seven subjects (four males and three females) who participated either in the laboratory condition experiment (5 participants) or the real-life condition experiment (2 participants). The difficulty of understanding the factors' names and relationships and any confusion regarding each factor were measured. According to these results, changes were made in the operational definition of some factors by using more easily comprehensible words and writing style.

After reviewing the results, we selected the most appropriate definition of the 19 UX factors based on their references. The usability of the voice command is the perceived ability of the Smart TV voice recognition function to provide sufficient and accurate control [12]. Stability is the degree to which users can use the Smart TV for a long time without defects of the device or completely discharging the remote controller battery [5, 23]. Relative salience is defined as the degree to which Smart TV feels relatively more innovative and prominent [2]. Real-life applicability is the degree to which users can use Smart TV appropriately in various situations [5]. Perceived sound quality is the degree of perceived sound quality output from the Smart TV [6]. Perceived security is the degree to which the Smart TV appears to safely handle personal information and avoid unnecessary exposure [14]. Perceived quality of 3D viewing can be defined as the perceived realism of three dimensional videos on the Smart TV. Perceived responsiveness is the degree of rapidity with which a product loads according to the user's requirement [8]. Perceived playfulness is the degree to which the use of a Smart TV gives the user enjoyment, amusement, or pleasure [8, 11]. Perceived picture quality is the degree of user perception when reading or seeing objects reproduced on a screen [8], and perceived helpfulness is the degree to which the Smart TV provides description or notification services to support user convenience [25]. Perceived aesthetics is the degree of aesthetic beauty of the user interface implemented on the screen [11]. Customized flexibility is the ability to which the user can easily change the setting of the Smart TV to suit his or her personal taste and convenience [28]. Ease of adaptation is the degree to which the Smart TV makes it easy for who to become familiar with watching and controlling the Smart TV [14, 16]. The controllability of the remote control is the degree to which the remote control is perceived as comfortable over a series of Smart TV control operations [30]. Content diversity is the degree to which a Smart TV provides various content (included apps) [23]. Connectivity is the degree to which the Smart TV smoothly connects with other devices or the Internet [5, 18]. Cognitive ease is intuitive or consistent provision of user interface elements (e.g., icons, buttons, or layout) in the Smart TV so that they are easy to understand [25]. Finally, appearance appropriate is the degree of suitability of the device exterior, such as thickness of the screen and its aesthetics [11].

STUDY 4: ONLINE SURVEY
Objective

An online survey targeting a large number of members was conducted to determine how each extracted UX factors con-tribute to the overall satisfaction level of Smart TV. In order to figure out the relationship between UX factors and users' satisfaction level, referring to the results of our prior studies, we developed a survey questionnaire that included 19 UX factors (perceived picture quality, appearance appropriate, interface aesthetics, relative salience, connectivity, perceived sound quality, controllability of the remote control, perceived quality of 3D viewing, perceived responsiveness, real-life applicability, content diversity, ease of adaptation, perceived usability of the voice command, customized flexibility, helpfulness, cognitive ease, stability, and perceived security) with user satisfaction as the dependent variable. The total number of questionnaire items was 115. Each UX construct included four to seven survey items to measure the effects of latent variables. We generated items on a seven-point Likert scale (with anchors from "Strongly disagree" to "Strongly agree") for each construct.

Method and Participants

After creating the questionnaire, we conducted a pilot test to determine whether the items had been appropriately configured for the purpose of the survey. A pilot test involving 33 Smart TV users was conducted to examine the psychometric properties of the measurement items and ensure their reliabilities and validities, both convergent and discriminant. Data was collected from the online survey responses. A total of 309 Smart TV users (168 males and 142 females) participated in the survey. The average age of the participants was 41.0 years, with a 10.74 year standard deviation.

Results

We tested the reliability and validity of the questionnaire items. First, we examined the reliability of the items and confirmed that all the constructs were highly reliable, i.e., all the reliability scores for Cronbach's alpha were higher than the standard

UX Factors	Mean (Stdev)
Perceived playfulness	4.91 (1.13)
Relative salience	5.24 (1.05)
Content diversity	4.78 (1.17)
Real-life applicability	4.84 (1.10)
Connectivity	5.16 (1.01)
Customized flexibility	4.59 (1.02)
Cognitive ease	4.59 (0.98)
Perceived quality of 3D viewing	4.22 (0.98)
Usability of the voice command	4.62 (0.77)
Perceived picture quality	5.49 (0.88)
Perceived aesthetics	4.77 (1.03)
Stability	4.86 (1.01)
Perceived sound quality	5.09 (0.99)
Ease of adaptation	4.97 (1.09)
Appearance appropriate	5.19 (0.90)
Controllability of the remote control	4.81 (1.20)
Perceived security	4.10 (1.09)
Perceived helpfulness	4.49 (1.10)
Perceived responsiveness	4.62 (1.20)

Table 5. Mean and standard deviation of the Study 4 results (bold: the highest and lowest score)

Predictors	β	t-value
Perceived playfulness	0.44	10.05**
Relative salience	0.26	6.45**
Content diversity	0.16	3.91**
Real-life applicability	0.09	1.91
Connectivity	0.06	1.69
Customized flexibility	0.06	1.46
Cognitive ease	0.06	1.37
Perceived quality of 3D viewing	0.04	1.32
Usability of the voice command	0.03	1.32
Perceived picture quality	0.03	0.88
Perceived aesthetics	0.02	0.71
Stability	0.01	0.23
Perceived sound quality	0.01	0.16
Ease of adaptation	0.00	0.02
Appearance appropriate	-0.01	-0.32
Controllability of the remote control	-0.01	-0.33
Perceived security	-0.02	-0.56
Perceived helpfulness	-0.04	-0.77
Perceived responsiveness	-0.12	-3.45*

Table 6. Multiple regression model for testing result of Study 4 (* p < .01, ** p < .001. Dependent Variable: User satisfaction)

Study	Major UX Factors
Study 1: Pre-test	Content diversity*
	Perceived picture quality*
	Connectivity*
	Real-life applicability*
Study 2: Think-Aloud	Controllability of the remote control
	Cognitive ease
	Perceived usability of the voice command
	Relative salience
	Perceived responsiveness
Study 3: Diary method	Controllability of the remote control
	Real-life applicability*
	Perceived picture quality*
	Content diversity*
	Perceived helpfulness
Study 4: Online survey	Perceived playfulness
	Relative salience
	Content diversity*

Table 7. Temporality of Smart TV UX: summary (* indicates the UX factors found in the pre-test expectations)

cutoff point of 0.7. The lowest Cronbach's alpha value was that of appearance appropriate(0.89), while the highest value was that of perceived playfulness(0.97). We then checked factor loadings and cross-loadings through factor analysis. All the factors satisfied the assumptions of factor analysis.

The statistical results are shown in Table 5. Perceived picture quality received the highest mean score, while perceived security received the lowest. A multiple linear regression analysis was performed to examine the effects of the UX factors on Smart TV user satisfaction. As listed in Table 6, multiple regression analysis showed that the regression model explains 86.0% of the variance in user satisfaction and the model is significant ($F(19, 290) = 94.02$, $p < .001$). Three UX factors, perceived playfulness($t = 10.05$, $p < .001$), relative salience ($t = 6.45$, $p < .001$), and content diversity ($t = 3.90$, $p < .001$) are statistically significant with a positive coefficient. Real-life applicability ($t = 1.91$, $p = .57$) and connectivity ($t = 1.69$, $p = .09$) are marginally significant. Perceived responsiveness, which is the reverse significant with negative t-value, indicated that the perceived product rapidity could not affect the user satisfaction of Smart TV.

OVERALL DISCUSSION

The objective of this study was to explore the elements of the Smart TV UX from various research methods and to identify the primary Smart TV UX factors over various time scales of usage. Specifically, we attempted to determine a comprehensive set of factors for the Smart TV UX by employing multiple qualitative methods and synthesizing the results from different research methods. In addition, we attempted to verify the validity of these factors by applying user satisfaction as the criterion variable in a regression model using data collected from online survey. The regression model results show that three primary Smart TV UX factors determine user satisfaction significantly.

The results of the multiple linear regression model reveal that user satisfaction is explained by the Smart TV UX factors identified by this research with a high explanatory power. The R-square value was 86%.

As shown in Table 7, a comparison of the UX factors found in all studies confirmed that the users' expectations were not sufficiently met in the early stage of product usage. Specifically, users usually expected the Smart TV to provide various contents, good picture quality, a high level of connectivity, and wide applicability in real-life. However, these expectations were not met to a satisfactory degree according to the results of the think-aloud laboratory experiment, with several negative responses being given. We confirmed that the users' expectations were satisfied over long-term usage, both in the real-life experiment and online survey.

We observed the different user responses over the usage life-cycle in our three different studies. In the laboratory condition experiment using the think-aloud method, which targeted the participants' first impression of Smart TV, the results showed that the most frequently mentioned factors such as controllability of the remote control, cognitive ease, perceived usability of voice command, and perceived responsiveness were related mostly to the control of the devices for executing Smart TV functions. In the real-life condition experiment using the diary method, which targeted users who had watched a Smart TV for about one month, the results showed that the controllability of the remote control was the most frequently mentioned factor, but factors related to usefulness, such as real-life applicability, content diversity, and perceived helpfulness were mentioned more frequently than in the think-aloud method. We found that long-term Smart TV users are usually interested in the usefulness of a product rather than only its ease of operation. Because the controllability of the remote control is the most commonly mentioned as an important factor of the Smart TV interface, we conclude that this factor requires continuous monitoring to improve user satisfaction in overall time periods. In the online survey, three significant factors were found to affect user satisfaction: perceived playfulness, relative salience, and content diversity. Previous studies (e.g., [7, 20, 34]) showed that the comments about UX changed from abstract to more concrete as usage time increased. Our results confirmed the prior research findings in terms of the variation of user responses over the product temporality.

In addition, prior UX research has identified affection (also called emotion) and aesthetics as key underlying factors in UX, and most UX guidebooks for designing products and services present design methods that encourage user affection and aesthetics [1, 15]. However, our qualitative studies show that aesthetics had a low percentage in the responses of user expectation (Study 1) and initial mentions (Studies 2 and 3). In addition, the results of our survey in Study 4 show that other factors, such as perceived playfulness ($\beta = .44$) and relative salience ($\beta = .26$), are more important than perceived aesthetics ($\beta = .02$) in the context of Smart TV UX. The results of previous studies show that product manufacturers not only met the customer expectations formed by the existing models and offer stable performance without mechanical errors or battery problems, but also deliver superior features and functions not found in prior and competitor's models. According to our study findings, aesthetics and affection-related factors are not as important as the factors that we extracted.

CONCLUSION
In this research, we empirically identified the primary factors that contribute to the overall Smart TV UX and verified statistically the validity of the discovered factors over various product temporalities. The UX factors revealed by this research together represent a comprehensive view of UX as it varies over different usage time periods, in contrast to prior television studies. In concrete terms, the result of the first study, a pre-test survey, showed that users highly expected a diversity of contents before encountering the product. Next, in Study 2, we conducted an experiment in a laboratory environment that asked users to mention their thoughts when they initially contacted the product. The result of Study 2 found that factors related to usability (e.g., the usability of the remote controller and cognitive ease) were frequently mentioned. In Study 3, we asked users in their living rooms to record a diary that included their emotions and thoughts about the Smart TV. The result of the third study, a real-life condition experiment with a diary, frequently presented not only usability but also various responses such as applicability in real-life, picture quality, and content diversity. Finally, in the online survey, major factors were mentioned, such as playfulness, relative salience, and content diversity, as factors that highly affected the users' satisfaction. Our sections of study followed the time stream from user's first contact with the product to long-term usage, and we found that the expectations of the product could be satisfied over the long-term use of a Smart TV. In addition, our research confirmed the results of existing studies in which elements that users mention gradually change from abstract elements to concrete elements.

Research on determining Smart TV UX factors is in its embryonic stage. To the best of our knowledge, our research is one of the first empirical investigations of Smart TV UX factors that uses a combination approach in which both qualitative and quantitative methods are applied. Our research procedure and model are expected to be easily generalizable to similar smart electronic products and home appliances. In addition, a quality assessment of new Smart TVs can be conducted using the factors and their metrics developed in this research. Future research can build on our studies to determine a tailored set of UX factors for new and innovative products that demand high levels of user engagement and quality experiences.

ACKNOWLEDGMENTS
This work was supported by Institute for Information & Communications Technology Promotion (IITP) grant funded by the Korea government (MSIP) (No. R2212-15-0027, K-Contents Search/Recommend Service Based on Social Taste Automatic Analysis Platform).

REFERENCES
1. Agarwal, A., and Meyer, A. 2009. Beyond usability: evaluating emotional response as an integral part of the user experience. In *Proc. 27th Int. Conf. Ext. Abstr. Hum. factors Comput. Syst. - CHI EA '09*. ACM Press, New York, New York, USA, 2919–2930.

2. Alba, J., and Chattopadhyay, A. 1986. Salience effects in brand recall. *J. Mark. Res.* 23, 4 (1986), 363–369.

3. Alben, L. 1996. Quality of experience: defining the criteria for effective interaction design. *Interactions* 3, 3 (1996), 11–15.

4. Bargas-Avila, J., and Hornbæk, K. 2011. Old wine in new bottles or novel challenges: a critical analysis of empirical studies of user experience. *Proc. 29th Int. Conf. Hum. factors Comput. Syst. - CHI 11* (2011), 2689–2698.

5. Batavia, A.I., and Hammer, G.S. 1990. Toward the development of consumer-based criteria for the evaluation of assistive devices. *J. Rehabil. Res. Dev.* 27, 4 (1990), 425–436.

6. Beerends, J.G., and De Caluwe, F.E. 1999. The influence of video quality on perceived audio quality and vice versa. *J. Audio Eng. Soc.* 47, 5 (1999), 355–362.

7. Bettman, J.R., and Sujan, M. 1987. Effects of framing on evaluation of comparable and noncomparable alternatives by expert and novice consumers. *J. Consum. Res.* 14, 2 (1987), 141.

8. Cao, M., Zhang, Q., and Seydel, J. 2005. B2C e-commerce web site quality: an empirical examination. *Ind. Manag. Data Syst.* 105, 5 (2005), 645–661.

9. Consolvo, S., and Walker, M. 2003. Using the experience sampling method to evaluate ubicomp applications. *IEEE Pervasive Comput.* 2, 2 (2003), 24–31.

10. Csikszentmihalyi, M., and Kubey, R. 1981. Television and the rest of life : A systematic comparison of subjective experience. *Public Opin. Q.* 45, 3 (1981), 317–328.

11. Cyr, D., Head, M., and Ivanov, A. 2006. Design aesthetics leading to m-loyalty in mobile commerce. *Inf. Manag.* 43, 8 (2006), 950–963.

12. Davis, F. 1989. Perceived usefulness, perceived ease of use, and user acceptance of information technology. *MIS Q.* 13, 3 (1989), 319–340.

13. Desmet, P., and Hekkert, P. 2007. Framework of product experience. *Int. J. Des.* 1, 1 (2007), 57–66.

14. Flavián, C., Guinalíu, M., and Gurrea, R. 2006. The role played by perceived usability, satisfaction and consumer trust on website loyalty. *Inf. Manag.* 43, 1 (2006), 1–14.

15. Hassenzahl, M., and Tractinsky, N. 2006. User experience - a research agenda. *Behav. Inf. Technol.* 25, 2 (2006), 91–97.

16. Heerink, M. and Kröse, B., Evers, V., and Wielinga, B. 2010. Assessing acceptance of assistive social agent technology by older adults: the Almere model. *Int. J. Soc. Robot.* 2, 4 (2010), 361–375.

17. Hess, J., Ley, B., Ogonowski, C., Wan, L., and Wulf, V. 2012. Understanding and supporting cross-platform usage in the living room. *Entertain. Comput.* 3, 2 (2012), 37–47.

18. Holz, C., Bentley, F., Church, K., and Patel, M. 2015. "I'm just on my phone and they're watching TV": Quantifying mobile device use while watching television. In *TVX '15*. 93–102.

19. Jokela, T., Ojala, J., and Olsson, T. 2015. A Diary Study on Combining Multiple Information Devices in Everyday Activities and Tasks. In *Proc. 33rd Annu. ACM Conf. Hum. Factors Comput. Syst. - CHI '15*. ACM Press, New York, New York, USA, 3903–3912.

20. Karapanos, E., Zimmerman, J., Forlizzi, J., and Martens, J.-B. 2009. User experience over time: An initial framework. In *Proc. 27th Int. Conf. Hum. factors Comput. Syst. - CHI 09*. ACM Press, New York, New York, USA, 729–738.

21. Karapanos, E., Zimmerman, J., Forlizzi, J., and Martens, J.-B. 2010. Measuring the dynamics of remembered experience over time. *Interact. Comput.* 22, 5 (2010), 328–335.

22. Kujala, S., Roto, V., Väänänen-Vainio-Mattila,K., Karapanos, E., and Sinnelä, A. 2011. UX Curve: A method for evaluating long-term user experience. *Interact. Comput.* 23, 5 (2011), 473–483.

23. Kuo, Y.F., Wu, C.M., and Deng, W.J. 2009. The relationships among service quality, perceived value, customer satisfaction, and post-purchase intention in mobile value-added services. *Comput. Human Behav.* 25, 4 (2009), 887–896.

24. Law, E.L.-C., Roto, V., Hassenzahl, M., Vermeeren, A.P.O.S., and Kort, J. 2009. Understanding, scoping and defining user experience: A survey approach. In *Proc. 27th Int. Conf. Hum. factors Comput. Syst. - CHI 09*. ACM Press, 719–728.

25. Lin, H.X., Choong, Y.-Y., and Salvendy, G. 1997. A proposed index of usability: A method for comparing the relative usability of different software systems. *Behav. Inf. Technol.* 16, 4-5 (1997), 267–277.

26. McCarthy, J., and Wright, P. 2004. Technology as experience. *Interactions* 11, 5 (2004), 42–43.

27. Meulen, R., and Pettey, C. 2012. Gartner Says 85 Percent of All Flat-Panel TVs Will Be Internet-Connected Smart TVs by 2016. (2012). `http://www.gartner.com/newsroom/id/2280617`.

28. Nidumolu, S.R. and Knotts, G.W. 1998. The effects of customizability and reusability on perceived process and competitive performance of software firms. *MIS Q.* 22, 2 (1998), 105–137.

29. Nielsen, J., Clemmensen, T., and Yssing, C. 2002. Getting access to what goes on in people's heads?: reflections on the think-aloud technique. In *Proc. Second Nord. Conf. Human-computer Interact. - Nord. '02*. ACM Press, New York, New York, USA, 101–110.

30. Quiring, O. and Schweiger, W. 2008. Interactivity: a review of the concept and a framework for analysis. *Communications* 33, 2 (2008), 147–167.

31. Rosenblatt, C.P., and Cunningham, R.M. 1976. Television Watching and Family Tensions. *Marriage Fam.* 38, 1 (1976), 105–111.

32. Roto, V., Law, E., Vermeeren, A., and Hoonhout, J. 2010. User experience white Paper: bringing clarity to the concept of user experience. *Dagstuhl Semin. Demarcating User Exp.* (2010), 12.

33. Shin, D.-H., Hwang, Y., and Choo, H. 2013. Smart TV: are they really smart in interacting with people? Understanding the interactivity of Korean Smart TV. *Behav. Inf. Technol.* 32, 2 (2013), 156–172.

34. Venkatesh, V. 2000. Determinants of perceived ease of use: Integrating control, intrinsic motivation, and emotion into the technology acceptance model. *Inf. Syst. Res.* 11, 4 (2000), 342–365.

Design Guidelines for Notifications on Smart TVs

Dominik Weber, Sven Mayer, Alexandra Voit, Rodrigo Ventura Fierro°, Niels Henze
VIS, University of Stuttgart – Stuttgart, Germany
{firstname.lastname}@vis.uni-stuttgart.de – °ro_venfro@hotmail.com

ABSTRACT

Notifications are among the core mechanisms of most smart devices. Smartphones, smartwatches, tablets and smart glasses all provide similar means to notify the user. For smart TVs, however, no standard notification mechanism has been established. Smart TVs are unlike other smart devices because they are used by multiple people - often at the same time. It is unclear how notifications on smart TVs should be designed and which information users need. From a set of focus groups, we derive a design space for notifications on smart TVs. By further studying selected design alternatives in an online survey and lab study we show, for example, that users demand different information when they are watching TV with others and that privacy is a major concern. We derive according design guidelines for notifications on smart TVs that developers can use to gain the user's attention in a meaningful way.

ACM Classification Keywords

H.5.m. Information Interfaces and Presentation (e.g. HCI): Miscellaneous

Author Keywords

Notifications; Smart TV; TV; Attention; Guidelines

INTRODUCTION

Today's mobile devices and traditional desktop computers inform about new messages, upcoming appointments, events, and general hints using notifications. Notifications are a well-established mechanism to inform a user about a diverse range of information. One of the main use cases is enabling asynchronous communication. A typical notification related to personal communication on all major platforms informs about the sender and shows a text excerpt. In recent years, notifications became one of the core mechanisms on a number of smart devices.

Notifications can provide time sensitive information. They, however, do not always reach the user in time, because the device is not in the user's range. Dey et al. [6], for example, showed that users' smartphones are only within arm's reach 53% of the time. Already in 2002, Want et al. [23] proposed to distribute notifications across different smart devices. Sahami et al. [21, 24] developed a system that forwards smartphone notifications to desktop computers. Recently, major smartphone platforms started to provide centralized notification mechanisms. Notifications are not only managed on a single device itself but collected and shared across smartphones, tablets, desktop computers and laptops. Furthermore, a number of new types of smart devices recently became available. The core feature of smartwatches and smart glasses is displaying notifications. Studying smartwatch users, Lyons [16], however, found that 24% of the 50 participants did not wear their watches at home.

Another highly successful type of smart devices are smart TVs. The main characteristic of smart TVs in comparison to regular TVs is the capability to process data and to connect with online services. Thus it is possible to stream videos and other content from the Internet. Unlike mobile operating systems, there is currently no dominant operating systems for TVs. There is, however, a clear trend towards platforms similar to mobile operating systems, including the possibility to extend the systems by installing apps from app stores. In contrast to other smart devices, current smart TVs have no established notification mechanisms. Displaying notifications on smart TVs poses a number of challenges. TVs are primarily used for watching content, including TV series, news and movies. Displaying notifications on top of the main content can result in distractions and therefore affect the TV experience. Furthermore, unlike smartphones or smartwatches, TVs are shared devices that are used by multiple people, often at the same time. Therefore, the notification mechanisms designed for other smart devices cannot directly be adopted for smart TVs. Instead, it has to be investigated how a pleasant notification experience on all devices can be achieved while respecting the users' attention and privacy.

In this paper, we develop design guidelines for notifications on smart TVs. The paper is structured as follows: Through a series of focus groups we first explore design alternatives that potential users envision. Informed by this design space we further study five different design alternatives in an online survey. Based on the results we develop a customizable smart TV application that is able to display notification whilst watching TV, which we use to conduct a lab study. Combining the findings of the focus groups, online survey and lab study, we derive design guidelines for notifications on smart TVs. These design guidelines can be used by developers of future TV systems to gain the user's attention in a meaningful way.

Permission to make digital or hard copies of all or part of this work for personal or classroom use is granted without fee provided that copies are not made or distributed for profit or commercial advantage and that copies bear this notice and the full citation on the first page. Copyrights for components of this work owned by others than ACM must be honored. Abstracting with credit is permitted. To copy otherwise, or republish, to post on servers or to redistribute to lists, requires prior specific permission and/or a fee. Request permissions from permissions@acm.org.
TVX'16, June 22–24, 2016, Chicago, IL, USA.
Copyright © 2016 ACM ISBN 978-1-4503-4067-0/16/06 ...$15.00.
http://dx.doi.org/10.1145/2932206.2932212

RELATED WORK

The main characteristic of smart devices is the ability to connect to other smart devices and the Internet. In the past years existing devices and everyday things got smarter. With mobile data networks it is possible to access the Internet on the go and with smartphones it can be carried in the pocket. Smartwatches and smart glasses extend smartphones and are always with the user. Smart TVs are able to stream content from the network, thus transforming the TV from a device that was used mainly for watching television to a large screen that is able to receive content from various sources. The connectivity of smart devices allows pushing messages to the devices which lays the foundation for notifications. When receiving a push message, smart devices can alert the user through multiple modalities, namely visual cues, auditory signals and tactile output.

On smartphones notifications are a central interaction mechanism. Most current mobile operating systems allow the list of pending notifications to be accessed from any screen with a simple gesture. Previous work studied the effect of notifications on desktop PCs, smartphones and smartwatches. In an in-situ study with 15 participants, Pielot et al. investigated how users interact with notifications. Over the course of one week participants received an average of 63.5 notifications per day, mostly from instant messaging and email applications [19]. Furthermore, the study showed that notifications are viewed within minutes, even when the smartphone was put in the silent mode. Sahami et al. conducted a large-scale analysis of smartphone notifications by collecting 200 million mobile notifications from 40,000 users [21]. They found that notifications are viewed in a timely manner, with 50% being viewed within 30 seconds. The results of the analysis show that notifications related to messaging, communication and calendar events are the ones that are most valued by users. Furthermore, the authors conclude that important notifications are about people and events.

Research on interruptions caused by notifications predates the current set of smart devices. Czerwinski et al. investigated the effects of interruptions on task switching on traditional desktop PCs [5]. According to studies conducted by Iqbal et al., notifications cause interruptions but are still valued by users because they provide awareness [12]. Research has shown that the disruptive effects of notifications can be reduced by timing notifications. By issuing notifications at the end of tasks it is possible to maintain high awareness and reduce the disruptive effects of notifications [1]. Fallman and Yttergren proposed a system for mobile phones that detects nearby users and chooses an appropriate notification modality accordingly [7].

Today, multiple devices are often used at the same time. Smartphones are, for example, becoming a second screen for the TV, offering interactivity through social networks [15]. Nathan et al. implemented CollaboraTV, a system for asynchronous interaction with the goal to bring people together even if they do not watch at the same time or place [17]. The results of a field study over the course of one month showed participants valued the system. Alaoui and Lewkowicz proposed a similar system for elderly to cope with loneliness [2].

Holz et al. found in a study that family members joined each other in the living room to be physically together [11]. Courtois found there are three types of TV watching behavior [4]. One type only focuses on the TV, the second type watches TV with second screens, for example tablets or laptops, and the third type uses seconds screens and even printed media.

Further work has been done in the field of program recommendation systems for TVs. Chang et al. give a literature overview and, based on the gained insights, propose a recommendation framework [3]. As recommendations are based on the user's interests this creates challenges for multiple users. One possible solution for these challenges is merging interest profiles from the people in front of the TV, as proposed by Shin and Woo [22]. Lee et al. proposed a system for smart TVs that can authenticate the user using face recognition [14]. This can be used to automatically change the program recommendations depending on the user in front of the TV. Furthermore, the researchers propose using hand detection to control the smart TV with natural hand gestures.

Regan and Todd explored a system that allows multiple users to access their instant messages while watching TV simultaneously [20]. They state that people often use their PC to communicate in addition to watching TV. They looked at the aspects of privacy and distraction caused by such a system when watching TV with multiple people in the same room. To make users aware of incoming messages they used pop-up alerts in the corner of the screen, similar to ones found on the PC. In a study they found that for some people access to instant messaging is important even when watching TV. In the study incoming messages were considered interrupting if they were not meant for the participant.

Hess et al. conducted empirical work on concepts for social TV experiences [10]. They state that through current technology the Web and TV is combined which enables users to share content and communicate with others over distance. They identified a trend that watching TV is supplemented by other media. Multiple devices are used simultaneously, e.g. for communicating with friends. In a workshop a group discussed notifications. Messages should be received on the smartphone but users should be able to decide whether a notification should be displayed on the smartphone, the TV or both. Neate et al. investigated how to draw attention to companion content on a second screen when watching TV [18]. They implemented several stimuli, including an icon shown in the corner of the TV. In a study conducted by Geerts et al. the need for a "do not disturb" mode was shown [8]. However, the researchers mention that users do not want to enable or disable this mode every time they do (not) want to be disturbed.

In summary, notifications are a core feature of current smart devices. They are used to alert to user through multiple modalities. While there is a corpus of work that investigated the use of smart TVs, no standard notification mechanism for smart TVs has been established. What is missing are design guidelines for the design of notifications on smart TVs.

FOCUS GROUPS

We conducted three focus groups to explore the design space of notifications on smart TVs. Each of the focus groups lasted approximately one hour and were held in a meeting room equipped with a white board and projector. We provided post-its and black whiteboard markers, magnets and felt-tip pens (in 3 different colors) as well as printouts of a TV on A4 paper. During the focus groups we provided snacks and beverages. We compensated the participants for their time with 10 EUR. In all groups, one researcher guided the discussion while another researcher took notes and wrote down participants' statements. In the following we first describe the procedure of the focus group which is based on Goodman et al. [9]. Afterwards, we provide information about the participants and their behavior in respect to smart TVs. Then we present results, followed by a summery and a discussion.

Procedure

Each focus group had the same structure and consisted of four parts, an introduction, a round of idea creation, an open discussion and finally a closing discussion with a summary.

Introduction

First, participants were given a short introduction to the topic of the focus group. We prepared slides that explain the current state of notifications on various smart devices, the lack of notifications on smart TVs and how we want to explore them. Furthermore, we encouraged the participants to speak freely during the session with the request to avoid talking at the same time. Afterwards, we asked them to introduce themselves. In the introduction round all participants first stated their names and told the group the kind of devices they own that are able to notify them and the last important notification they can think of. Furthermore, the participants stated whether or not they own a TV and briefly talked about their TV watching behavior.

Idea creation

After the introduction round we asked the participants to imagine a TV that can notify them about events, like messages, emails or calendar reminders. We handed out sheets of paper with a TV printed on them and asked participants to sketch ideas how such a system should look like and how it should behave. We asked them to consider multiple factors including the content, size, position and display duration of notifications. After approximately 10 minutes we asked the participants to discuss their ideas with the person next to them. We instructed them to talk about positive and negative aspects of their ideas and to pick the ideas they like the most.

Open discussion

After the idea creation, we collected all sketches that were selected by the participants and pinned them to a whiteboard. Figure 1 shows one of the focus groups in the discussion phase. We asked the participants to explain their ideas to the rest of the group. Subsequently, we asked the rest of the group about their thoughts on the idea, including the advantages and disadvantages. If not brought up by any of the participants, we asked them how their ideas would work when watching TV alone compared to watching TV with others.

Figure 1. Participants of one of the focus groups discussing their selected ideas on a whiteboard.

Closing discussion and wrap-up

After discussing the ideas of all participants, we explored with the group how far we can go with notifications on TVs. We asked them what they think about showing advertisements, weather forecasts, reminders or product recommendations and openly discussed their concerns and suggestions. This discussion concluded the focus group.

Participants

We recruited students from a university campus to participate in the focus groups. In total 19 students showed interest in participating and we divided those in three groups. The age of the participants was between 21 and 31 years ($M = 25.7$, $SD = 2.8$). The first group consisted of four female and four male participants and was held in English. The second group consisted of six male participants and was held in German. The third group consisted of one female and four male participants and was again held in English.

All participants owned a smartphone and either a desktop PC or laptop, or both. Nine (47.37%) participants stated that they own a tablet and ten (52.63%) participants that they own a TV. Streaming was the participants' preferred way to watch movies, series and news. Consuming those streams was not limited to the TV, instead participants also watched them on their tablets and laptops. When asked about the last important notification they received, the participants mentioned email, instant messaging and calendar notifications.

Results

In the following sections we describe the analysis of the idea creation and discussion parts.

Notification styles

To analyze the ideas created by the participants, three researchers went through all sketches and derived factors that distinguish them. Afterwards, they agreed on one set of factors and described each sketch according to these factors. In total we collected 46 sheets of paper, with 37 containing sketches of notification styles and 9 containing written comments. The most popular notification style with 19 sketches was the toast notification style known from desktop and mobile operating

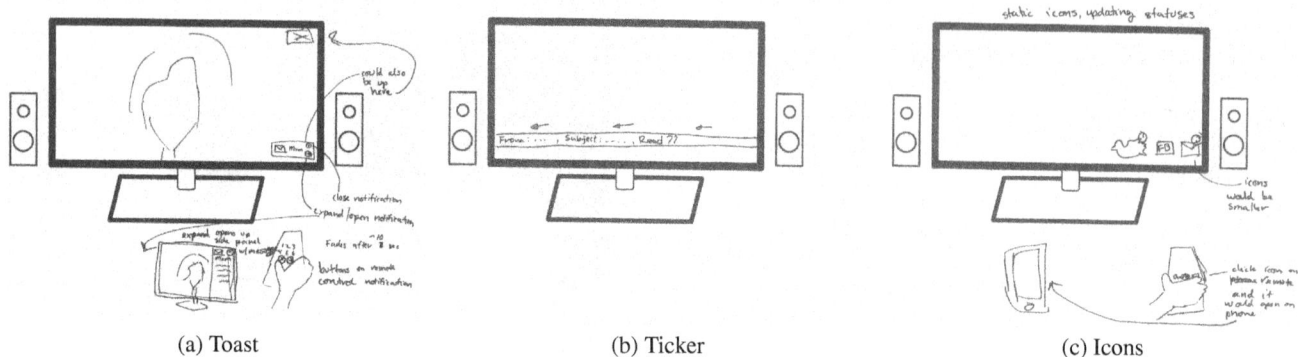

Figure 2. Sketches of notification styles created by the participants of the focus groups.

systems (see Figure 2a). Toast notifications overlay parts of the screen and typically consist of a box with an icon and two or more lines of text. On existing operating systems these notifications are typically only shown for a couple of seconds before disappearing again. On some sketches it is mentioned that after a toast notification disappears, a less intrusive indicator should be shown on the screen, e.g. an app icon. In most sketches the toast notifications were placed in the top right or bottom right corners of the screen.

The second most popular suggestion was a news ticker style at the top or bottom of the screen. Variants of the ticker style were found on 6 sketches. Figure 2b shows a sketch of a ticker notification at the bottom of the screen that scrolls the content from the right to left. While not exactly the same, this style is similar to the notification ticker used in Android prior to version 5.0, which temporarily replaced the status bar at the top of the screen with a ticker that scrolled through the received message content. A concern that came up in the group discussion was that this style would cover subtitles when placed at the bottom of the screen.

Another option that was also suggested 6 times, was to only show icons, similar to the status bar at the top of the screen of Android devices or the system tray area on desktop operating systems. The suggested place for these icons was, similar to the toast notifications, in the top right or bottom right corner. Participants mentioned that the icons could be enhanced by adding a badge to the icons that indicates the number of pending notifications for a certain application. Figure 2c shows three icons in the bottom right of the screen, with badges showing the number of notifications.

The fourth category of suggestions was about embedding a LED in frame or base of the TV. This variant was found 5 times on sketches. Participants suggested that the LED could change the color depending on the app that issued a notification, or depending on the importance of the notification. This option would be similar to notification LEDs found on smartphones.

One participant stated that the TV should be used as smart home hub, showing notifications and other information in full screen when the TV is not in use. Another participant suggested using a screen panel with a wider horizontal resolution that is reserved for notifications. This would allow for

a persistent notification stream on the TV without covering content. Independently from the notification style, all participants agreed that sound should be completely optional and configurable. Furthermore, participants agreed that notifications should sync with other devices, thus dismissing them on one device should dismiss them on other devices, too.

Concerns

Participants raised a number of concerns regarding notifications on TVs. A concern was occlusion of content. Notifications should be transparent to a degree, so nothing important is hidden. Examples were subtitles and score boards of sport broadcasts. Participants were concerned about bright pop-ups in an otherwise dark movie.

Another concern that was brought up in every focus group was the difference in watching TV alone in contrast to watching TV with others. The participants disliked the idea of notifications that show the sender and parts of the message while watching TVs with other people. One participant compared this with the scenario of giving a presentation and stated that he is always cautious to disable all notifications when giving a presentation. A "family mode" was suggested that hides the content or disables the notifications completely when watching TV with others. Furthermore, participants stated that notifications should be context aware. First, it should be detected if other people are in front of the TV, so notifications can be adjusted or disabled automatically. Also the idea of too many notifications was regarded as annoying, so only important notifications should be shown. Additionally, notifications should not be shown during truly immersive movies but a summary of missed events after the movie or during slow moments would be acceptable.

In the closing discussion some participants stated that if the notifications were used to display advertisements, they would disable the notifications. Others mentioned that if advertisements would allow them to watch movies or series for free, they consider them acceptable. Recommendation notifications, for example that the successor to the movie that is being watched is currently shown in the cinemas, was considered tolerable, as long as it not overused. The participants agreed that calendar reminders might be useful.

Summary and Discussion

In this section we described the procedure of three focus groups we conducted in order to explore the design space of notifications on smart TVs. The focus groups consisted of four parts, an introduction round, idea creation, open discussion and a closing discussion. In the idea creation part, participants drew sketches of possible notification mechanisms on smart TVs. Categorizing these sketches resulted in four categories for notification styles. The most popular styles were toast notifications, followed by ticker and icon-based notifications. Further variants include embedding LEDs in the TVs frame or base and using the TV as a hub for smart homes. In addition to this visual cues, sound could be used. However, sound should be optional and configurable.

Participants were concerned about privacy aspects of showing notifications on the TV when watching with other peoples. It was suggested to adjust the information shown depending on the number of people in front of the TV. Another concern was occultation of the screen content and distraction caused by notifications. Therefore, notifications should be only used for important events, for example messages from important contacts or calendar reminders.

ONLINE SURVEY

Based on the findings from the focus groups, we further investigated how much content should be shown in notifications on smart TV. To gain results from a wide variety of people we designed an online survey.

Therefore, we created five notification variants with varying amounts of information. The variants are shown in Figure 3. We focused on the amount of information shown rather than the design itself. Because of this, we decided to show all notifications as toast notifications, as this style was the most popular in the focus groups and is common in desktop setups to present notifications. Another preference from the participants of the focus groups was the positioning in the top right or bottom right corner. Accordingly, we displayed all notification variants in the top right corner. Apart from the variants we decided on one scenario. Therefore, we created videos for the five variants. Each video played back the same video content, each video was $25\,sec$ long. While the video was playing three notification popped up, the timing was the same for all variants, namely at 4, 15 and 18 seconds after the start. The displayed notification are an email, an instant message and second email notification.

In *Variant 1* a generic notification icon is shown and a badge on the icon keeps track of pending notifications (Figure 3a). *Variant 2* uses app-specific icons instead of the generic icon and the name of the app that created the notification is briefly shown (Figure 3b). *Variant 3* behaves similar to the second variant, however the sender of a message is also shown (Figure 3c). Furthermore, in *Variant 4* an excerpt of the message is shown below the sender, thus showing the most information (Figure 3d). These four variants are persistent until dismissed. *Variant 5* also displays the sender and the message excerpt, however no icon is left behind (Figure 3e).

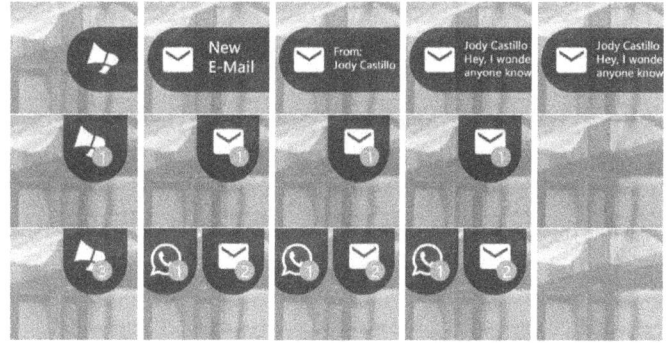

(a) Variant 1 (b) Variant 2 (c) Variant 3 (d) Variant 4 (e) Variant 5

Figure 3. The five notification variants with varying amounts of content, as shown at 4, 6 and 23 seconds in the video (from top to bottom).

We designed an online survey to receive feedback for the notification variants. The online survey was distributed via mailing lists, social networks and online communities.

Procedure

The online survey was answered by the participants in their web browser and consisted of three parts. First, we asked participants about demographic data, TV watching behavior and devices they are notified on. In the second part all notification variants were rated by the participants. The notification variants were counter-balanced (displayed in random order). For every notification variant a short textual description text was provided along with an embedded YouTube video.

For each condition the participants were asked to rate the following five statements from "Strongly disagree" to "Strongly agree" on a 5-point Likert scale.

(Q1) With this notification mechanism, I have the feeling that I am not missing a notification anymore.

(Q2) This notification mechanism provides me the information that I want.

(Q3) This notification mechanism disturbs my TV-watching-experience.

(Q4) I'd feel comfortable using this notification mechanism when I am watching TV alone.

(Q5) I'd feel comfortable using this notification mechanism when I am watching TV with others.

Finally, the participants should rate the two statements "It is important for me to know how many notifications from each application do I have.". At last the participants could comment our notification variants.

Participants

In total 167 people (50 female, 117 male) completed the survey. They were between 15 and 76 years old ($M = 28.8$, $SD = 10.2$), with 58% being students, 35% employees and 7% others. The online survey was available in English, German and Spanish. The English version was completed 46 (27.54%) times, the German version 105 (62.87%) times and the Spanish version 16 (9.58%) times. The size of the participants' households had a notable variety. 19.7% participants

	$0h$	$< 0.5h$	$0.5 - 1h$	$1 - 2h$	$2 - 3h$	$3 - 4h$	$> 4h$
Alone	19.1%	26.3%	13.7%	23.3%	10.7%	1.1%	5.3%
Others	26.3%	20.3%	20.9%	19.1%	7.7%	2.3%	2.9%

Table 1. Hours spent per day watching TV alone and with others.

stated that they live alone, 25.1% with another person, 24.5% in a three person household, 22.1% in a four person household and 6.0% live with five or more persons. 2.3% did not state the size of their household.

We asked "How many hours per day on average do you watch TV alone?" and "How many hours per day on average do you watch TV in company with other people?". In Table 1 we present the participants' TV usage.

We also asked the participants what kind of devices they own, on which devices they receive notifications and on which devices they actually read notifications. Possible options were smartphone, tablet, Internet-enabled TV, TV without Internet, desktop PC, laptop, smartwatch, fitness tracker and none. On smartphones, tablets and PCs notifications are a well-known paradigm to receive the attention of the user. Current smartwatches and fitness trackers often connect to a smartphone. Figure 4 shows the responses. 95.81% own a smartphone, 57.49% a tablet, 51.50% a TV with an Internet connection, 40.72% a TV without an Internet connection, 61.08% a desktop PC, 90.42% a laptop, 14.97% a smartwatch and 11.38% a fitness tracker. One participant stated that he does not own any of these devices. Generally, participants receive and read notifications on all smart devices with smart TVs being a notable exception.

Results

We analyzed all subjective ratings of the five conditions (Figure 5) using a Friedman test. We also analyzed the ratings for each rating using the Friedman test and Wilcoxon signed-rank post hoc tests with an applied Bonferroni correction, resulting in a significance level of $p < 0.005$.

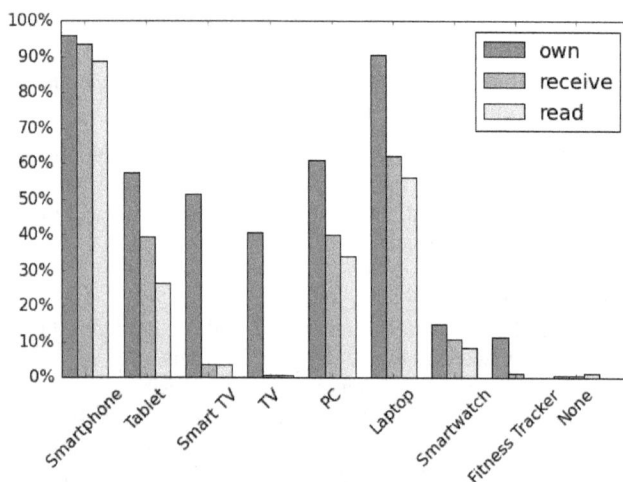

Figure 4. Devices which participants of the online survey own, receive notifications and read notifications.

(Q1) Not missing notifications: We found a significant difference for Q1, $\chi^2(4) = 115.020$, $p < .001$. For this statement Variant 3 ($M = 4.40$, $SD = 1.08$) and Variant 4 ($M = 4.40$, $SD = 1.13$) received the highest ratings, followed by Variant 2 ($M = 4.07$, $SD = 1.22$), Variant 5 ($M = 3.78$, $SD = 1.36$) and Variant 1 ($M = 3.38$, $SD = 1.34$). The rating of the variant with the generic icon is significantly lower than all other variants (1vs2 $Z = -6.322$, $p < .001$, 1vs3 $Z = -7.436$, $p < .001$, 1vs4 $Z = -7.436$, $p < .001$, 1vs5 $Z = -2.860$, $p = .004$). Variant 5 is significantly lower rated than Variant 3 ($Z = -5.326$, $p < .001$) and Variant 4 ($Z = -5.464$, $p < .001$).

(Q2) Provides wanted information: We found a significant difference for Q2, $\chi^2(4) = 123.015$, $p < .001$. For this statement Variant 3 ($M = 3.99$, $SD = 1.29$) received the highest rating, followed by Variant 4 ($M = 3.96$, $SD = 1.28$), Variant 5 ($M = 3.86$, $SD = 1.32$), Variant 2 ($M = 3.45$, $SD = 1.36$) and Variant 1 ($M = 2.86$, $SD = 1.22$). Again, Variant 1 received a significantly lower rating all other variants (1vs2 $Z = -5.798$, $p < .001$, 1vs3 $Z = -7.922$, $p < .001$, 1vs4 $Z = -7.022$, $p < .001$, 1vs5 $Z = -6.953$, $p < .001$). Also, Variant 2 (app icons, no text) received a significantly lower rating than variants with text, namely Variant 3 ($Z = -4.325$, $p < .001$) and Variant 4 ($Z = -3.409$, $p = .001$).

(Q3) Disturbs TV experience: We found a significant difference for Q3, $\chi^2(4) = 17.560$, $p < .001$. For this statement Variant 4 received the highest disturbance rating ($M = 3.74$, $SD = 1.36$), followed by Variant 3 ($M = 3.56$, $SD = 1.35$), Variant 2 ($M = 3.49$, $SD = 1.37$), Variant 5 ($M = 3.42$, $SD = 1.38$) and Variant 1 ($M = 3.38$, $SD = 1.40$). Variant 1, which displays only a generic icon, received the lowest disturbance rating. Variant 4, with sender and message excerpt, was rated significantly more disturbing than all other variants (5vs4 $Z = -3.533$, $p < .001$, 2vs4 $Z = -3.073$, $p = .002$, 3vs4 $Z = -3.018$, $p = .003$, 1vs4 $Z = -3.751$, $p < .001$).

(Q4) Comfort alone: We found a significant difference for Q4, $\chi^2(4) = 22.216$, $p < .001$. For this statement Variant 5 received the highest rating ($M = 3.93$, $SD = 1.36$), followed by Variant 3 ($M = 3.81$, $SD = 1.38$), Variant 2 ($M = 3.78$, $SD = 1.35$), Variant 4 ($M = 3.75$, $SD = 1.37$) and Variant 1 ($M = 3.41$, $SD = 1.38$). Variant 2-5 are not significantly different. Variant 1 has a significantly lower rating than Variant 2 ($Z = -3.398$, $p < .001$), Variant 3 ($Z = -3.654$, $p < .001$) and Variant 5 ($Z = -4.014$, $p < .001$).

(Q5) Comfort with others: We found a significant difference for Q4, $\chi^2(4) = 60.511$, $p < .001$. For this statement Variant 2 received the highest rating ($M = 3.19$, $SD = 1.36$), followed by Variant 1 ($M = 3.18$, $SD = 1.39$), Variant 3 ($M = 2.89$, $SD = 1.26$), Variant 5 ($M = 2.77$, $SD = 1.23$) and Variant 4 ($M = 2.59$, $SD = 1.10$). Variant 2 is significantly different to all variants except Variant 1 (2vs3 $Z = -3.415$, $p = .001$, 2vs5 $Z = -4.108$, $p < .001$, 2vs4 $Z = -5.236$, $p < .001$). Variant 1 is significantly different to Variant 3 ($Z = -3.059$, $p = .002$), Variant 5 ($Z = -4.127$, $p < .001$) and Variant 4 ($Z = -5.008$, $p < .001$). Also, Variant 3 is significantly different to Variant 4 ($Z = -3.636$, $p < .001$).

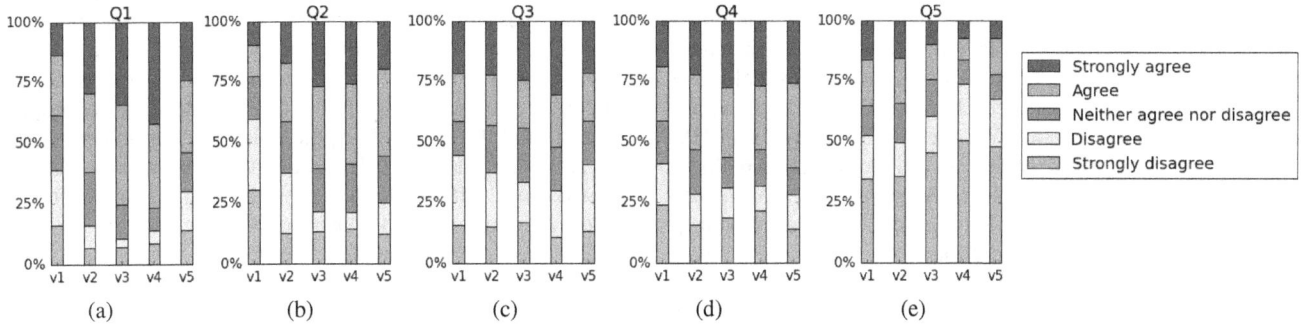

Figure 5. Ratings of the five statements (Q1-5) of the online survey for each notification variant (v1-5).

Optional comments

The last part of the online survey included a free text field that allowed the participants to enter a comment independent of the previous tasks. Two researchers translated comments written in Spanish and German to English and filtered comments without usable feedback. This resulted in 55 comments that were subsequently categorized by their content.

Thirteen participants explicitly stated that they would not use a notification system on their TV under any circumstances. Two participants stated that they do not want to be disturbed when watching TV at all and thus silence their smartphones. Three other participants were not as opposed to receive notification on the TV. Instead, they stated that it depends on the importance of the notification, which in return depends on the urgency or person sending the message. An interesting category of comments from 7 participants distinguished between watching a movie and "entertainment programs", for example quiz shows "where you do not have to actively focus on the program to follow it" *(Translated from German.)*. Two participants suggested displaying notifications after a movie.

In the survey we asked the participants how comfortable they would feel using this notification style alone compared to using it when other people are around. In the free text field 5 participants addressed this issue. They suggested multiple modes that can be switched depending on how many people are around. One mode would display notifications without restrictions, whereas the "private" mode would only display notification hints. Customization is another topic that was addressed by 13 participants. They suggested changes to the notification shown in the videos and overall options they would like to see, from the color of the notification to the screen corner that should be used.

Summary and Discussion

In this section we described the online survey, where we evaluated five notification variants with a varying amount of content. For each notification variant, we asked participants to rate their agreement to five statements and asked them what they like and dislike. Furthermore, we asked them in a free text field to give us general feedback to notifications on smart TVs. The participants owned a number of smart devices, on which they receive and read notifications. However, an exception to this poses are TVs and smart TVs on which most participants did not receive or read notifications.

Figure 6. The setup for the lab study. A participant is customizing the notification toast on the TV using a remote.

The results of the online survey indicate participants prefer to see the sender or the sender in addition to a message excerpt in the notification. Participants are concerned about missing notifications if no indicator is left behind and showing only a generic icon is not enough information for the participants. However, persistent indicators and showing more text in the notification increases the occluded display space. Therefore the participants stated that the variants with text disturb the TV watching experience the most. Four of our tested variants left an icon behind and not doing that could decrease the disturbance created by the text. When watching alone, participants liked all variants except the generic app icon. When watching with others, participants liked the variants that show the sender or message less.

LAB STUDY

In the online survey we investigated the amount of content which should be shown in notifications on smart TVs. One major result is that notifications should be customizable by the user. To further investigate in this direction, we conducted a lab study where participants had the task to customize a toast notification. Therefore, we set up a room in our lab with a sofa and a TV (see Figure 6). We implemented an application which enables us to push notifications to the TV while a video is playing. Derived by the results from the online survey there is a need to investigate in the customization while watching alone and with others. Therefore, we conducted the lab study with two groups, one group watching alone and the other watching together with a second unknown person. This was done to see if participants choose different settings. In the following we describe the study as well as the results.

Design

To get insights into the differences between watching television alone and with other people, we ran the study in a between subjects design. The participants of one group (A) sat alone in front of the TV, while the second group (B) watched a video in presence of a researcher. We used a 55" Philips Full HD TV connected to an Amazon Fire TV box to achieve a realistic TV experience. The Amazon Fire TV enabled us to push notifications on top of a video and also enabled the participant to customize them. Another limitation of the online survey was that we created an exemplary scenario, resulting in notifications that were not meaningful for the participants. Therefore, we developed a smartphone application for Android devices to log all notifications shown on the device. All notifications shown in the lab study were therefore notifications the participants recently received. The notifications were selected randomly from the log files and varied from instant messaging notifications to system messages.

For the lab study itself we developed a second Android application that was installed on the Amazon Fire TV. This app is capable of playing back a video while showing a overlay with a notification. Furthermore, it allows the user to control the representation of the notification with nine different settings. The GUI of the settings menu is shown on the left side in Figure 7. These settings are: position, size, icon, theme, opacity, duration, content, lines and sound. The *position* setting controls where notifications appear on the screen, with nine possible options from the top left to the bottom right. The *size* setting allows to scale the notification from small (225dp), medium (300dp) to large (375dp), using Android's density-independent pixels (dp) metric. The *icon* setting allows to show the icon of the app in full color and gray scale, a generic-app icon in color and gray scale, or no icon at all. The *theme* setting allows to set the background of the notification to white (light theme) or black (dark theme). The *opacity* allows to set the opacity to 25%, 50%, 75% or 100%. The *duration* setting controls how long the notification is shown, from 1 second to 25 seconds. The *content* setting controls how much of the logged text is shown. Possible options are to only show the name of the app, to include the title/sender, and to show title/sender and message. The *lines* setting depends on the content setting, because it controls how many lines are shown, with possible values being 1-5 or unlimited. The *sound* setting can be either enabled or disabled, and plays a default sound when enabled.

Procedure

We invited the participants two times. The first time to sign a consent form and to set up the notification logger. Two days later we invited them the second time to our lab. First, we asked them to fill in a demographic data form and seated them on a sofa in front of the TV ($3\,m$ between screen and participant). Then we explained that we built an application for the TV that would display random notifications from the past two days while an episode of the series "Big Bang Theory" was playing. For group A it was explicitly stated that they would watch the episode alone, without anyone in the room. For group B it was stated the researcher would stay in the room. We opened the settings screen and briefly introduced the participants to the nine available settings. At this point no

setting was configured yet. Therefore, the participants were asked to explore the settings by themselves. After configuring all settings, a preview notification appeared that allowed the participants to make further adjustments. When participants decided that the notification's representation was appropriate, we started the first half of the episode. For group A the researcher left the room. Ten notifications were shown at predefined times. The predefined times for displaying notifications were randomly chosen by us and the same for each participant. After the first half finished, the episode was paused and the settings page was opened automatically. The participants had the opportunity to change their settings for the second half of the episode. In the second half ten additional notifications were shown. After watching the full episode, the settings page opened again and participants were asked to adjust the settings one more time. Finally, we asked participants to rate the importance of each setting on a 5-point Likert scale.

Participants

In total 14 participants (5 female) took part in the study all were recruited on our university's campus. They were between 22 and 32 years old ($M = 25.86$, $SD = 2.95$). Twelve of the participants were students, one participant was a PhD student, one participant was a promoter.

Results

In Figure 8 the agreement to the importance of the settings is shown, highlighting the need for customization of notifications. The three most important settings to customize the notifications were the *position* ($M = 4.79$, $SD = 0.43$), size ($M = 4.71$, $SD = 0.47$) and *content* ($M = 4.50$, $SD = 0.65$). Followed by *duration* ($M = 4.29$, $SD = 0.83$), *lines* ($M = 4.01$, $SD = 0.62$), *opacity* ($M = 3.93$, $SD = 1.14$), *icon style* ($M = 3.64$, $SD = 0.84$) and *sound* ($M = 3.50$, $SD = 1.83$). The *theme* setting received neutral ratings ($M = 3.00$, $SD = 1.24$). However, statistics did not reveal any significant difference between people, who watched alone or together with other people.

Derived from the participants' final settings the following values are the most popular. For the nominal setting values we will report the *modus* and for the duration as a scale we report M and SD. This results in a *most popular* notification style, which is represented as follows: The notification is in a dark themed box in the upper right corner displayed for $M = 4.93$, $SD = 2.6$ seconds with 75% opacity. Including a colored app icon, the sender and two/three/unlimited lines of the message, with a small font and no sound. The visual representation is shown on the right side of Figure 7.

Position: Nine participants preferred the position in the upper right corner, two participants chose the bottom left corner and another two participants chose the bottom right corner. There are no significant differences between both groups. It is important that notifications are positioned in a way that provides visibility, but also does not hide the content or program inserts [P4, P8]. Two participants argued, that they chose the position because they are used to it from their smartphones and laptops [P11, P12].

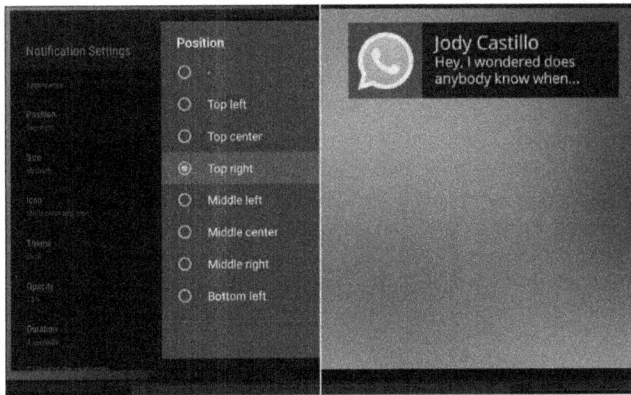

Figure 7. The study app on the Amazon Fire TV. The left side shows the settings with the *position* options dialog. The right side shows an exemplary *WhatsApp* notification with the *most popular* settings.

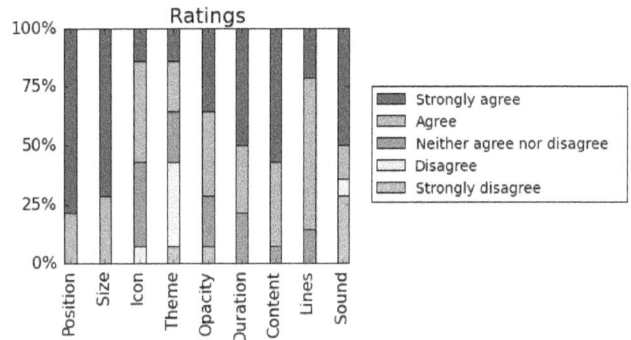

Figure 8. The importance ratings for the nine different settings we investigated in the lab study.

Size: Ten participants chose a small representation of the notification, 4 the medium size and none the large size. There are no significant difference between both groups. The notifications should be big enough to read and small enough to not hide the content [P8]. Too big overlays are annoying [P4, P14] and the size should depend on the TV's size and the distance to TV, too [P2].

Icon: The selection of the used icon depends on the two groups. Participants, who watched together with a researcher have chosen an icon, which belongs to the incoming notification. The app icon in color was chosen by 5 participants and 2 participants used the app application icon in gray scale. Participants, who watched alone chose dissimilar icons. Only 3 participants chose the app icon in color. Two participants used a generic icon for an incoming notification and two others decided to hide the icon completely. The usage of an application icon helps to the judge importance of the notification, which generated the notification [P1, P3, P9, P10, P11].

Theme: Ten participants set the dark variant and four the light one. Two participants mentioned that the contrast is important [P1, P4] and two other participants think there is not much of a difference between the light and the dark theme [P9, P12].

Opacity: Participants who watched alone all chose a high opacity, 6 of them used the 75% opacity and 1 participant used the 100% opacity. From the participants who watched together with a researcher, one chose 25% opacity and two participants chose 50%, 75%, and 100% respectively. The notification should not block the TV content [P8, P12] and not be too transparent [P3, P12]. This setting is important for minimal distraction [P11]. One participant thinks an opacity with 25% or 50% is too transparent [P3], while another participant said the opacity should be between 25% and 50% to not block the TV content [P8].

Duration: Participants who watched alone chose longer durations for displaying the notifications. One participant used a duration of $3 sec$, one participant used a duration of $4 sec$, 4 participants used a duration of $5 sec$ and one participant chose a duration of $13 sec$. However, 2 of the participants who watched together with a researcher chose a duration of $3 sec$, 2

participants used $4 sec$ for the duration and 3 participants chose a duration of $5 sec$. The setting for the duration of displaying the notification is a balance between being long enough to read the message and short enough so the notification is not a nuisance [P11]. The opinions to the duration diverges, too. One participant who watched alone thinks, more than $10 sec$ are too much for displaying the notification [P3]. However, a participant who watched with a researcher commented $2 - 3 sec$ are enough for displaying the notification [P8]. Another participant prefers that there should be a standard duration and user can terminate to read or skip by pressing a button [P2].

Content: From the participants who watched alone 1 participant chose to display the sender only, 6 of them chose to display the sender and the message of the notification. For the participants who watched together with a researcher 4 participants chose to display only the sender and 3 of them chose to display the sender and message of the notification. No one of the participants chose the option to display only the name of the application. The participants said that is important to decide what should be displayed on the screen because of privacy issues [P1, P8, P12]. There will be some people who want to read the notification only on their phone [P2], but other people might want to read the notification on the TV [P2]. When more text is displayed, longer attention is required and so you could miss what you are watching [P9] but also affects to what extend you are informed [P10].

Lines: From the nine participants who chose to display the message of their notifications, three chose two, three and unlimited lines of text respectively. These include participants who watched together with a researcher, one of them chose 2 rows and two others 3 rows for the message. The length of the displayed content is a privacy setting as well and depends on who could see the notification [P8, P10]. Another participant suggested a meaningful reduction of the displayed content, when full text is too much for a short insert [P4].

Sound: All participants but one disabled the sound for an incoming notification. They argue that the sound makes no sense [P1], is not necessary [P2] and distracting [P11]. Three participants perceived the sound as annoying [P4, P10, P12]. One participant thinks that the sound might bother some people but might help to remember acting on the notification after watching TV [P9].

Summary and Discussion

In this section we described our lab study, where we invited 14 participants to customize notifications while watching TV. The lab study revealed a clear need for customization. Participants rated the importance for all settings on average at least to *neither agree nor disagree*. We also reported qualitative feedback regarding the provided settings. Furthermore, we presented the *most popular* configuration of settings which can be used as an initial setting for further studies. One limitation of the "watching with a researcher" approach is the relationship between the participant and the researcher. In future studies differences between watching with friends, family or the partner should be investigated.

DESIGN GUIDELINES

Based on our findings from the focus groups, the online survey, and the controlled lab study we derived the following guidelines for notifications on TVs. The guidelines can be used by developers to gain the user's attention on smart TVs in a meaningful way.

Evaluate the importance

Developers should evaluate the importance of notifications instead of creating a stream of notifications as it is currently the case on other smart devices. Related work on smartphone notifications has shown that important notifications are about people and events [21]. Insights gained in the focus groups and the online survey confirmed this. For some people nothing is important enough to distract them from their immersion when watching TV. Because of this, notifications on smart TVs should always be optional.

Privacy considerations

Privacy aspects on smart TVs differ from other smart devices. TVs are typically shared devices and are used by multiple people, often at the same time. Unlike other smart devices it is therefore not recommended to simply display message excerpts in notifications. An idea brought up in the focus group was using multiple profiles depending on how many people are in front of the TV. One profile could be used for watching TV alone with no restrictions to the displayed information. Another profile could be used when watching TV with others. In this "private" profile, notifications could show various levels of information. For example, not showing the message excerpts, excluding the sender or using a default application icon. We suggest a system that detects people in front of the TV and uses this knowledge to automatically adjust the amount of information shown in the notifications. If an automated solution is not possible, it should be at least possible to switch between a public and private mode with ease.

Time interruptions

Multiple participants of the online survey mentioned that they like the idea of notifications on the TV. However, the notifications should not be shown during movies, as this was regarded as distractive. Instead, participants suggested to show notifications after a movie. Previous work on timing notifications has shown that notifications are less distractive if they are shown in between tasks [1]. Apart from the end of a movie we suggest notifying the user during advertisement breaks and, in the case of video on demand movies, when the movie is paused.

Be subtle

Notifications on smart TVs should be subtle. Effects and animations should be used with care to avoid distracting the user. Participants of our lab study disliked the idea of playing a sound. The size, opacity, display duration and text length have to be balanced in order to maximize readability and minimize occlusion of the content.

Allow customization

In all studies participants agreed that it must be possible to customize how notifications are displayed. As stated above, the amount of information to be displayed should be customizable. Furthermore, the position of the notification and display duration on the screen is something that participants were not in agreement, thus should be configurable.

CONCLUSION AND FUTURE WORK

In this paper we developed guidelines for notifications on smart TVs. Through a set of three focus groups we collected insights about users' attitude towards notifications on TVs. The design space includes the presentation of notifications, the displayed content, the application causing the notification, the number of received notifications, and how long a notification stays on the screen. We further studied selected design alternatives in an online survey to get more information about the displayed content of notifications on smart TVs. With these findings we implemented an application which enables us to display notifications on the TV while a video is playing and conducted a lab study. In the lab study we investigated the difference in the settings between watching alone and watching together with other people. From the findings, we have elaborated our design guidelines for displaying notifications on a TV. Only notifications truly important for the user should be shown. Furthermore, users' privacy should be considered especially if multiple people share the TV. Notifications could mainly be shown during breaks and be presented in a subtle way. Finally, users should be enabled to easily customize the presentation.

In the future, further insights could be gained by implementing a system that shows notifications on smart TVs and conducting a field study by installing the system in peoples' living rooms. In particular, it would be interesting to use a system that is able to determine the number of viewers, for example through the use of depth sensing cameras. The system could adjust the settings and types of notifications shown according to the viewers. Furthermore, means to interact with notifications shown on smart TVs should be investigated. Important notifications often inform about messages and users therefore might expect that they can directly react to them using the smart TV. A further direction are ambient visualizations that display notifications in a subtle way. A potential approach is to use technologies such as Ambilight and IllumiRoom [13] that allow visualizations in the surrounding of the TV.

ACKNOWLEDGMENTS
This work is supported by the German ministry of education and research (BMBF) within the DAAN project (13N13481) and by the DFG within the SimTech Cluster of Excellence (EXC 310/2).

REFERENCES
1. Piotr D. Adamczyk and Brian P. Bailey. 2004. If Not Now, when?: The Effects of Interruption at Different Moments Within Task Execution. In *Proceedings of the SIGCHI Conference on Human Factors in Computing Systems (CHI '04)*. ACM, New York, NY, USA, 271–278. DOI:http://dx.doi.org/10.1145/985692.985727

2. Malek Alaoui and Myriam Lewkowicz. 2013. A Livinglab Approach to Involve Elderly in the Design of Smart TV Applications Offering Communication Services. In *Proceedings of the 5th International Conference on Online Communities and Social Computing*. Springer-Verlag, Berlin, Heidelberg, 325–334. DOI: http://dx.doi.org/10.1007/978-3-642-39371-6_37

3. Na Chang, Mhd Irvan, and Takao Terano. 2013. A TV Program Recommender Framework. *Procedia Computer Science* 22 (2013), 561–570. DOI: http://dx.doi.org/10.1016/j.procs.2013.09.136

4. Cédric Courtois and Evelien D'heer. 2012. Second Screen Applications and Tablet Users: Constellation, Awareness, Experience, and Interest. In *Proceedings of the 10th European Conference on Interactive Tv and Video (EuroiTV '12)*. ACM, New York, NY, USA, 153–156. DOI: http://dx.doi.org/10.1145/2325616.2325646

5. Mary Czerwinski, Eric Horvitz, and Susan Wilhite. 2004. A Diary Study of Task Switching and Interruptions. In *Proceedings of the SIGCHI Conference on Human Factors in Computing Systems (CHI '04)*. ACM, New York, NY, USA, 175–182. DOI: http://dx.doi.org/10.1145/985692.985715

6. Anind K. Dey, Katarzyna Wac, Denzil Ferreira, Kevin Tassini, Jin-Hyuk Hong, and Julian Ramos. 2011. Getting Closer: An Empirical Investigation of the Proximity of User to Their Smart Phones. In *Proceedings of the 13th International Conference on Ubiquitous Computing (UbiComp '11)*. ACM, New York, NY, USA, 163–172. DOI:http://dx.doi.org/10.1145/2030112.2030135

7. Daniel Fallman and Björn Yttergren. 2005. Meeting in Quiet: Choosing Suitable Notification Modalities for Mobile Phones. In *Proceedings of the 2005 Conference on Designing for User eXperience (DUX '05)*. AIGA: American Institute of Graphic Arts, New York, NY, USA, Article 55. http://dl.acm.org/citation.cfm?id=1138235.1138299

8. David Geerts, Pablo Cesar, and Dick Bulterman. 2008. The Implications of Program Genres for the Design of Social Television Systems. In *Proceedings of the 1st International Conference on Designing Interactive User Experiences for TV and Video (UXTV '08)*. ACM, New York, NY, USA, 71–80. DOI: http://dx.doi.org/10.1145/1453805.1453822

9. Elizabeth Goodman, Mike Kuniavsky, and Andrea Moed. 2012. *Observing the User Experience, Second Edition: A Practitioner's Guide to User Research* (2nd ed.). Morgan Kaufmann Publishers Inc., San Francisco, CA, USA.

10. Jan Hess, Benedikt Ley, Corinna Ogonowski, Lin Wan, and Volker Wulf. 2011. Jumping Between Devices and Services: Towards an Integrated Concept for Social Tv. In *Proceddings of the 9th International Interactive Conference on Interactive Television (EuroITV '11)*. ACM, New York, NY, USA, 11–20. DOI: http://dx.doi.org/10.1145/2000119.2000122

11. Christian Holz, Frank Bentley, Karen Church, and Mitesh Patel. 2015. "I'M Just on My Phone and They'Re Watching TV": Quantifying Mobile Device Use While Watching Television. In *Proceedings of the ACM International Conference on Interactive Experiences for TV and Online Video (TVX '15)*. ACM, New York, NY, USA, 93–102. DOI: http://dx.doi.org/10.1145/2745197.2745210

12. Shamsi T. Iqbal and Eric Horvitz. 2010. Notifications and Awareness: A Field Study of Alert Usage and Preferences. In *Proceedings of the 2010 ACM Conference on Computer Supported Cooperative Work (CSCW '10)*. ACM, New York, NY, USA, 27–30. DOI: http://dx.doi.org/10.1145/1718918.1718926

13. Brett R. Jones, Hrvoje Benko, Eyal Ofek, and Andrew D. Wilson. 2013. IllumiRoom: Peripheral Projected Illusions for Interactive Experiences. In *Proceedings of the SIGCHI Conference on Human Factors in Computing Systems (CHI '13)*. ACM, New York, NY, USA, 869–878. DOI:http://dx.doi.org/10.1145/2470654.2466112

14. Sang-Heon Lee, Myoung-Kyu Sohn, Dong-Ju Kim, Byungmin Kim, and Hyunduk Kim. 2013. Smart tv interaction system using face and hand gesture recognition. In *Consumer Electronics (ICCE), 2013 IEEE International Conference on*. IEEE, 173–174. DOI: http://dx.doi.org/10.1109/ICCE.2013.6486845

15. Mark Lochrie and Paul Coulton. 2011. Mobile Phones As Second Screen for TV, Enabling Inter-audience Interaction. In *Proceedings of the 8th International Conference on Advances in Computer Entertainment Technology (ACE '11)*. ACM, New York, NY, USA, Article 73, 2 pages. DOI: http://dx.doi.org/10.1145/2071423.2071513

16. Kent Lyons. 2015. What Can a Dumb Watch Teach a Smartwatch?: Informing the Design of Smartwatches. In *Proceedings of the 2015 ACM International Symposium on Wearable Computers (ISWC '15)*. ACM, New York, NY, USA, 3–10. DOI: http://dx.doi.org/10.1145/2802083.2802084

17. Mukesh Nathan, Chris Harrison, Svetlana Yarosh, Loren Terveen, Larry Stead, and Brian Amento. 2008. CollaboraTV: Making Television Viewing Social Again. In *Proceedings of the 1st International Conference on Designing Interactive User Experiences for TV and Video (UXTV '08)*. ACM, New York, NY, USA, 85–94. DOI: http://dx.doi.org/10.1145/1453805.1453824

18. Timothy Neate, Matt Jones, and Michael Evans. 2015. Mediating Attention for Second Screen Companion Content. In *Proceedings of the 33rd Annual ACM Conference on Human Factors in Computing Systems (CHI '15)*. ACM, New York, NY, USA, 3103–3106. DOI: http://dx.doi.org/10.1145/2702123.2702278

19. Martin Pielot, Karen Church, and Rodrigo de Oliveira. 2014. An In-situ Study of Mobile Phone Notifications. In *Proceedings of the 16th International Conference on Human-computer Interaction with Mobile Devices & Services (MobileHCI '14)*. ACM, New York, NY, USA, 233–242. DOI: http://dx.doi.org/10.1145/2628363.2628364

20. Tim Regan and Ian Todd. 2004. Media Center Buddies: Instant Messaging Around a Media Center. In *Proceedings of the Third Nordic Conference on Human-computer Interaction (NordiCHI '04)*. ACM, New York, NY, USA, 141–144. DOI: http://dx.doi.org/10.1145/1028014.1028036

21. Alireza Sahami Shirazi, Niels Henze, Tilman Dingler, Martin Pielot, Dominik Weber, and Albrecht Schmidt. 2014. Large-scale Assessment of Mobile Notifications. In *Proceedings of the SIGCHI Conference on Human Factors in Computing Systems (CHI '14)*. ACM, New York, NY, USA, 3055–3064. DOI: http://dx.doi.org/10.1145/2556288.2557189

22. Choonsung Shin and Woontack Woo. 2009. Socially Aware Tv Program Recommender for Multiple Viewers. *IEEE Transactions on Consumer Electronics* 55, 2 (May 2009), 927–932. DOI: http://dx.doi.org/10.1109/TCE.2009.5174476

23. Royu Want, Trevor Pering, Gunner Danneels, Muthu Kumar, Murali Sundar, and John Light. 2002. The Personal Server: Changing the Way We Think about Ubiquitous Computing. In *UbiComp 2002: Ubiquitous Computing*, Gaetano Borriello and LarsErik Holmquist (Eds.). Lecture Notes in Computer Science, Vol. 2498. Springer Berlin Heidelberg, 194–209. DOI: http://dx.doi.org/10.1007/3-540-45809-3_15

24. Dominik Weber, Alireza Sahami Shirazi, and Niels Henze. 2015. Towards Smart Notifications Using Research in the Large. In *Proceedings of the 17th International Conference on Human-Computer Interaction with Mobile Devices and Services Adjunct (MobileHCI '15)*. ACM, New York, NY, USA, 1117–1122. DOI: http://dx.doi.org/10.1145/2786567.2794334

Who Has the Force?
Solving Conflicts for Multi User Mid-Air Gestures for TVs

Katrin Plaumann   **David Lehr**   **Enrico Rukzio**
Institute of Media Informatics
Ulm University, Ulm, Germany
<firstname>.<lastname>@uni-ulm.de

ABSTRACT
In recent years, mid-air gestures have become a feasible input modality for controlling and manipulating digital content. In case of controlling TVs, mid-air gestures eliminate the need to hold remote controls, which quite often are not at hand or even need to be searched before use. Thus, mid-air gestures quicken interactions. However, the absence of a single controller and the nature of mid-air gesture detection also poses a disadvantage: gestures preformed by multiple watchers may result in conflicts. In this paper, we propose an interaction technique solving the conflicts arising in such multi viewer scenarios. We conducted a survey with 64 participants, asking them about their TV viewing habits, experienced conflicts and opinions on conflict solving strategies. Based on the survey's results, we present a prototype for multi viewer gestural controls for TVs which solves possible conflicts.

ACM Classification Keywords
H.5.2 Information Systems: User Interfaces

Author Keywords
multi user gesture control;
mid air gestures; conflicts; TV gesture control; multi user;

INTRODUCTION
In recent years, mid-air gestures have become a viable alternative for controlling and manipulating digital content. One popular example is using gestures to control TVs instead of traditional remote controls [2, 5, 7, 8]. Low cost gesture recognition sensors and toolkits found their way into modern living rooms. Nowadays, even consumer products are shipped with gesture controls, allowing users to use gestures to navigate menus and manipulate content [6].

One of the main differences between gesture controls and traditional remote controls is that gesture controls do not require users to hold a dedicated device for interacting with the TV. This poses several advantages over traditional remote controls.

For instance, remote controls are not always at hand and have to be grabbed first before a command can be given. This is omitted with gesture controls, where users just perform the gesture for a corresponding command. Another advantage of gesture controls is that they cannot be lost or hidden like remote controls. Additionally, gesture controls are more hygienic, since no surface needs to be touched by multiple persons.

However, gesture controls constitute a different problem, which was not at all a problem with traditional remote controls: it is now possible for more than one person to manipulate content at the same time, simply by simultaneously performing gestures. This leads to several conflicts, both technical and social. Technical conflicts arise since the system needs to interpret all given commands and decide which should be executed. Social conflicts arise when users perform contradicting gestures, but also when the solution for a technical conflict is not satisfying for all.

Despite of the substantial body of work covering mid air interaction and recent works showing that co-watchers influence interaction [5, 8], solving conflicts in multi user gesture control scenarios has not been extensively researched in the past. The few works focussing on this topic mostly focus on interaction on tabletops and collaborative work scenarios [1, 4]. To fill this gap in knowledge, we developed three conflict solving strategies based on previous work. Those strategies were assessed by 64 participants in an online survey. This survey also showed that gesture controls are a feasible alternative for remote controls, and participants reflected upon conflict prone scenarios. Based on the survey's results, we implemented a prototype preventing technical as well as social conflicts. Our contributions therefore are:

- An online survey assessing multi watcher scenarios and conflict prone situations for mid-air interaction for TVs as well as conflict solving strategies based on previous work
- A prototype implementation for solving and preventing conflicts for mid-air interaction applicable not only to TVs, but digital content in general

The remainder of this paper is structured as follows: First, we will give an overview over related work. Subsequently, we will describe possible interaction techniques for solving conflicts based on prior work, the survey we conducted to assess conflicts from user perspective, and our prototype for solving conflicts in multi user mid-air interaction scenarios.

Permission to make digital or hard copies of all or part of this work for personal or classroom use is granted without fee provided that copies are not made or distributed for profit or commercial advantage and that copies bear this notice and the full citation on the first page. Copyrights for components of this work owned by others than ACM must be honored. Abstracting with credit is permitted. To copy otherwise, or republish, to post on servers or to redistribute to lists, requires prior specific permission and/or a fee. Request permissions from permissions@acm.org.

TVX'16, June 22-24, 2016, Chicago, IL, USA.
Copyright © 2016 ACM 978-1-4503-4067-0/16/06 ...$15.00.
http://dx.doi.org/10.1145/2932206.2932208

RELATED WORK

Gesture Controls for TVs

There exists a substantial body of work covering gesture detection as such and especially for TVs. One of the many projects showing that in the context of watching TV, gestures detection works quite reliable was conducted by Lee et al. [2]. However, they solely focussed on the detection of gestures, not on interaction concepts. This was done by Vatavu [7], who developed a gesture alphabet for interacting with TVs using a user elicitation study. Yet they only regarded single watcher scenarios, while we focus on multi watcher scenarios and their possible conflicts.

Multi User Gestural Interaction

Morris et al. [3] researched cooperative gestures for co-located groupware. Cooperative gestures are gestures were the gesture of a single team member contributes to a command given by the whole team. This type of gestural interaction impose a certain degree of teamwork. Besides focusing on mid-air gestures, we also focus more on the conflicts arising from multi user gestural interaction than on cooperation.

In the context of watching TV, multi user scenarios were researched by Ruiz et al. [5]. They developed gesture alphabets for omnidirectional videos using user elicitation, including both single user and multi user scenarios. One of their findings was that the gestures used to interact are performed slightly different in multi user scenarios. However, they did not further analyse conflicts arising in multi user scenarios or how they could be solved.

Zoric et al. [8] further analysed gesture based interaction for controlling TVs in multi user scenarios. In their study, co-watchers could manipulate content with various gestures. Observations of participants' behaviours showed that performing gestures contributed to the social watching experience. Therefore, the authors argue, social needs should be considered when designing interaction concepts. While our scenario is similar to the scenario of Zoric et al., our work differs in focusing on solving conflicts.

Conflict Solving Strategies

To the best of our knowledge, the most elaborate work proposing conflict solving strategies for multi user gesture controls have been both conducted with touch based interaction on tabletops, and not mid-air gestures. FlowBlocks [1], for example, is an interface especially developed for crowd interaction around multitouch tabletops. Besides at set of constraints simplifying crowd interaction, FlowBlocks also prevents conflicts by increasing mutual awareness of other users intents and physically blocking actions represented by user interface elements.

Morris et al. [4] researched conflict scenarios in co-located co-operative work scenarios. Based on their observations of such scenarios, they argue that simply relying on social protocols does not sufficiently solve conflicts and thus propose several conflict solving strategies.

CONFLICT SOLVING INTERACTION TECHNIQUES

Based on the conflict solving strategies used in previous work, three different interaction techniques were developed. Those three techniques are *master user*, *rank*, and *voting*. In the following, each technique is explained in detail.

Master User

This technique is based on the proactive coordination policies proposed by Morris et al. [4]. It also corresponds to the interaction concept proposed in FlowBlocks [1], and a variant was implemented by Zoric et al. [8].

Comparable to holding a remote control, only one person is in control of the content, and is thus the master user. With this strategy, conflicts are completely avoided. The only thing that needs to be negotiated is who the master user is. This negotiation could occur at the beginning and the result being in effect for the complete watching session, or renegotiated like in Zoric et al. [8]. The first approach leads to a *permanent master user*, while the latter leads to *varying master users*.

The main advantage of this strategy is its conformity to using remote controls, leading to a system behaving according to user's expectations. Yet the interaction time is longer, since becoming the master user requires an additional interaction step.

Rank

Another possibility for solving conflicts is ranking users. In case of a conflict, the gesture performed by the higher ranked user will be regarded by the system. This strategy was previously described by Morris et al. [4], and requires to rank the users beforehand. *Rank* could be implemented by assigning a rank to each person in the household and leveraging for example facial recognition to identify them. This implies a *fixed rank* of all watchers, that is household or family members. Another more flexible implementation could require co-watchers to assign a new rank each time they watch TV. Instead of being set explicitly, ranks could be assigned implicitly, for example by assigning the first person starting to watch the highest rank while the second person joining is assigned to the second highest rank and so on.

Rank leads to shorter interaction times, since users only need to execute the control gesture. Also, as long as the watcher's ranks are obvious, the system behaves as users would expect. However, especially with *fixed ranks*, and depending on the implementation of the ranking process, watchers could feel discriminated and being without a chance to control the content.

Voting

As in the co-located cooperative work scenario with tabletops described by Morris et al. [4], voting could also be applied for mid-air interaction for TVs. As soon as a user performs a gesture, the system would ask all users to either *approve* of or *veto* against the gesture. When approval is needed, all watchers agreeing to the gesture have to perform an approval gesture. If this is the majority, the associated action is triggered. When users are allowed to veto, they also perform a special gesture to express their will. If this is the majority, the associated action is not triggered.

Obviously, this is the most democratic strategy for solving conflicts, since every user can express their opinion. However, the time it takes to execute an action (or not) is longer, and the outcome not as predictable as with the other two proposed conflict solving strategies.

Incidence of discussions about ...						
Number of co watchers (amount of answers)	1 (5)	2 (27)	3 (19)	4 (11)	>4 (2)	Total (64)
Remote control as such	2	2	2	4	4	2
Volumn	2	2	3	3	4.5	3
Channel	5	3	4	4	4.5	4
Menu settings	1	1	1	1	1	1

Table 1. The median ratings of incidence of discussions about remote controls as such, as well as volume, channel and menu settings. Participants gave their rating on six point Likert scales, with 1 resembling "never" and 6 resembling "always". The results are given per number of average watchers and in total.

SURVEY

Participants and Procedure

To further asses multi watcher scenarios, behaviour and conflict prone scenarios, we conducted an online survey. The link to the survey was made available to members of our local institution and local clubs through mailing lists. Participation was voluntary. 64 persons participated in the survey, of whom 30 were female. The average age was 21.75 (8.97 SD). The average amount of persons sharing a TV with our participants was 3.47 (1.13 SD). Participants reported to have at average 2.67 (0.96 SD) co-watchers.

After giving consent and providing us with their demographic data, participants answered several questions regarding their opinion on gesture controls for TVs, possible conflict scenarios, and which of the three previously mentioned conflict solving strategies they preferred. Questions were answered on six point Likert scales. Additionally, participants could express their opinion, upsides and downsides in free text fields for each Likert scale.

Results

Potential conflicts in multi-watcher scenarios

Table 1 shows the median ratings regarding incidence of discussions, with 1 resembling "never" and 6 resembling "always". As Table 1 shows, an increase of co-watchers is accompanied by an increase of discussions. Discussions most often cover the selection of channel, volume settings, and the remote control as such.

When asked about how conflicts were solved, participants answers showed that a variety of strategies were applied. Those strategies included rank, where the most senior family member decided, and fixed master user, where the owner of the remote control decided. A third strategy was to discuss e.g. the channel and find a solution satisfying for all co-watchers. If a compromise was not satisfying for all, the concerned participants tended to avoid further conflicts by e.g. starting to watch their channel on a different device, do something else or stay and accept the decision.

Gesture controls as alternative

The median ratings of gesture controls as alternative input modality are shown in Table 2. The results are given split by age group and in total. As can be seen, most participants could well imagine to use gestures to control their TV and also find this applicable. Yet still, they are not tending to prefer gesture controls over traditional remote controls. This contradiction was clarified in the free text fields. Participants were concerned with technical issues, making mid-air interaction unreliable and

Participants found mid air interaction as means for controlling TVs ..						
Age groups (amount of answers)	<18 (21)	18-20 (20)	21-24 (14)	25-39 (3)	>39 (6)	Total (64)
imaginable	4	4	4.5	4	3	4
applicable	4	4	4	4	2.5	4
preferable	3	3	3	3	2	3

Table 2. The medians for the Likert scale items regarding how imaginable, applicable, and preferable mid-air interaction for controlling TV is, with 1 resembling "not at all" and six resembling "definitely". The results are given per age group and in total.

error prone. Gestures recognised as but not being intended to be control gestures were seen as problematic. Gestures should be easy to perform and simple. Most participants expressed the wish to use mid-air gestures when traditional remote controls were not at hand, impracticable or inconvenient.

Possible conflict scenarios for multi-user gesture controls

Figure 1 shows various scenarios potentially harbouring conflicts, and the percentage of participants rating them as conflict prone. As can be seen, most participants found scenarios involving contrary commands of two watchers most conflict prone. Note that the majority of participants rated scenarios were both watchers performed the same gesture as not prone of conflicts, although it could result in a conflict when the system executes the command associated to the gesture twice. This should be accounted for by system implementers, for example by ignoring a gesture when performed at the same time or shortly after the same gesture was performed.

Preferred conflict solving technique

Figure 2 depicts participants ratings regarding the usefulness of the previously presented conflict solving techniques. 56% of the participants at least tended to see *Voting* as useful. However, the number of participants rating this strategy as not useful

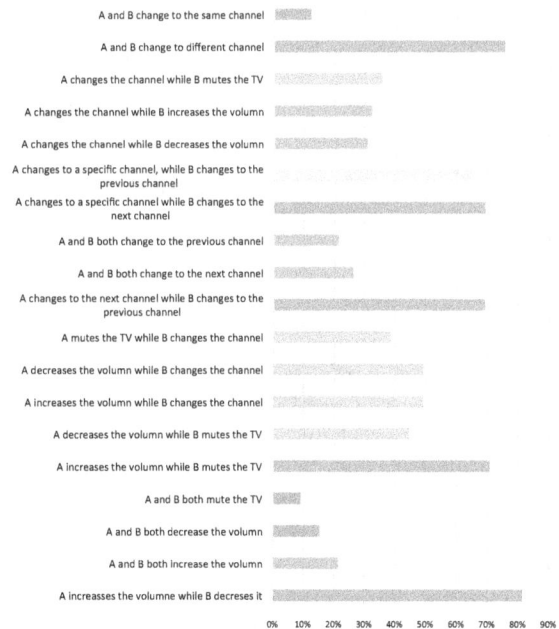

Figure 1. Potential conflict scenarios and the percentage of participants rating them as potential conflict scenarios.

Figure 2. Rating of the usefulness of each conflict solving strategy. Participants rated the usefulness on a six point likert scale ranging von 1 (not usefull) to 6 (useful).

was the largest. This is substantiated by the free text comments: participants acknowledged the fairness and entertainment factor, but also criticize its impracticability and the time it takes to come to a decision.

Rank, on the other hand, was tended to be seen as useful and not useful by nearly the same amount of participants (49% and 51%, respectively), yet this is the strategy rated as at least "rather not useful" by most participants. Interestingly, most of the participants expressing a positive opinion on rank where either in the youngest or in the oldest age group. As positive aspect they mentioned that it is always clear who is in control. Yet most of the comments were rather negative. Participants were concerned that the ranking of persons would cause more conflicts than solve. It was seen as unfair, and enabling or strengthen power games between the co-watchers.

The third alternative, *master user*, was rated the most at least "tending to useful" and the least "not useful" conflict solving strategy. Participants mentioned that the concept was not so different to traditional remote controls. This was both seen as positive and negative. Positive, because conflicts are avoided, communication between co-watchers is promoted, and falsely detecting control gestures is avoided. Negative aspects are that still only one watcher at a time could control the TV, and this person should have to somehow release the control to other users.

Discussion

The survey results show that conflict scenarios exist. So far, those conflicts were mostly solved through social protocols. Conflicts are also expected to occur when mid-air gestures are used. Conflict prone scenarios are mostly changing channels and volume settings. Changing channels and volume settings might also be the most often performed use cases when watching TV.

Regarding mid-air gestures as input modality for TVs, our results show that mid-air gestures are at least today not likely to replace traditional remote controls. For this, especially the technical concerns are too great. However, mid-air interaction could well serve as an equal alternative to traditional remote controls. The decision between gestures and remote controls could be made depending on the situation, with users choosing the input modality more convenient for each situation.

As for conflict solving strategies, our results show that albeit being the closest to traditional remote controls, *master user* is a feasible solution. It is most accepted by users, and prevents not only social but also technical conflicts by recognising control gestures only from one person at a time. However, attention needs to be paid to a proper implementation. Instead of *fixed*

Figure 3. The design of our proposed user interface. At the top of the video, a line is displayed. On this line, a sphere for every watcher is shown. The spheres' positions resembles the relative position of the viewers to each other. The current master user is marked with a larger sphere. Upon the detection of a gesture, the sphere changes its opacity from the default 45% to 100% when the gesture is completed. Icons in the upper right corner visualize the action triggered by the detected gesture.

maser user, users are more likely to accept *varying master user*, were the master user can change over time.

PROTOTYPE

The prototype user interface was designed based on the results of our survey, thus using the varying master user strategy for preventing conflicts. That means, that watchers have to perform a special gesture to become master user. They have the option of releasing control by performing another special gesture. To avoid one watcher never releasing control, we set a timeout, after which control automatically is released. Gesture recognition was implemented using a Microsoft Kinect 2 and its SDK. Video playback was implemented as a WPF application. In the following, the used gestures and the design of the user interface are explained. Figure 4 shows a screenshot of the prototype.

Gestures

Since changing channels and volume were seen as most conflict prone interactions, changing to the next and previous channel as well as increasing and decreasing the volume were implemented. For changing to the next and previous channel, swiping to the left and right respectively were implemented. The volume could be increased by moving the hand up and decreased by moving the hand down. Those gestures are similar to the ones describe by Ruiz et al. [5] and Vatavu [7] for the same functions. By default, no one is master user. Watchers can become master user by performing a special gesture: they have to outstretch their arm, form a fist and move their fist back to their shoulder. After a configurable timeout, the master user is revoked of their privileges and all watchers can become master users again. It is also possible to actively return ones master user privileges by performing the reverse gesture: moving the closed fist from the shoulder forward until the arm is outstretched, and opening the fist.

Graphical User Interface

Particular attention was paid to giving appropriate feedback to watchers. First, it should always be clear who the master user is. We therefore decided to show representations of users at the top of the video, as can be seen in Figure 3. Every user is

Figure 4. A screenshot of the final application. The spheres on the top of the video represent the watchers and their relative positions to each other. The watcher represented by the orange sphere is the master user, thus the sphere is larger than the others. The sphere is opaque, what indicates that a control gesture was detected, and the icons on the right upper corner of the video show that the volume was adjusted.

resembled through a uniquely coloured sphere. The positions of the spheres resemble the relative positions of the detected watchers to each other. The sphere of the master user is clearly distinguishable from the others through its larger diameter (blue sphere in Fig. 3). The second concern was giving appropriate feedback when gestures are recognized. Therefore, the already present spheres were leveraged. When no gesture is detected, the user's sphere has an opacity of 45%. When a gesture is detected, this changes up to full 100% opacity. This allows user to tell whether a gesture is detected, and how big it should be. When a gesture is recognized, the action triggered is further visualized through icons at the upper right corner.

CONCLUSION

This paper focused on conflict solving for multi user mid-air interaction for TVs. Mid-air interaction as input modality for TVs is getting more and more attention, and multi user scenarios are likely to occur when gestures are used to control TVs. Despite having several advantages over traditional remote controls, conflicts are more likely to arise with gesture controls. Thus, we proposed three conflict solving interaction strategies based on previous work. Further, we assessed multi watcher behaviour, potential of gesture controls and conflict prone scenarios in an online survey with 64 participants. Based on the results, we implemented a prototype preventing social and technical conflicts.

Albeit we focused on interaction with TVs in this paper, our proposed prototype and conflict solving strategy could also be used for manipulating other digital contents. For example, viewing images, viewing and manipulating 3D graphics, or manipulating objects in virtual reality. Also, the conflict solving strategies presented in this paper can not only be applied to gesture controls, but also to voice input and usage of multiple hardware controls like mobile devices.

Future plans regarding conflict solving strategies for multi user mid-air interaction include evaluating our proposed prototype in a user study, and implementing it for other digital content.

ACKNOWLEDGMENTS
This work was conducted within the context of the projects SenseEmotion (BMBF) and SFB/TRR 62 (DFG).

REFERENCES

1. Florian Block, Daniel Wigdor, Brenda Caldwell Phillips, Michael S Horn, and Chia Shen. 2012. FlowBlocks: a multi-touch ui for crowd interaction. In *Proc. of UIST '12*. ACM, 497–508.

2. Sang-Heon Lee, Myoung-Kyu Sohn, Dong-Ju Kim, Byungmin Kim, and Hyunduk Kim. 2013. Smart TV interaction system using face and hand gesture recognition. In *Proc. of ICCE '13*. 173–174.

3. Meredith Ringel Morris, Anqi Huang, Andreas Paepcke, and Terry Winograd. 2006. Cooperative gestures: multi-user gestural interactions for co-located groupware. In *Proc. of CHI '06*. ACM, 1201–1210.

4. Meredith Ringel Morris, Kathy Ryall, Chia Shen, Clifton Forlines, and Frederic Vernier. 2004. Beyond social protocols: Multi-user coordination policies for co-located groupware. In *Proceedings of the 2004 ACM conference on Computer supported cooperative work*. ACM, 262–265.

5. Gustavo Alberto Rovelo Ruiz, Davy Vanacken, Kris Luyten, Francisco Abad, and Emilio Camahort. 2014. Multi-viewer Gesture-based Interaction for Omni-directional Video. In *Proc. of CHI '14*. ACM, New York, NY, USA, 4077–4086.

6. Samsung. 2015. Samsung Smart TV - TV has never been this smart. (2015). http://www.samsung.com/us/experience/smart-tv/ Last accessed: 2015 - 01- 20.

7. Radu-Daniel Vatavu. 2012. User-defined Gestures for Free-hand TV Control. In *Proc. of EuroiTV '12*. ACM, New York, NY, USA, 45–48.

8. Goranka Zoric, Arvid Engström, Louise Barkhuus, Javier Ruiz Hidalgo, Axel Kochale, and others. 2013. Gesture interaction with rich TV content in the social setting. (2013).

Rivulet: Exploring Participation in Live Events through Multi-Stream Experiences

William A. Hamilton[1,2], John C. Tang[1], Gina Venolia[1], Kori Inkpen[1], Jakob Zillner[1,3], Derek Huang[1]

[1]Microsoft Research
Redmond, WA USA
{johntang,ginav,kori}@microsoft.com
derekahuang@hotmail.com

[2]Interface Ecology Lab
Texas A&M University
College Station, TX USA
bill@ecologylab.net

[3]VRVis Research Center
Vienna, Austria
jakob.zillner@vrvis.at

ABSTRACT

Live streaming has recently emerged as a growing form of participatory social media. While current live streaming practice focuses on single stream experiences, there are increasing instances of events covered by multiple live streams. In order to explore how to support communication and participation in multi-stream experiences, we present the design and evaluation of Rivulet, an end-to-end mobile live streaming system designed to support participatory multi-stream experiences. Rivulet affords simultaneously watching multiple live streams and incorporates existing feedback mechanisms of text chat and hearts with a novel push-to-talk audio modality. By recruiting viewers through Mechanical Turk, we were able to conduct a study of Rivulet at scale. We found that Rivulet afforded new engaging experiences for participants and led to an impromptu sense of community.

Author Keywords

live streaming, multi-stream, video, push-to-talk, telepresence

ACM Classification Keywords

H.5.2 User Interfaces

INTRODUCTION

During the past decade, live streaming has emerged as a new form of participatory social media. Live streaming has come to refer to live, streaming, video as well as a set of communication media that enable viewers to interact with each other and the streamer. The emerging popularity of live streams is attributed to their ability to enable remote viewers to engage and participate in shared live experiences [10].

The typical live streaming experience consists of a streamer broadcasting a single video stream accompanied by a

Permission to make digital or hard copies of all or part of this work for personal or classroom use is granted without fee provided that copies are not made or distributed for profit or commercial advantage and that copies bear this notice and the full citation on the first page. Copyrights for components of this work owned by others than the author(s) must be honored. Abstracting with credit is permitted. To copy otherwise, or republish, to post on servers or to redistribute to lists, requires prior specific permission and/or a fee. Request permissions from Permissions@acm.org.
TVX'16, June 22 - 24, 2016, Chicago, IL, USA
Copyright is held by the owner/author(s). Publication rights licensed to ACM.
ACM 978-1-4503-4067-0/16/06...$15.00
DOI: http://dx.doi.org/10.1145/2932206.2932211

dedicated chat channel. However, multiple, simultaneous, live streams provide an interesting opportunity to experience events. For example, on Periscope multiple streamers commonly stream simultaneously or within minutes of each other while attending events like concerts or conventions [24]. Similarly, on Twitch, streamers frequently play games together, while they both broadcast independent streams and their viewers' chat in separate chat channels [10].

Despite this trend there is minimal support for identifying and participating in these *multi-stream experiences*. There are a number of 3rd party sites that support embedding multiple live streams together, but do not provide much support beyond the visual aggregation of live streams and their separate chat channels. There are a number of research projects looking at combining multiple live streams [1, 3, 5, 6, 7, 8, 22, 23, 29], but these do not examine audience participation and the resulting experiences.

In this work, we explore how to support communication and participation in multi-stream experiences. In particular, we are interested in the following research questions.

1. How will people experience a collection of streams coming from a live event?
2. How will people use new and existing communication modalities to participate across different streams that are part of an event?

We designed and prototyped Rivulet, an end-to-end mobile live streaming system for multi-stream experiences, as a technology probe for investigating these questions [12]. Rivulet incorporates common live stream modalities including live video, text chat, and hearts (as seen in Periscope). However, we extended these modalities to specifically support a more integrated multi-stream experience, for example all of the streams share an event-wide chat channel. Rivulet also enabled us to explore push-to-talk (PTT) audio from any viewer to the stream, a higher fidelity communication modality that we hypothesized might be more engaging for participants.

To observe and explore realistic participation in multi-stream experiences through Rivulet, we conducted an at-scale field study with eight local Periscope streamers who streamed a local music event. Four participants streamed the event using

31

Rivulet while the other four streamed the event using Periscope. We also recruited 226 viewers on Mechanical Turk to watch live on both Rivulet and Periscope. This led to a brief, but realistic, multi-stream experience.

We found that by aggregating multiple streams together Rivulet helped participants find interesting streams to watch and participate in. It also afforded new engaging live experiences for viewers and streamers, engendered a stronger sense of community, and helped participants better understand what was happening at the event as a whole. Finally, despite some technical issues, PTT audio proved to be an engaging communication modality, which afforded unique participatory opportunities for viewers.

We start with a discussion of related work around live streaming media and practice. We then present the motivations and a detailed description of Rivulet's design. Next, we present the design of our field study of Rivulet along with the results of the study and a discussion of their implications for the design of live streaming experiences.

RELATED WORK
We present related prior work in the context of live streaming, live participation modalities, and multi-stream environments. We also briefly present the sensitizing concept of hot and cool media.

Live Streaming
While there are currently a number of popular live streaming platforms including Periscope, Meerkat, YouTube Live, and Twitch, live streaming has been emerging as a new form of social media over the past decade. In 2010, Juhlin et al. presented a detailed investigation of some previously popular mobile live streaming services including Qik, Bambuser, Flixwagon, and kyte.com [15], most of which are now effectively defunct. At the time, it was clear that mobile live streaming was still in its infancy. They found that streamers had a difficult time finding interesting topics to stream and there were many technical issues around how to manage the camera. As a result, they prescribed a need for more support on mobile devices and the web for better production of live streams [15]. Live streaming practice has evolved significantly during the past six years. There are now thousands of both professional and amateur live streamers streaming every day across the various platforms.

Live streaming as a medium for civic engagement was studied by Dougherty [4] who did a qualitative analysis of live streams on Qik. She found that much of the civic content on Qik focused on political or activist topics [4]. We see emergent multi-stream experiences around events as a potentially new form of civic engagement for both streamers and viewers. For example, many live streams are often shared during political events like protests and debates. We expect multi-stream experiences to potentially increase the impact and reach of communities around streams.

In 2014, Hamilton et al. reported on findings around Twitch, a video game live streaming site, which emerged from the now shutdown Justin.tv [10]. They found that, while video game content was a major factor for the success of Twitch, what really defines Twitch streams is viewer participation and how that leads to forming communities around live steams. Given this finding, we aim to support audience participation in multi-stream experiences through the design of the Rivulet prototype.

Participatory Live Modalities
A number of research projects have explored interaction and communication modalities that afford audience agency and participation. Jo and Hwang [13] explored viewpoint control and direct sketching on video to support viewer communication and participation during live calls. Kim et al. [18] found that providing contextual information, such as maps and high resolution photographs, during live experiences enabled viewers to actively participate in the experience by pointing out things invisible to or unnoticed by a remote streamer. Yonezawa and Tokuda [30] designed a system which helped connect musical performers with their audience by enabling remote viewers to control the light and camera angle of the broadcast. They found that these modalities engaged viewers and increased the connection between performers and their audiences. In the Rivulet prototype, we explore how to augment and combine existing communication modalities within a multi-stream environment to afford greater viewer participation.

Blast Theory recently designed a participatory live streaming experience that takes the form of a game where performers simultaneously stream live video and engage with online viewers [21]. They prescribe the "thickening" of online connections between streamer and online connections by making viewer messages more prominent and incorporating new communication modalities [21]. Additionally, Webb et al. in their recent investigation of distributed live performances identified a need to develop new modalities to serve as subtle feedback mechanisms between audiences and performers [12]. Through Rivulet, we aim to thicken the connections between audiences and streamers by redesigning existing and including additional communication modalities.

Multi-Stream Environments
To support multiple live stream experiences around an event, Rivulet supports dynamically aggregating streams. We note that a number of third party sites exist, especially in the context of Twitch, that support the combination of multiple streams into a single aggregated view [11, 16]. However, these sites generally only allow the user to collect streams and their separate chat channels together visually. We argue that, to meaningfully support multi-stream experiences, communication modalities must be designed to support participation across as well as within individual streams.

Tazaki proposed one of the first multi-stream systems [25]. The system, although never implemented, was designed to engage participants in not viewing, but contributing and curating live video in a shared multi-stream experience. Bentley and Groble later designed TuVista, a live video

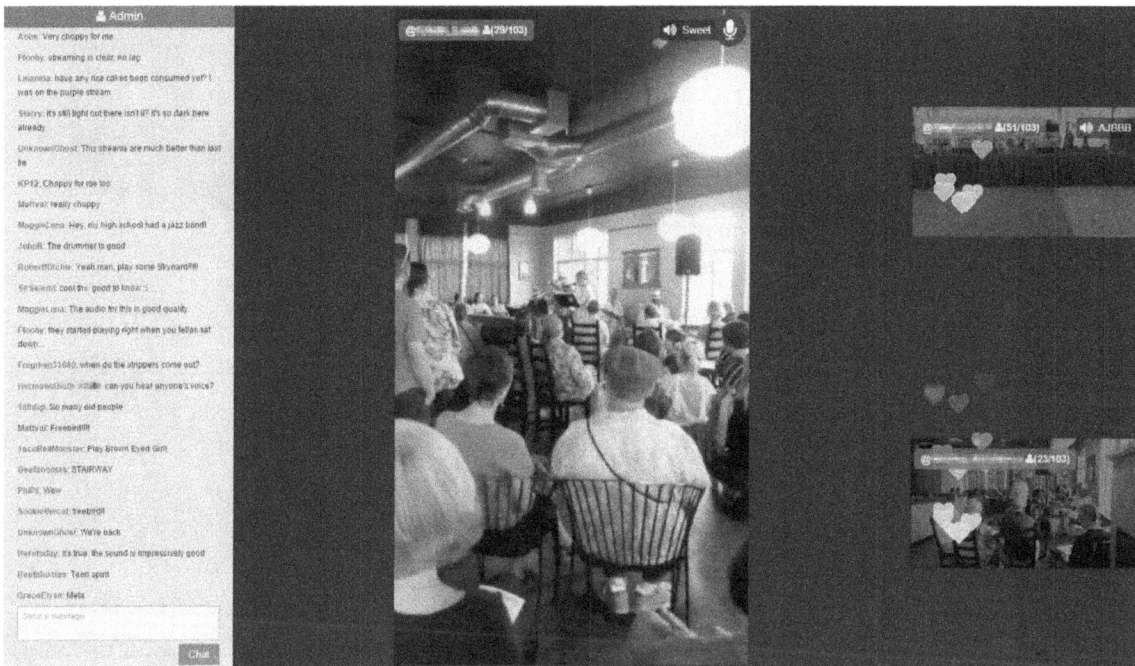

Figure 1. Screenshot of Rivulet viewer client during the Jazz Walk study. Viewers could focus on and listen to one stream at a time and see previews of the other live streams. Viewers shared an event-wide chat with usernames color coded by the stream they were watching. Viewers could send hearts to their focused stream, and see hearts sent to any stream. Viewers could send push-to-talk audio to their focused stream by clicking on the microphone icon in the upper right of the live stream.

production system meant to facilitate the real-time composition of multiple live streams from a sporting event [1]. Similarly, Engström et al. presented a multi-stream system that supported the collaborative contribution and composition of mobile video streams in a night club setting [5]. Engström went on to explore several projects which explored the live mixing and production of mobile live streams [6, 8]. Juhlin et al. also investigated the production practices of professional [7] and amateur [14] live broadcasters to inform the design of live video applications. Recently, Sa et al. designed a live streaming application that helped mobile live streamers collaboratively produce live experiences by providing awareness of other nearby streams [22]. Numerous other works have investigated how to enable crowds to compose and edit video both live [3, 23, 29] and after the fact [1, 9, 17, 27]. These works have focused on issues such as event coverage [9, 17], automated organization [3, 17, 27], collaborative orchestration and organization [1, 3, 9, 23, 27], and privacy [1] around event contexts like concerts [17] and sporting events [111, 9]. In the Rivulet prototype, we do not directly support the composition or production of multiple live streams, but rather we take the approach of supporting viewers in experiencing, selecting from, and participating in multiple live streams simultaneously.

Sensitizing Concept: Hot and Cool Media

In their analysis of live streaming media in the context of Twitch, Hamilton et al. drew on McLuhan's concept of Hot and Cool media to describe how text chat and live video afforded participatory live experiences [10, 19]. McLuhan

described *cool media* as those which are typically low fidelity and afford high levels of participation. Inversely, he described *hot media* as high fidelity and affording little participation [19]. In the context of live streaming, Hamilton et al. describe live video as *hot*. It is high fidelity and affords the sharing of rich live experiences, but alone offers little opportunity for participation. Conversely, text chat is *cool*, affording much greater opportunity for participation through a lower fidelity medium. They argued that together, these *hot* and *cool* modalities afforded the shared history and participatory experiences at the core sense of community in many live streams [10]. We draw on this concept to discuss the qualities of the hearts and push-to-talk communication modalities and their resulting role in Rivulet.

RIVULET PROTOTYPE

The Rivulet prototype implements an end-to-end live streaming service. The prototype consists of a custom Android video streaming application, web based viewer client, and web service. By developing each of these components we were able to design a holistic multi-stream experience aimed at engaging participants through novel communication modalities. We present the design and motivations for each of the components of Rivulet.

Viewer Client

The viewer client (Figure 1) was implemented as an online web-based interface. This enabled us to recruit a large group of viewer participants through the web who could use the system by simply navigating to a URL. The client enables participants to watch multiple streams simultaneously, engage in a global chat, give feedback in the form of hearts to streamers, and broadcast PTT audio.

Broadcaster Client

We developed a custom Android application that enabled streamers to broadcast video from either the front- or back-facing camera (see Figure 2). Participants could also rotate the orientation of their phones while streaming as the viewing client dynamically rotated the streaming video for viewers. Video was broadcast at a resolution of 576 x 320 (the same resolution used by Periscope) and was encoded at a data rate between 1.5 – 2.0 Mbps using H.264. The encoded video was streamed to a cloud based Wowza streaming engine server using the Real Time Messaging Protocol (RTMP). During the course of the presented study, video was uploaded over cellular LTE connections. We will describe how the broadcaster interface integrates each of the explored communication modalities in the following sections.

Supporting Multi-Stream Experiences

To support participants in watching and participating in multiple streams, they first needed to be able see them all and choose which one to focus on. While viewers could see a live preview of all of the active streams in the experience, they could only focus on one. The focused stream appears in the middle of the interface and audio plays for that stream (see Figure 1). Previews of other streams appear smaller and darkened on the right side of the interface. To focus on another stream, viewers simply click on a preview to swap its place with the currently focused stream in the interface. At the same time, the new stream's audio is played instead of the previously focused stream's audio. As streams started and stopped broadcasting, they were dynamically added to and removed from the interface. When the client is first opened, and if the stream that the viewer is focused on ends, the system randomly selects a stream to play.

Each stream is labeled with the name of the streamer as well as a fraction indicating the portion of all viewers of the event who are watching this stream. We intended this to help viewers understand how other viewers were selecting which stream to watch. This fraction also shows the streamer how many viewers are watching them compared to participating in the event as a whole (see Figure 2). Additionally, each stream is algorithmically assigned a unique color, which is helps differentiate each stream's viewers in the global chat.

We used a custom Adobe Flash Player to stream and render each video stream. The total delay from broadcaster to viewer was typically between 2 and 5 seconds, which is equal to or less than most current live streaming platforms. While viewers could watch each of the streams, streamers were unable to see other live streams during the study. While streamers could not directly maintain awareness of other streams, they would be indirectly aware through viewers' comments in the provided communication modalities.

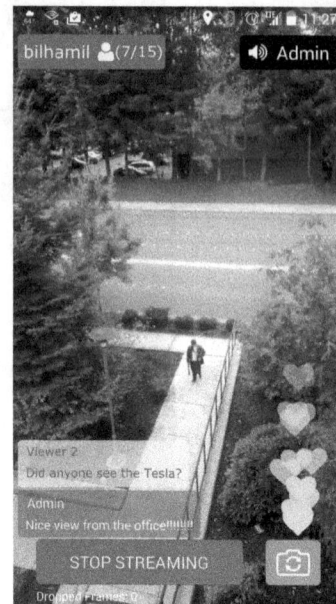

Figure 2. The mobile client enabled sharing live video and audio and monitoring viewers, hearts, chat, and PTT audio.

Event-Wide Text Chat

Our second research question focuses on how to participants experience communication modalities in multi-stream environments. We were particularly interested in how to support viewers using text chat in a multi-stream experience. Rivulet associates all of an event's live streams with a single event-wide text chat. This differs from associating a single stream with its own text chat, as seen on Twitch, Periscope, Meerkat, and many other streaming platforms. We expected that participants would discuss and experience the event as a whole instead of in disjointed conversations around each stream. However, we still wanted participants to be able to make comments localized to particular streams and make sense of who was watching what stream. In the chat, viewers' usernames were color coded with the live stream they were watching when they made the comment.

Similarly, we hypothesized, for streamers, text chat from viewers focused on their stream would have more immediate value than chats from other viewers. Thus, while all text chats would briefly appear on the streaming interface, chats from the streamer's viewers would be highlighted with the color associated with their stream (see Figure 2). Chats from viewers of other streams appeared with a gray background.

Hearts

For the Rivulet prototype, we adopted the hearts communication modality featured in Periscope. Hearts are an ephemeral mechanism that enable users to send lightweight feedback to streamers. A viewer simply clicks on the stream to send one heart, which appears on the video stream and briefly floats up before disappearing. This can be done rapidly, and often is, to send a stream of hearts. To help viewers maintain awareness of each stream, viewers can see hearts appearing on each stream separately (see Figure 1).

Hearts are roughly color coordinated with viewers. While the heart shape implies love, their exact meaning is ambiguous.

Hearts are an interesting emerging communication modality because they provide extremely ephemeral and localized feedback about a live stream. They provide quick, positive feedback to the streamer about their viewers. However, taken beyond the context of just one stream, hearts might help other viewers identify interesting activity in a multi-stream environment. Considering hearts within the framework of *hot* and *cool* media, they are extremely *cool*. They are very low fidelity in that they only have one particular form. At the same time they afford ample opportunity for participation, as any number of participants can send as many hearts as they wish at any point in time without being clearly identified.

Push-To-Talk Audio

Our goal with the incorporation of PTT audio was to further explore our second research question by examining how participants engage in a multi-stream experience using a relatively novel communication modality. The PTT modality is not common to live streaming practice and lies somewhere between *cool* text chat and *hot* live video on McLuhan's spectrum. We designed PTT to afford viewers a higher level of impact on the experience, while affording more opportunity to participate than live video.

In Rivulet, any viewer with a microphone can broadcast audio on the stream they are currently focused on by clicking and holding on the microphone icon displayed on the stream (see Figure 1). The audio is captured and encoded in the browser, streamed to the Rivulet web service, and then pushed to the streamer's broadcasting client. On the mobile client, the audio is played back immediately to the streamer and also mixed into the right channel of the outgoing stream's stereo audio. This allowed viewers of that stream to hear PTT audio from other viewers in sync with when the streamer heard it. An indicator appeared in the video stream during showing who was talking (see PTTs from *AJBBB* and *Sweet* in Figure 1). This indicator was also displayed on the broadcaster client (see PTT from *Admin* in Figure 2). To prevent feeding the PTT back to the person who spoke it, they heard only the left channel from the video stream for the duration of the PTT. Streamers wore headphones to prevent PTT audio from leaking into the left channel of the broadcast.

We limited PTT broadcasting to only one viewer at a time per stream. We also set a maximum of 10 seconds for PTTs to prevent any viewer from dominating the modality by continuously broadcasting. The system also ensures a 5 second break between every PTT to give the streamer a chance to respond. When a viewer tries to start a PTT, if the channel is clear, a start chime is played and a 10 second countdown starts. After 10 seconds, if the viewer has not stopped broadcasting the system plays a disconnect chime and stops the transmission. If the viewer tries to PTT when the channel is not clear, they see a wait signal until it is clear. If multiple viewers are trying to PTT simultaneously, the system places them into a wait queue.

We explicitly intended PTT to be a communication modality at the single stream level. Only viewers of a particular stream would be able to hear PTTs sent to that stream. We also expected PTT to be easier for streamers to pay attention to while still engaging in the shared event, since they did not have to look at their device to perceive the incoming audio.

STUDY DESIGN

We designed a study of Rivulet to explore our research questions around communication modalities and emergent behaviors in multi-stream experiences. Through the study, we aimed to create a multi-stream experience that was as ecologically valid as possible. To this end, we recruited experienced streamers to broadcast at a local event to an audience of live viewers. We also worked to recruit an online audience of reasonable scale. In the following sections, we describe our process for selecting and organizing an event, recruiting participants, and evaluating the experience.

The Jazz Walk Event

We wanted to find an event which would be interesting to the streamers and viewers and had multiple concurrent activities to provide ample opportunity for streamers to share different perspectives of the event. We also had to consider the availability of robust cellular network connections as a prior study failed due to cellular network issues. We chose a local jazz festival called The North City Jazz Walk, which historically attracts several hundred attendees. The event featured 10 local musical groups playing in different venues across a 3 block area. Venues included bars, parking lots, a coffee shop, a church, and a club house.

Live Streamers

Prior to the event, we recruited local Periscope streamers. By recruiting experienced streamers, we aimed to have participants who were comfortable conducting a live stream and interacting with viewers. We also expected that streamers would be able to provide insights into how their experience with Rivulet compared with Periscope.

We identified local Periscope streamers by collecting geocoded Periscope Tweets from the local area over a four-day period. From the resulting 250 streamers, we were able to contact approximately 50. We also asked these streamers to forward the study information to any local streamers they knew. We successfully recruited 7 participants to attend the Jazz Walk and added one personal contact who was familiar with live streaming. Participants were offered a 250 USD gratuity for taking part in the study.

Prior to the study, we met the streamer participants outside the event area where we administered a short pre-questionnaire and divided the participants into two groups of four. Four participants were asked to stream using Periscope [P1-P4], the other four were asked to use Rivulet [R1-R4]. The Rivulet streamers were given a brief tutorial on how the system worked. While the Periscope streamers used their own devices, we gave the Rivulet participants Android phones to use during the study. We asked that participants

Likert Questions
Q1 I was aware of all the streams offered by the people streaming at the Jazz Walk today.
Q2 I enjoyed being able to choose different streams at the Jazz Walk.
Q3 I was aware of what the other streamers at the Jazz Walk were covering compared to what I was watching.
Q4 I felt like I was able to influence the live streams using the push-to-talk feature.
Q5 I felt like I was able to influence the live streams using text chat messages.
Q6 I felt like I was able to influence the live streams by sending hearts.
Q7 I was able to easily find a view that was interesting to watch.
Q8 Using [Periscope, this Prototype] to view the Jazz Walk event was fun.
Q9 I felt like I was part of a community of people enjoying the Jazz Walk.
Q10 I felt connected to the people streaming the the Jazz Walk.
Q11 I felt connected to the other people viewing the Jazz Walk event.
Q12 I felt like I could control what I viewed of the Jazz Walk event.

Table 1. Summary of Likert questions asked in each condition. Note that Q4 was only asked in the Rivulet condition.

attend the event for approximately an hour and a half and that they stream for at least a quarter of the time. The Periscope streamers were asked to publish a tweet with the hashtag #MSRJazzWalk anytime they started streaming, so they could be found. We placed no other restrictions on what or how they streamed. We only asked that they do what they would normally do. During the study, a researcher was available at the event for technical assistance. After the study, we met with the streamers again and briefly discussed the experience and asked them to complete a short survey.

Mechanical Turk Viewers

We aimed to recruit an audience of reasonable scale to observe during the study. We argue that this is critical for observing meaningful engagement and communication during a live streaming experience. Thus, we recruited viewer participants through Amazon's Mechanical Turk. Approximately 15 minutes after sending the streamer participants into the event, we published two Human Intelligence Tasks (HITs): one to recruit viewers to watch the experience on Rivulet, and the other for Periscope.

Participants in both conditions were shown a brief video explaining how either Rivulet or Periscope worked. Viewers were also given a link to the Jazz Walk website. Rivulet participants were directed to the viewer client through a link. Since the web-based Periscope client does not afford sending hearts or chats, Periscope participants were asked to use their smart phones (downloading the Twitter and Periscope mobile apps if needed). They were told they could locate streams by searching for #MSRJazzWalk on Twitter.

Participants in both conditions were asked to watch streams for at least 20 minutes and as long as they liked beyond that. After watching, participants in both conditions were asked to fill out a short questionnaire composed of a series of Likert questions (see Table 1). We also asked participants to rate

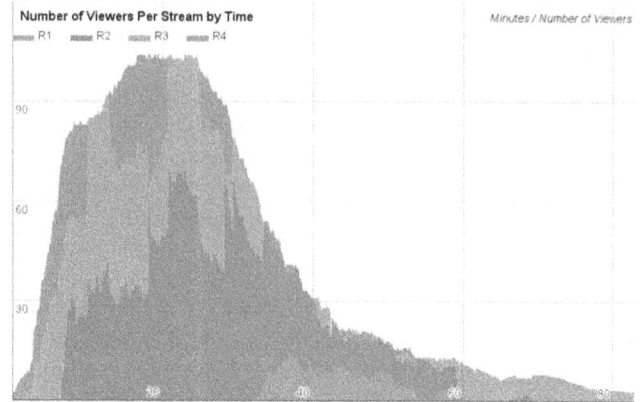

Figure 3. Viewers per stream in Rivulet over the course of the study, showing how viewers switched among streams.

the usefulness of the communication modalities in each condition using a semantic differential and answer a series of open-ended questions. We expected that viewer participants would be engaged in the task between 35 minutes to an hour. Thus, participants in each condition were offered an 8 USD compensation (in keeping with a 10 USD hourly wage). 120 HITs were published for each condition.

Data Logging

Besides serving the page content and managing real-time messaging, the Rivulet web server also logged user actions and relevant metadata in a database for later analysis. We were not able to log periscope user interactions, so we are not able to present a quantitative analysis comparing conditions.

RESULTS AND DISCUSSION

Despite the complex nature of the presented study, we experienced relatively few issues, resulting in an engaging and rewarding experience for both streamers and viewers. We present the results of the study and discuss the implications of our findings. We first provide a brief description of the recruited viewership and streams shared during the event. Next, we provide a discussion of how each of the communication modalities were used, and draw implications from our observations. We then discuss how participants engaged in multiple streams and the implications of multi-stream live experiences around events. We also discuss the emergent sense of community we observed. Finally, we discuss implications related to our study design.

Viewership

After publishing the Mechanical Turk HITs, participants quickly flooded into the study. Figure 3 illustrates the number of viewers over time in the Rivulet condition. Within 20 minutes over 100 viewers were watching on Rivulet. In total, we had 115 participants in the Rivulet condition [RV1-RV115] and 111 in the Periscope condition.

Live Streams

During the study, some of the streamers in different conditions decided to stream together. Consequently, there were similar streams in each condition. We provide a brief description of what was streamed by each of the streamers.

R2, P2, and P3 were a group of high school boys and were friends prior to the study. They walked and talked together while simultaneously streaming 3 different streams almost continuously for the duration of the study. Before entering the event, they first went to a nearby grocery store and purchased some rice cakes and water. This proved to be a fairly humorous diversion for many viewers. They then started walking around the event and stopped at several different musical performances. While they walked they focused on interacting with their viewers and with each other. R2's stream received the most chat messages per minute and the second most PTTs per minute.

P1 and R3 are a brother and sister in their thirties. For most of the study they streamed from a bar that was hosting one of the musical performances, later walking to another bar hosting a performance. They used their front-facing cameras for much of their streams to interact with their viewers with less focus on the jazz performances. R3 throughout the study made humorous faces and noises trying to get a reaction from her viewers. At one point, she started encouraging viewers to tell jokes on her stream. She also pretended to eat the hearts viewers were sending her. P1's stream was more subdued, and he streamed both the musical performances and himself while he interacted with viewers. P1 and R3 frequently interacted with and streamed each other during the study.

R1 and P4 were two men in their early twenties and were friends prior to the study. During the study they streamed at different outdoor performances and while walking between performances. They interacted with their viewers to a much lesser degree than the aforementioned streamers. At one point the pair got up and started dancing while a band played a cover of the Peanuts' theme song. While P4 streamed for most of the duration of the study, R1 only streamed for a short duration toward the end of the event.

R4 was by himself for most of the study. He frequently responded to viewer chats, but generally his stream focused on the musical performances at the event. He never showed his face on stream during the study, and often just streamed different performances. At one point, he did stream himself walking down the street, but minimal interaction occurred with viewers during this time.

Text Chat
During the study, a total of 862 chat messages were sent among the Rivulet viewers, and all but 17 of our 115 Rivulet viewers sent at least one chat message. Figure 4 illustrates the distribution of viewers based on how frequently they chatted. As may be expected given the tendencies of lurkers [20], a large number of viewers, 87 out of 115, chatted either not at all or less than twice every five minutes. However, the remaining 28 viewers chatted regularly, one as often as 3 times a minute.

Chat messages were of varying content including comments and questions about the event directed at the streamer or other viewers. Some viewers and streamers reported that at some points the chat was moving too fast for them to effectively read every message, a known issue within large live streaming chat channels [10]. We conducted a coding analysis of chat messages to build an understanding of the conversation. Codes emerged through the analysis relative to our research questions. The most common codes included viewer responses to other participants (13.8%), commentary on the experience (13.6%), discussing the prototype (13.6%), viewer reactions to events (10.9%), and questions about the experience (9.7%). Interestingly, viewers often made requests (7.4%) of the streamers via text chat suggesting how they should stream or participate in the event:

> *Turn the phone sideways* RV71, to R1.
> *Go to the nearest venue!* RV72, to R2.
> *haha...[R3], somebody else is livestreaming at the same venue as you, you should find them!!!!* RV94, to R3.
> *Can you ask him where he got that hat?* RV108, to R4.

These requests illustrate the level of engagement some viewers had with the streamers in shaping how the event was covered. It even included coordination among the streamers, as viewers recognized other streamers at the event.

Understanding Event-Wide Text Chat
We were particularly interested in evaluating how participants understood the global text chat and its impact on the experience. Many viewers indicated that, while they were able to understand which viewers were watching each stream, it was confusing. Many viewers also expressed wanting to see only chats from viewers on the same stream or at least be able to filter out chats from other streams. When asked to rate the usefulness of the text chat modality, 90% of viewers responded positively in the post questionnaire that being able to see chat messages from the same stream they were watching was useful, only 57% reported that seeing chat messages from viewers in other streams was useful. The event-wide chat did enable viewers and streamers to maintain awareness of what was going on in other streams. R4 reported he experienced *"greater awareness about the event as a whole and what other streamers were doing via event wide chat."* While an event-wide chat has clear benefits, viewers and steamers need to be able to quickly identify messages in their active stream.

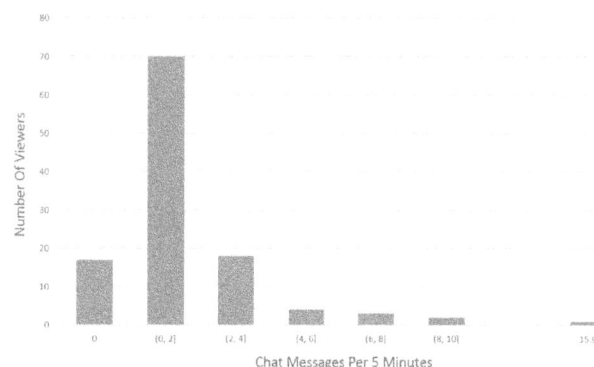

Figure 4. Distribution of chat frequency among viewers.

Despite some initial confusion, 3 of the 4 Rivulet streamers indicated that they could easily understand which chats were coming from their viewers. The binary nature (only 2 colors) of the chat visualization on the broadcasting client (Figure 2) made it easier to understand which chats were coming from viewers of their stream.

Push-To-Talk Enables High Profile Participation

PTT was used by significantly fewer viewers than text chat. Only 14 out of the 115 recruited viewers attempted to broadcast audio. Furthermore, 50% of the messages failed to be understood by the streamer or viewers. This was due to a number of issues including viewers' microphone configurations, the system prematurely cutting off participants' audio, or the audio being too quiet to hear. Since the Jazz Walk was a live music event, the ambient noise level at the event frequently drowned out incoming PTT audio.

For the half (42 out of 83) of the PTT messages that were comprehensible, messages ranged from asking questions, making jokes, commenting on the stream, asking if the speaker could be heard, or simply saying *"Hi!"*. In several instances a streamer and viewer were able to have a short conversation through the stream audio and PTT. Unlike chat, PTTs were mostly directed at the streamer, not other viewers.

When asked what they liked about PTT, many viewers indicated that they liked the instant, high profile communication with the streamer. According to RV18: *"It's loud and heard, so it's easily recognizable. It would be easy to make a point that stands out above the wall of text."* Other viewers seemed to appreciate others' use of PTT. RV45 indicated that: *"While I did not personally use it, listening to other people interact with the streamer was neat. Being able to influence their decision making was the best part."*

Other viewers had concerns about the value of PTT. RV63 felt like PTT would *"just encourage people to act out"*, and R3 indicated that she would like the option to mute particular viewers who were trolling her. While we did not explore this issue directly, there is a clear need to support boundaries of use for such a high-impact communication modality.

We transcribed and coded PTT messages for content and to whom they were directed. This revealed that PTT messages were integrated into the conversation in the stream where almost all messages either clearly implied a response from the streamer, or were in direct response to the streamer. This is in contrast to text chat, which more often was just commentary that did not respond to or imply a response.

While there does not appear to be a direct correlation between the number of chats a user sent and how often they used PTT, 12 of the 14 PTT users were in the top 35% of the most frequent text chatters during the event. This leads us to suspect that PTT appeals to already engaged viewers, who are looking for a more direct means to participate.

Our timing strategy of allowing only 10 seconds of speaking time seemed to keep people from dominating the channel and gave the streamers an opportunity to respond. None of the streamers indicated that they felt overwhelmed by the incoming audio. We also suspect that PTT audio may be socially intimidating and thus self-regulating. RV34, who sent the third most chats during the experience, but not any PTTs, indicated that s/he was scared to use the feature.

Despite technical issues, the results indicate that PTT audio provided new opportunities for participating in live streaming experiences. PTT proved to be *hotter* than text chat. It is high fidelity and affords a unique means for highly engaged participants to have impact. Furthermore, PTT is *cooler* than live video, with more space for participation.

Hearts are Noisy

The hearts feature was used extensively in both the Rivulet and Periscope conditions. While we do not have exact numbers for the Periscope streams, a total of 24,523 hearts were sent through Rivulet. While 22 viewers did not send any hearts, 21 viewers sent more than 200 hearts over the duration of the study. Ultimately, we observed it was very easy for the hearts modality to be dominated by a few viewers. For example, one outlier alone sent 8686 hearts.

When we asked Rivulet viewers if they thought hearts were useful to send or see using a five point Likert scale, responses averaged 3.26 (s=1.18) and 3.19 (s=1.32) respectively. Results in the context of Persicope were similar. This lukewarm perception of hearts seems counter-intuitive given the apparent popularity of the feature in Periscope. However, what we did find is that 6 of the 8 streamers thought hearts provided useful feedback to them about their streams (the other 2 were neutral). This leads us to suspect that hearts, at least in their current form, are more meaningful to streamers.

Despite this finding, hearts played a significant role in informing viewers when they should switch streams. RV82 reported that *"when people would hit hearts on other streams I would pop over and see what was going on."* However, since hearts were so easy to generate in rapid succession, it was easy for one viewer to create a potentially distracting signal with hearts. As RV102 reported *"I think the hearts were more the result of someone clicking for no reason than the video's content."* Similarly, in the case of R3's stream, when she pretended to eat incoming hearts, sending hearts became more of a game and less a signal of interesting content. Given the noisy nature of sheer heart throughput, a more valuable signal might be derived by normalizing the number of hearts by the viewer's typical heart sending rate or from the number of unique heart senders at one time.

Viewing Multiple Streams

We found that being able to view multiple live streams and readily switch between them had several immediate impacts on viewers' experience of the event. Drawing from participant responses to Likert questions in the post questionnaire, we found the significant benefits of the Rivulet prototype over Periscope (see Table 2). The results

Likert Question	Periscope-μ	Rivulet-μ	Mann-Whitney U	p-value
Q1	3.68	4.21	4320	<.001
Q2	3.45	4.15	3698	<.001
Q7	3.80	4.25	4630	<.001
Q9	3.71	4.10	5059	<.004
Q10	3.60	4.03	4788	<.001
Q11	3.47	4.15	3804	<.001
Q12	3.15	3.83	4081	<.001

Table 2: Comparison of selected Likert response means across conditions, with 1 = Strongly Disagree and 5 = Strongly Agree. The difference in responses across conditions were analyzed for significance using Mann-Whitney U non-parametric tests with Bonferroni correction applied.

for Q1, Q2, Q7, and Q12 indicate that Rivulet effectively enabled participants to watch several live streams simultaneously. We describe the impact of multiple streams through a discussion of how and when viewers switched streams, how viewers were able to find interesting streams to watch, and emergent multi-stream experiences.

Switching Streams

We logged how often participants voluntarily switched between different streams in Rivulet, removing automatic stream switches that occurred when a stream ended. Figure 5 shows the distribution of viewers by how often they switched streams. While many viewers switched infrequently or not at all, a significant portion switched streams regularly. On average, 32% of viewers switched streams at least every 2 minutes. One extreme viewer switched streams a total of 42 times. During the first 60 minutes of the study, we observed a diverse distribution of viewers across the streams. As shown in Figure 3, viewers actively switched to new streams when they appeared.

Being able to watch and switch between multiple streams enabled viewers to find and participate in streams that were of interest to them. Despite covering the same event, each stream was different in content and activity from the others. R1 and R4 focused more on the musical performances while R2 and R3 focused more discussing the event and interacting with viewers. Different viewers reported enjoying both of

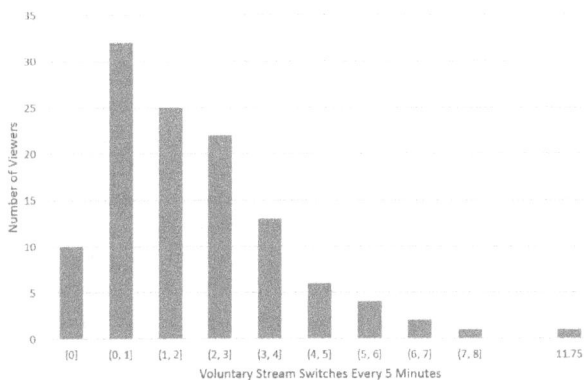

Figure 5: Distribution of Viewers by Rate of Stream Switches.

these types of streams and switching streams for an experience that was of most interest to them.

This observation that viewers' personal interests drove their varied viewing behavior is consistent with prior work such as Velt et al. [26] who also explored a music festival. Hamilton et al. [10] also observed that viewers are drawn to certain streams either for their content (such as live music) or to primarily interact with the stream and its community. We argue that by combining different kinds of streams and enabling viewers to explore and participate in them simultaneously, we can support live experiences that are more personally meaningful to individual viewers.

Viewers used a combination of signals to inform switching between the different streams. Many viewers indicated that they switched streams when they saw an interesting conversation occurring in chat. RV66 reported *"being able to see the different conversations from the different streams let you know which stream was the hottest at that moment"* (hottest meaning most interesting, not McLuhan's *hot*). Other viewers reported monitoring the live previews to watch for interesting content. RV13 reported *"when there was a change of scenery, or when someone changed the camera angle to their face, it made me switch to see what was going on, to hear the audio."* Despite the ambiguity of hearts, many viewers reported choosing streams based on heart activity (see *Hearts are Noisy*). Viewers also returned to streams of viewers they had been watching previously. In several cases, we observed viewers exclaiming in chat *"[Streamer] is back!"* after a streamer restarted their stream.

Cross-Stream Experiences

The multi-stream nature of the Rivulet prototype enabled several experiences that viewers noted as exciting. In one case, viewers noticed that R3 and R4 were streaming at the same part of the event and they could see R4 through R3's stream. They pointed out R4 to R3, and one viewer switched over to R4's stream and suggested that he go over and talk to R3. In a similar case, R3 and R2 randomly encountered each other while walking down the sidewalk. They then streamed each other for a while and had a short discussion about the event. RV20 reported that *"the most interesting thing that happened while I was watching was when two "hosts" met each other. It was a little surreal."*

We note that without aggregating live streams together, these kinds of cross-stream experiences are virtually impossible in existing platforms. By coordinating streams and communication modalities together around an event, viewers are more aware of stream and can interact across streams.

Sense of Community

Over the course of the experience, it appeared as if a temporary sense of community emerged within the audience of the Rivulet experience. When answering Q9, 94 of the 115 Rivulet viewers agreed (37 strongly agreed) that they felt like they were part of a community. This feeling was significantly greater in Rivulet compared to Periscope (See Table 2: Q9).

We also found that viewers in Rivulet felt significantly more connected to the people streaming than those in Periscope (See Table 2: Q10), and more connected to other viewers (See Table 2: Q11). Many viewers also indicated in their free responses that they felt they were part of community during the experience. As RV110 said:

"What I liked best was how easy it was for the streamers to interact with viewers and the close-knit feeling that I gained from watching several streams. It felt like I was a part of the community."

Study Design Implications

Recruiting a relatively large number of viewers from Mechanical Turk enabled us to observe a live experience at-scale through the Rivulet prototype. However, given that both streaming and viewing participants were compensated to participate in the event, the study cannot be considered an organically emerging experience. Thus, there are some inherent issues with the ecologic validity of the experience.

For example, while 100% of the participants watched for at least the requisite 20 minutes, only 12 Rivulet viewers watched longer than 30 minutes. It appears that most participants left after the minimum required viewing time in the HIT. By 45 minutes into the study, only about 20 viewers remained, resulting in a relatively short window of time when Rivulet had a reasonably sized audience. Future work could look at different ways to design this kind of study to engender more ecologically valid viewer behavior.

Additionally, looking at the length of streams shared during the study, almost all of the streamers (both on Rivulet and Periscope) were active for most of the study duration. This contrasts to the brief (5-10 minute) streams typically seen on Periscope. It is unclear if this was because they had more viewers than they were accustomed to or they felt like they were expected to because of the study.

We also note that during the study a significant amount of chats mentioned Mechanical Turk (6.7%). While these messages might have distracted from the shared experience, they may also have helped participants connect through their shared experiences on Mechanical Turk. Further work is needed to investigate the social implications of using turkers as participants in live social systems.

CONCLUSION

We built and field tested at-scale the Rivulet prototype for experiencing multiple streams of an event. Viewers used all modalities (text chat, PTT, and hearts) to engage with the streamers and with the viewers within and across streams in the event. Their engagement included shaping the way that streamers were covering the event and working to inform other viewers as streams started or stopped. Taken together, we see evidence that multi-stream experiences around events afford new opportunities for participating in and forming impromptu communities. We reflect here on our second research question, namely how people used the various

communication modalities in Rivulet on the spectrum of *cool* to *hot* media [10, 19].

It is apparent that lightweight, *cool* signals, like hearts, are a compelling emerging participation modality. While we saw many people engaging through the hearts modality, displaying all those hearts may imply more importance than is warranted. When used in isolated live streams, as in Periscope, hearts may give meaningful feedback to the streamer and viewers. But in the context of multiple streams, people used them as a cue to switch to a stream, only to find out they did not indicate what they expected. We argue that work needs to be done further refine these types of modalities. For example, visualizing the proportion of people that give hearts, rather than the total number of hearts, may be a more useful signal of which streams are interesting.

Text chat is a warmer communication modality that is used less than hearts. We redesigned text chat as a communication modality to bridge across multiple streams, and foster an event-centric experience. We found that this approach had clear benefits, leading to interesting cross-stream interactions. However, there is a need to more clearly present which chats are from people watching the same stream versus other streams.

Additionally, we found that new modalities like PTT, a modality *hotter* than text chat and *cooler* than live video, supported compelling new participatory experiences. While only a small subset of highly engaged users sent PTTs, they engendered a higher level of engagement by immediately responding to or evoking responses from streamers. PTT afforded a new opportunity for higher impact participation. We argue that there is a need for continued investigation of new communication modalities to understand the roles they can play in participatory live experiences.

Finally, with regards to our first research question, we found that multi-stream experiences led to interesting cross-stream interactions. Viewers were excited about encounters involving multiple streamers. They were also able to easily find and participate in streams that addressed their interests and desire for engagement.

We note that we were only able to observe interactions in the context of this one event. Future work could examine multi-stream interactions around different types of events such as parades, conventions, sporting events, political debates, or protests at both larger and smaller scales than what we observed. We expect that different events at different scales will exercise communication modalities in different ways, helping us further learn how to support participation in multi-stream events. Rivulet also did not explore streamer-to-streamer communication, which could become more important in events with more streams. As live streaming continues to evolve and practices emerge, we believe that supporting interaction among multiple streams from the same event is an important, new form of social media communication that is ripe for future work.

REFERENCES

1. Edward Anstead, Steve Benford, and Robert Houghton. 2016. MarathOn Multiscreen: Group Television Watching and Interaction in a Viewing Ecology. In Proceedings of the 19th ACM Conference on Computer-Supported Cooperative Work & Social Computing (CSCW '16). ACM, New York, NY, USA, 405-417. DOI=http://dx.doi.org/10.1145/2818048.2820003

2. Frank R. Bentley and Michael Groble. 2009. TuVista: meeting the multimedia needs of mobile sports fans. In Proceedings of the 17th ACM international conference on Multimedia (MM '09). ACM, New York, NY, USA, 471-480. DOI=http://dx.doi.org/10.1145/1631272.1631337

3. Michael S. Bernstein, Joel Brandt, Robert C. Miller, and David R. Karger. 2011. Crowds in two seconds: enabling realtime crowd-powered interfaces. In Proceedings of the 24th annual ACM symposium on User interface software and technology (UIST '11). ACM, New York, NY, USA, 33-42. DOI=http://dx.doi.org/10.1145/2047196.2047201

4. Audubon Dougherty. 2011. Live-streaming mobile video: production as civic engagement. In Proceedings of the 13th International Conference on Human Computer Interaction with Mobile Devices and Services (MobileHCI '11). ACM, New York, NY, USA, 425-434. DOI=http://dx.doi.org/10.1145/2037373.2037437

5. A. Engström, M. Esbjörnsson, and O. Juhlin. 2008. Mobile collaborative live video mixing. In Proceedings of the 10th international conference on Human computer interaction with mobile devices and services (MobileHCI '08). ACM, New York, NY, USA, 157-166. DOI=http://dx.doi.org/10.1145/1409240.1409258

6. Arvid Engström, Mark Perry, and Oskar Juhlin. 2012. Amateur vision and recreational orientation:: creating live video together. In Proceedings of the ACM 2012 conference on Computer Supported Cooperative Work (CSCW '12). ACM, New York, NY, USA, 651-660. DOI=http://dx.doi.org/10.1145/2145204.2145304

7. Arvid Engstrom, Mattias Esbjornsson, Oskar Juhlin, and Mark Perry. 2008. Producing collaborative video: developing an interactive user experience for mobile tv. In Proceedings of the 1st international conference on Designing interactive user experiences for TV and video (UXTV '08). ACM, New York, NY, USA, 115-124. DOI=http://dx.doi.org/10.1145/1453805.1453828

8. Arvid Engström, Goranka Zoric, Oskar Juhlin, and Ramin Toussi. 2012. The mobile vision mixer: a mobile network based live video broadcasting system in your mobile phone. In Proceedings of the 11th International Conference on Mobile and Ubiquitous Multimedia (MUM '12). ACM, New York, NY, USA, , Article 18 , 4 pages. DOI=http://dx.doi.org/10.1145/2406367.2406390

9. Martin D. Flintham, Raphael Velt, Max L. Wilson, Edward J. Anstead, Steve Benford, Anthony Brown, Timothy Pearce, Dominic Price, and James Sprinks. 2015. Run Spot Run: Capturing and Tagging Footage of a Race by Crowds of Spectators. In Proceedings of the 33rd Annual ACM Conference on Human Factors in Computing Systems (CHI '15). ACM, New York, NY, USA, 747-756. DOI=http://dx.doi.org/10.1145/2702123.2702463

10. William A. Hamilton, Oliver Garretson, and Andruid Kerne. 2014. Streaming on twitch: fostering participatory communities of play within live mixed media. In Proceedings of the SIGCHI Conference on Human Factors in Computing Systems (CHI '14). ACM, New York, NY, USA, 1315-1324. DOI=http://dx.doi.org/10.1145/2556288.2557048

11. Hamrick, B. MultiTwitch. http://www.multitwitch.tv/.

12. Hilary Hutchinson, Wendy Mackay, Bo Westerlund, Benjamin B. Bederson, Allison Druin, Catherine Plaisant, Michel Beaudouin-Lafon, Stéphane Conversy, Helen Evans, Heiko Hansen, Nicolas Roussel, and Björn Eiderbäck. 2003. Technology probes: inspiring design for and with families. In Proceedings of the SIGCHI Conference on Human Factors in Computing Systems (CHI '03). ACM, New York, NY, USA, 17-24. DOI=http://dx.doi.org/10.1145/642611.642616

13. Hyungeun Jo and Sungjae Hwang. 2013. Chili: viewpoint control and on-video drawing for mobile video calls. In CHI '13 Extended Abstracts on Human Factors in Computing Systems (CHI EA '13). ACM, New York, NY, USA, 1425-1430. DOI=http://dx.doi.org/10.1145/2468356.2468610

14. Oskar Juhlin, Arvid Engström, and Elin Önnevall. 2014. Long tail TV revisited: from ordinary camera phone use to pro-am video production. In Proceedings of the SIGCHI Conference on Human Factors in Computing Systems (CHI '14). ACM, New York, NY, USA, 1325-1334. DOI=http://dx.doi.org/10.1145/2556288.2557315

15. Oskar Juhlin, Arvid Engström, and Erika Reponen. 2010. Mobile broadcasting: the whats and hows of live video as a social medium. In Proceedings of the 12th international conference on Human computer interaction with mobile devices and services (MobileHCI '10). ACM, New York, NY, USA, 35-44. DOI=10.1145/1851600.1851610 http://doi.acm.org/10.1145/1851600.1851610

16. kbmod. kbmod multistream. http://kbmod.com/multistream/.

17. Lyndon Kennedy and Mor Naaman. 2009. Less talk, more rock: automated organization of community-contributed collections of concert videos. In

Proceedings of the 18th international conference on World wide web (WWW '09). ACM, New York, NY, USA, 311-320. DOI=http://dx.doi.org/10.1145/1526709.1526752

18. Seungwon Kim, Sasa Junuzovic, and Kori Inkpen. 2014. The Nomad and the Couch Potato: Enriching Mobile Shared Experiences with Contextual Information. In Proceedings of the 18th International Conference on Supporting Group Work (GROUP '14). ACM, New York, NY, USA, 167-177. DOI=http://dx.doi.org/10.1145/2660398.2660409

19. McLuhan, M. Understanding media: the extensions of man. McGraw-Hill, 1964.

20. Blair Nonnecke and Jenny Preece. 2000. Lurker demographics: counting the silent. In Proceedings of the SIGCHI conference on Human Factors in Computing Systems (CHI '00). ACM, New York, NY, USA, 73-80. DOI=http://dx.doi.org/10.1145/332040.332409

21. Stuart Reeves, Christian Greiffenhagen, Martin Flintham, Steve Benford, Matt Adams, Ju Row Farr, and Nicholas Tandavantij. 2015. I'd Hide You: Performing Live Broadcasting in Public. In Proceedings of the 33rd Annual ACM Conference on Human Factors in Computing Systems (CHI '15). ACM, New York, NY, USA, 2573-2582. DOI=http://dx.doi.org/10.1145/2702123.2702257

22. Marco Sá, David A. Shamma, and Elizabeth F. Churchill. 2014. Live mobile collaboration for video production: design, guidelines, and requirements. Personal Ubiquitous Comput. 18, 3 (March 2014), 693-707. DOI=http://dx.doi.org/10.1007/s00779-013-0700-0

23. Guy Schofield, Tom Bartindale, and Peter Wright. 2015. Bootlegger: Turning Fans into Film Crew. In Proceedings of the 33rd Annual ACM Conference on Human Factors in Computing Systems (CHI '15). ACM, New York, NY, USA, 767-776. DOI=http://dx.doi.org/10.1145/2702123.2702229

24. John C. Tang, Gina Venolia, and Kori Inkpen. Meerkat and Periscope: I Stream, You Stream, Apps Stream for Live Streams. In Proceedings of the 34th Annual ACM Conference on Human Factors in Computing Systems (CHI '16). ACM, New York, NY, USA, in press.

25. Tazaki, A. InstantShareCam: Turning Users From Passive Media Consumers to Active Media Producers. Workshop Investigating new user experience challenges in iTV: mobility & sociability, 24th Annual ACM Conference on Human Factors in Computing Systems (CHI '06).

26. Raphael Velt, Steve Benford, Stuart Reeves, Michael Evans, Maxine Glancy, and Phil Stenton. 2015. Towards an Extended Festival Viewing Experience. In Proceedings of the ACM International Conference on Interactive Experiences for TV and Online Video (TVX '15). ACM, New York, NY, USA, 53-62. DOI=http://dx.doi.org/10.1145/2745197.2745206

27. Sami Vihavainen, Sujeet Mate, Lassi Liikkanen, and Igor Curcio. 2012. Video as memorabilia: user needs for collaborative automatic mobile video production. In Proceedings of the SIGCHI Conference on Human Factors in Computing Systems (CHI '12). ACM, New York, NY, USA, 651-654. DOI=http://dx.doi.org/10.1145/2207676.2207768

28. Andrew M. Webb, Chen Wang, Andruid Kerne, and Pablo Cesar. 2016. Distributed Liveness: Understanding How New Technologies Transform Performance Experiences. In Proceedings of the 19th ACM Conference on Computer-Supported Cooperative Work & Social Computing (CSCW '16). ACM, New York, NY, USA, 432-437. DOI=http://dx.doi.org/10.1145/2818048.2819974

29. Stefan Wilk, Stephan Kopf, and Wolfgang Effelsberg. 2015. Video composition by the crowd: a system to compose user-generated videos in near real-time. In Proceedings of the 6th ACM Multimedia Systems Conference (MMSys '15). ACM, New York, NY, USA, 13-24. DOI=http://dx.doi.org/10.1145/2713168.2713178

30. Takuro Yonezawa and Hideyuki Tokuda. 2012. Enhancing communication and dramatic impact of online live performance with cooperative audience control. In Proceedings of the 2012 ACM Conference on Ubiquitous Computing (UbiComp '12). ACM, New York, NY, USA, 103-112. DOI=http://dx.doi.org/10.1145/2370216.

Analysis of User Behavior with a Multicamera HbbTV App in a Live Sports Event

Marc Aguilar
Media Internet Area
I2CAT Foundation
Barcelona, Spain
marc.aguilar@i2cat.net

Sergi Fernández
Media Internet Area
I2CAT Foundation
Barcelona, Spain
sergi.fernandez@i2cat.net

David Cassany
Media Internet Area
I2CAT Foundation
Barcelona, Spain
david.cassany@i2cat.net

ABSTRACT

This paper describes the results of a large-scale live pilot test of an HbbTV multicamera application. In this pilot test, carried out during an association football match, the interactions of 6203 user devices with the application were logged. An exploratory statistical analysis was performed on the dataset, to better understand the behavior of the users on the application. The analysis yielded conclusions that can be useful to those seeking to build a successful multicamera service, with insights on issues of suitability of program genres, multicamera content selection, audience segmentation, and the structure of data stream traffic.

Author Keywords

Connected TV; HbbTV applications; user behavior; multi-camera; live video

ACM Classification Keywords

H.5.1. Information interfaces and presentation: Miscellaneous; H.5.1. Information interfaces and presentation: Evaluation/methodology

INTRODUCTION

In the last years, there has been a growing interest in the patterns of user consumption of innovative TV experiences. It is being increasingly recognized that the hybridization of broadcasting with Internet technologies is altering traditional TV viewing patterns to a large degree [3]. In a multiplatform environment, the determinants of important user decisions such as watching a particular program are shifting. Audiences are no longer focused on a single content source, and take into account multiple external factors in their decision making, such as peer recommendations on social media and on-demand content availability [1]. This convergence of television and the internet is profoundly changing the audio-visual market. As key players become aware of the fact that chang-

es in viewer habits and consumption patterns are poised to redefine business models in the coming years, the demand for fresh insights into user experiences and consumption patterns is likely to grow [12].

In parallel to these trends in the Connected TV arena, there is a rising perception that emerging digital technologies can add significant value to the field of sports events, not just for improving decision making but also for the TV broadcasting of competitive sports [14]. In the last years, a number of studies have attempted to shed light on the user experience with sports-related interactive TV, giving rise to a modest research agenda focused on this issue [2,7].

This paper attempts to contribute to ongoing discussions from the insights generated in a European Commission-funded innovation project, TV-RING. A major goal of this initiative was the implementation of a large-scale live pilot of a multicamera HbbTV application. The pilot took place during a football match, in which audiences were monitored as they interacted with the multicamera application. This pilot yielded a rich dataset on the audience usage of the application during the event, from which a series of insights can be extracted with an analysis of this dataset. We believe our results will be relevant for broadcasters, application developers and content producers, most particularly in the audiovisual sports domain.

PILOT METHODOLOGY

As delineated in the TV-RING piloting plan, a sequence of tests was carried out over a thirteen-month period [13]. This constituted the final phase of a larger user-centered design process, which had previously involved users in two rounds of requirements analysis and three iterations of prototype refinement [11]. First, four small-sample controlled pilots were executed from December 2014 to June 2015. This phase involved twenty households in the town of Gurb, in central Catalonia. Each household was given an HbbTV 1.5 device capable to play MPEG-DASH and last generation services. Test users were connected to a monitored fibre network of 100Mb/s using a local controlled content delivery network (CDN), from which detailed analytics could be monitored. At this stage, the goal was to fine-tune the usability of the test application, sort out any outstanding technical issues, and obtain market data on the most attractive contents for

Permission to make digital or hard copies of all or part of this work for personal or classroom use is granted without fee provided that copies are not made or distributed for profit or commercial advantage and that copies bear this notice and the full citation on the first page. Copyrights for components of this work owned by others than ACM must be honored. Abstracting with credit is permitted. To copy otherwise, or republish, to post on servers or to redistribute to lists, requires prior specific permission and/or a fee. Request permissions from permissions@acm.org.
TVX 2016, June 22–24, 2016, Chicago, IL, USA.
© 2016 ACM ISBN 978-1-4503-4067-0/16/06...$15.00.
http://dx.doi.org/10.1145/2932206.2932210

users to be used in larger experiments. The contents for these tests were a singing contest show, a special news report on the Spanish local elections, and two football matches.

This first phase of controlled-sample pilot tests set the stage for the two large-scale open pilots. A preparatory pilot was carried out in September, with news coverage of the Catalan national day rally, to ensure the successful deployment of the envisioned live pilots. The selected contents for the live pilots were two FC Barcelona football matches in September and November 2015. These open live pilots were followed by an audience of about 4000 and 6200 TV devices which accessed the project's HbbTV application, representing an audience of thousands of users interacting with the offered multicamera services. For the second test, a data collection framework was in place, to obtain and store user data via cookies and server request logs.

The evaluation plan for the open live pilot experiment provided for two kinds of data to be collected from the audience of the live sports event. Quantitative data was collected from the content delivery network system logs. This dataset contains information on every request made by specific devices for each particular audiovisual data stream. More specifically, it collects data on each request's time, device IP, stream URL, and total bytes transferred. This data was subjected to an exploratory statistical analysis, to reveal the structure of the distribution of the variables and uncover causal relationships (or the lack thereof) between these variables. Also, qualitative data was collected via an online questionnaire and the textual analysis of Twitter feeds. These sources of information were used during the analysis phase to contextualize the quantitative data.

HBBTV MULTICAMERA APPLICATION PILOT

The multicamera pilot application, developed by TV-RING partner Televisió de Catalunya (TVC), consisted of two main scenarios or areas of work. First, a video on demand (VoD) service displayed programs that could be accessed interactively from one or two different points of view or 'renditions'. Second, a live service allowed the broadcaster to offer to audiences a set of multiple renditions on an ongoing live TV show. Content was accessed using MPEG-DASH in all cases, providing for seamless and instantaneous timeline shifting in the first case, and actual live content in the second case. All contents were offered in three different qualities, ranging from the highest 7Mbps at HD, to an intermediate 5Mbps, to the lowest 3Mbps at SD.

The application was made up of different screens. The user entry point for the application was composed of a screen with the available list of live and VoD contents. The user could interact with the application using the remote control of the HbbTV-compliant TV set device, enabling the user to select content, control video playback and specify video renditions. Finally, in the start menu, the user had the option to display a help screen by pressing the blue button on the remote control.

In the figure below, a workflow of the application can be found to better describe the different GUI interactions.

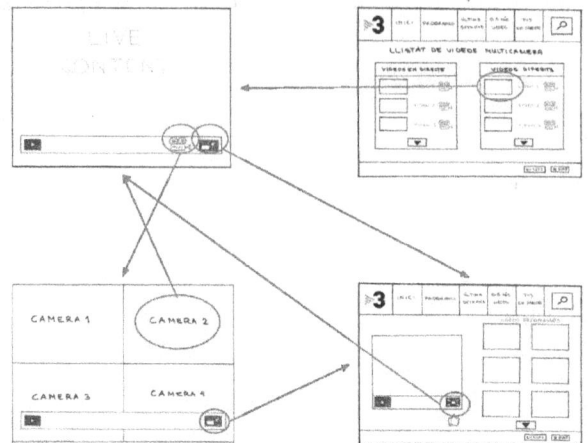

Figure 1. Multicamera application basic interaction pattern

Early on during the user evaluation activities, it was found that traditional remote controls offer very poor usability for users accustomed to more agile handheld device navigations. Several approaches to replace or complement the traditional remote control have been successfully implemented, such as speech and gesture recognition controls [17,4], or geospatial navigation designs which implement location flipping concepts [8]. In the TV-RING project multicamera pilot, a Second Screen solution was selected as the most suited to the specificities of the application tested on field trials. This remote control functionality allowed users to control the HbbTV application using a mobile device of their choice as remote control.

For the live pilot test from which the user behavior data was collected, the application allowed audiences to select between four different cameras. These four cameras were the live match broadcast (Stream 1), a camera which followed the three attacking FC Barcelona stars (Stream 2), a camera which centered on FC Barcelona's coach (Stream 3), and a fourth camera which gave an overview of FC Barcelona's attacking formation (Stream 4). This content was delivered to the user via five separate streams: the four views, plus the mosaic. The pilot content (an association football match) ran from 19:45 to 21:30 UTC on November 24, 2015. The football match consisted in two 45-minutes halves, with a 15-minute half time period in the middle.

DATA ANALYSIS

A dataset with more than 2.1M individual audiovisual stream requests was collected, representing the interactions of a total of 6203 unique TV devices with the application over the course of 2 hours of live pilot test. The total population of HbbTV 1.5-compliant devices in the Catalan territory was estimated by the broadcaster to be, at the point of the experiment, at about 35000 TV devices.

Figure 2. Screenshots of multicamera application mosaic and start page

Therefore, this estimation means that the data was obtained from a sample of 18% of the total potential population of available TVs. With these figures, the confidence interval for the statistics reported in this chapter should be estimated at plus/minus 1.13, for a confidence level of 95%.

As regards the questionnaire data, responses were obtained from a sample of 37 individual users. Out of an estimated population of 35000 valid devices, this constitutes a sample size of 0.1%. For a confidence level of 95%, the confidence interval of all reported statistics is plus/minus 16.11%. The very small sample and correspondingly large standard error place limits on the reliability of these statistics. Therefore, it is recommended that the results coming from the analysis of qualitative data are rather interpreted as broad orientations on audience preferences and perceptions.

Exploratory statistical analysis

The page requests dataset was subjected to an exploratory analysis. Statistical analysis of datasets generated at user experiments has followed a variety of multivariate statistical techniques, such as experimental design t-tests [6] or even cluster analysis of natural language codes derived from user diary studies [15]. Other authors researching large-scale TV consumption patterns have opted for highly sophisticated multivariate analyses, with the goal to derive conclusions from the distribution of data on key sociodemographic variables, i.e. age, gender, and household composition [5]. Notwithstanding their diversity and ingenuity, the common thread in all these approaches is that their authors follow an exploratory analysis strategy. This analytical strategy is char-

acterized by not letting prior choices of theoretical framework dictate the direction of hypotheses, but rather subjecting the data to a rigorous battery of tests which allow the structure of the data to emerge, in a fashion similar to what grounded theory approaches implement in qualitative research (see [10] for further reference).

TV Manufacturer	Unique Visitors	%	Page Views	%
LG	2,341	37.7	10.899	36.0
Sony	1,428	23.0	7.289	24.1
Panasonic	1,298	20.9	6.898	22.8
Samsung	922	14.9	3.848	12.7
Philips	69	1.1	486	1.6
Toshiba	55	0.9	310	1.0
Other	37	0.6	286	0.9
Total	**6,203**		**30.265**	

Table 1: Unique visitors and page views per TV manufacturer

Table 1 above presents the data on unique visitors and page views on the application, broken down by the manufacturer of the users' TV device. This manufacturer data may be useful to infer the market penetration of each manufacturer in the Catalan territory, in the segment of HbbTV 1.5-compliant devices. If we proceed with an analysis of this data, we can observe that there is a very strong correlation, in the order of $R^2=0.9898$, between the number of unique visitors and the number of page views requested. To explore more in depth this relationship, a more accurate non-parametric statistic of variance (the One-way ANOVA or Kruskal-Wallis H test) was calculated. The TV manufacturer of each device was introduced as the independent variable, while the total seconds spent in each page (a continuous and more accurate variable than just page views) was added as dependent variable. The test outcome revealed that there is indeed a statistically significant difference across groups, with a Chi-square statistic of 56.256. Because of the lack of comparable studies in the literature, it is not possible to compare the research significance of this Chi-square value with those of other experiments. The associated Median test carried out in the same analysis confirmed that audiences stayed on the application slightly longer depending on their TV models, but with such small observed differences that these can be regarded as insignificant for theory building purposes.

In Figure 3, we can see how total number of user and total data usage strongly correlate with the beginning of the match and the mid-time. Users did not watch so much in the midst of the bustle of the sport event, but rather in the starting minutes of each half. The highest usage peak occurred during the ten minutes before and the ten minutes right at the start of the match. A second, gentler peak can be observed in the minutes around the start of the second half. The size of these usage peaks is approximately five times and three times larger than during the rest of the match.

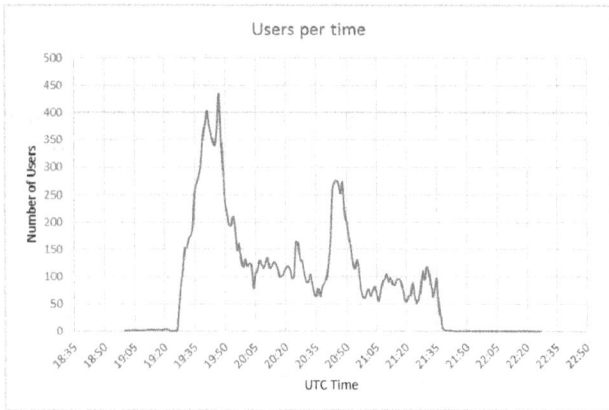

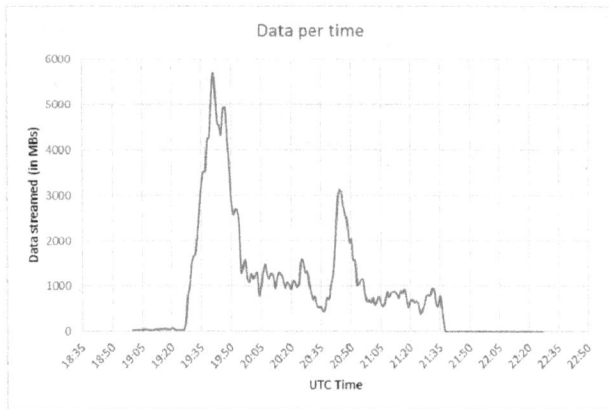

Figure 3. Users and data streamed along time during live pilot, total

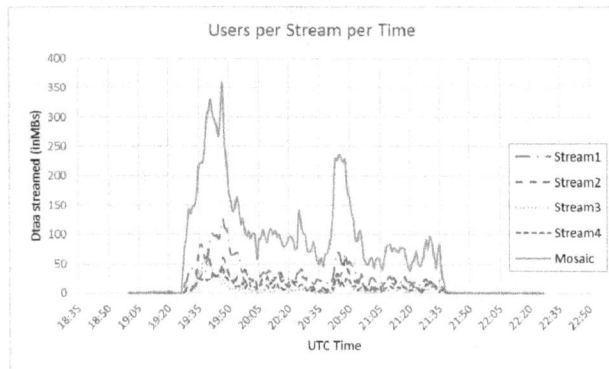

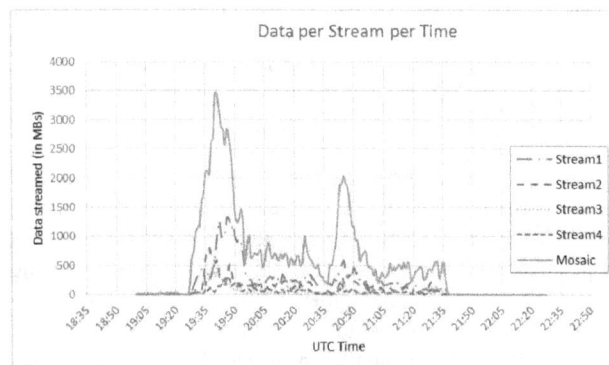

Figure 4. Users and data streamed along time during live pilot, breakdown by stream

Figure 4 above displays the volume of data transmitted during the pilot test at each of the five audiovisual data streams that could be requested by the multicamera application. It can readily be noticed that the mosaic was the most watched stream, accounting for over 80% of the total data traffic. The broadcast (indicated as Stream 1 in the graph) came next. The rest of streams (Stream 2 with the three stars, Stream 3 with the coach, and Stream 3 the overview of the attack) were only watched sporadically.

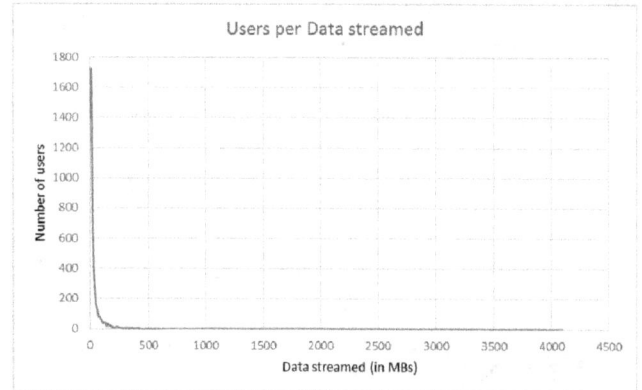

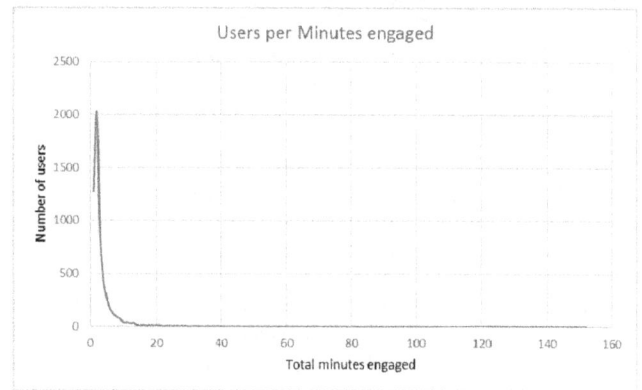

Figure 5. Number of users by total data streamed and total minutes engaged

The graphs in Figure 5 bin the 6203 pilot test users by their total usage of the application, in terms of total data streamed during the match and total minutes engaged on the application. As we can readily see, both variables have very non-normal distributions, strongly skewed to the left. These are long right tail variables, where an overwhelmingly majority of the cases are concentrated in the left side of the graph. In connection with our analysis of user behavior in the pilot test, the implications are that 95.02% of users were engaged in the application for less than ten minutes, and 74.65% of users were engaged for less than three minutes.

Contextual qualitative analysis

It must be acknowledged that the robustness of our qualitative results is negatively affected by the large error margin of the computed statistics. This is a direct consequence of the very small sample obtained, of only 37 respondents. Nevertheless, even allowing for the likelihood of a 16-percentualpoint mismatch between the population parameters and the sample statistics reported below, these results can give a general guidance on certain relevant issues. Most importantly, the user-generated statements and comments obtained via the questionnaire and program Twitter feed can provide vital contextual information to complement the analysis of the CDN log data.

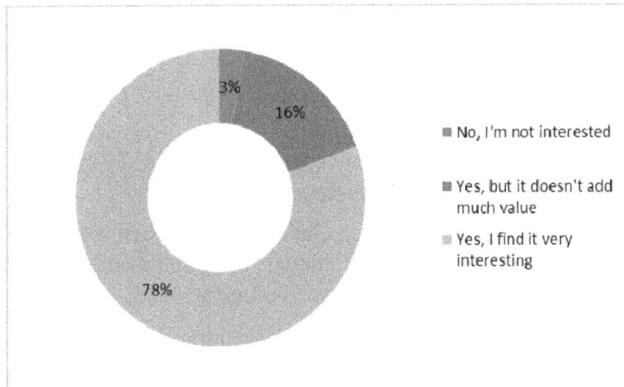

Figure 6. Perceived value of multicamera services in live football broadcast

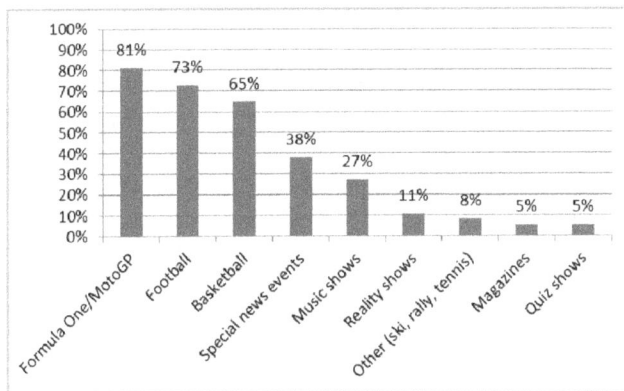

Figure 7. Stated preference of program contents for multicamera application

Figures 6 and 7 provide an indication of the perceived value of the piloted multicamera services, and their suitability for an range of program contents. Error margin notwithstanding, the large differences between the results of different response categories allow for the identification of certain facts. First, multicamera services can indeed be perceived as value-adding by a majority of users. And second, that the nature of the program content is a significant factor in the audience's decision to use such services.

DISCUSSION OF RESULTS

A number of insights emerge from the analysis of the data obtained during the multicamera pilot test. Firstly, it is significant to notice that users did not watch *during* the sport action, but mostly used the multicamera service when there was a moment of lesser activity in the course of the match. Thus, the current level of excitement of the match seems to be the main factor in shaping the level of engagement of users with

the service. The more exciting the moment of the match, the less likely is that users will be using the multicamera application. This finding is in line with the outcomes of previous studies on usage patterns of sports-related TV applications [9].

The selection of the streams is also very important. Not all multicamera views are born equal: some will experience much heavier usage than others. To a very large extent, the choice of available views determines the dynamics of camera switching of the users. In the pilot's case the most watched were the mosaic and the broadcast. The other three specific streams were watched occasionally, and for very short periods, usually just a few seconds. The qualitative analysis hinted at the fact that many users favorite view was actually the mosaic, because they felt they were "losing information" if they focused on just one of the views. The broadcast similarly gave them this sense of "being in control" of all that was happening in the match.

A key insight of this study has to do with the clustering of sports audiences on the basis of their multicamera application usage pattern. A large majority of users can be expected to be "dabblers", just trying out the application out of curiosity, but not interacting with the system in a sustained and meaningful way. At the other end of the distribution, there will be as well a small group of "very engaged" users, using the application on a regular (but not necessarily predictable) basis. If we set the threshold for engagement at 10 minutes of active usage, for our pilot test the relative size of both groups can be estimated at about 95% and 5% of the total audience of app users. Identifying and reaching this very small user group is critical for market research purposes.

Last but not least, an adequate selection of the program contents has been found to be critical for the success of a multicamera HbbTV application. Program genres in which the relevant action may happen simultaneously in several locations provide the best fit for a multicamera service. Sports such as football, basketball or tennis, and racing events like the Formula One or MotoGP competitions have been identified as particularly suitable contents for multicamera. Other kinds of contents such as special informative events (i.e. demonstrations, election days) and song contests were piloted during the course of the TV-RING project. The audience's reaction to these programs was fairly positive as well. Nevertheless, a lesser level of interest was detected, as many users did not see the value of multicamera services for those kinds of programs vis-à-vis the broadcast content produced by an experienced audiovisual producer.

CONCLUSION

The live pilot test of a multicamera HbbTV application generated extensive data on the patterns of usage of the application, technical performance parameters and several metrics of user satisfaction. An in-depth analysis of these data has yielded rich information on HbbTV market penetration in the Catalan market, models of user segmentation and clustering on the basis of multicamera application usage patterns, and analytics on the user's behavior in real-life settings. These have implications for service providers, broadcasters and manufacturers.

ACKNOWLEDGMENTS
The research leading to these results was carried out in the TVRING project and has received funding from the EC CIP-PSP Program under grant agreement 325209.

REFERENCES
1. Abreu, J., Almeida, P., Teles, B., Reis, M.: Viewer Behaviors and Practices in the (New) Television Environment. In *EuroITV 2013* (pp. 5-12), Como, Italy (2013).

2. Anstead, E, Benford, S., Houghton, R.J.: Many-Screen Viewing: Evaluating an Olympics Companion Application. In *Proc. TVX 2014* (pp. 103-110). Newcastle, UK (2014).

3. Barkhuus, L., Brown, B.: Unpacking the Television: User Practices Around a Changing Technology. ACM TOCHI 16, 3 (2009), 15.

4. Bobeth, J., Schrammel, J., Deutsch, S., Klein, M., Drobics, D., Hochleitner, C., Tscheligi, M.: Tablet, Gestures, Remote Control? Influence of Age on Performance and User Experience with iTV Applications. In *Proc. TVX 2014* (pp. 139-146). Newcastle, UK (2014).

5. Chaney, A.J.B., Gartrell, M., Hofman, J.M., Guiver, J., Koenigstein, N., Kohli, P., Paquet, U.: A Large-Scale Exploration of Group Viewing Patterns. In *Proc. TVX 2014* (pp. 31-38). Newcastle, UK (2014).

6. Costa, D., Carriço, L., Duarte, C.: The Differences in Accessibility of TV and Desktop Web Applications from the Perspective of Automated Evaluation. Procedia Computer Science Volume 67, 2015, 388–396.

7. Engstrom, A., Esbjornsson, M., Juhlin, O., Perry, M.: Producing Collaborative Video: Developing an Interactive User Experience for Mobile TV. In *Proc. UXTV 2008* (pp. 115-124). Silicon Valley, CA, USA (2008).

8. Fritzsche, T., Müller, S., Berger, A., Eibl, M.: Location Based Video Flipping: Interactive Prototype navigated by HbbTV remote control In: TVX 2014. Newcastle, UK (2014).

9. Fyrvald, N.: Usage Patterns of a Sports Related Second Screen Application. A Qualitative Case Study During Live Sport Games. Royal Institute of Technology Degree Thesis. Stockholm, Sweden (2015). https://goo.gl/akQ1BX

10. Glaser, B. (2008) Doing Quantitative Grounded Theory. Sociology Press, Mill Valley, CA.

11. Glaser, S. et al: D3.2 Intermediate Evaluation Report. Public report, TV-RING project (2014). http://www.tvring.eu/wp-content/uploads/2014/12/D3.2-Intermediate-evaluation-report.pdf

12. Medina, M., Herrero, M., Guerrero, E.: Audience behaviour and multiplatform strategies: the path towards connected TV in Spain. Austral Comunicación, 4, 1 (2015).

13. Pamplona, P. et al: D4.2. Pilot Execution Report. Public report, TV-RING project (2015). http://www.tvring.eu/wp-content/uploads/deliverables/D4.2-Pilot-Execution-Report.pdf

14. Petrović, L.T., Milovanović, D., Desbordes, M.: Emerging Technologies and Sports Events: Innovative Information and Communication Solutions. Sport, Business and Management: An International Journal 5,2 (2015), 175-190.

15. Rhiu, I., Rhie, Y.L., Shin, G.W., Yun, M.H.: Cluster Analysis on Self-reported Emotional Experiences of Smart TV-viewing, The Japanese Journal of Ergonomics, Vol. 51 (2015), S410-S413.

16. Tsekleves, E., Whitham, R., Kondo, K., and Hill, A. Investigating Media Use and the Television User Experience in the Home. Entertainment Computing 2, 3 (2011), 151–161.

17. Vanattenhoven, J., Geerts, D., De Grooff, D.: Television Experience Insights from HbbTV. In *Proc. TVX 2014* (pp. 32-34). Newcastle, UK (2014).

Connecting Living Rooms: An Experiment in Orchestrated Social Video Communication

Manolis Falelakis
Aristotle University of Thessaloniki
Greece
manf@issel.ee.auth.gr

Marian F. Ursu
University of York
United Kingdom
marian.ursu@york.ac.uk

Erik Geelhoed
Falmouth University
United Kingdom
erik.geelhoed@falmouth.ac.uk

Rene Kaiser
JOANNEUM RESEARCH
Austria
rene.kaiser@joanneum.at

Michael Frantzis
Goldsmiths, University of London
United Kingdom
m.frantzis@gold.ac.uk

ABSTRACT

Consumer live video communication has now become an established communication medium, but the current systems are still quite limited in their ability to support natural communication in more complex interaction setups. What new features might be required to further expand live video communication? This paper suggests: "orchestration" – i.e. the ability to automatically and in real-time (re)configure the communication system to the needs of the interaction context. The inspiration for communication orchestration is television production through mixing views from different cameras and camera reframing. This paper reports a specific study of orchestration carried out in the social setting of a group of friends communicating from three separate living rooms through television screens and multiple cameras. The orchestrated experience was evaluated against a static (split screen) connection, and was carried out via a questionnaire, analysis of automatic logs and interviews. In this case study, orchestration has been identified as providing for more intimate conversations, whereas, the static solution emerged to be better for conveying group awareness.

Author Keywords

Videoconferencing; Telepresence; Mediated communication; Group communication; Communication orchestration; Virtual Director; Video; Live; Group;

ACM Classification Keywords

H.4.3. Communications Applications: computer conferencing, teleconferencing, and videoconferencing

Permission to make digital or hard copies of all or part of this work for personal or classroom use is granted without fee provided that copies are not made or distributed for profit or commercial advantage and that copies bear this notice and the full citation on the first page. Copyrights for components of this work owned by others than the author(s) must be honored. Abstracting with credit is permitted. To copy otherwise, or republish, to post on servers or to redistribute to lists, requires prior specific permission and/or a fee. Request permissions from Permissions@acm.org.
TVX'16, June 22 - 24, 2016, Chicago, IL, USA
Copyright is held by the owner/author(s). Publication rights licensed to ACM.
ACM 978-1-4503-4067-0/16/06...$15.00
DOI: http://dx.doi.org/10.1145/2932206.2932215

INTRODUCTION

Consumer videoconferencing has now become an established communication medium. Applications like Skype, FaceTime and Hangouts are increasingly used to keep in touch with each other, to connect with the workplace, for meetings, job interviews, and sometimes just for fun. This expansion is not entirely the consequence of better underlying technology, it is also partly due to people's ability to adapt their behavior [14] and find ways to overcome the current limitations of the communication systems [13]. In fact, videoconferencing systems have not evolved that much at all in terms of the affordances they provide. To date, most of the technology advancements concerned mainly the quality of the audio and video content: better cameras and microphones, better encoding algorithms, more bandwidth, better transmission protocols, more effective rendering on better screens and speakers, all resulting in clearer and richer pictures and sounds. In the past few years, however, research has started to look beyond this. Now a rapidly growing research field [15], it is increasingly concerned with the development of new technological capabilities to allow live video communication to properly *expand into more complex communication setups* and *provide for more natural interactions* – to support new affordances.

Complex setups imply greater information spaces that cannot be dealt with anymore by brute force algorithms. Seeing and hearing everything that is captured from all the other locations, is not a feasible proposition anymore in a complex setup, nor is the expectation that one webcam and one microphone could capture from a complex location everything that is relevant to the overall communication. What is needed, we believe, is systems' ability to identify and capture the most important aspects of the communication and to aggregate and present this information in effective ways – in other words, *awareness of the context of each particular conversation* and *knowledge and ability to adapt in real time to the needs of the particular conversation*. We refer to this capability as *orchestration* [9, 23]. In this approach, it is the *system* that is able to dynamically adapt to the communication context, rather than the *people* adapting and finding ways to overcome its limitations.

Orchestration is inspired by television production: the use of multiple cameras and microphones, controlled in real time, feeding into audio and vision mixers to construct optimal representations of the covered event. Unlike television, though, orchestration is driven by communication rather than narrative needs and is required concurrently for all the inter-connected locations, rather than constituting a single unidirectional stream. It is not about passive content consumption, but rather a two-way real-time process where participant interaction influences mixing decisions and vice-versa.

Orchestration, as reasoning, subsumes two main processes: (i) *understanding* the continuously changing context of the communication taking place, and (ii) *deciding* upon optimal audiovisual representation to mediate the particular communication contexts identified. The former uses sensors and feature extraction modules to infer higher-level aspects of the communication, such as the person who has the conversational turn. The latter, by applying screen-language conventions, responds to this information by determining how to control the cameras and mix the available live content. It is important to note that this screen language needs to be created – it can draw on the language and grammars of TV and film, but, as already noted, it is radically different, as it serves communication rather than narration.

Existing commercial systems, such as Skype and Hangouts, have started to incorporate basic orchestration behavior, but this is essentially a mere "talking heads" [17] paradigm: each node is equipped with one camera and one screen, assumes one "talking head" in front of the camera, and some logic based on audio activity decides how to represent the group conversation in each node – normally the nodes from which audio activity is dominant are given visual prominence. This is only a basic example in a vast space of orchestration behaviors: there is an endless space regarding context understanding, as well as an endless space in addressing it, dynamically, with various system configurations. To this, we should add the countless communication setups possible, which could be considered along coordinates such as number of connected locations, cameras per location, screens, people, and activities they undertake. All in all, this is a potentially huge research landscape.

Refining and validating orchestration knowledge is not straightforward. On one hand, orchestration knowledge can be regarded as a combination of rules with potentially strong inter-dependencies. Its study, therefore, is radically different from that of the effect of a single variable (such as the size of the head) upon the mediated communication. On the other hand, orchestration is not a *general* recipe to any video-mediated communication setup. Each particular setup requires its own specific orchestration logic. Yet, more generic bodies of orchestration knowledge, applicable to wider communication setups, need to be identified, if the whole approach of orchestrated communication is to be feasible and effective. There is tight coupling between choosing the communication setup and refining the corresponding orchestration knowledge, each influencing the other. These aspects create a highly non-deterministic space, very dynamic and quite challenging for experimental enquiry.

There are no published studies that expose the logic and algorithms used in intelligent communication orchestration and their impact upon the quality of the resulting communication experiences for the commercial systems capable of orchestration and very few acquired through research prototypes (see the Related Work section). The experimental enquiry reported here continues the line of investigation into orchestration presented in [6, 9, 23, 24]. It is a comparative study between an orchestrated a non-orchestrated video-mediated communication taking place within a social setting: friends interacting from three remote locations. Orchestration has been identified as providing for more intimate conversations, but the non-orchestrated solution emerged to be better for conveying group awareness. The relationship of this study with prior research, the details of the experiment, the detailed findings and a discussion interpreting the findings are presented in the remainder of this paper.

RELATED WORK

Research in videoconferencing and telepresence (we suggest needing to be labeled more generically as "live video-mediated communication") is a rapidly growing field of research. However, when it comes to creating new features and functionalities, it faces a great challenge: the prototypes required for experimental investigation need robust and complex infrastructures, not easily available on research projects [15]. Therefore, rather than 'inventing the future' research is trying to 'get around' limitations of existing technology to do something creative [15]. Our research addresses this challenge: the investigation of a possible "future feature", orchestration, on a prototype system developed for this purpose.

The framework for telepresence research presented in [10] contextualises our work. It proposes seven design dimensions, of which we address 'vision' and 'communication', and seventeen scenario types, 'talking socially' being the one addressed in our study.

Although research into video expression and representation in videoconferencing started as early as the nineties [12 and self-references], orchestrated communication is a rather new area of research, with very little orchestration knowledge evaluated and published. However, each of the two main reasoning components of orchestration – context understanding and directing video expression – has significant bodies of related research. There is substantial work regarding the understanding of conversation dynamics and social signals, but this has not been linked, yet, to directing cameras and vision mixers for live video communication. Conversely, there is significant expertise and knowledge regarding directing cameras and mixing content, but this is geared towards film, TV and, more recently, games, not towards context-aware, adaptive communication. A brief survey of these two areas made from the perspective of their relevance to orchestration was published in [24]. The techniques and technologies for conversation analysis [21] and social signal processing [7] provide an excellent foundation for context understanding in orchestration. Screen-language for TV, film and video games provide great inspiration for screen grammar in videoconferencing.

Research that connects the two main reasoning components of orchestration is scarce. [1] investigated the identification of 'floor control' (see also [3]) in group meetings, using a multi-modal approach that combines patterns of speech (e.g., the use of discourse markers) with visual cues (e.g., gaze exchanges). Identifying who has control of the floor has been used in this research for information retrieval and summarization from audio-video recordings, not on live video communication. Further, the work focused on the definition of a model, using manual annotations of audio and video recordings, and not on its implementation. Nevertheless, floor control is an important dynamic cue that can inform orchestration decisions. [18] reported a study that employed principles from television production to capture meetings of small groups. Events such as 'speaker change', 'posture change' and 'head orientation' are mapped, according to an internal logic, onto different types of shots, such as 'close-up', 'two-person' and 'overview'. Automatically compiled representations were compared with representations compiled by a film crew. This work is very closely related to orchestration, but its overall aim is to better recount meetings (to passive viewers), not to provide for real-time communication between participants. [1] and [18] consider face-to-face communication and aim to develop better ways for their recording and recounting, whereas orchestration considers mediated communication. Also, [1] and [18] are set in the more structured space of meetings, whereas orchestration, here, is studied within the less structured space of social interaction.

Research regarding the understanding of user needs for live video-mediated communication has direct relevance to orchestration. [20] argue that research into telepresence in social communication settings has to give more emphasis to emotional connection, as people tend to describe their experiences with such references, e.g., feeling close, feeling connected. [2] complements the investigation of user needs, shedding light on the differences between private and professional communication. These examples illustrate the complexities of the social interaction space that ought to be supported by systems for live video mediated communication. They informed our system design decisions.

Orchestration research

The work reported in [11] is directly relevant to orchestration. Two groups of people have a meeting across a video link. One direction of communication was orchestrated, employing one mobile camera, whereas the other one was 'conventional', using a static wide shot. The orchestration logic was refined by analyzing TV debate programs. Eight types of shots were refined, including 'speaker', 'listener' and 'speaker and listener'. The duration of each shot was clocked and so a frequency distribution was compiled from the TV content. The orchestration logic was subsequently expressed as two-shot transition tables, each specifying the probability of transition from any shot to any other shot. This is inspiring work, but the setup was limited: context understanding was not automatic; only one direction of communication was orchestrated; and the interaction context was that of a structured meeting. Benefits of the orchestrated communication have been observed, such as better conveyance of the feelings and intentions of the active speaker, but also benefits of the conventional link have been noticed, such as making the situation easier to grasp. The conclusion of the study was that orchestration could be a way of improving the quality of communication in structured meetings. However, interestingly, the study hypothesized that this paradigm is not portable to the less structured conversations of the social space, as speaker identification is not portable to situations when people take short turns or speak over each other. We are challenging this hypothesis in our research, as we believe, with backing up evidence from [9, 23, 24], that the paradigm can be ported to social spaces. A subsequent study [12], however, revises the initial conclusion stating that 'the suitable video expression may be different depending on the kind of meeting' and suggesting that a 'more variety of video expression should be examined'.

The experimental enquiry reported here continues the line of investigation into orchestration for social interaction between family and friends reported in [6, 9, 23, 24]. [7] and [9] are earlier accounts of aspects of orchestration, [7] describing an automatic reasoning process and [9] reporting on the first experimental investigation of orchestrated live video communication behavior. The research reported in [23] explored the concept of orchestration in a specific social setting: a group of friends playing social games and have idle chats from two separate living rooms. Both communication directions were orchestrated, the system employing four fixed cameras per location, each able to provide one particular functional shot. The orchestration logic was expressed as a set of rules, but the corresponding reasoning process was carried out by human operators. The orchestration logic was based not only on 'conversation turns' (similar to active speaker in the previously cited work), but also on other features of conversation analysis, such as 'crosstalk' and 'quick turn taking'. The study concluded that orchestration can improve the quality of communication and interaction in social settings.

The research reported in [24] continued this line of investigation by employing a completely automatic system (no manual intervention) in a similar social communication context to [23]. It is the first published study of a completely automatic orchestrated communication system that exposed the logic of interaction and followed its effect upon the mediated interaction. It was based on a slightly simpler orchestration rule set than [23], but it employed the same conversation features (conversation turn, cross-talk and quick turn taking) [19] to describe the dynamic context of communication and three rather than four functional shots (a wide and two mid-shots, one per participant). The activity at the center of the social interaction was the guessing game *Articulate*. The study employed two main experimental conditions for the main research question: *automatic orchestration*; and *static connection* (one camera, one shot, no dynamic adaptation) mimicking the capabilities of the current systems. It also employed two other conditions for further analyses: manual orchestration, based on the same rule set; and a randomly mixed shots condition. The main finding of this study was that social task efficiency – reflecting the ability to win social games– can be improved through orchestration. However, it was inconclusive with regards to the subjective evaluation of the experience. Yet, by challenging the questionnaire used which, allegedly, was insufficiently refined to identify differences it formulated the hypothesis that orchestration is probably better at conveying closeness and intimacy, the static connection being better at maintaining group awareness. . It also hypothesized that the benefits of orchestration might become more apparent in more complex communication setups.

Building on these grounds, the study reported in this paper investigated orchestration by using a different questionnaire in an expanded communication setup. To this end, differences in the way participants experience each condition were measured by employing a questionnaire refined specifically for this purpose. Furthermore, the experiment involved groups of people socializing with each other from 3 interconnected living rooms, in effect doubling the amount of camera shots available for display in each location. This however came at the expense of dropping the manual orchestration condition, as the technical infrastructure needed to support it became overly complex.

In addition to the subjective experience the study attempted to monitor how conversational behavior is affected by orchestration, by automatically logging and analyzing a number of conversational cues together with their corresponding mixing decisions. Finally, the orchestration logic was the same and so were the types of (functional) shots used.

EXPERIMENT DESCRIPTION

Communication Setup

Three rooms, each measuring about 12 m^2, were connected via a videoconferencing system that was purpose-built as part of the Vconect research project[1]. The room layout is depicted in Figure 1 . Although for practical reasons the rooms were in close proximity, there was no natural sound leakage from one to another. The rooms featured comfortable seating in such an arrangement that directional audio could be determined accurately.

Each room featured one 50" TV display and participants sat at a distance of about 2m from it. One Sony EVI-HD1 PTZ camera was positioned centrally just below the display and two Panasonic AG-AC160 (fixed) cameras were placed on tripods on either side and close to the bottom of the display. The Return Transmission Time (RTT), the standard measure of round-trip delay, was found to be constant and of the same value between all 3 rooms, and measured 650 milliseconds.

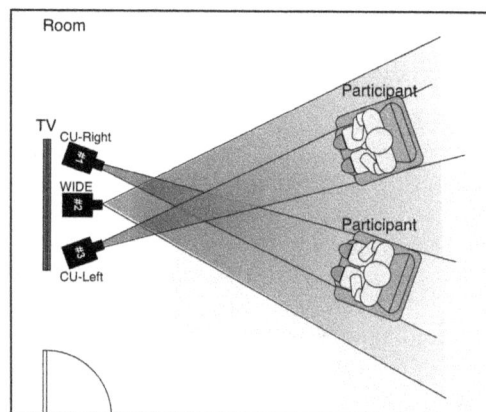

Figure 1. Room layout for each of the three connected rooms.

In each room the position of the person speaking was determined automatically via audio analysis, using an array of four condenser microphones. This cue was then processed via a rule-based system which resulted in automatically editing/orchestrating the video output, which in turn resulted in different composition for each room. As a conscious design decision to limit the complexity of the space, participants were not able to see themselves, e.g. via Picture in Picture (PiP), nor were they able to derive feedback as to how (or if) they were shown on the screens of the other two rooms.

Orchestration logic

In the context of the current experiment, orchestration logic was designed with the aim to follow and give visual prominence to the active speaker, while trying to maintain a balanced view of all people involved in the conversation and ensuring that the visual continuity of the representation is preserved. To this end, the understanding module of the

---

[1] http://vconect-project.eu/

system was based on the concepts of *turn shift, short turn taking* and *cross talk*, which were automatically inferred from a more primitive cue, namely 'start voice activity by person P'. The definition of the concepts is given below:

A *turn shift* occurs when there is significant (i.e. lasting more than 400ms) voice activity from a person who does not currently have the turn, excluding the case of a cross talk. The turn is maintained, even if there are some short (i.e. lasting no more than 500ms) gaps in the speech of a participant. Only one person can have the turn at any moment. A *cross talk* occurs when a person starts speaking at a point when another person has the conversational turn. There is a *pattern of short turn taking* if 3 or more turn shifts occur within 5 seconds. These thresholds were chosen based on a number of small-scale experiments.

For the dynamic adaptation of visual representation, a small set of types of shots was considered to be sufficient in each room: a *wide shot*, framed to include both people in the room (Figure 2 c), allowing them also a bit of space for movement, and two tighter shots, *mid-shots*, one for each person in the room, as depicted in Figure 2 (a-b). This gave the orchestration system a total of six shots to choose from at each point, i.e., three coming from each one of the other two rooms. Orchestration was done solely through the mixing of these shots (i.e., there was no camera reframing) and using only clean-cut transitions.

The mixing logic, expressed as rules in natural language, is described in Table 1. The rules are stated from the point of view of the room/screen *for* which the mixing is taking place; therefore, the persons referred to in the rules are from the other two rooms.

1. If person P starts a conversational turn (i.e., a turn-shift to P occurs), show the medium shot of P.
2. If there is a pattern of short turn taking within a room, then show the wide shot of that room.
3. If there is no turn shift for 5 seconds, then show the wide
4. No change of shot is allowed within 2 seconds of the previous cut (highest priority, when there are conflicts)

Table 1. Orchestration rules.

Conditions

There were two experimental conditions:

For the first, *orchestrated* condition, the aforementioned orchestration logic was employed in order to select in real-time from the six available shots coming from the other two rooms, as described in the previous section.

The second, *static* condition, involved using one static camera per room and the participants in each room could see the four other participants in the remote rooms as a group. This was anticipated to afford good group awareness, including being able to identify where vocal backchannels came from but would fall short on feedback through facial expressions. To this end, a screen showed

one remote room at the top and the other at the bottom of the screen in a geometrically consistent configuration, i.e., if the participants in room 1 see room 2 at the top and room 3 at the bottom then the participants in room 3 should see room 1 at the top and room 2 at the bottom. An example of this layout is illustrated in Figure 2 (d).

We chose to use static as our control condition, refraining from the use of an orchestrated commercial system. This is partially due to the fact that the algorithms driving camera-selection in commercial systems are not publicly available, but mainly because a traditional context-unaware setup can assist the evolution of orchestration logic in a controlled fashion.

Figure 2. Screen layouts - (a), (b) and (c) orchestrated condition: two mid-shots and a wide (d) static condition.

All participants took part in both conditions in one of two orders, in a counter-balanced manner. For one condition, participants were asked to generate a list of seven items between them pertaining to "what constitutes an ideal holiday" using a maximum of 5 minutes and then using another maximum of 5 minutes to prioritize and agree upon a group list of these seven items. A (deliberately) small piece of paper and a pencil was provided to each participant. For the other condition the task was to generate and prioritise seven items pertaining to an "ideal home".

The topics for the task are relatively neutral and people of different backgrounds are equally able to carry it out. In addition there is (practically) no learning curve, as such participants perform equally well in the first as in the second session. The task is highly repeatable across a number of synchronous and asynchronous experimental paradigms, i.e. the experimental validity is high. In addition, the task elicits highly interactive behaviour around trivial topics in a way that mimics (some) communication through social media and thus we might argue that there is a reasonable ecological validity.

Sessions and Participants

The experiment involved 24 participants, 18 of which female (mean age 22.89, SD 3.86) and 6 male, (mean age 22.83, SD 3.25). All participants were students of Goldsmiths, University of London, therefore constituting a study group younger and probably more technology-savvy than the average population. There were four experimental sessions and each session involved two participants per room, i.e., six per session.

Evaluation Measures

After experiencing each condition, participants were asked to answer 16 questions about aspects of telepresence. We adapted an existing questionnaire that a vendor for videoconferencing systems had been using previously [8]. Using graphic rating scales [22], participants had to mark on a line between 'not at all' (receiving a score of 0) and 'very' (= 100). Below is an example of a rating scale question:

How close did you feel to people in the other rooms?

Not at all   Very
|_____|

Participants were asked to make a mark on the scale between (and including) the two extremes. The questions asked about well-established aspects of telepresence, adverse effects on conversational parameters and group interaction (see Table 2).

1. How much was looking at the people in the other rooms like looking through a window?
2. How much was looking at the people in the other rooms like watching a TV panel discussion?
3. How lifelike were the people in the other rooms?
4. How close did you feel to people in the other rooms?
5. How much did you notice the facial expressions of people in the other rooms?
6. How much did you feel you had eye contact with people in the other rooms?
7. How much did it distract from the group conversation when you spoke to the person sitting next to you in your room?
8. How well could you see the persons in the other rooms?
9. How much did you notice a delay in the communication, i.e. it looked like the people in the other rooms heard you a little while after you spoke?
10. How disruptive did you find the delay?
11. How often did it happen that someone in your room and someone in one of the other rooms started talking at the same time?
12. How often were there awkward silences between the three rooms?
13. How lively were the discussions between all of you?
14. How similar to a face-to-face meeting was this session?
15. How easy was it to keep track of the discussion?
16. How well did you feel you came across to the other rooms?

Table 2. Experience assessment questionnaire.

The questionnaire data were analysed using SPSS, identifying statistical descriptions. Analysis of variance was used to explore differences, correlations and Multi Dimensional Scaling were used to analyse similarities.

Further to the questionnaire, the evaluation was enhanced by the use of *orchestration logs*, captured automatically, and reflecting the events inferred in real-time by the Orchestration Engine software component.

Finally, short unstructured group *interviews* were carried out after the experiment (i.e. after both conditions), asking about likes, dislikes and wishes of the technologies used.

Comments on the Design

For the contextualization of the results and the subsequent discussions, some of the experiment design choices ought to be explicitly highlighted. The orchestrated condition was intentionally chosen to force differences between (1) the provision of detailed representations (itself) against (2) an overall representation of the whole communication setup (static). Thus, for example, the orchestrated condition did not include the split screen showing both rooms in its set of possible visual representations, nor other global representation of all the people involved in the interaction. The orchestrated condition, therefore, might be regarded as "incomplete". The activity that drove the social interaction was chosen to generate an animated conversation, reflected, for example, in patterns of quick turn taking. This suited well with the age group of the participants and also allowed the choice of a relatively short period of interaction in each condition (10 minutes). The participants were not briefed on the conditions they were going to experience in order to not present the temptation of reverse engineering the behavior of the system and "play" with its capabilities. Finally, with regard to the number and positioning of the cameras, there were certainly many more options to have more comprehensive cover of the communication setup However, this would have potentially made the interpretation of the results more complex, therefore we opted for an incremental approach starting with a simpler configuration.

EVALUATION RESULTS

This section is divided into two parts: while results based on the questionnaire primarily focus on the subjective experience aspect of our research question, results based on the software component's logs relate to the objective participant behaviour. We chose to report results from the unstructured group interviews only in the discussion section to underline certain findings.

Questionnaire

Descriptive statistics

In the orchestrated condition the responses could be grouped in three bands of scores, as illustrated in Figure 3: High ratings were given for the ability to see their conversational partners, the ability to notice their facial expressions, for the conversation involving many simultaneous starts, and being lively and for remote partners seeming lifelike. Mid ratings indicated that the display configuration reminded participants (somewhat) of a TV panel show, they were distracted by side conversations with the person who was co-present (in the same room), they could keep track of the conversation, felt relatively close to remote partners, felt they came across reasonably well, found the display disruptive and they noticed the delay. They did not judge the communication to be like a face-to-face meeting, it was not like looking through a window, eye contact was poor and there were few awkward silences.

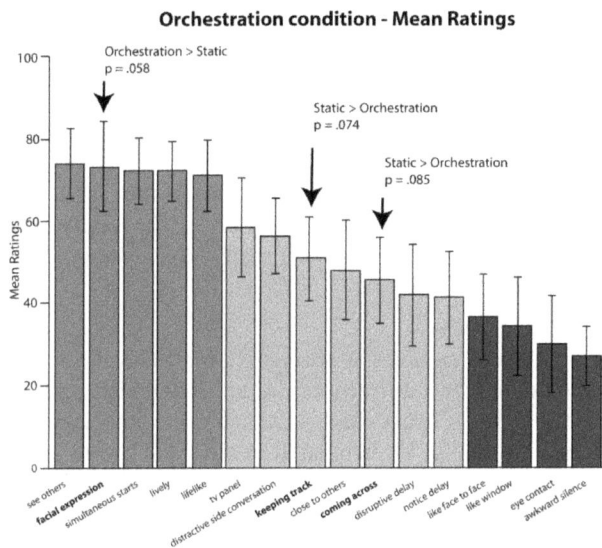

Figure 3. Mean ratings for the orchestrated condition.

On the other hand, in the static condition, there were four bands of scores, depicted in Figure 4. High ratings were given for remote conversational partners being lifelike, they experienced a high number of simultaneous starts, the sessions were lively and they could see their remote conversational partners well. The band of high-mid ratings indicated that participants were able to see the facial expressions relatively well, could keep track of the conversation, they thought they came across well, felt close to remote partners, thought the visual representation resembled a TV-panel but were also distracted from the conversational flow by side conversations with the co-present participant, i.e. the person in the same room. Poorer ratings were given to how like a face-to-face meeting the mediated session was; the configuration was not like looking through a window and seeing the remote partner. On the other hand delay was not noticed particularly and was not found to be overly disruptive. Low ratings were given for eye contact and participants rated the occurrence of awkward silences low.

Two-Way ANOVAS, Like for Like comparisons
A series of two way ANOVAs was carried out comparing the survey questions (repeated measures, main effect for the two experimental conditions) in a "like for like" manner with order of presentation as a between subjects factor. As there were equal numbers of subjects per condition/cell, we used a type III error. In addition to the F-ratio and p-value we also provide the effect size: Cohen's partial eta-squared (η_p^2).

In most cases, the differences between the static and orchestrated conditions were not profound. However, adopting an alpha level of 10%, we observed a significant effect for being able to see facial expressions, which was rated higher in the orchestrated condition than in the static one. On the other hand, in the static condition it was easier to keep track of the conversation and participants thought they came across better than in the orchestrated one. We choose to focus on these three questions to examine the findings of the main and order effects.

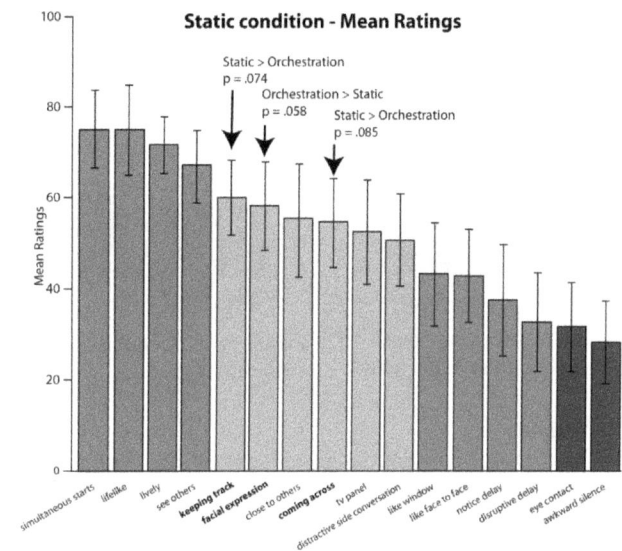

Figure 4. Mean ratings for the static condition.

Figure 5 shows the means for the static and orchestrated conditions for Order 1 (static – orchestrated) and Order 2 (orchestrated – static).

Main effect: static vs. orchestrated: For being able to see "Facial Expressions" (Figure 5) we found a near significant main effect, $F_{(1,22)}$=4.006, p=.058, η_p^2=.154, seeing facial expressions was rated higher in the orchestrated condition than in the static condition.

Order effect: There was significant Order effect, $F_{(1,22)}$=6.864, p=.016, η_p^2=.238. The mean ratings for seeing facial expressions were highest (irrespective of condition) when the orchestrated condition was second.

Being able to keep track of the conversation (Figure 6) was on average rated higher in the static condition, $F_{(1,22)}$=3.522, p=.074, η_p^2=.138. There was a significant interaction, where in the second session of Order 1 (the orchestrated condition) and in the second session of Order 2 (the static condition) lower ratings were given.

On average, participants felt they came across better in the static condition (Figure 7), $F_{(1,22)}$=3.263, p=.085, η_p^2=.129. There were no order effects in this question.

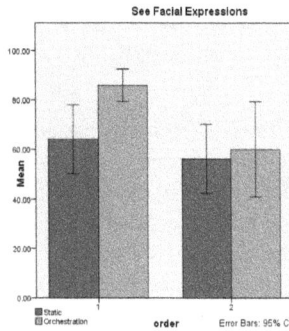

Figure 5. Noticing facial expressions order effect

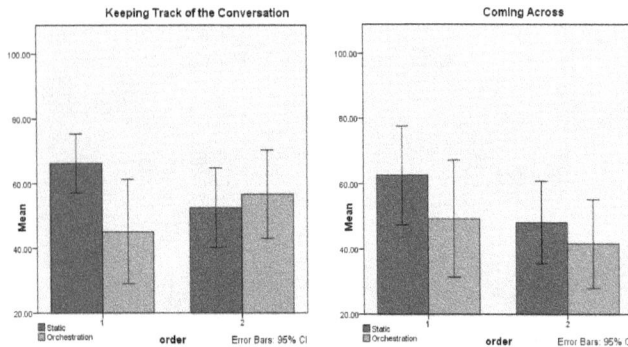

Figure 6. Keeping track of the conversation order effect.

Figure 7. Coming across order effect.

Correlations
We carried out correlations tests between the responses to all 16 questions in both conditions. The most significant result within the subset of the three questions that we chose to focus on was the positive correlation between recognising facial expression in the orchestrated condition and keeping track of the conversation in the static condition, r=0.509, n=24, p=0.011. This could indicate that those who better rate higher facial expressions in the orchestrated condition are also those who identify the ability to keep track of the discussion as being better in the static one. Thus participants seem to be consistent in identifying the qualities of each condition.

Orchestration Logs
The system logged a number of conversational parameters as well as editing (orchestration) actions undertaken by the system (in the orchestrated condition only), based on detecting the voice activities of the participants. Hereby we report only on the occasions where significant differences were observed across conditions, namely on turns and cross talks.

Turns
Comparing the frequencies of turns using paired chi-squared tests, we found that there were more conversational turns in the orchestrated condition (mean 258.75, SD 74.4), than the static one (mean 233.50, SD 65.43), a pattern that was consistent across the sessions. This leads to the total of conversational turns across sessions in the orchestrated

condition being significantly greater than the static one, with $\chi^2(1)$=5.181, n=24, p<.05.

We classified turns according to their duration into *short* (less than one second), *medium* (between one and four seconds) and *long* (more than four seconds). When comparing their frequencies across conditions we observe a consistent pattern for short turns. More specifically, the orchestrated condition consistently involves more short turns (mean 67.75, SD 42.97) than the static one (mean 56.25, SD 36.53), with $\chi^2(1)$=4.266, n=24, p<.05.

With regard to overall turn durations between the orchestrated (mean 2.14, SD 1.85) and the static condition (mean 2.23, SD 2.13), paired chi-squared tests do not indicate significant differences on a per session basis. However, in the orchestrated condition turns are consistently shorter on average that in the static one. Consequently, the duration of turns in the orchestrated condition is significantly shorter than in the static one, with $\chi^2(1)$=4.453, n=24, p<.05.

Cross talks
Comparing the number of cross talks across conditions, we found significant differences in all individual sessions, indicating more cross talks in the orchestrated condition (mean 174, SD 73.19) compared to the static (mean 142.25 SD 61.68). This resulted in a significant overall difference, with the number of cross talks being higher in the orchestrated condition with $\chi^2(1)$=12.750, n=24, p<.001.

FINDINGS
Although the subjective evaluation questionnaire did not lead to dramatic differences between the two conditions, it did show near to significant differences with regards to two aspects: (1) ability to see facial expressions, enhancing a level of telepresence of the active speaker and providing a sense of intimacy; and (2) keeping track of the conversation and group awareness.

Unsurprisingly, the former came up strongly in the orchestrated condition and the latter in the static condition. They were overwhelmingly backed up by interview data, with participants combining both aspects in their responses; e.g.: *"I preferred the [orchestrated condition] because of the clarity of it, expressions and everything ... but in a way it was more distracting..."* and *"The [static] one was easier to follow the discussion, although you could not see their facial expressions"*. This can be partially attributed to the reduced face size as a result of the inherent restrictions in screen space posed by the use of split screen. On the other hand, there were also individual voices that challenged the overall trend: *"The dual screen was a bit difficult. Could just about get used to it with regular conversations, but if more than one person is talking, where do you look?..."* and *"The second [orchestration] one didn't feel live. It felt like they have been interviewed before."*

There seemed to be a preference trend to the static condition with regards to the feeling of coming across to the other rooms. This could be explained by the assumption that the static condition provides a more predictable and controllable sensation, as the participants seem to feel confident that they are shown in a wide shot. However, it was expressed in interviews more as a drawback of the orchestrated condition than a strength of the static one: "... *didn't like the zoom as I didn't know when it was close-up on myself*" and "*I was not sure whether I have attracted attention, which means I am not sure if they have their eyes on me*".

There is an interesting order effect pattern regarding the three aspects in which the two conditions most significantly differed (i.e. facial expression and telepresence of active speaker; keeping track of the conversation; and feeling of coming across in the other space). The order "static fist, orchestrated second" led to more significant differences between the two conditions than the reversed order.

The analysis of the automatically captured logs indicates that in the orchestrated condition there are higher frequencies of conversation turns, as well as short turns, while their average duration is shorter compared to the static condition. Furthermore, the orchestrated condition is also characterised by a significantly higher amount of cross talks. It is generally considered that higher frequency of shorter conversational turns, interruptions and backchannels is indicative of a healthy and lively (group) conversation. On the other hand, longer turn duration has been associated with poorer telepresence [16, 5, 4], while more formal and structured floor control generally denotes an attempt by users to adjust to the system's limitations in the audio-visual representation. From this perspective, the automated logging data point to a livelier conversation in the orchestrated condition. The interview data leads to a similar conclusion: "*I liked the [orchestrated one] because it became less formal... there was less pressure to perform*". However, we cannot dismiss the converse interpretation, also possible but not suggested by this experiment data, that the short turns and cross talks indicate a problem with keeping track of the conversation – "*I think people talked over each other a lot more*", although the interview data backs up the former interpretation.

The interview data provides further insights. The orchestration logic is the main point of discussion. Some participants noticed delays in the system's response to conversational cues: "*...first I could hear the voice then afterwards came the image*" and "*it [the system] was behind the conversation*". This might indicate drawbacks in the validation of the orchestration logic of the communication system's behaviour.

Various improvements to the orchestration logic have been alluded to through interviews. Seeing all the people involved in the communication, not their spaces, was a suggestion: "*see everybody's faces there, so you can see other's people reactions to what they're saying as well*" and "*if could have like show all four faces that would have been*

cool". Complementing the orchestrated condition with aspects that represent the whole group has also been suggested in interviews: "*maybe if there were something that was a bit more a combination of the two. The images changed too much*" and "*you cannot see two people at the same time ... I think we should see two voices and two pictures at the same time*". There are also aspects that the current orchestration logic ignores, such as ability to address someone, ensuring eye contact and being able to (partly) control the system's behaviour. The interviews back them up: "*I was asking a question to someone, but it was showing someone else ...*", "*basically I struggle with everything that does not have eye contact. Even Skype is difficult*", and "*... I should have a set of controls to choose where I was looking*".

CONCLUSIONS

This paper reported on the experimental evaluation of *orchestration*, a possible new feature of group live video communication, carried out via a dedicated prototype system. The evaluation was carried out within a generic setup, where groups of 6 people sat in 3 rooms, each equipped with 3 HD cameras and a large TV screen. Participants were exposed to two different mediation conditions; during the first one the content of each screen was automatically mixed based on a specific orchestration logic, whereas the second offered a static wide view of both other locations.

The evaluation results did not reveal dramatic differences between the two conditions, thereby not confirming the hypothesis that in a more complex setup the effects of orchestration would be more beneficial, therefore more visible.

Regarding the main research question behind this experiment, they did, nevertheless, provide some clear indications on their effect. According to these, the orchestrated mediation contributes to a livelier and more intimate interaction that comprised more frequent turn-taking and unstructured floor control. On the other hand, the static condition seems to benefit from its ability to provide better spatial awareness and track of the conversation, while having a more predictable and controllable nature in terms of self-representation in the other rooms. Note that these conclusions have been drawn only for the chosen communication setup (3 rooms, 6 people, etc.). In fact, we need to point out that this evaluation assumed a specific communication setup coupled with a relatively simple orchestration logic and also note that a different group in terms of age and technical fluency might have led to slightly different results.

In future work, we plan to focus on improving the capabilities of the orchestrated condition with regard to keeping up with the speed of conversation and providing spatial awareness. To this end we plan to enhance the orchestration logics in order to improve context understanding by performing the calculation of conversation metrics in real time and by investigating the use of longer states in reasoning. Finally, we are also interested in improving adaptation by supporting automated switching between more complex layouts, essentially yielding the static layout as part of the orchestration options, in an attempt to combine virtues of both worlds.

ACKNOWLEDGMENTS

The research leading to these results has received funding from the European Community's Seventh Framework Program (FP7/2007-2013) under grant agreements no. ICT-2011-287760 and ICT-2007-214793. We thank all partners who contributed to this study.

REFERENCES

1. Aggarwal, D., Ploderer, B., and Vetere, F. Understanding Teleconsultation through Different Perspectives. *Everyday Telepresence workshop ACM CHI 2015.*

2. Brubaker, J., Venolia, G., and Tang, J. 2012. Focusing on shared experiences: moving beyond the camera in video communication. *Proc. ACM DIS 2012*, 96-105.

3. Chen, L., Harper, M., Franklin, A., Rose, T. R., Kimbara, I., Huang, Z., Quek, F. 2006. A multimodal analysis of floor control in meetings. In *Machine Learning for Multimodal Interaction*, 36-49.

4. Clark, H. H. 1996. *Using language.* Cambridge University Press.

5. Cohen, K. 1982. Speaker interaction: Video tele-conferences versus face-to-face meetings. *Proc. of Teleconf. and Electronic Communications,* 189-199.

6. Falelakis, M., Kaiser, R., Weiss, W., and Ursu, M.F. 2011. Reasoning for video-mediated group communication. *Proc. IEEE ICME* 2011, 1-4.

7. Gatica-Perez, D. 2009. Automatic nonverbal analysis of social interaction in small groups: A review. Image and Vision Computing 27.12 (2009): 1775-1787.

8. Geelhoed, E., Parker, A., Williams, D.J., Groen, M. 2009. Effects of Latency on Telepresence. *HP labs technical report: HPL-2009-120, 2009.*

9. Groen, M., Ursu, M., Michalakopoulos, S., Falelakis, M., Gasparis, E. 2012. Improving video-mediated communication with orchestration. *Computers in Human Behavior* 28 (5), 1575-1579.

10. I. Rae, G. Venolia, J. Tang, and D. Molnar. 2015. A Framework for Understanding and Designing Telepresence. *Proc. ACM CSCW 2015*, 1552-1566.

11. Inoue, T., Okada, K. and Matsushita, Y. 1995. Learning from TV programs: Application of TV presentation to a videoconferencing system. *Proc. ACM UIST 1995*, 147-154.

12. Inoue, T., Okada, K., Matsushita, Y. 1999. Effects of video expression in videoconferencing. Proceedings of the 32nd Annual Hawaii International Conference on Systems Sciences (HICSS) 1999.

13. Kirk, D. S., Sellen, A., and Cao, X. 2010. Home video communication: mediating 'closeness'. *Proc. ACM CSCW 2010,* 135-144.

14. Kleij, van der, R., Schraagen, J.M., Werkhoven, P., & De Dreu, C.K.W. 2009. How Conversations Change Over Time in Face-to-Face and Video-Mediated Communication. *Sm. Group Research* 40(4), 355-381.

15. Neustaedter, C., Challenges for Telepresence: Design, Evaluation and Creativity. *Everyday Telepresence workshop ACM CHI 2015.*

16. O'Conaill, B., Whittaker, S., & Wilbur, S. 1993. Conversations over video conferences: An evaluation of the spoken aspects of video-mediated communication. *Human-computer interaction, 8(4),* 389-428.

17. Oduor, E., Neustaedter, C., Venolia, G., and Judge, T. K. Moving beyond talking heads to shared experiences: The future of personal video communication (workshop). *Proc. ACM CHI 2013*, 3247-3250.

18. Ranjan, A., Birnholtz, J. and Balakrishnan, R. 2008. Improving Meeting Capture by Applying Television Production Principles with Audio and Motion Detection. *Proc. ACM CHI 2008*, 227-236.

19. Sacks, H., Schegloff, E. A., Jefferson, G. 1974. A simplest systematics for the organization of turn-taking for conversation. *Language,* 50, 1974, 696-735.

20. Schlager, M., and Wang, Y., Reframing and Researching Everyday Telepresence for Families. *Everyday Telepresence workshop ACM CHI 2015*

21. Sidnell, J., Conversation Analysis: An Introduction. Wiley-Blackwell, 2010.

22. Stone, H., Sidel, J., Oliver, S., Woolsey, A. and Singleton, R.C., 1974. Sensory evaluation by quantitative descriptive analysis. *Descriptive Sensory Analysis in Practice*, pp.23-34.

23. Ursu, M.F, Groen, M, Falelakis, M, Frantzis, M, Zsombori, V, and Kaiser, R. "Orchestration: TV-like mixing grammars applied to video-communication for social groups" *Proc. ACM Multimedia 2013*, 333-342.

24. Ursu, M.F., Falelakis, M., Groen, M., Kaiser, R., Frantzis, M. Experimental Enquiry into Automatically Orchestrated Live Video Communication in Social Settings. *Proc. ACM TVX 2015.*

Confessions of A 'Guilty' Couch Potato

Understanding and Using Context to Optimize Binge-watching Behavior

Dimph de Feijter
NHTV, Breda University of
Applied Sciences
Breda, The Netherlands
feijter.d@nhtv.nl

Vassilis-Javed Khan
Eindhoven University of
Technology
Eindhoven, The Netherlands
v.j.khan@tue.nl

Marnix S. van Gisbergen
NHTV, Breda University of
Applied Sciences
Breda, The Netherlands
gisbergen.m@nhtv.nl

ABSTRACT

Viewers more frequently watch television content whenever they want, using devices they prefer, which stimulated 'Binge-watching' (consecutive viewing of television programs). Although binge-watching and health concerns have been studied before, the context in which binge-watching takes place and possibilities to use context to optimize binge-watching behavior have not. An in-situ, smartphone monitoring survey among Dutch binge-watchers was used to reveal context factors related to binge-watching and wellbeing. Results indicate that binge-watching is a solitary activity that occurs in an online socially active context. The amount of time spent binge-watching (number of episodes) correlates with the amount of free time and plays an important role in the effect of binge-watching on emotional wellbeing. Considering the difficulty viewers have to create an optimal viewing experience, these context factors are used as a framework to be able to design and promote a recommendation tool for TV streaming services to create a more optimal binge-watching experience.

Author Keywords

Binge-watching; Context; Mobile survey; Health-implications; Self-regulation; TV viewing behavior.

ACM Classification Keywords

K.4.m. Computers and society: Miscellaneous.

Permission to make digital or hard copies of all or part of this work for personal or classroom use is granted without fee provided that copies are not made or distributed for profit or commercial advantage and that copies bear this notice and the full citation on the first page. Copyrights for components of this work owned by others than ACM must be honored. Abstracting with credit is permitted. To copy otherwise, or republish, to post on servers or to redistribute to lists, requires prior specific permission and/or a fee. Request permissions from Permissions@acm.org. *TVX'16*, June 22-24, 2016, Chicago, IL, USA
© 2016 ACM. ISBN 978-1-4503-4067-0/16/06...$15.00
DOI: http://dx.doi.org/10.1145/2932206.2932216

INTRODUCTION

New digital technologies stimulate different ways of television viewing. Viewers are not limited to one screen anymore, in which specific content can only be viewed at fixed time slots. Instead, they can watch television shows in succession whenever and wherever they want, which is referred to as binge-watching [3]. Prior to video-on-demand (VOD) and online streaming services such as Netflix, the viewing of many TV shows in succession was stimulated by the introduction of DVD-box sets [9,15,20]. The term "Binge-watching" became popular when in 2013 Netflix released an entire season at once instead of episode by episode [9]. Netflix popularized the term binge-watching as "watching between 2-6 episodes of the same TV show in one sitting" [22]. A recent study, conducted by research agency DVJ Insights revealed that around 40% of the Dutch population is 'binge-watching'; men more often than women [7]. However, a dilemma also arises, related to finding the optimal balance between pleasure in viewing more television programs in a row versus a decrease in experience. Research shows that physical fatigue and depression can occur due to the viewing of too many television programs consecutively [6]. It is unclear whether viewers are capable of recognizing the optimal viewing duration themselves and can act on it accordingly. Such a dilemma is already addressed in domains in which "binge" signifies a self-harming overindulgence as in 'binge drinking' and 'binge eating'. Overindulgence of media content might result in a so-called 'guilty pleasure', similar to that of binge eating, in which pleasure turns into something negative during or after the consumption [17]. Binge-watching may stimulate inactive behavior, turning viewers into so-called (feelings of being) 'couch potatoes'. However, driven by the popularity of binge-watching, combined with the fear of losing subscribers, content providers feel forced to change along with the trend of binge-watching, further stimulating users to 'overindulge' [1], without knowing the most optimal viewing time. TV streaming services are already criticized for promoting unhealthy binge-watching behavior and some viewers even claim they feel 'manipulated' by related services [6].

Aims and contribution

This study is not aimed to stimulate a discussion on whether binge-watching has serious negative health consequences and who should be responsible for acting on it when health is at stake. However, with this study, we do want to raise awareness for possible advantages of promoting and creating more 'healthy' binge-watching experiences. Promoting 'healthy' binge-watching means to look for factors that can create a better viewing experience, in which it might be beneficial to help viewers to plan and act on a binge-watching strategy, even if this means stimulating the viewing of fewer television episodes in a row.

To do this, one needs to understand the context in which binge-watching takes place. However, as binge-watching is a relatively new phenomenon, there is little knowledge regarding which contextual factors have an influence on binge-watching behavior and feelings of wellbeing. This study provides insights into the viewing behavior of Dutch binge-watchers between the age of 18 and 34. More specifically, we aim to make the context in which binge-watching takes place more explicit. By means of observing viewers in their natural environment and daily lives, we want to analyze context factors that influence the experience, and in doing so gain more understanding of binge-watching behavior [26,12]. This study reveals the context in which binge-watching occurs on two dimensions: (a) the physical context (time, location, social context, and activities) and (b) the psychological context (mood and feelings). By having a better understanding of the context, we can potentially create a framework to design products and solutions to optimize the binge-watching experience.

BACKGROUND

There are few studies that research the context of binge-watching. The contribution we seek to make with studying the context of binge-watching is to identify when the behavior occurs. In the following sections, context factors related to binge-watching are discussed.

Activity context

In general TV viewing is considered a habitual and passive activity. Nonetheless, research shows that viewers are often doing other activities simultaneously, characterizing TV viewing as either a primary or secondary activity [13]. Diary studies among television viewers reveal that most of these activities are related to passive behavior, such as eating and drinking, that require little effort and focus [8]. Several possible health related risks connected to longer TV viewing durations and inactive behavior patterns are identified [8,25]. Risks that range from an increase in (unhealthy) eating behavior to planning issues that stimulate sleeping problems and the increase in sedentary behavior leading to physical [10,11,23] and social health problem [14,19].

It is, however, unclear whether binge-watching is conducted in the same way as 'regular television viewing'. On the one hand, binge-watching may stimulate longer viewing times due to viewers being more immersed and as more attention is required to understand the narratives. In which case no other activities are conducted or activities are more on a secondary level. On the other hand, binge-watching might just replace regular viewing time and stimulate activities while watching, such as an increase in social activities to share experiences or activities that need to be done simultaneously in order to be able to view for a long time.

Next to that, previous studies that focus on negative effects related to longer TV viewing times, have not always taken into account the emergence of smartphones and tablets in which relative easier multitasking activities are promoted [8]. These new media developments might stimulate a healthier demeanor of binge-watching: decreasing feelings of loneliness and/ or increasing active behavior. New media multitasking when binge-watching might also provide opportunities to plan and communicate optimal-binge watching experiences (possibilities such as giving signals to stop or continue watching or having a break). However, the context in which binge-watching takes place has not been researched to account for all these changes and as such it remains unclear whether or not viewers are multitasking.

Social and location context

Contemporary streaming services change the context of TV viewing, and in doing so, potentially affect social interaction during and after television watching. With binge-watching it is likely that viewers will not watch particular content simultaneously with friends or peers [16]. Hence, compared to 'regular' television watching, binge-watching might be connected to a more solitary context. A consequence could be that a collective social experience of television viewing will decrease in a similar manner as that non-linear television viewing seems to reduce social time [6,16,17]. However, prior studies do not make clear whether fewer people are physically and/ or digitally present (for instance via social media apps) when binge-watching. Recent studies suggest that binge-watching isn't necessarily an experience viewers prefer to do alone. Results from a Netflix Survey indicated that 51% of the binge-watchers (viewers that stream multiple episodes of a TV series in a row) like to watch with at least one other person compared to 38% that prefer to watch alone. In addition, 39% of TV streamers who "save" TV shows to watch at a later date, choose to do so to be able to watch with another person. These results seem to indicate that binge-watching does not stimulate 'unhealthy' solitary behavior and stimulating 'other' persons to be part of a binge-watching session might often increase a binge-viewing experience.

It remains unclear how social context of binge-watching is connected to a specific location. On the one hand, binge-watching seems to occur often at home and late in the evening, encouraging binge-watching as a solitary activity. On the other hand, home is where people tend to view with others, often family, as well. Moreover, new technologies make it possible to access and view content on different locations, which might change the dominant physical location from the domicile perimeters via television, to mobile viewing in socially active locations such as at the beach or at work or school [16]. These technologies might stimulate appropriate viewing behavior in social spaces as well as inappropriate viewing behavior during class or work time. The dominant location(s) in which binge-watching takes place is unclear. As such it remains unclear how social context and location has an effect on the optimal binge-watching experience and therefore can be used to create socially healthier binge-watching experiences.

Emotional and health context

An image of negative emotional context that surrounds binge-watching is stimulated by previous studies claiming that "guilty" psychological states of binge-watching are not that different from other 'binge behaviors' such as binge eating [6,21,28]. Although these studies have not confirmed whether a negative mood state precedes or follows the binge behavior [28], it is reported that psychological states in binge-eating such as anger, depression and guilt are similar to those connected to binge-watching behavior [23]. Several studies have shown that the mood of heavy TV viewers is the same or worse after viewing [18]. A recent study indicates that loneliness, depression and lack of self-control are associated with binge-watching [23]. In addition, studies showed that viewers who are feeling more depressed tend to 'binge-watch' more TV shows [14]. Additionally, they might even feel more depressed after binge-watching in the same way that that the mood of binge eaters tends to become even more negative after a binge eating episode [28]. However, other studies do not show that binge-watching causes more feelings of loneliness or depressions, or even indicate that watching a TV show reduced feelings of loneliness [5]. Thus, more research is needed to identify whether binge-watching negatively affects mood and emotions.

Although previous studies often concentrated on regular television watching, they reveal important contextual factors, related to activity, social and physical location, and emotional state, that can potentially have an effect on binge-watching experiences as well. However, it remains unclear how these factors manifest within the context of binge-watching.

METHOD

In order to identify the context in which binge-watching takes place, a research design was chosen in which viewers could immediately reflect on the viewing context after they finished watching television. To do so, a design was chosen

in which viewers were prompted to participate in a survey via their personal mobile device each time they finished a viewing session. They participated for a period of ten days: eight working days and a weekend (11-20th, May 2015). Each day participants received an SMS reminder to fill in the survey. Participants were briefed and instructed to complete the surveys without any delay subsequent to their viewing session. Whenever participants ended a television session they immediately filled in a survey (which often resulted in participating in several surveys per day). To we used Tempest, a tool specifically designed for mobile surveys and diary methods [2]. Tempest is a web-based system, allowing the researcher to configure and tailor a mobile survey. All participants received a unique code, to identify the collected data. In addition, the participants received a unique URL redirecting them to the corresponding survey. Before starting the survey, a pilot was executed, to make sure that the mobile survey was accessible. On average it took participants around two to three minutes to fill in each questionnaire.

Participants

Dutch males and females between the age of 18 and 34 participated in the study which is the main target group for binge-watching [8]. Participants were recruited using an online questionnaire that was distributed via social media. Only viewers that already had experience with binge-watching could participate. As stated in prior literature, we defined binge-watching as having watched three or more episodes in succession, regardless whether the episodes belonged to one or more shows [21,22]. A total of 32 participants were selected based on demographics, viewing behavior and availability to watch TV series in the aforementioned fieldwork period. Only the answers related to watching three or more episodes at once were analyzed, resulting in 18 (out of 32) participants and 66 (out of 132) filled in questionnaires. The age of these participants varied between 18 and 33 years old (M=24.9, SD=3.7). Male and female participants were equally distributed and the number of completed surveys per participant varied between one and ten (M=3.7, SD=2.9, Median=3). Five participants (Table 1) also participated in a one-hour interview after the ten-day survey period ended. Participants were selected for the interviews based on the survey results regarding the

	Gender	Age	Occupation	Frequency (t)
P1	Female	23	Student	4 (8)
P2	Female	25	Full-time job	3 (5)
P3	Male	21	Student/ Part-time job	3,36 (5)
P4	Male	28	Full-time job	4,2 (12)
P5	Female	20	Student/ Side job	11,25 (12)

Table 1: Background interviewees. Frequency is the average amount of episodes binge-watched per session and the total amount of viewing sessions (t).

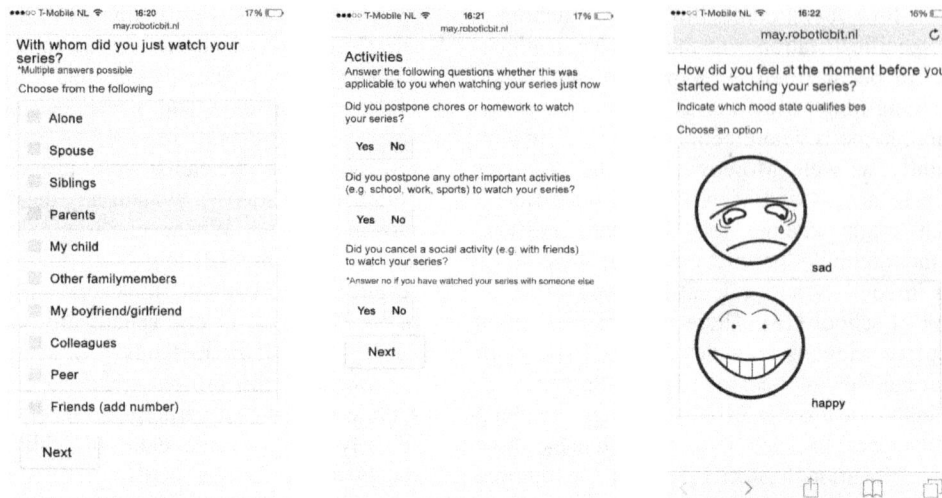

Figure 1. Example screens of the Experience Sampling Form on Safari - iOS8, iPhone 6. The left screen displays a multiple answer question concerning the social context of the participant's viewing session. The middle screen shows yes or no questions with relation to postponing activities for their viewing session. Finally, the screen on the right displays a mood question, designed for quick reply, as touching the mood face immediately redirects you to the next screen.

large number of episodes watched (P5), the amount of binge-watched time spent during free time (P4), noteworthy viewing locations (P2, at work), and having primarily negative feelings (P3) or positive feelings before and after a binge session (P1).

Measurements
The mobile survey contained 34 questions that measured the quality of the viewing experience, divided into three sections (i.e., before, during, and after a binge session). The survey is designed with the Experience Sampling Method in mind [12]. The questions varied from multiple choice questions regarding *viewing location*, *companionship* and *device*, to open-ended questions related to *(secondary) activities*, and dichotomous questions concerning *responsibilities* and *self-regulation*. The mobile survey concluded with asking participants to choose between bipolar adjective pairs related to the *emotional state* of their binge session (i.e. happy-sad; cheerful-irritable; friendly-hostile; sociable-lonely; active-bored; relaxed-tensed) (Figure 1). This last item was modified from an Experience Sampling Form designed to enable participants to select a mood instantaneously [4].

During the interviews, participants were confronted with their mobile survey responses regarding the *experience, viewing behavior, content, activities, self-regulation,* and *awareness of own behavior* topics. They were asked to further elaborate on the answers they provided in the survey as well as to try to explain *why* they acted as reported in the mobile survey. In doing so, we tried to get a better understanding of the reasons behind the observed binge-watching behavior, as well as obtain personal reflection on the observation to better comprehend how they interpreted

relatively complex items used in the survey such as emotions.

RESULTS

Number of episodes and viewing time
Over 50 different series were reported with *Game of Thrones* being the most frequent viewed series. Other popular series include *Grimm, Supernatural, The Blacklist, The Returned* and *Entourage*. On average around three to four episodes are viewed within one binge-watch session. The median, being the representative number of the distribution's balance, seems to justify that three consecutive episodes is probably the right threshold to identify binge-watching behavior (Mean=3.8, SD =4.5) (Figure 2). Although the average lies around three to four episodes, the interviewees state they do not have a specific number of episodes planned when deciding to start binge-watching. The duration and number of episodes viewed depends on the day and time, the type of show (e.g., suspense in drama stimulating longer viewing behavior), content strategy (being closed or open-ended episodes, and with or without cliff-hangers) and available episodes. For instance, one interviewee (P5) revealed that she'd rather not watch series that have already released several seasons, as she is aware of her lack of self-control. She states that it is usual for her to view up to 20 episodes (of less than 20 minutes each), as was shown during the ten-day survey period (viewing 31 episodes in one day). Although viewers do not plan the number of episodes beforehand, they seem to have a preference for 3 to 4 episodes. Within this number they feel most immersed and relaxed. Viewers tend to lose focus and start engaging in other activities when 5 or more episodes are watched. However, the preferred number seems to depend on the variance between series being

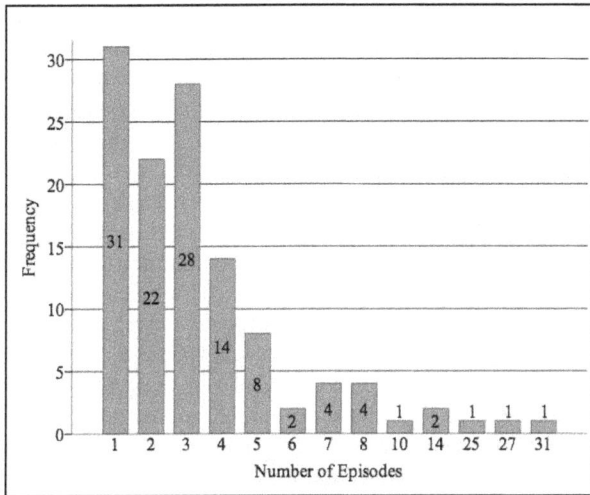

Figure 2: Frequency distribution of number of episodes resembles a geometric distribution. Note that this is the only graph that we included 'less than three viewed' episodes in the analysis (N=119).

watched. In case episodes of different shows are watched, the optimal binge-watching experience seems to encompass more episodes than the preferred amount of 3 to 5 "*I rather watch episodes separately, as it cultivates desire and anticipatory pleasure for next week's episode*" (P1).

Activity context results

Activities were coded as being maintenance activities (i.e., related to one's subsistence such as eating), productivity activities (e.g., work), active leisure activities (e.g., sports) or passive leisure activities (e.g., mobile messaging) [12]. All types of activities are conducted before and after binge-watching. While almost 11% of the participants *prefer* to do nothing *while* watching, maintenance and passive leisure activities seem common when binge-watching. Even more so, "passive leisure" activities seem to double during a viewing session compared to before and after the session (see **Fout! Verwijzingsbron niet gevonden.**). Examining in more detail the type of "passive leisure" activities, the most performed activities while watching are WhatsApp usage, social media usage, and eating. Participants provided several *reasons* why they are active. An important explanation is given by P4 as he believes that activities like WhatsApp, and browsing the Internet are not distracting. He explains that he often sits on his couch, carrying out swift activities on his smartphone while binge-watching. P3 argues that using the phone might be a little distracting and thus he would not interrupt a show that requires a lot of attention such as a drama series. However, he would multitask during programs that need less attention, such as sitcoms. P5 does not agree and has an outspoken opinion: "*I believe that if you multitask, you are not able to fully focus on the content*". She always pauses an episode when she starts other activities, taking a short break to focus and react

on her WhatsApp messages. Whether using the phone is distracting or not, digital devices are used while binge-watching and thus can be utilized to create an optimal binge-watching experience.

Results showed that activities are postponed due to binge-watching sessions. More specifically, in 58% of the binge-watching viewing sessions, other planned activities were postponed. A female participant (P5) provides an example in which she intended to workout but instead stayed in bed for the rest of the day, watching an entire season of Entourage. The main activities postponed are chores (61%), school assignments, work activities & sports (26%) and social activities (13%). Most of the time viewers postpone these activities because they become completely immersed in the series. They lose control and often are not able to plan and commit to a certain viewing time. Postponing activities happens consciously as well as unconsciously. P1, for instance, described a conscious situation in which she watched her favorite series late in the afternoon realizing she still has to do the dishes but deciding it could be done later in time as well. In addition, she recalls an unconscious situation in which she ended up late for a visit to her father because she was incapable of stopping to watch the series. Some viewers already take this immersion effect into account. For example, P3 ensures that all of his chores are finished, prior to binge-watching. Most of the interviewees indicated a feeling of guilt when postponing activities such as a workout. P5 states that the feeling of guilt after binge-watching is predominantly caused by canceling or postponing activities. Also P4 gives examples of not feeling relaxed when finished watching his series as chores were stacking up.

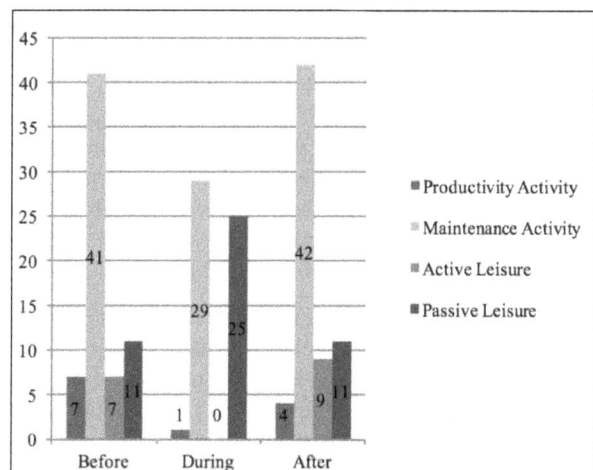

Figure 3: Type of activities before, during and after a viewing session.

63

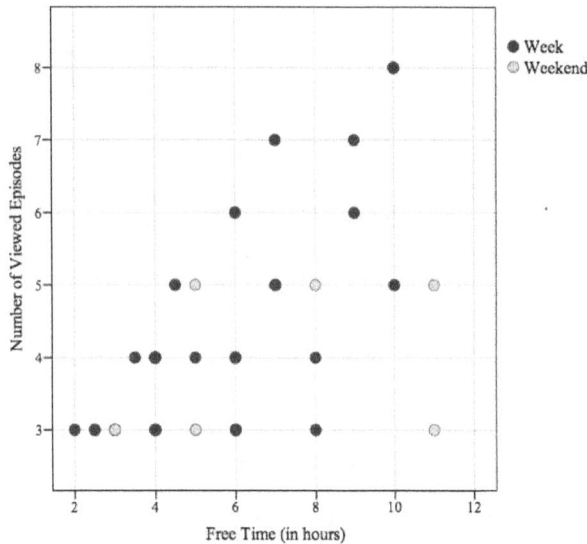

Figure 4: There is a strong positive correlation (r=.674**) between the viewed number of episodes and free time during a day (n=45). This is a result after eliminating outliers in number of episodes watched and available free-time (r=.31**, when all scores are included).

Social, location and time context results

The reported average daily *free time*, in the sampling period, was 10 hours (min=2, max=24, SD=7.1). The results show a strong positive correlation number of episodes viewed and the amount of free time (r=.674**, Figure 4).

Unsurprisingly, the *most common viewing location* was at home in the living room or bedroom (Figure 5). One participant binge-watched at work as well. Watching also occurs in a combination of home settings as illustrated by one of the participants (P3), who uses his free time during the day to view series in the living room and continues watching in the bedroom late in the evening. Another combination of locations is illustrated by a participant (P2) that binge-watched at work and continued watching in the evening on her tablet at home in the living room before she moved to the bathroom and bedroom to finish her fifth and final episode of that day. Apparently to stay within the ideal binge-watching experience of 5 episodes.

Viewing devices play a significant part in understanding the context of binge-watching related to the viewing location. The results showed that TV is the primary binge-watching viewing device (59%), followed by a laptop (30%) and tablet (11%). None of the participants reported to view on a smartphone during the survey, although one participant (P1) did state to occasionally binge-watch on her smartphone when traveling by train in the morning on her way to her internship. However, she stated that she did not prefer this screen, due to the small size.

Related to viewing time, the evening is the most preferable *viewing moment* (Figure 5). Series are most often watched

in the evening, as could be expected due to responsibilities during the day. Interestingly, night and afternoon share second place as being most used moments to binge-watch. The most mentioned reasons to watch at night are related to health issues (such as not able to sleep and psychological issues); working schedules; immersion (i.e., not being able to stop viewing); and preferred ways to organize activities (e.g., P5 explains she frequently watches her series at night when she has no obligations the following day). Although binge-watching is positively correlated to free time, most binge-watching sessions (88%) happened during a weekday and not in the weekend. One explanation is that in weekends priority is given to social activities with friends and family. Free time in the evening during working days is spent on watching series. *"I mainly watch series in the evening after work, however, I don't watch as much in the weekend, as I spend more time with my friends"* (P4).

Binge-watching mainly seems to happen in a *solitary social context*. The results showed that, of the total binge-watching sessions, 77% was watched alone; 11% was watched with a partner and/ or spouse; 8% with one or more family members and in 4% a friend was present. Although these results are, of course, connected to the living situation of the participants (39% lives alone, 22% lives with 'significant other' or roommate and 17% lives with family), it clearly shows a high number of times binge-watching happens in a solitary context (which is confirmed in other studies as well). This is important as watching alone seems to correlate with watching more episodes, which does not seem to fit with an optimal binge-watching experience. Our results showed that when participants binge-watched alone, almost always seven or more consecutive episodes were being watched (Figure 6).

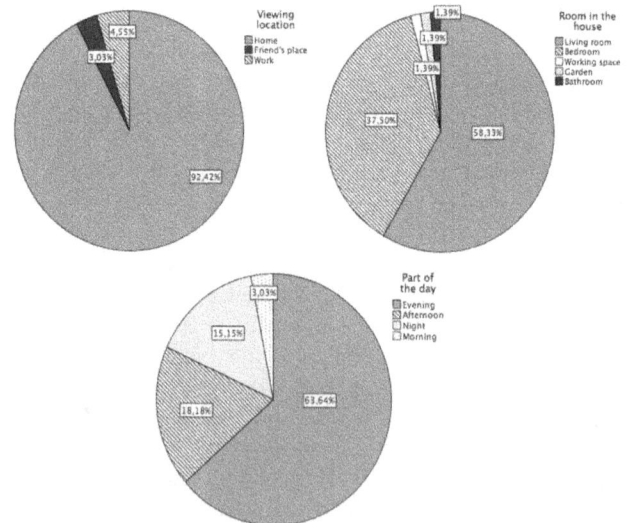

Figure 5: Distribution of cases concerning the viewing location (left), and the preferred room in the house (right). The most common viewing location is at home, preferably the living room. Regarding the time of viewing the majority of sessions takes place in the evening (middle) (N=66).

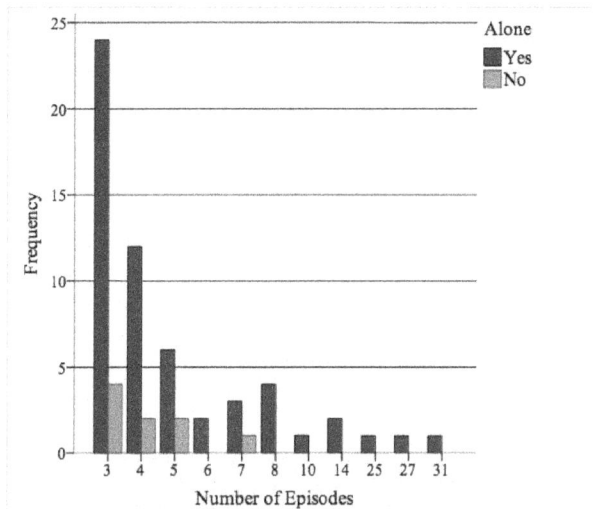

Figure 6: Number of episodes clustered according to social context (alone or watching with company).

Emotional and health context results

The results showed that viewers do not have, and are not able to create a clear image of their own binge-watching behavior. Sometimes binge-watching time was less than expected (*"Well, that's not that bad... is it? I expected it to be a lot worse"* (P1); *"Oh I expected it to be a lot worse"* (P2). Sometimes it was more than expected (*"Ouch, this is not good"* (P3); *".... it was kind of shocking"* (P4). Furthermore, the awareness of their own (binge-watching) behavior created a new emotional context in which often an intention to change the observed behavior emerged; wanting to reduce the number of binge-watching hours (e.g., P3, P4 and P5) or change the binge-watching location (e.g., not at work anymore). The intention to decrease viewing time matches the observed behavior: in 56% of the binge-watching sessions, participants found it hard to stop watching. In addition, during 47% of the binge-watching sessions, participants watched longer than intended and in 27% of all sessions participants claimed they were unable to stop watching. Reasons given for this unintended extended viewing time are the high suspense level; the autoplay feature (*"without autoplay my viewing experience would be disrupted"* (P4)), the available amount of free time, and the absence of obligations. Although some interviewees did not feel a tremendous urge to cut down viewing time, feelings of guilt did arise when they did not have a lot of time on their hands. These results indicate that it will be hard for viewers to plan and act towards creating an optimal binge-watching (viewing-time) experience, partly due to a lack of control. Although this seems to be a plea for help in creating the optimal experience, participants also struggle with the question when to (get the advice to) stop viewing and/ or plan new viewing moments, as they also like the sustained immersion.

Although the *emotional context* is hard to grasp via monitoring of behavior, the interviews seemed to confirm the connection between an increase in binge-watching time and feelings of negativity or depression as well as reveal 'social healthy' encouragements. Two male interviewees (P3 and P4) did confirm that feelings of depression or pessimism were connected to long binge-watching sessions. The reasons to watch at work were also connected to feelings of boredom and unhappiness, leading to inappropriate viewing during work and feelings of irritation due to work obligations. On the other hand, one female participant (P5) explicitly stated that it is impossible to binge-watch when feeling really depressed; *"I remember feeling depressed once. I tried to seek distraction, but I was not even able to concentrate on my favorite series"*. Furthermore, another female participant revealed that binge-watching a certain series helps her to sustain social relationships *"I always ask...Have you seen the latest episode, it was so exciting!"* (P2).

DISCUSSION AND CONCLUSION

With this study, we acquired more knowledge concerning the context in which binge-watching occurs that can be used to design solutions to promote 'healthier' viewing behavior for streaming services that offer binge-watching experiences. Using a ten-day in-situ smartphone survey to monitor behavior combined with interviews, made it possible to better understand the context of binge-watching and filter out important context factors that can be used to be used to optimize binge-watching experiences.

Without having the intention to stimulate less time spent on consecutive viewing, results did show that viewers often cannot plan or control their binge watching behavior and in addition revealed specific context factors of binge-watching that could be of help to create a more enjoyable (healthy) experience when binge-watching.

Furthermore, we observed a dominant binge-watching pattern connected to contextual factors. The results indicated an optimal binge-watching experience around three to five episodes. Watching more than five succeeding episodes seems to decrease pleasure, increase guilt and passive leisure activities (i.e. Instant Messaging, eating, and social media). As a result, viewers might lose focus of substantial details of the story – dialogue and plot points – that are essential for the contemporary complex TV narratives. More awareness and control over viewing time, avoiding overrunning the optimal number of episodes being watched, seems to be key to increase the binge-watching experience. Specialists claim that as with any "overindulgence", moderating one's behavior is not only beneficial to the users, but also for the content providers, stating that excess viewing could lead to a loss of appreciation of the show [27].

Although we did not explicitly ask in our survey questions regarding physical health issues, in our results we do observe pre-conditions that lead to an unhealthy lifestyle. For example, in 77% of all binge-watching sessions participants were alone, passive leisure activities spike during watching and free time is positively correlated with binge-watching. The aforementioned results could lead to an increasingly sedentary, solitary lifestyle. This passive, physical state that we observed is in compliance with the study of Hwang, Kim and Jeong [13], and is known to increase the risk for health issues associated with sedentary behavior [10,11,25].

As our findings imply that many viewers lack awareness of their own viewing behavior, as well as a lack of control over viewing time, often leading to longer viewing times than planned, a first step in designing solutions to promote a more optimal binge-watching experience would be to increase awareness of short and long term viewing behavior. A potential system should provide viewers with the opportunity to plan their session before watching and compare planned and actual viewing time while adding and monitoring experience scores. Based on these results, signaling the viewer when the optimal viewing time has been reached or passed (which seems to happen above five episodes) could further increase the experience.

In our results, the most common viewing location is at home using the television, despite studies suggesting a strong increase in different locations due to new technologies [16]. This finding implies that an app for all viewing devices at home could be the most effective solution to monitor viewing behavior, provide feedback and enhance the overall viewing experience accordingly. Likewise, since secondary activities increase with viewing time and most of the passive leisure activities include a mobile device, there is an opportunity for identifying the behavior -in combination with other findings (e.g., number of viewed episodes and time of the day). As binge-watching wellbeing challenges seem to occur mainly during weekdays, a design recommendation would be to differ feedback options based on weekends and working days (evenings). For instance, allowing a longer duration in weekends before the recommendation appears to stop watching and automatically plan a new viewing moment. The same goes for providing help mainly when viewing alone, as an unaccompanied context is the most dominant viewing situation and is predominantly connected with viewing time above the ideal binge-watching duration (the optimal number of episodes viewed).

The goal, with reference to promoting healthy viewing behavior, is to reduce feelings of guilt while preserving full immersion by eliminating undesired distractions, which might result in a better viewing experience. Providing direct contextual feedback concerning the viewer's behavior, can positively affect beliefs and therefore develop an intention to change towards the most optimal binge-watching experience. Further research is necessary to verify findings using a larger sample. However, taking into account the challenge viewers have to create an optimal viewing experience, we strongly believe that our study provides a solid framework to develop, design and test a recommendation tool aiming to create a more 'healthy' binge-watching experience based on viewing context. This tool would incorporate important contextual factors that are specified and divided across activity, social & location and emotional & health dimensions in this study. Future studies should monitor viewing time, immersion and feelings of guilt to establish a more robust optimal binge-watching experience, taking into account different genres and persona's (target groups) as well as effects of different binge-watching scenario's to further create an optimal context to enjoy binge-watching.

ACKNOWLEDGMENTS
We would like to express our gratitude to Nikolaos Batalas, developer of Tempest for his extensive assistance in setting up and running the mobile diary. Moreover, we would like to extend our gratitude to our participants.

REFERENCES
1. Adams, D. (2014, September - October). Binge Viewing: For your convenience. *CSIMagazine*. 13-16. Retrieved from http://www.csimagazine.com/DigitalEdition/CSISeptOct2014

2. Batalas, N., & Markopoulos, P. (2012, October). Introducing tempest, a modular platform for in situ data collection. *In Proceedings of the 7th Nordic Conference on Human-Computer Interaction: Making Sense Through Design* (pp. 781-782). ACM.

3. Cook, C. I. (2014). *Netflix: A Stepping Stone in the Evolution of Television*. (Unpublished master thesis). University of South Florida St. Petersburg

4. Csikszentmihalyi, M., & LeFevre, J. (1989). Optimal experience in work and leisure. *Journal of personality and social psychology, 56*(5), 815.

5. Derrick, J. L., Gabriel, S., & Hugenberg, K. (2009). Social surrogacy: How favored television programs provide the experience of belonging. *Journal of Experimental Social Psychology, 45*(2), 352-362.

6. Devasagayam, R. (2014). Media Bingeing: a qualitative study of psychological influences. *Proceedings of the Marketing Management Association*. Spring2014, P40

7. DVJ Insights. (2014). *Binge-watching onderzoek*. Retrieved from http://dvj-insights.com/nl/binge-watching-onderzoek/

8. Foehr, U. G. (2006). *Media Multitasking among American Youth- Prevalence, Predictors and Pairings*. Menlo Park, CA: Kaiser Family Foundation.

9. Giuffre, L. (2013, September). The Development of Binge-watching. *Metro Magazine, 178*, 101-102

10. Grøntved, A., & Hu, F. B. (2011). Television viewing and risk of type 2 diabetes, cardiovascular disease, and all-cause mortality: a meta-analysis. *Jama, 305*(23), 2448-2455.

11. Hamilton, M. T., Hamilton, D. G., & Zderic, T. W. (2007). Role of low energy expenditure and sitting in obesity, metabolic syndrome, type 2 diabetes, and cardiovascular disease. *Diabetes, 56*(11), 2655-2667.

12. Hektner, J. M., Schmidt, J. A., & Csikszentmihalyi, M. (Eds.). (2007). *Experience sampling method: Measuring the quality of everyday life*. Sage.

13. Hwang, Y., Kim, H., & Jeong, S. H. (2014). Why do media users multitask?: Motives for general, medium-specific, and content-specific types of multitasking. *Computers in Human Behavior*, 36, 542-548.

14. International Communication Association. (2015, January 29). Feelings of loneliness and depression linked to binge-watching television. Retrieved from http://www.eurekalert.org/pub_releases/2015-01/ica-fol012615.php

15. Jenner, M. (2014). Is this TVIV? On Netflix, TVIII and binge-watching. *New Media & Society*, 1461444814541523.

16. Jones, E. (2009). Network Television Streaming Technologies and the Shifting Television. *Media in Transition 6*.

17. Kubey, R. W. (1996). Television dependence, diagnosis, and prevention. *Tuning in to Young Viewers-Social Science Perspectives on Television*. Thousand Oaks, CA- Sage, 221-260.

18. Kubey, R., & Csikszentmihalyi, M. (2002). Television addiction. *Scientific American*, 286(2), 74-81.

19. Matrix, S. (2014). The Netflix Effect: Teens, Binge-watching, and On-Demand Digital Media Trends. *Jeunesse: Young People, Texts, Cultures, 6*(1), 119-138.

20. Pinto, D. (2014, June 1). *The big binge: Viewers marathon episodes of television shows is a new obsession*. Retrieved from http://www.dnaindia.com/lifestyle/report-the-bigbinge-viewers-marathon-episodes-of-television-shows-is-a-new-obsession-1992675

21. Ramsay, D. (2013). *Confessions of a binge watcher*. CST Online. Retrieved from http://cstonline.tv/confessions-of-a-binge-watcher

22. Spangler, T. (2013). Netflix survey: binge-watching is not weird or unusual. Retrieved from Variety website: http://variety.com/2013/digital/news/netflix-survey-binge-watching-isnot-weird-or-unu-sual-1200952292/

23. Sung, Y.H., Kang, E.Y. & Lee, W. (2015). A Bad Habit for Your Health? An Exploration of Psychological Factors for Binge-Watching Behavior. to be presented at the 65th Annual International Communication Association Conference, San Juan, Puerto Rico, 21-25 May 2015.

24. Thorp, A. A., Owen, N., Neuhaus, M., & Dunstan, D. W. (2011). Sedentary behaviors and subsequent health outcomes in adults: a systematic review of longitudinal studies, 1996– 2011. *American journal of preventive medicine, 41*(2), 207-215.

25. Van den Bulck, J. (2000). Is television bad for your health? Behavior and body image of the adolescent "couch potato". *Journal of Youth and Adolescence, 29*(3), 273-288.

26. Visser, F. S., Stappers, P. J., Van der Lugt, R., & Sanders, E. B. (2005). Contextmapping experiences from practice. *CoDesign, 1*(2), 119-149.

27. Wagstaff, K. (2014, February 14). *Binge-Watch 'House of Cards; on Valentine's Day at Your Own Risk*. Retrieved from NBC News website: http://www.nbcnews.com/tech/internet/binge-watch-house-cards-valentines-day-your-own-risk-n29566

28. Wegner, K. E., Smyth, J. M., Crosby, R. D., Wittrock, D., Wonderlich, S. A., & Mitchell, J. E. (2002). An evaluation of the relationship between mood and binge eating in the natural environment using ecological momentary assessment. *International Journal of Eating Disorders, 32*(3), 352-361.

Understanding Video Rewatching Experiences

Frank Bentley
Yahoo
Sunnyvale, CA USA
fbentley@yahoo-inc.com

Janet Murray
Georgia Institute of Technology
Atlanta, GA USA
jmurray@gatech.edu

ABSTRACT

New video platforms have enabled a wide variety of opportunities for rewatching video content. From streaming sites such as Netflix, Hulu, and HBO Now, to the proliferation of syndicated content on cable and satellite television, to new streaming devices for the home such as Roku and Apple TV, there are countless ways that people can rewatch movies and television shows. But what are people doing? We set out to understand current rewatching practices across a variety of devices and services. Through an online, open-ended survey to 150 diverse people and in-depth, in-person interviews with 10 participants, we explore current rewatching behaviors. We quantify the types of content that are being rewatched as well as qualitatively explore the reasons and contexts behind rewatching. We conclude with key implications for the design of new video systems to promote rewatching behaviors.

Author Keywords
Video; Transmedia; Television; Movies; Rewatching

ACM Classification Keywords
H.5.m. Information interfaces and presentation (e.g., HCI): Miscellaneous

INTRODUCTION

The willingness of viewers to watch the same video content multiple times has been foundational to television as an industry and as a cultural form. [3,14] Rewatching of television content has been possible since the 1950s, when it was based on scheduled re-runs of serialized content, allowing broadcasters additional advertising revenue from the same content. As television stations increased, first as broadcast and then as cable, reruns became an important commodity with television shows seeking to stay on the air long enough to reach the 100-episode level at which they became marketable in the secondary serialization market. The dependable appeal of previously aired popular series from many eras has supported multiple cable channels, and is identified as an important cultural phenomenon that helps to shape collective memory, generational identity, and cross-generational communication and understanding. [15]

Permission to make digital or hard copies of all or part of this work for personal or classroom use is granted without fee provided that copies are not made or distributed for profit or commercial advantage and that copies bear this notice and the full citation on the first page. Copyrights for components of this work owned by others than ACM must be honored. Abstracting with credit is permitted. To copy otherwise, or republish, to post on servers or to redistribute to lists, requires prior specific permission and/or a fee. Request permissions from permissions@acm.org.
TVX 2016, June 22–24, 2016, Chicago, IL, USA.
© 2016 ACM ISBN 978-1-4503-4067-0/16/06...$15.00.
http://dx.doi.org/10.1145/2932206.2932213

The advent of the VCR opened up wider possibilities for timeshifting broadcast and cable offerings, but also for rewatching content, and for purchasing and consuming television not as weekly episodes but as yearly series. Digital technologies have further intensified these possibilities, creating hardcopy archives of DVDs and on-demand access to streaming archives of series which may originate online instead of on broadcast or cable channels, and may be released as a complete season rather than a discrete episode. This "publishing model" of television provides more control to the viewer and encourages closer attention to the content, supporting formal strategies that create greater narrative complexity. [6]

Digital delivery is now ubiquitous, creating the practice of "binge viewing," encouraging still-frame and replay investigation of television content, and encouraging episode-level amateur and professional commentary distributed online. YouTube has further expanded the possibilities of repeatable TV experiences by allowing targeted replay and sharing of excerpts, with easy access to commenting and distribution on social media. [13] Although the internet has introduced economic disruption into the cable business model [12], it has only increased the public's access to the repeat viewing experience [4], turning the second decade of the 21st century into an age of "spreadable" media. [2] In short, television is no longer an ephemeral experience, and access to on-demand retrieval and replay is now an assumed aspect of our consumption of digital video, marking a significant change in a cultural practice that is foundational to traditional sources of viewing pleasure and to the role of shared moving images as a form of social connection.

Given this new accessibility, what do viewers choose to rewatch? What motivates re-viewing and what rewards does it offer? We set out to answer these questions and to explore the rewatching habits of 160 individuals through an online survey and in-depth, in-person interviews to understand recent occurrences of video rewatching.

RELATED WORK

Previous work has explored aspects of rewatching specific forms of video content. Metcalf explored the changing practices of television consumption that came with the consumption of series on DVDs. [5] He saw the boxed set of DVDs as making the experience of viewing a television series as similar to reading a novel, starting with a hard copy object that sits on a shelf, always available to rewatch. Bentley and Groble [1] allowed viewers to rewatch sports highlight videos in their TuVista system and identified the fan practice of celebratory rewatching of key moments in the game after a win.

Several researchers have explored how increasingly complex narratives are encouraging people to rewatch video content. Mittell describes a "publishing model" of television replacing the broadcast model of ephemeral content, and he includes digital files distributed online as instances of publishing along with boxed sets of DVDs. Both afford more control to the viewer and encourage consumption of serial content as repeatable and part of larger continuous story arcs. [7] Murray created custom-built applications to allow following complex narratives in programs such as Justified and Game of Thrones. [8, 9] These applications allowed users to rewatch key scenes and follow particular characters through the episodes.

Other researchers have theorized the cultural significance of rewatching [15, 5, 6]. In particular, Weispfenning [15] observed that shared television viewing can shape generational identity as well as develop shared points of understanding between generations, contributing to our collective memory and helping to provide social continuity, making reruns particularly reassuring in changing times. In addition, familiar programs provide a type of parasocial activity, connecting viewers with characters that they learn to know and love throughout a long running series. Finally, Weispfenning noted that watching an episode can provide a "dependable pleasure" since the story is constructed to evoke certain emotions.

While this existing literature has identified particular behaviors of rewatching, it has been mostly focused on professionally-produced broadcast and cable television programs, and was mostly conducted in the era before streaming services with large catalogs were in wide use, and before social media offered alternate channels for distributing and commenting on video. Many questions remain after this review of the literature. We were interested in knowing the types of videos that were rewatched using today's platforms, which devices were used for rewatching, as well as the motivations for, and outcomes of, rewatching incidents.

STUDY DESIGN

Our study contained two main components, an online open-ended survey distributed to 150 diverse participants and in-depth, semi-structured interviews with 10 diverse individuals in the San Francisco Bay Area. Data from both studies was combined and analyzed to produce the findings below, which explore current video watching behaviors both quantitatively and qualitatively.

The survey was deployed online, and participants represented a wide range of the American population. Participants lived in 24 different states, were 46% female, 42% were college graduates, and they held varied occupations such as a Risk Manager, Freelance Artist,

Theater Staff Member, Writer, Preschool Teacher, Holistic Canine Nurse, Janitor, Librarian, Lawyer, Casino Dealer, Bank Teller, Accountant, Chemical Engineer, etc.

We asked survey participants to think about the past two times that they rewatched any piece of video, from TV shows to movies or online videos. For each instance, we asked for details of the particular situation: what prompted the rewatching, who they were with, how many times they had seen the video before, etc. We also asked them to list up to five television shows and movies that they have watched multiple times, to get a better idea of how genre, release date, or actors might play into rewatchability.

Ten interviews were conducted in the San Francisco Bay Area. Similar to the online survey, we asked participants to think of several recent examples where they had rewatched videos. In addition to the basic questions about what prompted the event and whom they were with, we followed up in more detail about each situation to better understand the circumstances of rewatching in greater detail than we could obtain from a few sentence response in a survey. Interview participants ranged in age from their early 20s through mid-50s and included six women and four men.

Qualitative data from both studies were combined and studied in a grounded theory based affinity analysis. Exact quotes from participants were used as the item-level nodes in the analysis, and were iteratively combined to find themes. Overall, we had 657 items for analysis. The sections in the findings below derive from these themes, and exemplary quotes are used in parallel with the quantitative data from the survey.

FINDINGS

We will begin by exploring what people rewatched and the circumstances of the rewatching. Each subsection will combine data from our survey and interview-based study to explore both current behavior as well as reasons for their current actions. Overall, video rewatching was a common occurrence, with 79% of participants having rewatched some type of video content in the past week, rising to 92% in the past month. No participant was recruited based on any aspect of previous video behaviors.

What People Are Rewatching

Participants rewatched a wide variety of video content. Figure 1 shows the types of videos that were watched again and the devices that were watched on. We defined these categories to be non-overlapping with YouTube videos consisting of non-TV, non-movie content posted on the site. Television shows and online videos were most commonly rewatched while computers (41%) and televisions (41%) dominated the devices used for rewatching across categories. Surprisingly, phones (8%) and tablets (10%) were not frequently used to rewatch, likely because 62% of video rewatching occurred with other people, making larger screens on computers and televisions more comfortable devices for people to watch together.

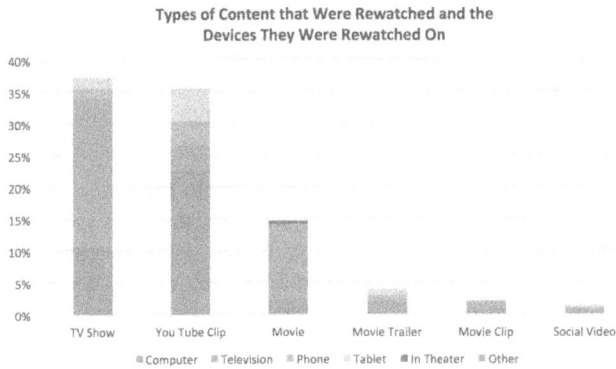

Figure 1: The content types that were watched and the devices that they were watched on. TV shows made up 36% of all videos watched, and most notably phones and tablets were rarely used for rewatching content.

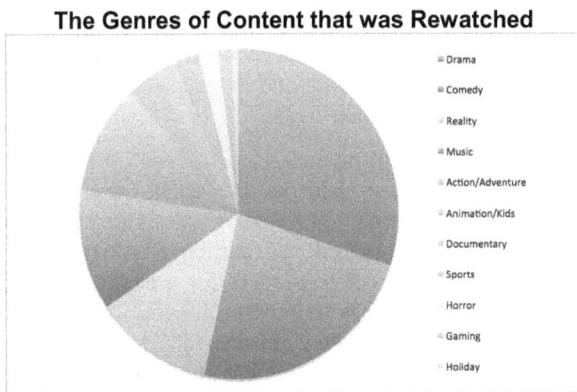

Figure 2: Genres of content that were recently rewatched by our participants. Note that Drama and Comedy make up greater than half of all videos, while Sports and Reality make up much smaller percentages.

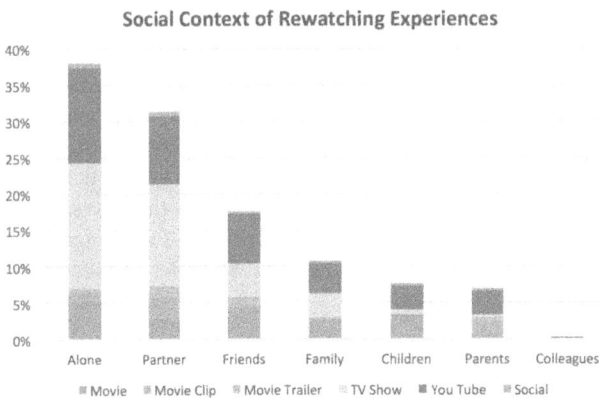

Figure 3: Social Context of Video Rewatching. 62% of the 300 total videos rewatched by our 150 diverse survey participants were watched with others present.

When we look at the specific genres that were rewatched in Figure 3, we see that Drama and Comedy cover more than half of all videos that were rewatched. However, this distribution is quite different from the content that is aired

Program Title	Viewers (M)
NBC Sunday Night Football	18.1
The Big Bang Theory	17.2
NCIS	15.5
The Voice	14.0
Sunday Night NFL Pre-Kick	13.4
The Voice (Tue)	12.7
60 Minutes	12.7
NCIS: New Orleans	12.1
Adele Live in New York	11.3
Life in Pieces	10.3

Table 1: Top Nielsen Ratings for US Broadcast Television from the week of December 14, 2015.

http://www.nielsen.com/us/en/top10s.html

Program Title	People
The Walking Dead	41
Game of Thrones	23
Breaking Bad	21
Friends	20
The Big Bang Theory	20
Star Wars	16
Seinfeld	16
The Office	16
The Simpsons	12
Lost	11
Family Guy	10
Roseanne	9
Titanic	9
Dexter	8
Parks and Recreation	8
Lord of the Rings	8
South Park	8
Scandal	8
Pulp Fiction	8
How I Met Your Mother	7

Table 2: Top 20 videos by participants who rewatched.

on television, which in recent years has skewed towards reality and sports content. If we look at the top television shows in the US according to Nielsen (Table 1), we can see that six of the top ten shows were reality, sports, news, or music, which only make up 26% of all rewatched content that we found in our study.

While cheaper to produce, much of this content does not have a high rewatch-ability. In contrast, many of the top rewatched programs in our survey (Table 2) have complex narratives and many characters, epitomized by *Game of Thrones*, the second most rewatched program, with 100+ active characters.

Social Rewatching

The most common motivation to rewatch video content was to show others, with 104 items of analysis under this theme. Of all videos that participants rewatched, 62% were watched with others (Figure 3). Motivations to show video content to others included getting others to like content, to see people's reaction to content, or to hand curate a particular piece of content for a particular person and situation.

Often, participants watched videos with others to get them to change their mind about the quality of a program. P149 wanted to get his friends excited about *Steve Jobs*: "I just wanted to show others the movie trailer. They thought it would be boring and had no desire to see the movie until they saw the trailer and learned it was about a lot more than Apple." P45 could not believe that her partner had not seen her "favorite movie" and felt compelled to show him.

This behavior was often related to a desire to see someone else's reaction upon watching video content for the first time. P13 rewatched some "bonkers, bonkers, bonkers YouTube" videos with a friend who had a "similar sense of humor." He "wanted to see the look on his face as the video played out." P147 talked about really enjoying rewatching a movie trailer with a friend as "my friend also seemed to like it, which enhanced my enjoyment even further."

Other times, participants had chosen a particular video or series to watch with a specific person. P113 was "telling my son about the show, as he is getting interested in survival shows and science fiction. He wanted to watch it, so we decided to stream it and watch it together, an episode or two every or most nights." P78 talked about some friends who had never seen *Breaking Bad*, and that he "couldn't believe it" so tried to get them hooked on the show as he knew they would like it. Sharing video content that they had enjoyed, and getting the other person excited about content that the sharer thought that they would like, is a prime motivation for rewatching content.

Rewatching to Change Mood
Frequently, specifically chosen video content was played to get the participant into a desired mood, covering 92 of the items for analysis in this broader theme. Most frequently, participants wanted to laugh and watched something that would lift their spirits, however, other times participants sought out content that would get them in other moods.

P108 discussed rewatching a sitcom: "It made me laugh all over again, as *Boy Meets World* always does." P49 discussed a similar incident of watching content to laugh: "My significant other thinks this video is so funny. I also do. It makes me laugh every time." P2 told us that "Really only comedies can be rewatched. The other stuff, once you watch it once, it lessens that impact of the show."

Other emotions were elicited by specific types of video content, and these were sought out to get the participant into a desired mood. P71 discussed watching a documentary: "I wasn't feeling tired and thought of how peaceful it is to watch *Planet Earth*...it's specifically great to watch and fall asleep to." P6 discussed watching a skateboarding video in preparation for going skating himself: "I just rewatched it to get pumped up to go skateboard." P61 watched a music video: "It was a mood. The maudlin music I was craving since I needed to calm down." Meanwhile, P27 watched some anime because "it just puts me in an excited good mood." Specific, previously-viewed content is often chosen to rewatch because of the specific moods it will produce.

Nostalgia
Highly related to mood, we often found participants talking about "nostalgia" as a reason for rewatching video. This was a word that they often used with us on their own, in a total of 31 items for analysis which fell under this category.

P121 told us that she "felt like watching stuff I liked when I was a kid last night." Watching older content was very entertaining for participants. P47 was driven to watch an old movie because he had "a feeling of nostalgia and wanting to be entertained."

Older content can also allow viewers to remember related people and a time in their life. P133 rewatched a sports clip and years ago he "was at the particular game the clip shows and it brings back good memories." However, sometimes these memories can be bittersweet. P148 watched a movie and was "reminded of when I watched it with a loved one that has now passed on." P146 decided to put on the movie *Las Vegas Bloodbath* "for nostalgic reasons" as "it's the best bad 80s movie ever made" and he used to play it whenever he had a party. P3 discussed rewatching the Soup Nazi episode of *Seinfeld* as "it's just kind of classic. It's really old, but it's still funny." And P111 rewatched a movie with her best friend "because it reminds us of our childhood." Movies and television shows have a great power to invoke reminiscing and nostalgia and take people back to other times in their lives.

Contexts for Rewatching
We will now turn to address the most frequent three contexts that promote rewatching described by our participants. We observed 28 participants choosing to rewatch content in order to prepare for a new season of a show or a sequel as a primary reason for rewatching one of the last two videos that they rewatched. P18 said: "When the new *Mockingjay* movie was coming out we wanted to refresh our memories" and rewatched the first part. P123 was getting ready to watch *Fast and Furious 7* and "wanted to remind myself of the last movie" so watched part 6. Frequently, we observed this behavior for television shows. P109 told us that "At the beginning of each *House of Cards* season, I will binge watch all of the prior seasons." Several participants were getting into the Netflix series *Jessica Jones* and wanted to watch a related Marvel show. P128: "Someone my wife works with mentioned that coming to this fresh off *Daredevil* might have some advantages and we really couldn't remember the show too well [so they rewatched it]." P119 was getting ready for a new season of a show to start and watched the previous season again "just to remind myself where the story was after not watching it for a period of months."

Sometimes, this rewatching occurred in preparation for upcoming experiences unrelated to new video content. P17: "My boyfriend and I are getting ready to go to Universal Studios Wizarding World of Harry Potter and thought it would be fun to do a Harry Potter movie marathon before hand." Related experiences such as theme parks or travel often can prompt rewatching. P27 was "feeling nostalgic about London [in preparation for a trip there] and wanted to watch someone drive through it."

Holiday seasons or traditions also prompted rewatching content, appearing in 11 items of analysis. Often, holidays brought about time with family and traditions to rewatch particular content together. P17 rewatched a *"Friends* Thanksgiving episode that I thought the family would enjoy yesterday for the holiday." P36 discussed watching "the Holiday episodes" of her favorite shows "whenever that holiday rolls around." She had just watched the Thanksgiving episode of *Buffy the Vampire Slayer* with her brother, as was a family tradition. The Thanksgiving holiday also brought about rewatching of football clips from games in previous years in some households.

The release of new episodes or sequels, preparing for travel or other related experiences, and holidays all brought about occasions for rewatching video content. This creates opportunities for richer transmedia experiences related to upcoming content, travel, or holiday time with family.

Discovering Content to Rewatch

Often, a recommendation system or comment from a friend prompted the rewatching of content as was seen in 43 items of analysis. Increasingly, content is not often explicitly searched for, but recommended or reposted on various forms of social media. P40 discussed watching a show after he "enjoyed watching it the first time, and when it came up as a suggestion on Netflix, I decided to watch it again." P8 finds "funny clips" on Tumblr by reading through his dashboard. Many of these he has seen before, but will watch again. P5 received a recommendation on Netflix and "just hadn't seen it in a long time." And her reaction was "like sure" and she watched it again. Finally, P115 was "on IMDB looking at a different movie when it suggested that I might be interested in *Flatliners*. I had completely forgotten about that movie and I used to be crazy about it, so I watched it again." This highlights the large potential for streaming sites to drive people into nostalgic content.

Other times, participants had a specific task in mind, and sought to rewatch videos to help them with this task. One relatively new form of video that drove many to rewatch was the tutorial video, with 14 participants recently rewatching these types of videos. P135 was "happy that with the tips in the video, I was able to cut my own bangs with great success." It took her a few watchings before she felt confident. P73 was about to dye her hair and rewatched a tutorial "to make sure I had the recipe correct and to see [again] how it was applied to the hair." P8 talked about the need to rewatch makeup tutorials: "It goes by so quick that you can't pause it on Instagram so you're watching the whole 15 seconds all over again … You have to watch it a few times and view for technique or whatever." P120 rewatched a gun tutorial to "see what the shotgun can do and the different ammo and chokes to use." Tutorial videos are becoming extremely popular, with the top videos making it into the double-digit millions of views[1].

---

[1] http://cosmeticsmag.com/news/2015/3/20/top-10-youtube-beauty-vloggers

Deep Connections to the Content

Many participants were driven to rewatch because they considered themselves a committed fan of a specific actor, director, or narrative, represented by 87 items. These attachments may reflect connoisseurship, affiliation with a fan community, or fascination with a performer, a cult classic, or a nostalgic favorite

Participants often followed specific actors and watched, and rewatched, everything that they made. P99 told us: "Daniel Day Lewis' acting was suburb. I love rewatching excellent acting to savor it." P150 really enjoyed *Catching Fire* and called it "great entertainment. Jennifer Lawrence is really good and the cast surrounding her all turn in great performances as well." Often, an admired actor can make for a movie that participants wanted to watch again and again. Viewers also followed the work of particular directors, seeking out their other works and rewatching familiar ones. P74 just saw another movie by his favorite director and "wanted to watch a funny review of his other works."

Some participants discussed wanting to rewatch a favorite movie in better quality. P87 rented a small private movie theater with his friends. P113 discussed connecting his computer to a television and surround sound speakers, which was "a better experience than when I initially watched it on a 19" boxy low res TV." Similarly, P134 saw a Blu-ray version of an old favorite, "It was significantly a much better experience on my new speakers! The Blu-ray audio was much more refined and sounded so much better." A new cut or new equipment can create a desire to rewatch.

There are programs that participants would watch dozens of times over many years. P58 discussed a movie that she watches with her partner: "We definitely have many favorite lines in this movie. So now when we watch, we will speak these lines out just prior to them actually being said in the movie." These traditions keep the movie fun and new even after many viewings. P1 watched *Batman* "probably like a hundred times." For him, as long as "the same parts are just as funny and the action's just as good" he'll keep watching. He had "two movies on my iPad and I know them almost line by line. I usually watch almost every other night." P145 discussed *The Hobbit* as "a pleasant way to spend the afternoon" and that she could "watch it twice a month really."

Story Complexity

The increasing complexity of narratives in television shows and movies [9] has led people to rewatch shows that they really liked, often to catch details that they missed the first time. P1 discussed Disney movies: "I love going back and just kind of like rewatching because you get a different meaning. A lot of people say when you watch Disney when you're younger it's a story. When you watch Disney as you're older it has a totally different meaning." She liked to "see new things in the movie and it kind of gives it a new meaning. Something else that may make you enjoy the movie more." P130 rewatched the complex drama *Lost*: "When I watched *Lost* the first time I missed some episodes and found it hard to pick up on exactly what had happened since I last saw it, but watching it now on Netflix where I never miss an episode it's very easy to follow."

One of P142's favorite movies is *The Godfather: Part II*. He said that "it feels brand new to me every time I watch that movie. So many life lessons to be learned just by watching the characters in the movie play their roles. Truly a movie inspired by real life events and lifestyle." P53 frequently rewatches a zombie movie to "look for mistakes that are often made such as a zombie missing a limb, then a minute later he has that limb!"

The connection between complex storytelling and reviewing can also be seen in the quantitative data. Several of the most rewatched programs are complex dramas such as *Game of Thrones*, *The Walking Dead*, and *Lord of the Rings*. Many of these shows require repeated viewing to fully understand the plots or the trajectories of characters.

IMPLICATIONS FOR DESIGN

The findings from this work have clear implications for the design of digital tools to enable rewatching video content as well as for creating the content itself. We will explore three areas for future research and development in this section.

Encouraging Rewatching

We observed many situations when participants wanted to rewatch content. These included preparing for a new release in a shared storyworld, following series across seasons and seeking familiar experiences to create a particular mood. Digital systems can easily support these situations through well-placed recommendations and notifications. When new seasons are about to start, or when a new sequel is about to be released, content systems can highlight the previous seasons of the show in the interface and through marketing. Systems can also push notifications to users with links to catch up on the older content in preparation for the new releases. Systems can also curate holiday viewing lists, with specific holiday episodes from the content in their catalogs, or holiday-specific movies such as It's a Wonderful Life and Miracle on 34th Street for Christmas. Emotions can also be supported by curating lists of content for specific moods, similar to the Yahoo Video Guide application that was recently released. Connections can be made with travel itineraries from email to promote content related to an upcoming in-person trip, such as the Universal Studios/Harry Potter example above. This can create an even more intense transmedia experience, moving beyond text and video to real-world experiences related to the content. Specific guides to visiting movie locations could also be delivered alongside the video content. As in the London example, trips to London could be advertised along with movies that feature that location.

Making Sense of Complex Storyworlds

Furthering the research of Murray et al [9], it is clear that many rewatching incidents are driven by the complex storylines of today's television and movie industries. Building applications that help support not only catching viewers up and reviewing key plot points and characters, but that also encourage rewatching particular scenes and character arcs could help people engage more deeply with the content and story. This is especially important for episodic dramatic series that unfold over multiple seasons or movie releases separated by many months or years. It is often desirable to rewatch the entire content in advance, and especially to engage socially with other friends who might be present while watching the new content in the future. This also creates the opportunity for context-sensitive story recaps that are more complete than the brief "Previously on" clips shown at the start of an episode and but less time-consuming than rewatching an entire season.

Social Connoisseurship

This leads to a larger opportunity to help people to share the video content that they enjoy with others who might enjoy it, since we observed that 62% of rewatching experiences that participants reported were with other people present. As P147 said above, seeing someone else's positive reaction to watching a program can enhance their own experience of viewing it again. We see a large opportunity in creating systems that create social experiences out of viewing, making it so viewers become "Together Alone" [10]. Moving beyond the first generation of Social Television systems (e.g. [16]) or large public broadcasting spaces such as Twitter [11, 10], we see the opportunity for systems that support personal suggestions to schedule the viewing of content with specific people that a person thinks will most enjoy watching. More personalized viewing frameworks could enable the synchronous and asynchronous sharing of emotional reactions keyed to specific moments in a curated narrative with chosen companions to create more meaningful shared experiences than currently available from the larger, spoiler-ridden, and noisy assemblages of current social media platforms.

CONCLUSION

We have explored the types of video content that people currently rewatch, as well as the motivations and context for rewatching. Through this quantitative as well as qualitative analysis of broader video rewatching across platforms, we have identified implications for the design of future video platforms. Rewatching content is something that 92% of our participants had done in the past month, and presents a rich and still largely unexplored opportunity for new interactive video experiences. Our implications for design highlight promising areas to explore in further research to promote rewatching behaviors.

REFERENCES

1. Frank R. Bentley and Michael Groble. 2009. TuVista: meeting the multimedia needs of mobile sports fans. In *Proceedings of the 17th ACM international conference*

on Multimedia (MM '09). ACM, New York, NY, USA, 471-480.
DOI=http://dx.doi.org/10.1145/1631272.1631337

2. Jenkins, H., et al. (2013). Spreadable media : creating value and meaning in a networked culture. New York ; London, New York University Press.

3. Kompare, Derek. Rerun nation: How repeats invented American television. Routledge, 2006.

4. Kompare, Derek. Reruns 2.0: Revising Repetition for Multiplatform Television Distribution. Journal of Popular Film & Television. Summer 2010, Vol. 38 Issue 2, p79-83

5. Metcalf, Greg. The DVD novel: how the way we watch television changed the television we watch. ABC-CLIO, 2012.

6. Mittell, J. (2015). Complex TV : the poetics of contemporary television storytelling. New York, New York University Press.

7. Mittell, Jason. "Narrative complexity in contemporary American television."The velvet light trap 58.1 (2006): 29-40.

8. Janet Murray, Sergio Goldenberg, Kartik Agarwal, Tarun Chakravorty, Jonathan Cutrell, Abraham Doris-Down, and Harish Kothandaraman. 2012. Story-map: iPad companion for long form TV narratives. In *Proceedings of the 10th European conference on Interactive tv and video* (EuroiTV '12). ACM, New York, NY, USA, 223-226.
DOI=http://dx.doi.org/10.1145/2325616.2325659

9. Janet H. Murray. 2012. Transcending transmedia: emerging story telling structures for the emerging convergence platforms. In *Proceedings of the 10th European conference on Interactive tv and video* (EuroiTV '12). ACM, New York, NY, USA, 1-6.
DOI=http://dx.doi.org/10.1145/2325616.2325618

10. Steven Schirra, Huan Sun, and Frank Bentley. 2014. Together alone: motivations for live-tweeting a television series. In *Proceedings of the SIGCHI Conference on Human Factors in Computing Systems* (CHI '14). ACM, New York, NY, USA, 2441-2450.
DOI=http://dx.doi.org/10.1145/2556288.2557070

11. David A. Shamma, Lyndon Kennedy, and Elizabeth F. Churchill. 2009. Tweet the debates: understanding community annotation of uncollected sources. In *Proceedings of the first SIGMM workshop on Social media* (WSM '09). ACM, New York, NY, USA, 3-10.
DOI=http://dx.doi.org/10.1145/1631144.1631148

12. Sharma, Amol, An Existential Crisis Hits TV's Rerun Business. Wall Street Journal, Eastern edition [New York, N.Y] 20 June 2014: B.1.

13. Zink, Michael, et al. "Watch global, cache local: YouTube network traffic at a campus network: measurements and implications." Electronic Imaging 2008. International Society for Optics and Photonics, 2008.

14. Williams, Phil, "The evolution of the television rerun." Journal of Popular Film & Television, 01956051, Winter 94, Vol. 21, Issue 4

15. Weispfenning, J, "Cultural functions of reruns: Time, memory, and television" JOURNAL OF COMMUNICATION, Volume: 53, Issue: 1, Pages: 165-177, MAR 2003

16. Crysta Metcalf, Gunnar Harboe, Joe Tullio, Noel Massey, Guy Romano, Elaine M. Huang, and Frank Bentley. 2008. Examining presence and lightweight messaging in a social television experience.*ACM Trans. Multimedia Comput. Commun. Appl.* 4, 4, Article 27 (November 2008), 16 pages.
DOI=http://dx.doi.org/10.1145/1412196.1412200

"I Kind of Had an Avatar Switch": The Role of the Self in Engagement with an Interactive TV Drama

Allie Johns
University of
Salford
Salford, UK

Adam Galpin
University of
Salford
Salford, UK

Joanne Meredith
University of
Salford
Salford, UK

Maxine Glancy
BBC Research
& Development
Salford, UK

ABSTRACT
This paper reports results from a study which examined viewers' cognitive and affective responses to an interactive TV drama. Ten participants were videoed interacting with 'Our World War' [1], and then interviewed about their experience using the video playback as a retrospective prompt. An interpretative framework was designed to guide analysis by probing themes of narrative engagement identified in previous literature. We report findings relating to five themes of engagement: cognitive, affective, perspective taking, competence and autonomy, and transportation. Our data adds to the existing literature on interactive stories by highlighting the pivotal role of the self in engaging with interactive drama, with self-reflection emerging within each theme. We conclude that two experiential states drive engagement: a transported experience; and one in which self-reflection limits transportation.

Author Keywords
Interactive TV; interactive narrative; interactive storytelling; self-reflection; self-determination theory

ACM Classification Keywords
•Human-centered computing→Human computer interaction (HCI); HCI design and evaluation methods; User studies;

INTRODUCTION
Television is no longer the dominant force it once was. Viewership in the UK, for example, amongst 16 to 34 year olds is declining [12]. This age group reports a preference for 'on demand' viewing, especially via hand-held media. Gaming too is growing in popularity, with 42% of UK adults now playing games [12]. Interactive TV dramas, defined as narratives in which the action is influenced by viewer interaction [15], offer new, immersive and self-defined experiences. Interactive narrativity presents both an opportunity and challenge for TV programme makers

Permission to make digital or hard copies of all or part of this work for personal or classroom use is granted without fee provided that copies are not made or distributed for profit or commercial advantage and that copies bear this notice and the full citation on the first page. Copyrights for components of this work owned by others than ACM must be honored. Abstracting with credit is permitted. To copy otherwise, or republish, to post on servers or to redistribute to lists, requires prior specific permission and/or a fee. Request permissions from permissions@acm.org.

TVX 2016, June 22–24, 2016, Chicago, IL, USA.
© 2016 ACM ISBN 978-1-4503-4067-0/16/06...$15.00.
http://dx.doi.org/10.1145/2932206.2932218

seeking to create TV dramas that viewers will value and are economic to implement [22]. It has the potential to open up a new TV format, which meets the needs of people who have grown up interacting with digital media and content through game playing and the Internet. Understanding the key drivers of interactive TV engagement will therefore be critical to the successful development of future interactive programming.

The study reported here was designed to understand the experiential aspects of engaging with an interactive drama in which viewers are asked to make decisions at key points in the narrative. As our stimulus, we used an online interactive narrative 'Our World War' developed by the BBC in 2014 that had not yet been evaluated from an audience engagement perspective and presented an opportunity to probe how viewers engage with an interactive TV episode (see 'Materials' section for more details).

THEORETICAL BACKGROUND
Few studies or articles explore the nature of interactive TV dramas [e.g. 6, 10, 22, 17], and there is a lack of data regarding viewer engagement with interactive TV narratives. In our approach, we reviewed the literature on interactive print narratives [9], linear narratives [e.g. 2, 7] and with video games [16, 21], to help us understand the factors involved in engaging with a visual, interactive narrative structure.

Exploring other worlds through the medium of storytelling may result in the sensation of transportation [7], where the reader or viewer experiences the sensation of becoming lost in a story, with their mental capacities and systems becoming focused on the characters and events. Transportation involves a shift into the world of the narrative, including a loss of awareness of current location, and a loss of self-awareness [2].

Part of a shift into the narrative world involves identification with a character [3], whereby the reader or viewer begins to lose their sense of self to be replaced by the perspective of the character with which they identify. Indeed, the more a viewer can lose themselves in the narrative, including experiencing the emotions of a character through empathic identification, the greater their enjoyment [2, 8].

In an interactive narrative, where a viewer is choosing the characters' actions, they may express a sense of responsibility for the outcomes in the story [9]. In the context of video games, Rigby and Ryan [16] propose that the player may not only experience emotions in relation to fictional events or characters, but also a sense of playing an integral role by influencing the storyline and outcomes. This also suggests the individual's ability to exercise agency over the narrative may also play a critical part in the viewer experience.

Such a sense of autonomy is a key aspect of motivated behavior according to Self-Determination Theory [SDT; 4], and has been found to predict enjoyment in video gaming [16, 21]. For example, Tamborini et al [21] found that both hedonic experience (arousal and affect) and non-hedonic needs (a sense of autonomy and a sense of competence) were predictive of enjoyment with video-games: players needed to feel capable and in control.

Within the context of an interactive TV drama, there is a need to identify the salient factors involved in engagement. Roth et al. [17] applied quantitative questionnaire methods to assess several measures of experience from the literature on narrative entertainment. Our study builds on this approach by using qualitative in-depth interviews to understand experiential aspects from the viewers' own perspectives. We sought to answer the question: how are the themes of narrative engagement, as identified in previous literature, experienced during interaction with an interactive TV drama?

METHODOLOGY

Design
The study used a qualitative interview design, which was analysed using a thematic framework [20]. Framework analysis allows the researcher to use previously identified themes to guide the analysis and allow the indexing of interview excerpts. The study was, therefore, deductive in its approach, with pre-defined themes of engagement used to inform the thematic coding.

Participants
Ten students of the University of Salford (7 female and 3 male) were recruited for the study, aged between 19 and 28 years. The sample was an opportunity sample, recruited through poster advertisement on the Salford campus.

Materials
The stimulus used for the study was 'Our World War' [1]. The interactive episode is accessed online and comprises three scenes featuring a small group of British soldiers in the First World War. The action centers on the dilemmas the soldiers faced during battle. The viewer takes the role of Arthur who comes into the role of a platoon leader after the commander is killed in the opening scene. In total, the viewer is asked to make 6 choices over the course of the interactive drama, under pressure of a countdown clock. Feedback is given on the appropriateness of each decision after the choice is made. 'Our World War' may be described as 'pseudo interactive' [22], since it invites viewers to make choices to influence the narrative, even though the narrative is actually pre-prepared, meaning that the decisions are not necessarily played out in the action. Instead the action reverts to what the author has predetermined to be the correct choice. The exception is the last scene in which the viewer's decision determines one of two possible endings. The episode lasts approximately 20 minutes.

Data collection of the stimulus interaction was facilitated by two video cameras, one directed to record the participants' facial expressions, and the other directed at a Microsoft Surface tablet screen they were using to access the interactive TV drama. Interviews were recorded for transcription on a digital voice recorder.

Procedure
Each data session took place in the Media Psychology laboratory at the University of Salford, which is designed to appear like a sitting room. Each session began by ascertaining background details of the participant's experience with video games, interactive television and 'Our World War'. The participant was then provided with the tablet to access and play 'Our World War'. They were then left alone to work through the interactive episode, with their facial expressions, verbal reactions and the tablet screen recorded. After completing 'Our World War', they were interviewed immediately post-play on their experience, with questions probing emotional and cognitive experience, their sense of control and their engagement with the narrative and characters. One problem with studying media engagement is when to measure the experience. If done during viewing or interacting, the true nature of the experience is interrupted by the questioning process. If done afterwards, the experience may be forgotten. We sought to reduce this problem by filming participant interaction and using the playback as a retrospective memory prompt to tie questions to the specific events in the narrative. Therefore, the second part of the interview involved playing back the video footage to use as a prompt to probe further about specific decisions or parts of the plot (e.g. *How did you feel about making that decision? Why was that?'*). A soft-laddering technique was used which probes deeper into answers by continually questioning 'why. This allows the researcher to move from discussion about a particular behavior (e.g. pausing over a decision or demonstrating an expression of frustration) to probing the psychological experience that underpins the behavior (e.g. I felt confused by what to do, or concerned about the consequences). Finally, participants were asked questions on their overall impressions of 'Our World War' and the concept of interactive TV dramas generally. Each session lasted between 1 hour and 1.5 hours depending on

the duration of their stimulus 'playing' and the semi-structured interview. The semi-structured interview data was then transcribed verbatim.

Analysis

Data analysis was conducted using thematic framework methodology [20]. Thematic framework methodology is a matrix based analytic method, which aims to "classify and organise data according to key themes, concepts and emergent categories" (p.220). For our analysis, the data were organized according to themes which emerged from the literature. Four factors of engagement were identified (affective, perspective taking, competence and autonomy, and transportation) and we added 'cognitive' as a fifth factor of engagement because the nature of the stimulus was designed to facilitate discovery about the First World War. The data were coded deductively according to these identified themes. However, while coding deductively, any emergent sub-themes, (e.g. 'self-reflection' and self-esteem') were additionally coded, and were added to the framework following initial coding. Once the themes and sub-themes had been identified, the data were then organized in a matrix, which allowed for all extracts which related to each theme and sub-theme to be identified.

RESULTS AND DISCUSSION

The thematic framework analysis is summarized in Table 1, below. The themes of engagement were probed through interview questions and used to code interview excerpts.

Themes of engagement	Sub-themes
1. Cognitive	Ease of cognitive access Learning Self-reflection
2. Affective	Arousal Sympathy Self-esteem
3. Perspective taking	Sympathy Identification (empathy) with characters
4. Competence and autonomy	Agency Challenge Self-esteem
5. Transportation	Narrative Emotional Identification

Table 1. The thematic framework, and factors of engagement which emerged within themes.

These interactive TV narrative themes and sub-themes are defined and discussed in turn, thus providing interpretations of participants' responses in relation to the stimulus and the wider theoretical context. Extracts are presented for each theme which are representative of those identified in the thematic matrix.

Theme 1: Cognitive experience

The theme 'cognitive experience' relates to how participants discussed the mental ease or difficulty of the experience, and what reflections or learning were prompted by the stimulus. Participants commented on difficulty assimilating the plot details: *'It was for me, hard to remember after that scene where they tell you who you are and what their job titles are. And then after that when you see them again, it's hard to remember who they were, like their names, you know.'* (P4, F). Such comments demonstrate the importance of building the necessary 'mental models' to support narrative comprehension and engagement [2]. Participants also commented on the usability of the interactive features: *'After the first act, it was quite simple.'* (P6, F). Together, these show that ease of cognitive access to both plot details, and interactive controls are salient to the experience of interactive TV dramas.

The data showed some evidence of response to the educational aspects of the narrative, with the informational content raising awareness: *'When the titles come up and it's giving you more information at the end and they're telling you about the amount of bodies that might be buried in High Wood... It's sad that people have to go through this kind of stuff.* (P7, F), or supporting existing beliefs: *'I guess it just kind of reinforced whatever feelings I had towards war.'* (P10, F). These experiences, however, did not emerge as key features of engagement.

In contrast, the amount of introspection expressed by participants on their own decision-making abilities was prominent in our data. Reflecting on their decisions and judging themselves seemed to be important: *'It seemed like I almost scored higher on the moral aspect, and I don't know whether that's a female instinct where you try to protect someone, which could be it. But I notice that I always opted for the safer choice, rather than sacrificing other people.'* (P4, F). The participant here suggests that perhaps it is her 'female' instinct that is leading her to make these choices. This is the only example where the participant's gender is made relevant in the data. Several other participants were prompted to reflect on their leadership skills as a result of the interactive decision-making: *'I wouldn't be a good (leader) because I don't have that, um, conviction to lead with authority'* (P8, F), and *'I feel that with the type of person that I am... I feel I'm able to take command of a group.'* (P5, F). The opportunity for self-reflection through interaction was explicitly appreciated: *"I think people enjoy those type of quizzes and games that show them something about themselves. (...)*

This is something that you can kind of learn a little bit about yourself." (P7, M).

Theme 2: Affective experience

The effectiveness of the storytelling in 'Our World War' is demonstrated through the heightened emotional experience reported by our participants: *'It was a rollercoaster that. As in it was upsetting'* (P3, M), *'It's quite intense (...) I felt quite emotional all the way through it.* (P2, F), and *'I felt kind of overwhelmed emotionally.'* (P1, M). The pressure to make decisions that impacted the narrative events was also arousing: *'I still feel some adrenaline pumping through my body. It's very difficult to make that decision with the clock ticking.'* (P9, F). Participants described the affective engagement as emotionally overwhelming and upsetting, yet when asked if they would recommend the experience, responses were positive: *"Absolutely. I have a lot of friends who would love it."* (P1, M). This demonstrates that mediated experiences can be appreciated even if characterized by negative mood states such as sadness. Several theorists [e.g. 13] propose that viewers can be motivated in their media choices beyond simple pleasure-seeking, sometimes valuing more meaningful and reflective experiences (eudemonic motivations). This is reflected in the following extract: *"It was very emotive and it did make you think and it's important to do those things, rather than staying as you are."* (P2, F).

Whilst the characteristics of affective engagement may be tied here to the particular narrative events or interactive features of 'Our World War', a more general point is that the self-reflection prompted by the interactive decision-making did not preclude sympathetic responses toward the events and characters: *'I was fighting back the tears when that poor lad died at the end.'* (P3, M) and *'I felt like I actually cared about them.'* (P5, F).

Theme 3: Perspective taking

Several extracts referred to how the interactive elements engendered an immersive identification with the characters and a loss of self: *'Because you are making major decisions, you become commander-in-chief, you become that person where you get to make the call'* (P4, F). This demonstrates more than the sympathetic response we observed in some other excerpts. Instead, it suggests an empathic state in which participants shared the characters' identity [3], seeing the events unfolding through their eyes and experiencing their emotions: *'I felt like I was experiencing, like the emotions they would be experiencing themselves'* (P6, F). Evidence from this study suggests some participants were readily able to identity with the characters; *'You do find something about a character you can relate to, um that you can identify with. And you can almost take on that identity.'* (P5, F). Thus, taken together, the data suggests dual experiences where the participants sometimes *became* the characters, whilst at other times maintained a sympathetic detachment. This shift between

modes is described by P1 as an *'avatar switch'*: *'I placed myself in his shoes. I kind of had an avatar switch.'* (P1, M).

Although gender differences were not explored as an objective of this study, the data suggests that gender may not be a strong influence to the extent to which the viewer experiences perspective taking. For example, even though the characters in this interactive drama are male, both male and female participants still slipped into identifying with the characters and willingly expressed their emotions in relation to them. Indeed, it appears that even when gender may not be matched between character and viewer, identification can be facilitated by other characteristics: *'I really kind of identified a bit with the cautious one (...) because I think I'm quite like him.'* (P7, F).

Theme 4: Competency and autonomy

Our data also revealed affective responses emerging from self-reflection based on the interactive decision-making involved in 'Our World War'. These responses can be viewed through the lens of Self-Determination Theory, which posits that a sense of autonomy is a foundation for motivated behaviour, as is a sense of challenge and the ability to experience our own competency [4]. The ability to interact fostered a sense of agency, described as a positive affective experience: *'I liked being able to choose the outcomes, and then learn from whether or not it was one of the good things to do'* (P8, M). This sense of autonomy was not compromised by the pseudo-interactive structure of the narrative: *'I felt like the decisions that I made were my decisions.'* (P5, F).

As discussed, 'Our World War' prompted self-reflection, demonstrating how the interactive elements allowed participants insight into their own competencies. Whilst the particular challenges may have been specific to the narrative (moral decision making and leadership), a wider implication is that the challenge related to the decision making in general allowed the participants to test their own abilities. Indeed, one participant commented that he would seek out other interactive episodes because of the inherent challenge in the decision making process: *"Oh yes, I will do that. Just to challenge myself. I like the whole score thing, the whole scenario and the decision process, it's something that makes you think."* (P1, M).

Conversely, competency may be experienced in a somewhat negative way when the decisions made are perceived to have led to an undesirable narrative outcome: *'I felt guilty straight away because I was gonna shoot somebody and he could've been a Brit and he was.'* (P3, M) and *'Then I chose to send the fastest guys, which was not appropriate. So then I felt a bit, uh, deflated. I began to question my tactical nouse then.'* (P1, M). Our data therefore suggest that the ability to make decisions that influence the unfolding narrative may prompt affective reactions linked to self-esteem. Ryan et al. [18] and Tamborini et al [21], theorize the important of competence and autonomy in the context of the gaming experience. Similarly, our data suggesting that viewers of interactive TV dramas will be driven to reflect on their own sense of worth by way of competency-based, agentic content.

Theme 5: Transportation

Our final theme considers the experience of transportation, i.e. becoming lost in the narrative, and unaware of surroundings [8]. Participants described being *'immersed in the game'* (P4, F), and *'in the moment'* (P2, F), and *'in the narrative'* (P9, F) suggesting transportation into the story world. This theme also draws upon evidence presented in earlier themes. For example, transportation is also closely linked to the concept of identification with characters, as evidenced by the *'avatar switch'* expressed by P1. Transportation also overlaps conceptually with 'presence', which is defined in the context of gaming as feeling in, and experiencing emotions relevant to the narrative world [16]. This is evidenced in our data through the sadness expressed by a number of participants to the narrative events. Whilst some participants discussed being *'in the narrative'* (P9, F), Kim and Biocca [11] describe presence as involving both 'arrival' in the mediated environment and 'departure' from the physical environment. This is described by some of our participants: *'When it came to the second act, I completely forgot where I was. I was engrossed in it.'* (P5, F), supporting the notion of transportation away from the real world.

Again, however, we observed a contrasting experience, with one participant feeling like a *'fly on the wall'* (P5, F) therefore positioning themselves as a detached observer. This lack of transportation seems not to be related to the production values, since the same participant also commented that *'It felt real... because I'm seeing the person, I'm hearing the person, I can see the person sweat. I can see the person, you know, their emotions.'* (P5, F). Whilst some participants seemingly retained a sense of detachment from the story world, this nevertheless did not prevent affective engagement: *'I don't think I lost a sense of where I was. I was very aware of where I was but I can also say that yes, I can say I was emotionally affected by it.'* (P10, F).

CONCLUSION

This study offers data which complements existing knowledge in relation to the experiential aspects of interactive storytelling, in particular highlighting the role of the self.

In the context of interactive storytelling, Roth et al. [17] collected quantitative data revealing that manipulating whether a game is played through a character impacts on the nature of the experience, leading them to conclude that "IS (interactive storytelling) environments may face a specific challenge with respect to user experiences, that is, allowing users to exert global control over story developments while keeping them immersed in story developments." (p.632). Our data supports this finding qualitatively, and further shows a key role for self-reflection in determining the type of narrative experience. We propose that the self-reflection prompted by the interactivity created an experiential state of self-awareness that is incompatible with character identification and with the loss of awareness of surroundings necessary for transportation. Our data links this self-reflection with the challenge inherent in the interaction. Indeed, supporting evidence from a study of engagement with an interactive narrative finds that frustration with gaming challenges was also a barrier to transportation [19].

Self-reflection and expressions of self-esteem as a factor of needs satisfaction in gaming [18] were manifest prominently in this study. Participants reflected on their abilities, and this emerged as a key factor in defining their experience with 'Our World War'. Participants appeared to be preoccupied with their own performance, finding challenge on a moral level, as well as on a practical level. The importance of challenge, involved in promoting a sense of competence [5], was also evidenced by this study. We propose, therefore, that challenge should be a strong consideration for scriptwriters and designers of interactive episodes. They should consider methods for scaffolding performance to ensure that audiences are both challenged and supported in their interactions, thus optimizing viewers' level of challenge and engagement.

Our data also suggest that engaging interactive experiences can be crafted even when a 'pseudo-interactive' narrative structure is used in which decisions do not actually influence narrative events. The results suggest that it may be the decision-making process itself that is important through fostering self-reflection and a sense of challenge.

The difference between a transported state and one characterized by self-reflection has been noted previously in media use in general [14]. Our data are consistent with this approach, demonstrating two broad classes of experience; one in which the viewer is immersed in the narrative world, and another in which they are driven to self-reflection through the challenge of interaction.

ACKNOWLEDGEMENTS

We thank all the participants who volunteered for this study, and the producers of 'Our World War' for their helpful discussions and insight.

ADDRESS FOR CORRESPONDANCE

Please address all correspondence to Dr. Adam Galpin: A.J.Galpin@Salford.ac.uk

REFERENCES

1. British Broadcasting Corporation (Producer). 2014. Our World War. [Website]. Retrieved from http://www.bbc.co.uk/programmes/articles/1kWsQcfTPFjfz9sdxfTGFhC/our-world-war-interactive-episode

2. Rick Busselle and Helena Bilandzic. 2008. Fictionality and perceived realism in experiencing stories: A model of narrative comprehension and engagement. *Communication Theory* 18 (2008). 255-280. doi:10.1111/j.1468-2885.2008.00322.x

3. Jonathan Cohen. 2001. Defining identification: A theoretical look at the identification of audiences with media characters. *Mass Communication and Society, 4,* 3 (2001). 245-264. doi: 10.1207/S15327825MCS0403_01

4. Edward L. Deci and Richard M. Ryan. 1985. Intrinsic motivation and self-determination in human behavior. New York: Plenum.

5. Edward L. Deci and Richard M. Ryan. 2000. Intrinsic and Extrinsic Motivations: Classic definitions and new directions. *Contemporary Educational Psychology* 25 (200). 54 - 67. doi: 10.1006/ceps.1999.1020

6. Inger Ekman and Petri Lankoski. 2003. Integrating a game with a story: Lessons from interactive television concept design. *Computers & Graphics* 20 (2003). 167 - 177. doi: 10/1016/j.cag.2003.12.002

7. Richard Gerrig. 1993. Experiencing Narrative Worlds: On the Psychological Activities of Reading. New Haven: Yale University Press.

8. Melanie C. Green and Timothy C. Brock. 2000. The role of transportation in the persuasiveness of public narratives. *Journal of Personality and Social Psychology,* 79, 5 (2001). 701-721. doi: 10.1037?0022-3514.79.5.701

9. Melanie C. Green and Keenan M. Jenkins. 2014. Interactive narratives: Processes and outcomes in user-directed stories. *Journal of Communication* 64 (2014). 479 - 500. doi: 10.1111/jcom.12093

10. Stacey Hand and Duane Varan. 2007. *Exploring the effects of interactivity in television drama in interactive TV: A shared experience.* Paper presented at proceedings of the EuroITV Conference, 24 - 25 May 2007. Amsterdam. doi: 10.1007/978-3-540-72559-6_7

11. Taoyong Kim and Frank Biocca. 1997. Telepresence via television: two dimensions of telepresence may have different connections to memory and persuasion. *Journal of Computer-Mediated Communication* 3, 2 (1997). doi: 10.1111/j.1083-6101.1997.tb00073.x

12. Ofcom. 2014. *Adults' media use and attitudes report.* Retrieved from http://stakeholders.ofcom.org.uk

13. Mary Beth Oliver and Arther A. Raney. 2011. Entertainment as Pleasurable and Meaningful: Identifying Hedonic and Eudaimonic Motivations for Entertainment Consumption. *Journal of Communication,* 61 (2011). 984–1004. doi: 10.1111/j.1460-2466.2011.01585.x

14. W. James Potter. 2009. Conceptualising the Audience. In M.B. Oliver & R. L. Nabi (Eds.) *The Sage Handbook of Media Processes and Effects.* Sage: London

15. Mark O. Reidl and Vadim Bulitko. 2013. Interactive narrative: An intelligent systems approach. *AI Magazine, 34, 1* (2013). 67 - 77. Retrieved from *www.aaai.org/ojs/index.php*

16. Scott Rigby, and Richard M. Ryan. 2011. Glued to games: How video games draw us in and hold us spellbound. Santa Barbara: Praeger.

17. Christian Roth, Ivar Vermeulen, Peter Vorderer, Christopher Klimmt, David Pizzi, Jean-Luc Lugrin and Marc Cavazza. 2012. Playing in or out of character: User role differences in the experience of interactive storytelling. *Cyberpsychology, Behavior, and Social Networking* 15, 3, (2012). 630-633. doi: 10.1089/cyber.2011.0621

18. Richard M. Ryan, Scott Rigby, and Andrew Przybylski. 2006. The motivational pull of video games: A Self-Determination Theory approach. *Motivation and Emotion* 30 (2006). 347 - 363. doi: 10.1007/s11031-006-9051-8

19. Angeline Sangalang, Jessie M. Quintero and Kate E. Ciancio. 2013. Exploring audience involvement with an interactive narrative: Implications for incorporating transmedia storytelling into entertainment-education campaigns. *Critical Arts: South-North Cultural and Media Studies,* 27, 1 (2013). 127-146. doi: 10.1080/02560046.2013.766977

20. Liz Spencer, Jane Ritchie and William O'Connor. 2003. Analysis: Practices, principles and Processes. In J. Ritchie & J. Lewis (Eds.), *Qualitative Research Practice: A guide for social science students and researchers* (pp. 199-218). London: SAGE.

21. Ron Tamborini, Matthew Grizzard, Nicholas D. Bowman, Leonard Reinecke, Robert J. Lewis, and Allison Eden. 2011. Media enjoyment as need satisfaction: The contribution of hedonic and nonhedonic needs. *Journal of Communication,* 61 (2011). 1025-1042. doi: 10.1111/j.1460-2466.2011.01593.x

22. Marian Ursu, Ian. C. Kegel, Doug Williams, Maureen Thomas, Harald Mayer, Vilmos Zsombori, Mika L. Tuomola, Henrik Larsson, and John Wyver. 2008. ShapeShifting TV: interactive screen media narratives. *Multimedia Systems,* 14, 2 (2008). 115 - 132. doi: 10.1007/s00530-008-0119-z

Enabling Frame-Accurate Synchronised Companion Screen Experiences

Vinoba Vinayagamoorthy
BBC R&D
London, United Kingdom
vinoba.vinayagamoorthy@bbc.co.uk

Rajiv Ramdhany
BBC R&D
London, United Kingdom
rajiv.ramdhany@bbc.co.uk

Matt Hammond
BBC R&D
London, United Kingdom
matt.hammond@bbc.co.uk

ABSTRACT

This paper describes the development and implementation of an open communication standard between Internet-connected TVs and companion screens, over the home network. Content providers know that the better Internet connectivity and prevalence of personal mobile devices is encouraging our audiences to seek more interactive experiences across multiple screens. In order to deliver a coherent integrated user experience, with content on all screens presented according to a common timeline, the application on the companion device needs to discover *what is being shown on the TV* and *what the timeline position is*. DVB-CSS provides a standardised way to enable this synchronisation between the TV and any personal device on the home network. We describe its development, use cases and early prototype implementation.

Author Keywords

Companion screen; connected experiences; interaction techniques; second screen; television; synchronisation.

ACM Classification Keywords

H.5.2 [Information Interfaces and Presentation (e.g., HCI)]: User Interfaces – User-centered design;

INTRODUCTION

"Direct communication between the TV and second device provides the most reliable, responsive and accurate means of providing synchronization. However, there is a significant challenge in incorporating this functionality into devices. Broadcasters and manufacturers need to collaborate to standardize any such communication APIs and ensure incorporation into new devices. It will take potentially many years for devices with these capabilities to become commonplace." - Quote from our CHI Case Study, 2012 [21]

TV viewing behaviour is changing: studies have shown that 87% of UK [17] and 77% of US viewers [20] use another device - usually a smartphone - while simultaneously watching TV. These companion screens can extend the TV experience. The BBC has been conscious of the challenges involved in trying to understand the usage of companion screens (hereafter, *CS*) from their audience's perspective and have been conducting research into emerging CS behaviour in an attempt to explore how audiences use personal devices to enhance their TV viewing.

CS use enables audiences to direct their own experience. Behaviours include searching for additional information, follow-up content discovery, exploring commercial opportunities, and social media [3][21]. Most companion screen users appear to use a variety of tools and applications to tailor their viewing experience as opposed to using a curated built-for-purpose programme companion app. A comparatively small proportion of programme apps or websites are currently updated and synchronised with a TV broadcast, to form CS content [3]. Previously, we suggested that direct communication - through standardised protocols, connecting TV and companion device - would provide "the most reliable, responsive and accurate" means to enabling synchronisation [21].

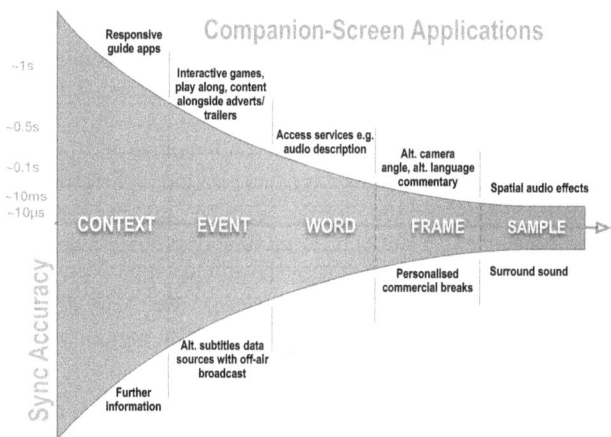

Figure 1: Synchronisation accuracy requirements in the companion screen experience landscape

Richer CS content generally demands synchronisation between devices, and each experience can tolerate only a certain level of asynchrony [10]. A CS experience showing alternative camera angles of a scene being presented on the TV will most likely require frame-level synchronisation accuracy while near frame-rate synchronisation accuracy may be sufficient for CS experiences comprising of

Permission to make digital or hard copies of all or part of this work for personal or classroom use is granted without fee provided that copies are not made or distributed for profit or commercial advantage and that copies bear this notice and the full citation on the first page. Copyrights for components of this work owned by others than the author(s) must be honored. Abstracting with credit is permitted. To copy otherwise, or republish, to post on servers or to redistribute to lists, requires prior specific permission and/or a fee. Request permissions from Permissions@acm.org.

TVX'16, June 22 - 24, 2016, Chicago, IL, USA

Copyright is held by the owner/author(s). Publication rights licensed to ACM. ACM 978-1-4503-4067-0/16/06...$15.00

DOI: http://dx.doi.org/10.1145/2932206.2932214

alternative directors' commentary. CS experiences that exploit spatial audio effects may have stricter synchronisation accuracy requirements such as sample-level accuracy. The variation of synchronisation accuracy requirements across a variety of experiences is illustrated in Figure 1.

To that end, the BBC, with partners in the DVB Project [19], have developed open standards for the network protocols needed for a TV and a companion device to communicate – the *Companion Screens and Streams specification (DVB-CSS)* published as an ETSI Technical Specification [8][9]. DVB-CSS is a standardised and interoperable framework that allows applications on smart devices to construct an integrated, synchronised content experience with the TV over the home network. The specification includes protocols that enable a TV to tell a companion device *'what content it is presenting'* and *'what the timeline position is'* thereby supporting reliable, accurate, and timely interactions over the home network.

Our prototype implementation of these protocols achieves frame-accurate synchronisation between a connected TV prototype and companion devices, and enables CS content to respond promptly to changes occurring on the TV, such as a channel switch, or pausing or fast-forwarding on a DVR (digital video recorder).

This paper presents the protocols we have been involved in standardising and our experience of building frame-accurate synchronised experiences using them. Although, the DVB-CSS specification defines the protocols and provides some implementation guidelines, there has been no reference implementation of the DVB-CSS protocols to date and no prior experience of building CS applications that utilise them until now. In this paper, we therefore first introduce the protocols and then elaborate on our experience in building applications on top of these. In particular, we highlight our choice of algorithms and software architecture and provide early results indicating synchronisation performance. Finally, we give an apercu of the possibilities for synchronised experiences that this suite of protocols enables, by describing our portfolio of prototypes that exemplify common use cases of CS experiences. We also develop further use cases and an empirical evaluation methodology.

OPEN STANDARDS FOR CS EXPERIENCES
A number of solutions exist to enable CS experiences, for example, audio watermarking/fingerprinting, QR-codes, DIAL [6] and Chromecast [2]. However, these solutions offer at most islands of functionality and pose significant challenges to broadcasters for mass-service deployment due to reasons such as vendor lock-in, licensing costs and fragmented device-support. Audio watermarking and audio fingerprinting solutions support up to word-level

synchronisation accuracy, work only if the TV audio can be successfully detected and require access to proprietary backend infrastructure for audio analysis [5]. Other solutions, such as Chromecast [2], allow content from the web and some video players to be 'casted' to the TV, but only support certain platforms. Because these solutions tend to be vertically integrated and device-specific, they often lead to market fragmentation - making it challenging for broadcasters to deliver a consistent CS-synchronised experience across a heterogeneous mix of devices.

As mentioned in [21], direct communication between the TV and the companion device provides the most reliable, responsive and accurate means of providing synchronisation. The BBC, alongside TV manufacturers, broadcasters, and platform operators within the DVB group[1], contributed to both the use-cases and commercial requirements for companion screen experiences (via DVB CM-COS Group [7]) and participated in subsequent standardisation activities leading to DVB-CSS [8][9]. This was a collaborative consensus-driven process, open to all DVB members. The detailed technical specifications produced permit the development of competing implementations of CS products that are interoperable.

HBBTV2.0
HbbTV is an open-standard for hybrid digital televisions and an industry standard for the delivery of interactive entertainment services to consumers on connected TVs, set-top boxes and multiscreen devices, from broadcast and broadband sources. Interactive services take the form of HTML and Javascript running in a browser engine and can co-exist with the presentation of broadcast content. HbbTV defines a profile of HTML, CSS and Javascript capabilities for TVs to support, and also defines APIs to control functionality specific to TV devices (such as controlling the broadcast tuner). HbbTV 2.0 adds a range of functionality to support interaction between the TV and a companion device [13]. Two of these mechanisms are described here.

Device Discovery
HbbTV 2.0 adopts the DIAL [6] protocol to allow the TV to be discovered on the home network by a CS application. The discovery operation is underpinned by the use of the SSDP protocol to locate DIAL servers on the local network segment and obtain access to a DIAL RESTful service on those devices. The DIAL RESTful service enables a DIAL client (the companion) to query, launch, and optionally stop applications on a DIAL server device (the HbbTV terminal). Endpoint locations for application-to-application communication and inter-device synchronisation are also discovered by a query to this interface.

---

[1] DVB [19] is an internationally accepted suite of open standards for digital television including those (e.g. DVB-

T2, DVB-S2, DVB-C2) that define the physical & data-link layer for data distribution via broadcast networks.

Application to Application (App-to-App) Communication Service

This is a communication service using WebSockets that facilitates direct communication between HbbTV apps and CS apps. It operates as a connection exchange service as it requires HbbTV and CS applications to create separate connections to itself and then pairs these separate connections to match HbbTV apps with their relevant CS applications. This decoupled approach ensures an interaction pattern that is familiar to web developers.

Inter-Device Synchronisation

HbbTV2.0 adopts the architectural abstractions, interfaces and protocols of DVB-CSS for synchronising one or more slave CS applications with a master TV terminal. The capabilities enabled by DVB-CSS are described in the following section.

THE DVB-CSS PROTOCOLS

The DVB-CSS specification defines the necessary concepts, functional roles, overall architecture and abstractions to deliver up to frame-accurate CS experiences bridging DVB-based broadcast services and companion content.

It defines protocols to communicate state information from TV to CS application, including content ID and timeline position. The CS experience is not streamed from the TV. The CS application determines for itself what content it should present and where to obtain that content from.

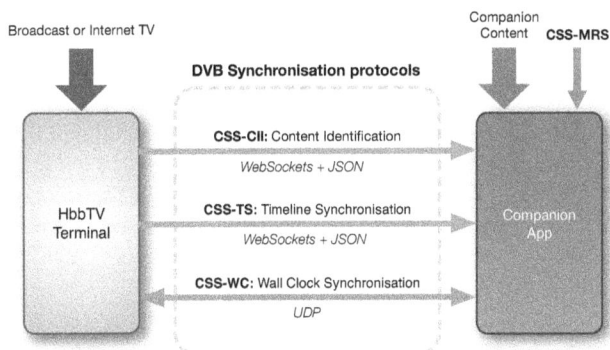

Figure 2: DVB-CSS protocols for inter-device synchronisation used by HbbTV 2.0

In particular, the DVB-CSS protocols (also shown in Figure 2) perform the following functions:

Content Identification – the CSS-CII protocol endpoint is signalled to CS devices during the DIAL-based TV discovery. It allows a hybrid TV to report, via JSON messages across WebSockets connections, the content it is currently showing in the form of a content identifier synthesised from the signalled metadata in the stream as well as its presentation status (paused, buffering, tuning or presenting normally). This takes the form of a URI.

WallClock Synchronisation – Timeline positions at the TV are reported as timestamps during the Timeline Synchronisation procedure. To account for latencies in network communication between TV Device and CS application, the timestamps exchanged make reference to a shared Wall Clock between the TV Device and the CS application. The Wall Clock synchronisation protocol (CSS-WC) provides the means to use a clock synchronisation algorithm to establish a best effort approximation of the TV's Wall Clock at the CS application. A client sends regular protocol requests to which the TV responds. Each request-response constitutes a measurement from which the TV Wall Clock can be estimated. The request-response message format and use of UDP for low latency and resilience makes it similar to NTP but it is optimised for simple master to client synchronisation, simplifying client side implementations. Clients are free to implement any algorithm for scheduling the request-response interactions and processing the resulting measurements. This application layer protocol is needed because there is no guarantee that the system clocks of the two devices are accurately synchronised to a reliable time source at all times (e.g. using NTP), and an application on a mobile device generally has no means to find out.

Timeline Synchronisation – the CSS-TS protocol is used by the TV to report time positions on its timeline (timelines that are signalled in the broadcast or derived from the streaming container format). These control timestamps also contain the Wall Clock time when the readings were taken, in effect specifying the correlation between the TV media timeline with the Wall Clock. Using these timestamps, the CS application can build an estimate of the TV content timeline and use it to drive its own media playback. A broadcast can contain multiple sets of timeline signalling, so this protocol allows the companion to select the one to use.

The **Material Resolution Service (MRS)** is a service used by the companion to resolve the information sent by the TV. This information is based on existing identifiers and signalling carried in the stream or broadcast and is therefore subject to its limitations. Taking the case of a broadcast: the content identifier will identify the channel but may not accurately identify the current show; and time zero will not be at the start of the programme for a broadcast timeline based on Presentation Timestamps (PTS) embedded by broadcast video encoders. The companion is unable to build an enhanced experience from this information alone. The MRS offers resolution as a service by providing time-mapping relationships between broadcast media timelines and companion content timelines. Using these time correlations, a CS application can determine the position within the companion content to begin playback in order to match the TV content's position. Typically, services for mapping programme metadata are provided separately via internet/cloud services and will be populated with data from the broadcasting system. Thus, broadcast streams need not carry companion metadata; resolution occurs in the realm of the companion.

Figure 3: Frame accurate synchronisation between a companion device and a CSSTV

BUILDING FRAME-ACCURATE SYNCHRONISATION PROTOTYPES

As well as contributing to standardisation activities, BBC R&D has been building prototypes to evaluate the CS synchronisation protocols. Our motivation for doing this is five-fold:

1) Facilitate adoption of the DVB-CSS by providing implementations of the protocols and demonstrating viable use cases to content creators.
2) Discover the practicalities in achieving frame-accurate synchronisation with the current generation of companion device platforms.
3) Characterise performance of the protocols to determine achievable synchronisation accuracy by audiences under different network conditions.
4) Explore diverse engaging experiences requiring CS synchronisation and determine their synchronisation accuracy requirements.
5) Determine the backend services required by broadcasters and resources needed to ease service development e.g. software libraries for CS application developers, tool chains for CS experience creators.

In this section, we describe our experience in building these prototypes and share lessons learnt.

CSSTV – a TV emulation platform

The 'CSSTV' was built to emulate a future manifestation of a connected TV with DVB-CSS protocols support. The core of the CSSTV is an Ubuntu based Linux implementation using Gstreamer framework [11] and a DVB PSI library (libdvbpsi) [15]. The protocol endpoints are implemented using a C websocket library [16]. The WallClock server, service DIAL discovery protocol and the app-to-app server are implemented as python processes.

This CSSTV is able to play DVB MPEG-2 Transport Streams whilst detecting the current selected channel and Presentation Time Stamp (PTS) data [14]. In this way the TV can dynamically populate the CSS-CII protocol with the Content ID of the currently displayed channel and the CSS-TS protocol with the current timestamp values derived from the internal Linux system clock and the PTS. It also simulates the existence of an interactive application running on the TV that, via the app-to-app mechanism, can be instructed to pause the presentation.

Transport Stream Multiplex Creation

Our CSSTV plays a single pre-generated MPEG-2 transport stream stored as a file, similar to the BBC's UK broadcasts, and changes between channels within that transport stream. The final transport stream contained the final episode of a three-part BBC nature programme "*Alaska: Earth's Frozen Kingdom*", the fifth episode in a six-part period drama "*Wolf Hall*" and a custom generated calibration sequence used to demonstrate the accuracy of the synchronisation protocols.

Companion Screen Applications

Our CS application prototypes can synchronise the playback of video/audio files (both streamed and local) and the presentation of web content with up to frame-level accuracy. Figure 4 illustrates the high-level architecture of the CS application.

CSS-CII: State Updates

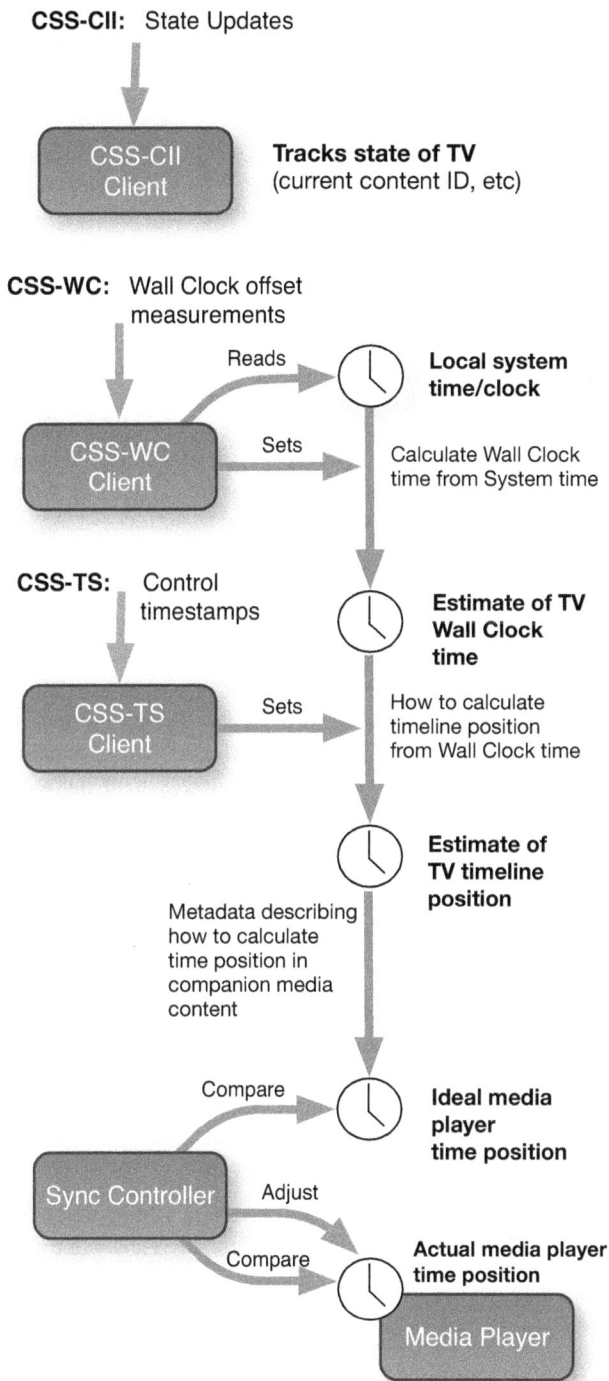

CSS-CII
Client

Tracks state of TV
(current content ID, etc)

CSS-WC: Wall Clock offset
measurements

CSS-WC
Client

Reads

Sets

Local system
time/clock

Calculate Wall Clock
time from System time

CSS-TS: Control
timestamps

CSS-TS
Client

Sets

Estimate of TV
Wall Clock
time

How to calculate
timeline position
from Wall Clock time

Estimate of
TV timeline
position

Metadata describing
how to calculate
time position in
companion media
content

Compare

Ideal media
player
time position

Sync Controller

Adjust

Compare

Actual media player
time position

Media Player

Figure 4: CS application Software Architecture

Through its CSS-CII protocol client, the CS application is able to receive content identification updates and track the state of the TV. The CSS-WC client makes regular measurements using the protocol (as described earlier). For each measurement, our client algorithm assumes symmetric network delays to estimate the Wall Clock, but also calculates the uncertainty bounds (dispersion). Dispersion is always at least half the round-trip time – reflecting the worst

case of total asymmetry – and grows over time due to the potential for clock drift. If a new measurement has lower dispersion, then it is adopted as the best estimate of the TV Wall clock. If it has higher dispersion, then it is discarded.

We use the notion of software clock objects to model timelines - flow of time in the world or in a piece of media - and to represent the relationships between them. The clock object is used to store a correlation and a multiplier constant (speed) with respect to a parent clock. The CS application's Wall Clock is therefore a clock that models the correlation between the CS application's and the TV's local times. As shown in Figure 5, this correlation (an offset) is regularly updated by CSS-WC protocol interchanges.

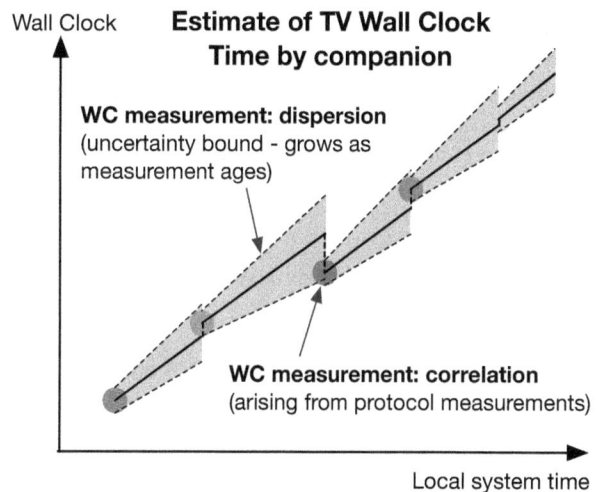

Figure 5: Estimate of TV Wall Clock time through Wall Clock synchronisation

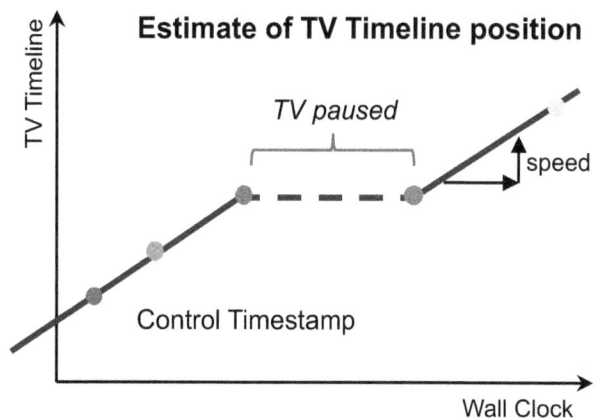

Figure 6: Estimate of the TV timeline position at the CS application through CSS-TS updates

Similarly, the TV content timeline is estimated locally at the CS application by a clock representing the correlation between the estimated Wall Clock time and the TV content time (see Figure 6). Control timestamps received by the CSS-TS client allow the CS application to update its estimate periodically or when the relationship between the TV content timeline and its Wall Clock changes (e.g. when the TV is paused). Using time-mapping metadata (companion content timeline to TV timeline) the CS application can infer the ideal media time player position at the current Wall Clock time. A *Sync Controller* object compares the ideal with the current media time player position. If necessary, it will then instruct the media player to align itself with the ideal timeline by adjusting its playout. The media player may speed up or slow down the playback to allow catch up or for large time differences execute a seek operation.

The Need for Device Calibration

DVB-CSS specifies that the Control Timestamps describe the time at which the light and sound should emit from the TV/Companion. This is later than the time at which software renders the video frame or audio samples, and needs characterising on a per-device-model basis, so that it can be compensated for. To measure these media decoding and rendering delays, a synchronisation-accuracy measurement system [12] was built using a micro-controller to collect light and sound samples from devices being characterised. The measurement system emulates the role of a CS application to measure delays on the TV i.e. it synchronises its local wall clock via CSS-WC and synchronises to a timeline using CSS-TS. The TV is then made to play a test video sequence in which the timings of light flashes and audio beeps are known; the times at which the flashes/beeps are detected by the system recorded. Based on expected and observed timings, an average offset accounting for pipeline and rendering delays is calculated. To measure delays on the CS application, the measurement system pretends to be a TV with an advancing timeline. It measures the light/sound coming out of the companion while the CS application uses control timestamps from the CSS-TS protocol to align its synchronisation timeline and drive its media playback. Our tools for precise timing measurement and calibration [12] are publicly available.

EARLY SYNCHRONISATION ACCURACY RESULTS

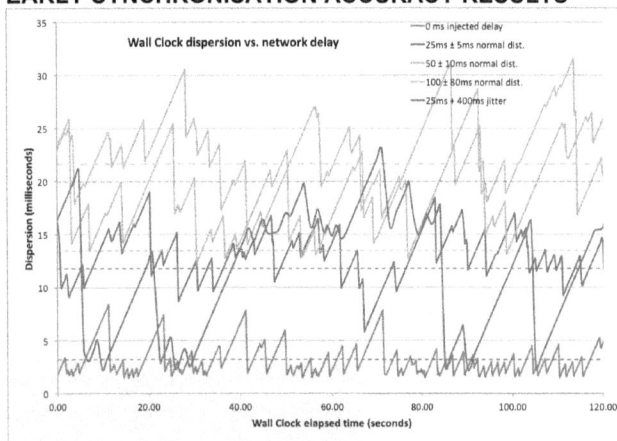

Figure 7: Synchronisation accuracy uncertainty bounds

The Wall Clock dispersion quantifies the amount by which the Wall Clock time at the CS application is inaccurate.

Because the CS application uses control timestamps from the TV (each being a Wall Clock time and content time pair) to estimate the TV timeline, values on this timeline will have an error largely contributed by the Wall Clock dispersion.

A simple evaluation exercise to determining synchronisation accuracy is therefore to measure the Wall Clock dispersion over time and to determine whether the values affect frame-level accuracy. By artificially injecting delays in network traffic and measuring the Wall Clock dispersion, it is further possible to surmise the effect of delay variation on sync accuracy. Using Linux's 'netem' network emulation tool, different types of delay variations were injected into network packets leaving the CSSTV's network interface namely, 1) 25 ± 5ms, 2) 50 ± 10ms, and 3) 100 ± 80ms with a normal distribution for variation in delay. To simulate realistic home WiFi conditions, further experiments were carried out with a delay of 25ms and jitter variation of up to 400ms

The results summarised in Figure 7, show that under 'low-delay' conditions (blue line), the CS application could potentially be, on average, about 3ms out of sync. In network conditions profiling more pronounced delay variations on a home network, the CS application asynchrony is less than or close to the duration of a video frame. (~20ms). These early synchronisation performance evaluation experiments exercise the protocols under a limited set of network conditions and show that synchronisation accuracy is affected by delay and delay variation. Further investigation is currently being carried out to measure actual delay variability in home networks and gauge its impact on synchronisation performance.

USE CASES

Different use cases require different degrees of accuracy of synchronisation. In creating a portfolio of demonstrations, we considered a spectrum of applications, enabled by different degrees of synchronisation accuracy, and implemented using DVB-CSS protocols. We included use-cases of:

1. Video to video synchronisation in which both the TV and the companion device play videos in a tightly synchronised fashion.
2. Video to audio synchronisation in which the companion device plays an audio track tightly synchronised to a programme on the TV.
3. Video to CS web application synchronisation in which the companion device presents relevant web content synchronised to the timeline of a programme on the TV.
4. Responsive active and passive control of the TV depending on user action on a CS web application.

The user journey, that we prototyped, begins with choosing the desired TV to synchronise with (Figure 8). This is made possible through the DIAL-based discovery mechanism mentioned previously. Once the TV is selected, the Content

ID (obtained from the CSS-CII protocol client) is used to discern which programme is being presented and the relevant companion experiences are proffered to the user (Figure 9).

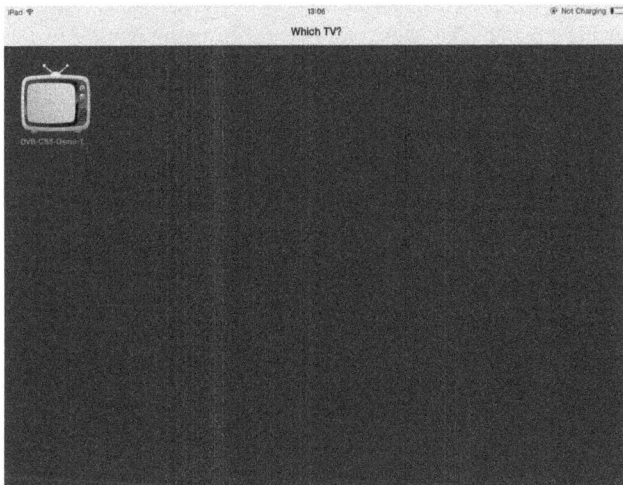

Figure 8: Discovering & choosing a TV on the home network.

Figure 9: Only experiences relevant to "*Alaska: Earth's Frozen Kingdom*" are proffered.

Video to video synchronisation

Figure 3 and Figure 10 depict the video to video synchronisation use case which requires frame accuracy (Figure 1) in order to be able to ensure consistency across screens especially if the video being played on both devices contains the same content albeit different sources. The frame accurate synchronisation is achievable due to a combination of the CSS-WC and CSS-TS protocols in conjunction with the calibration process.

Although, users have indicated parallel viewing of media as a desirable feature to have in companion experiences [1], a more interesting option is to provide users, watching a sporting event on the TV, to also be able to watch the same event from a different camera angle. The ability to enable frame-accurate synchronisation affords the user the option of listening to the sound tracks from both devices thereby

alleviating some of the concern surfaced in previous works [1][21].

Figure 10: Video to video synchronisation use case

Alternative audio streams

Playing alternative audio is not a novel idea. The audio streams may be alternative language commentaries covering an event, a directors' cut for a show, a broadcasters' audio description, a preferred presenter commentary etc. Synchronising an audio stream on a companion device to a video on the TV, requires at least word-level accuracy (Figure 1).

Audio Description

Access Services are very important to the BBC [21] and as such the BBC delivers narrative audio description to aid visually-impaired users. Figure 11 shows the companion device playing audio description tracks for the 5th episode of "*Wolf Hall*" synchronised to the TV. The user can listen to the audio description track on their personal companion device, through headphones, while listening to the original audio track being played on the TV, allowing a viewer to use the audio description service without disturbing other viewers in the same room.

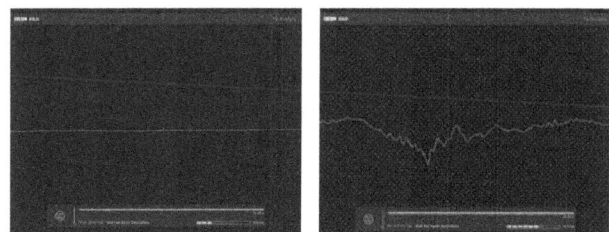

Figure 11: Visualisation of audio description track at 31.98s and 44.42s of "Wolf Hall". The visualisation is a feedback to the user to signal the presence of alternative audio.

Interactive content

One of the foremost use cases that comes to mind for companion experiences is an interactive web application which augments the TV program with relevant and synchronised information about the scene [4][10][18]. Over time, the BBC has produced a comprehensive collection of historical and factual information on King Henry VIII and the people who played major roles around his reign. In order to craft an interactive web application, we turned to this existing online collection and the branded programme pages associated with "*Wolf Hall*" [22] to manually craft companion content.

Figure 12: Images relevant to scenes in "*Wolf Hall*"

Backdrop information – Reusing & discovering content
Additional information about the locations at which scenes were filmed, cast information, behind the scenes candid photos and facts relating to the historical real life figures were sourced from BBC web (Figure 12 and Figure 14). Now and then, certain phrases were used in the programme which were in keeping with the period but not widely known to the layman. These were clarified to give the user a more in-depth understanding (Figure 13).

In this way, existing content created for previous period dramas on the same subject or educational aids were reused and resurfaced for the user. In keeping with the idea of interweaving our experience with already established behaviours exhibited by users looking for clarification or more in-depth relevant content.

Synopsis of previous episode – catch-up
Fans of a TV programme with an episodic narrative tend to create online Wikipedia pages or blogs to accompany the narrative and keep track of events [18].

As the story-telling becomes more complex in an episodic programme, such as "*Wolf Hall*", characters are seen to build relationships with each other but if you miss previous episodes, it is hard to understand the progression of the relationship. When scenes in the current episode related to a scene from a previous episode, we provided one or more clips to allow the user to catch up. In addition to providing the clips, we also provided information about where to access the previous episodes.

Remote Control: Active and Passive
One of the challenges in crafting companion experiences is managing the visual attention of the user. There has been negative feedback from users about their inability to relax during what is essentially a form of entertainment. Using the app-to-app communication channel, we chose to pause the TV if the user played a video clip on the companion device or interacted with an embedded webpage.

The user was given feedback to remind them the TV was paused through an unobtrusive text message. The progress of the timeline along the programme was also shown to the user through the progress bar at the top of the screen (Figure 12 to Figure 14). The user was also given an indication of the TV's pause/play state by surfacing the functionality to toggle the state (see play/pause button in Figure 13).

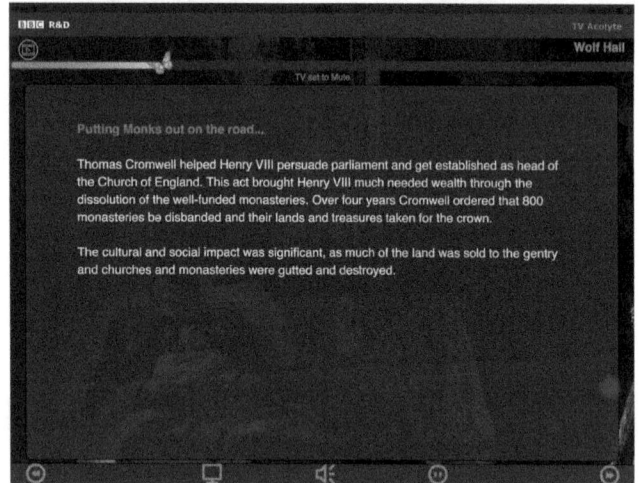

Figure 13: Text to explain interesting conversations

It has been suggested that users would want control of when the TV pauses or plays as opposed to being paused when the user clicks on the video clip presented on a companion screen, especially if they were watching with someone else [18]. In the prototype, we elected to pause the TV automatically but we let the user choose when to resume play.

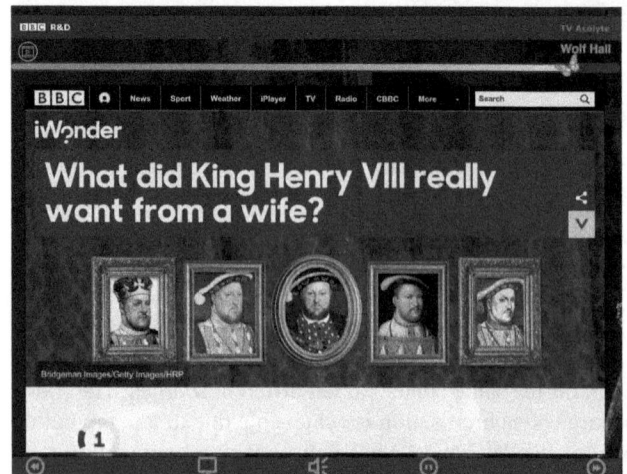

Figure 14: Existing BBC page

We also gave the user the ability to rewind or forward the programme by 10 seconds in case they missed the last part of the conversation between the characters on the TV. Figure 12 to Figure 14 show the control bar at the bottom of each screenshot. We also included rudimentary volume control (Figure 13).

FURTHER WORK

As HbbTV 2.0 compliant televisions become available, use of these specifications comes with a low barrier to market [13].

In future iterations of the prototype, we would like to include functionality to jump to a particular segment (chapters) in the program especially in conjunction with nature programmes. If a user was particularly interested in 'dolphins', they could request to watch everything to do with the mammal only. Furthermore, we plan to investigate other CS experiences that span across multiple devices in the home. With sophisticated interactions between the devices, there is a need for advanced synchronisation semantics to build such experiences. In order to make CS experiences part of programme-making, it is important to understand how the making of companion content might fit into existing production processes and how, in real broadcast contexts, the MRS is integrated with existing broadcaster metadata systems. Other than these technical considerations, we plan to explore the user's perception of different companion screen experiences and their tolerance induced synchronisation errors across different types of content. We hope to be able build a characterisation of what types of experiences work best in what circumstances. The most crucial aspect of developing second screen applications is finding the right balance between engagement and distraction [10].

CONCLUSION

This case study has presented recent BBC research and development work on the frame-accurate synchronisation of companion devices with our emulation of a connected TV using standardised DVB-CSS protocols which, through their adoption in HbbTV 2.0 are expected to appear in commercially available connected TVs in the near future. We have created a portfolio of non-commercial research prototypes as proof-of-concepts and as a platform to push forward research in this area. Given the rapidly developing technological landscape in the companion device space, it is important to anticipate technical opportunity and conduct some user-centred explorations.

ACKNOWLEDGEMENTS

We thank all our collaborators and colleagues in the BBC who have given us valuable insight. Particular thanks to the creator of the CSSTV, our colleague Dr. Nigel Earnshaw.

REFERENCES

1. Edward Anstead, Steve Benford, Robert J. Houghton. 2014. Many-Screen Viewing: Evaluating an Olympics Companion Application. In *Proceedings of the 2014 ACM international conference on Interactive experiences for TV and online video (TVX 2014)*, 103-110.
http://dl.acm.org/citation.cfm?id=2602299.2602304.

2. Chromecast. Google. Retrieved October 9, 2015 from https://www.google.com/intl/en_uk/chromecast/.

3. Santosh Basapur, Hiren Mandalia, Shirley Chaysinh, Young Lee, Narayanan Venkitaraman, Crysta Metcalf. 2012. FANFEEDS: Evaluation of Socially Generated Information Feed on Second Screen as a TV Show Companion. In *Proceedings of the 10th international interactive conference on Interactive television (EuroITV 2012)*, 87-96.
http://dl.acm.org/citation.cfm?id=2325616.2325636

4. Alison Button. 2012. Second Screens: How people are actually using them to enhance their TV viewing. Retrieved September 29, 2015 from http://audiencesportal.co.uk/article_list/digital_media_articles/second_screens.aspx.

5. M. Oskar van Deventer, Hans Stokkinh, Matt Hammond, Jean Le Feuvre, Pablo Cesar. 2016. Standards for Multi-Stream and Multi-Device Media Synchronization. In *IEEE Communications Magazine – Communications Standards Supplement.* 54, 3 (2016), 16-21.

6. DIAL. Netflix. Retrieved October 9, 2015 from http://www.dial-multiscreen.org/

7. Digital Video Broadcasting (DVB) – CM-COS Group. Retrieved January 13, 2016 from https://www.dvb.org/groups/CM-COS.

8. Digital Video Broadcasting (DVB); Companion Screens and Streams; Part 1: Concepts, roles and overall architecture. 2015. DVB BlueBook A167-1, ETSI TS 103 286-1. Retrieved September 29, 2015 from https://www.dvb.org/standards.

9. Digital Video Broadcasting (DVB); Companion Screens and Streams; Part 2: Content Identification and Media Synchronization. 2015. DVB BlueBook A167-2, ETSI TS 103 286-2. Retrieved September 29, 2015 from https://www.dvb.org/standards.

10. David Geerts, Rinze Leenheer, Dirk De Grooff, Susanne Heijstraten, Joost Negenman. 2014. In Front of and Behind the Second Screen: Viewer and Producer Perspectives on a Companion App. In *Proceedings of the 2014 ACM international conference on Interactive experiences for TV and online video (TVX 2014)*, 95-102.
http://dl.acm.org/citation.cfm?id=2602299.2602304.

11. GStreamer: Open source multimedia framework. Retrieved October 8, 2015 from http://gstreamer.freedesktop.org/.

12. Matt Hammond. 2015. Standardising companion screen synchronisation - tools and testing. Retrieved October 9, 2015 from http://bbc.in/1z2JNg5.

13. HbbTV Specification FAQ. HbbTV. Retrieved October 9, 2015 from https://www.hbbtv.org/wp-content/uploads/2015/07/HbbTV-Specification-2.0-FAQ.pdf.

14. ISO/IEC 13818-1:2015: Information technology - Generic coding of moving pictures and associated audio information -- Part 1: Systems. 2015. Retrieved October 8, 2015 from http://bit.ly/ISO13818.

15. libdvbpsi. VideoLAN. Retrieved October 8, 2015 from http://www.videolan.org/developers/libdvbpsi.html.

16. libwebsockets. Libwebsockets.org. Retrieved October 8, 2015 from https://libwebsockets.org/trac/libwebsockets.

17. Gavin Mann, Francesco Venturini, Robin Murdoch, Bikash Mishra, Gemma Moorby, Bouchra Carlier. 2015. *Digital Video and the Connected Consumer*. Accenture. Retrieved September 29, 2015 from http://bit.ly/TechRepAccenture_2015.

18. Abhishek Nandakumar, Janet Murray. 2014. Companion Apps for Long Arc TV Series: Supporting New Viewers in Complex Storyworlds with Tightly Synchronised Context-Sensitive Annotations. In *Proceedings of the 2014 ACM international conference on Interactive experiences for TV and online video (TVX '14)*, 3-10. http://dl.acm.org/citation.cfm?id=2602317.

19. The DVB Project – about page. DVB. Retrieved September 24, 2015 from https://www.dvb.org/about.

20. The New Multi-screen World: Understanding Cross-platform Consumer Behaviour. Google. Retrieved September 24, 2015 from https://think.withgoogle.com/databoard/media/pdfs/the-new-multi-screen-world-study_research-studies.pdf.

21. Vinoba Vinayagamoorthy, Penelope Allen, Matt Hammond, Michael Evans. 2012. Researching the User Experience for Connected TV – A Case Study. In *CHI'12 Extended Abstracts on Human Factors in Computing Systems (CHI 2012)*, 589-604. http://dl.acm.org/citation.cfm?doid=2212776.2212832.

22. Wolf Hall. BBC. Retrieved October 9, 2015 from http://www.bbc.co.uk/programmes/p02gfy02.

Mining Subtitles for Real-Time Content Generation for Second-Screen Applications

Johannes Knittel
Institute for Visualization and Interactive Systems
University of Stuttgart
knittejs@visus.uni-stuttgart.de

Tilman Dingler
Institute for Visualization and Interactive Systems
University of Stuttgart
tilman.dingler@vis.uni-stuttgart.de

ABSTRACT

Using mobile devices while watching TV is becoming increasingly common. Most of the so-called second-screen apps provide additional information and services for a specific TV program. App content is mostly manually curated by the program or app publishers. In this paper we present an approach for automatically extracting keywords from subtitles in order to retrieve and provide highly relevant additional program content. Over the course of 4 months we recorded more than 45.000 hours of TV shows, on which we based an entity linking algorithm to extract relevant keywords and automatically trigger Wikipedia look-ups. Our system includes a second-screen app which proactively displays these contents with hindsight to time and position in the current TV show. We then conducted a user study with 30 participants investigating the relationship between app usage while watching documentaries and effects on comprehension, recall, and subjective experience. We confirmed user distraction while using the app, but noticed an increase in subjectively reported comprehension compared to when users triggered web-searches via a smartphone browser. The content extracted, linked and proactively presented by our system turned out to be highly relevant.

Author Keywords

second-screen app; entity linking; subtitles; content generation, real-time content delivery; context-awareness

ACM Classification Keywords

H.5.m. Information Interfaces and Presentation (e.g. HCI): Miscellaneous

INTRODUCTION

The ubiquity of mobile devices increasingly affects our TV experience. 90% of smartphone owners use their mobile device while watching TV, about 50% of this group browses the web while 30% use it for looking up additional information about the show, topic, and people involved [8]. Often times people use a second device, *i.e.* phone or tablet, for looking

Permission to make digital or hard copies of all or part of this work for personal or classroom use is granted without fee provided that copies are not made or distributed for profit or commercial advantage and that copies bear this notice and the full citation on the first page. Copyrights for components of this work owned by others than ACM must be honored. Abstracting with credit is permitted. To copy otherwise, or republish, to post on servers or to redistribute to lists, requires prior specific permission and/or a fee. Request permissions from Permissions@acm.org.

TVX'16, June 22-24, 2016, Chicago, IL, USA
2016 ACM. ISBN 978-1-4503-4067-0/16/06 $15.00
DOI: http://dx.doi.org/10.1145/2932206.2932217

Figure 1. TVInsight is a second-screen app that shows additional program information by triggering web searches and Wikipedia look-ups in real-time. Left: general program information. Right: Wikipedia content for extracted people entities.

up keywords online and gather additional information with relevance to the current TV program. In 2012 the PEW Research Center assessed the parallel usage of second-screen devices while watching TV and the relevance of that activity to the current program [30]: from almost 2000 participants, 22% used their cell phone to check facts mentioned in the program, 35% visited a related website, 20% looked up relevant social comments, and 19% posted their own comments about the program they were watching. However, the process of looking up relevant information can be quite slow, cumbersome and is error-prone; coming up with appropriate search keywords, correct spelling, and individually evaluating each search result can be time consuming and requires mental effort, which distracts attention away from the current show.

A great number of commercial second-screen apps usually focus on one particular show or program. These apps are often hosted by the TV station itself or by an exclusive partner, so access to content is restricted to the particular app. Users who follow more than one show end up with a fragmented collection of apps on their devices. For content providers on the other hand, curation can be expensive while content can be extracted in an automated way by intelligently linking existing resources together. Such an approach is cheaper and further allows live-shows to be augmented with additional information.

An increasing number of TV stations broadcast subtitles alongside their program. These subtitles bear great potential for content extraction algorithms, since they contain crucial information about topics and people involved. Such contents can be used to augment the TV experience independent from the channel users are watching. Additional information can be purely informative, but can also be of educational use, especially while consuming foreign language shows, as they are often watched with the goal of language acquisition. Castillo *et al.* [6], for example, proposed a system that automatically analyzed subtitles to find relevant news articles for a given news program. Most systems and studies, however, are based on a very topic-specific domain, therefore limiting their general applicability in a diverse TV program environment.

In this work we set out to assess the feasibility of automatically generating relevant content to improve the TV experience in real-time. We describe our approach of using an extended entity linking algorithm to extract important keywords from subtitle streams, linking them to highly relevant Wikipedia articles, and delivering them to a proprietary second-screen app called *TVInsight* (Fig.1), which displays additional information in a context-sensitive way. For the entity linking algorithm to work efficiently, we collected a corpus of subtitles from 30 TV stations over the course of 4 months resulting in more than 45.000 hours of TV shows.

In a comprehensive user study we then evaluated our system with hindsight to its effects on the TV experience, the user's comprehension of the program's content, and its distracting nature as compared to conventional look-ups performed on a second device. Therefore, we started out collecting user feedback through an online study to gain insights into what kind of information people look for when using second-screen apps, how frequently they use it and from which sources they tend to gain their information. We then elicited a number of features for a working prototype which harnesses live TV streams to pinpoint the current program and exact program location to mine its subtitles in real-time and performs online look-ups autonomously. Hence, the contribution of this paper is as follows:

1. Findings from an online survey informing the design and feature space of second-screen apps.

2. A system that parses TV subtitles (closed captions) and uses entity linking in real-time to perform web look-ups for pushing relevant content to a second-screen app.

3. Results from a comprehensive user study showing the utility of the information provided and its effects on comprehension and overall TV experience.

RELATED WORK
Our work is based on previous research on second-screen apps in general, user attention and distractions, as well as automatic content creation by linking existing resources.

Some first guidelines for second-screen apps were formulated by Robertson *et al.* [28] who introduced a system connecting a Personal Digital Assistant (PDA) with a television device, where the TV was used more as an additional screen

real estate. Utilizing the hardware of each connected device creates synergy effects that extend the experience of each device by itself. Cruickshank *et al.* [9] also looked at PDAs as second-screen device capable of browsing the TV program and changing channels.

In recent years a multitude of second-screen apps have commercially entered the market. They provide additional content, invite users to participate in real-time surveys, or comprise social features, such as social check-ins or sharing content. The market is fragmented with numerous shows and channels offering their proprietary second-screen app, mostly tailored to run on mobile devices. Geerts *et al.* [13] found that a general second-screen app is preferable with regard to every show providing its innate application while barriers to find additional program information should be kept at a minimum. Second-screen content should not solely mirror the program content, but provide additional information. Further, the program progress should be taken into account.

By splitting functionality across devices the issue of diverting attention became more prevalent. Fleury *et al.* [12] found that users generally appreciate second-screen apps to draw their attention to additional content, but this should be done in an unobtrusive way. Van Cauwenberge *et al.* [31] looked into media multitasking and how using a search engine to answer questions while watching a documentary affects comprehension. They found that the increased cognitive load by using the search engine as a secondary task lead to participants not being able to comprehensively recite the facts of the documentary and performed worse on comprehension tests. A study by Google reported that 22% of second-screen usage was complementary to the current program [14]. Holz *et al.* [17] on the other hand found that most of the app usage was not program related. Especially during formats that inform and educate, the audience's focus was generally higher and less concerned with second-app usage.

About 27% of TV show-related searches is about the characters and their relations, closely followed by searches about the plot with 23%, according to a survey conducted by Nandakumar *et al.* [23]. They created a companion second screen prototype that displayed synchronized and context-sensitive information mainly about the characters and found that this enhances comprehension when used by first-time viewers of a late season episode.

To reduce distractions, attempts have been made to automatically detect the current program running in the background. Therefore, Chuang *et al.* [7] developed a smartphone app using audio fingerprinting to recognize the current show in order to provide additional content by analyzing the video- and audio stream.

While most additional content is manually curated, especially for canned user studies, Castillo *et al.* [6] showed an approach for automatically analyzing subtitles to find relevant news articles for a news program as well as music titles through mining song lyrics. Their algorithm was used in Yahoo!'s service *IntoNow* which was discontinued in 2014. Additional content can further be created by linking existing and relevant content together. Allan [2] formulated the need for automated procedures to link paragraphs to relevant documents in an automated way. Redondo *et al.* [27] performed named entity recognition on subtitles for news broadcasts and used structured data from DBpedia to generate a comprehensive set of relevant context items.

Shen *et al.* [29] give a comprehensive overview of common entity linking features coming to the conclusion that most algorithms are highly domain specific. Mihalecea *et al.* [10] presented a linking model integrating *Wikipedia* articles. To increase recall and precision values, other works have included PageRank values [21], the number of incoming links, or a combination of different features and classifiers [11]. Odijk *et al.* [26] made specific use of subtitles for linking Wikipedia articles by using a context graph based on dynamic assembly of anchor phrases. However, the analysis of their approach was based on a curated set of well-defined topics but lacked an evaluation 'in the wild'.

Subtitles are traditionally used to make content accessible to people with hearing impairments. However, subtitles have increasingly been subject to research focusing on word frequency analysis [18, 19, 25] showing that subtitles approximate spoken language. Hayati *et al.* [15] showed that displaying subtitles in foreign language movies improves auditory comprehension when shown in native as well as in foreign languages. Similarly, Mitterer *et al.* [22] found that subtitles in a foreign language support language perception and strengthen vocabulary. Kovacs *et al.* [20] developed a video player for foreign language learners which enhanced the traditional subtitles display by allowing users to jump back and forth through the video by clicking on the corresponding subtitle. Brasel *et al.* [4] investigated displaying advertisements in users' native language with subtitles and their effects on eye movements and recall showing that participants were able to recall more of the advertisement brands shown. However, they also showed a negative effect for recalling visual program elements.

Concluding, people seem to use a great number of apps and browser-based strategies to look up information based on the TV program they currently watch. But at this point there is not a comprehensive solution proactively providing relevant content across TV programs. Manual curation would be unfeasible, which is why we focus on automated content generation techniques. By harvesting the availability of subtitles and our proprietary entity linking algorithm, we are able to automatically generate additional program content. The solution we propose is independent from any particular channel or show. It prevents the user from having to download a variety of apps, but at the same time offers highly topic-relevant content. By proactively retrieving content, users have the information at their fingertips as they launch the app rather than actively having to look for content. This reduces potential diversion from the actual TV program. Limited distractions should benefit the TV experience - *e.g.* through immersion - and improve content comprehension. Inspired by previous work in language learning we explore learning scenarios as application cases for context-sensitive second-screen apps.

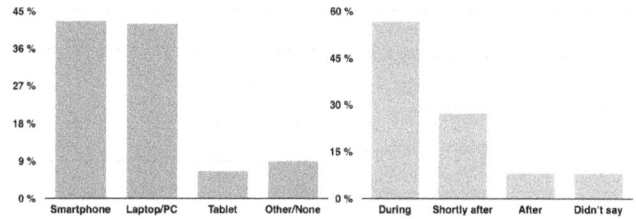

Figure 2. Types of devices used for web searches and the timing of the searches relative to the show watched.

FEATURE ELICITATION

To elicit features for a second-screen app we conducted an online survey in February 2015 focusing on how people go about web searches while watching TV. We were interested in what type of information people look up, on which devices and the timing of their searches. We were further interested in how they use subtitles, how frequently they are used, as to why and for which types of shows.

We set up an online survey using LimeSurvey[1] running on one of our servers. After a brief explanation of the purpose of the survey and granting consent for the data collection, participants were redirected to three blocks of questions focusing on demographics, TV information search, and usage of subtitles. The survey was announced through university mailinglists and social networks. Over the course of two weeks we recorded survey responses of 136 participants (60 females) with a mean age of 27 ($SD = 8.4$). 54% indicated to be students while 41% were working professionals. 40% stated they watched TV on daily basis, 88% at least once per week. Filling in the survey took less than 5 minutes, participants were not rewarded.

Results

The collected data provides insights into how people search the web while watching TV as well as in what way they make use of subtitles.

Web Search

19.9% stated they had looked up something online related to a TV show in the last 24 hours, 58% within the last week, and 80% within the last month. As to what they were searching, 48.5% named people that were mentioned in the program, 28.7% searched for a terminology or had a specific question, and 10.3% looked up the current show's topic. Fig.2 depicts the device types used during triggering a search and at which point in time: most people used their Smartphone (42.6%) or Laptop/PC (41.9%) to look up information, mostly while watching the show (56.6%). Fig.3 shows the program types in which participants usually use web searches according to what search category (terminology/question, people, topic) they look for. Participants indicated to mostly search the web during TV shows (33.5%), movies (19.1%) and documentaries (11.8%). Especially during shows and movies people seem to look up people, during documentaries there is a tendency to look up terminologies. As to where people end up when looking up such information, 61% indicated Wikipedia as number one while 10.3% named movie portals, such as

---

[1]http://limesurvey.org/

95

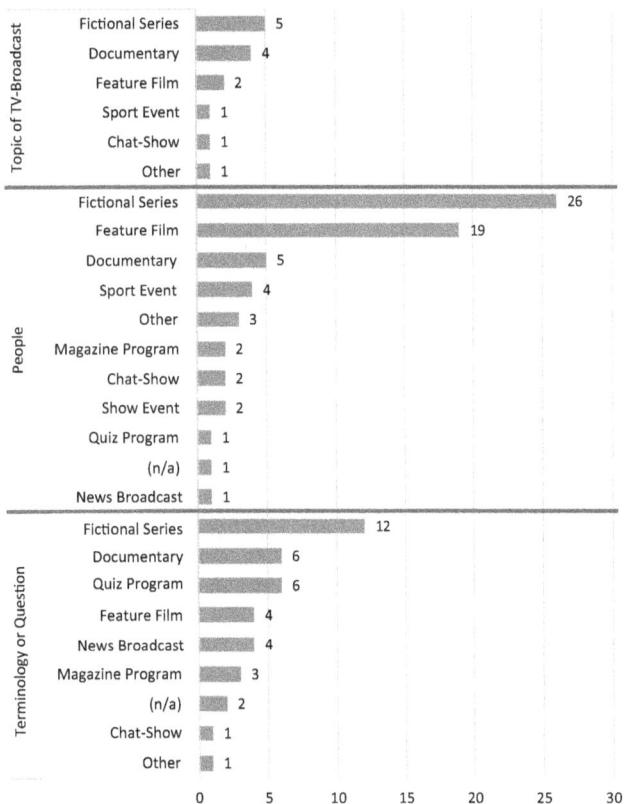

Figure 3. Types of shows according to search categories.

topics is to be found. It makes sense then to populate a second screen app with contents from or direct links to Wikipedia.

Participants noted that often they did not undertake web searches due to not having correctly heard a name or not knowing the wording of a topic. Thus, a second screen app should be aware of the program context including content specifics so that additional information can be provided as it becomes relevant to the current program position.

Not surprisingly, subtitles seem to be mainly used for supporting comprehension of foreign language content. As related research states, subtitles often distract from the visuals. They do, however, provide important content keywords, which can be used as a starting point for web searches. A second-screen app can take advantage of the information contained in subtitles to automatically collect and provide additional information in real-time.

SYSTEM OVERVIEW

Based on the insights from the online survey we designed and implemented the second-screen app TVInsight. It provides additional information to the current TV program independent from the type of program or channel. Therefore, it needs to be aware of the current program context, i.e. the position, its content, trigger automated web searches, and compile the resulting information to a comprehensive and easily accessible second screen experience.

Content Generation

An increasing amount of TV programs are broadcast with subtitle streams to make content accessible for people with hearing impairments. Our goal was to develop an entity linking algorithm specifically designed for the real-time analysis of subtitles that works across a wide range of different TV-programs and genres. There are publicly available subtitle databases, such as *opensubtitles.org*, but they usually focus on movies and TV series and miss out on popular TV-program formats, such as live shows, chat shows, news broadcast, or documentaries. Hence, we developed a software which directly receives data streams from a TV tuner to decode and store subtitles broadcast via Teletext. Our system taps into cable TV streams using a DVB-C (Digital Video Broadcasting - Cable) extension card. For each transponder, the respective MPEG-2 transport stream multiplexes various data, video and audio streams [1]. We decode the Teletext streams and filter out packets containing subtitles. Furthermore, we receive the Electronic Program Guide (EPG), which our software uses to associate subtitles with the corresponding TV program and store further meta data.

Our software is written in C# and runs on a server which currently receives 30 TV channels. An admin interface (see Fig.4) shows current tv programs and most recently extracted subtitles. Here we can also tune to different frequencies or scan the transponder to list available channels.

We wanted to train our algorithm on a broad spectrum of TV programs. Hence, we let our server collect data over the

IMDb[2], and only about 3% end up on the direct website of the TV channel or program. Most survey participants agreed that searches did not take too much time and usually satisfied their information need.

Subtitle Usage

Direct usage of subtitles was rather uncommon among participants. In Germany, where most survey participants resided, foreign media content is usually dubbed. More than 40% indicated to have never or more than a year ago made use of subtitles. 33% stated they activated subtitles within the last month, only 8.8% within the last 24 hours. Subtitles seemed to be used mostly during movies (45.4%) and TV shows (38%), sometimes during documentaries (9.3%). In 84% of the usage cases, the program watched contained foreign language content, in 40% they were explicitly used for language learning purposes, the same amount accounts for a better understanding of acoustics.

Discussion and Feature Elicitation

Many consumers use secondary devices while watching TV for looking up additional program information mostly concerning people and the corresponding topic. Smartphones and Laptops seem to be the preferred devices, which confirms previous findings. The majority of web searches leads to Wikipedia where additional information about people and

---

[2]http://www.imdb.com/

course of 4 months, which resulted in 45.000 hours of subtitled programs from 30 channels and a corpus of 136 million words in total. A word frequency analysis yielded about 1 million unique words (no stemming applied) and more than 200.000 words that appeared more than 10 times. We focused on German channels, but similar corpora can be created using channels in other languages.

Entity Linking

Entity Linking describes the process of retrieving and linking phrases to their counterparts in knowledge databases. We created an algorithm that continuously analyzes incoming subtitles in real-time and finds corresponding content on Wikipedia. To do this, we downloaded the publicly available german Wikipedia content[3] (~14GB), from which we extracted the links between articles, cleared out redundancies, extracted titles, definitions, images, and marked people entities. We wrote the algorithm from scratch in C#. Our approach is made up of 3 consecutive steps:

1. Extract Candidates

Similar to previous approaches like [26], we used the collection of anchor texts (the displayed text linked to a specific page) to extract potential candidates. This step produced quite a number of candidates since commonly used words like 'this' and 'here' are often used as anchor texts within Wikipedia. On the other hand, anchor texts provide an extensive and high-quality list of synonyms and variant spellings of the same topic. We used stop words to immediately reduce the number of very unspecific candidates.

2. Select Target Page

For each candidate there may be multiple possible destination pages. The page to which the corresponding anchor text was most often linked to within Wikipedia, was picked as the first page candidate. In most cases, this was already the best target page. Garcia *et al.* [11] achieved a combined accuracy of 75% on several disambiguation datasets this way. To improve this, we took into account contextual information: to determine the second page candidate we intersected the context sets, comprised of the words of the first paragraph of the article on the one side, and the most recent words in the subtitle stream (sliding window approach) on the other side (ignoring stop words). The page whose intersection contained the least common word was considered the second candidate (if applicable). We used the word frequency of the generated subtitle or Wikipedia corpus, whichever was higher, to determine the least common word. In case there was a second page candidate, a neural network decided which one was more relevant. To train the network, we manually annotated a set of about 2000 items which were randomly picked instances from our recorded set. Thus, we first extracted the candidates from our vast subtitle database, selected those with two page candidates, filtered out very common anchor texts like *'this'*, and manually annotated a subset of randomly picked candidates.

3. Determine Candidates To Be Linked

For each candidate and its chosen target page we used a second neural network to decide whether an annotation between

---

[3]http://dumps.wikimedia.org/dewiki/latest

candidate and target site should take place. As stated before, the number of candidates extracted in the first step is huge, thus, we had to narrow it down to items that were considered highly relevant for the respective scene. Again, to train the network we randomly picked about 3500 candidates from our vast subtitle collection, performed the disambiguation and manually marked the items that should be linked.

Features

For the neural network classifiers, we elicited the following set of features based on previous work such as [26] and [11], and further added some features to make the algorithm better suited for the analysis of subtitles.

- Word frequencies of anchor text and context intersection based on our subtitle corpus and Wikipedia

- Probability that anchor text is linked to this page

- Probability that anchor text is an anchor within Wikipedia

- Indegree: how often the page is being linked within Wikipedia

- Outdegree: number of anchor links on the page

- Is the TV program mentioned on the page?

- Is the anchor text equal to the page name?

- Does the first paragraph contain the anchor text?

- Similarity metrics between anchor text and page title as well as context words and page title

Performance

An in-memory directed word graph is created to efficiently extract the candidates and retrieve target page candidates. The run time of the classifier is negligible. Our implementation needs approximately 25GB of memory, but processes subtitles extremely fast since the time complexity lies in approximately $O(1)$ per word. We optimized for performance rather than memory usage, since available memory is usually less of an issue anymore, especially in server environments.

Results

In contrast to previous work we make heavy use of domain knowledge about subtitles, including relative word frequencies of the subtitle corpus and meta information about the corresponding TV program. To the best of our knowledge, our approach is the first one based on a comprehensive data set taken from subtitles of a great variety of TV program genres.

Compared to the approach by Odijk *et al.* [26] for processing subtitles, the algorithm presented here performs better (precision = 0.79, recall = 0.77 vs. R-Precision = 0.71). The reported precision and recall values of our approach are the respective means of the 5-fold cross-validation runs. Further limitations of [26] are the presentation of multiple possible destination sites rather than definite decisions and the fact that their training data was solely based on manually annotated and topic-separated content from talkshows, which generally limits the external validity of their approach.

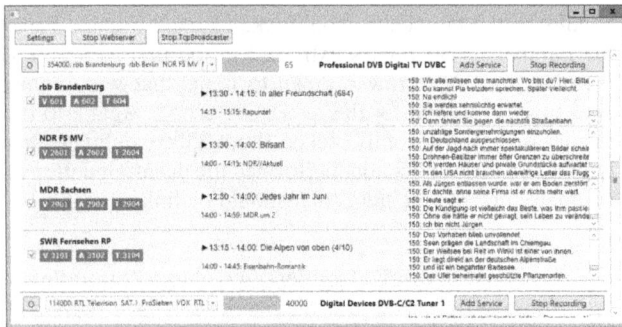

Figure 4. Admin view of the server software showing current TV programs and most recently extracted subtitles.

A Second-Screen App: TVInsight

The purpose of the entity linking algorithm described is to provide relevant Wikipedia articles based on an analysis of the current TV program's subtitles. The resulting articles are delivered through a second-screen app - which we called *TVInsight* - with the goal of supporting web-based searches during TV consumption. Therefore, we created a native Windows Phone 8.1 application which proactively displays relevant content.

The frontend contains 4 menu items where consumers can choose between different categories of information (see Fig.1 and 5):

- *info*: general information about the current TV program including channel, program times and a short description (as provided by the EPG).

- *people*: Wikipedia articles regarding people entities including an article preview and portrait picture. A tap opens the corresponding Wikipedia page in a browser view.

- *wiki*: topic-relevant Wikipedia articles including an article preview.

- *google*: keyword suggestions relevant to the current program. A tap opens up a browser view showing a list of corresponding Google results.

As subtitles are broadcast and received on our server, they are being processed in real-time and the generated content is timestamped. The keyword search suggestions are based on the anchor texts of the detected annotations.

Our goal is to offer a feed of articles that convey a much richer and more content-focused experience compared to traditional program information services (e.g. mobile EPG solutions), since we extract people and topic entities from what is said on the program and not just from official cast listings and short summaries.

For synchronizing the app content with the currently watched TV channel, audio fingerprinting has been proposed [7]. However, to ensure stable and equal conditions among all study sessions of our study with recorded the documentaries in advance and synchronized the video player with the app content according to the current viewing position through the network connection. As incoming subtitles are processed in

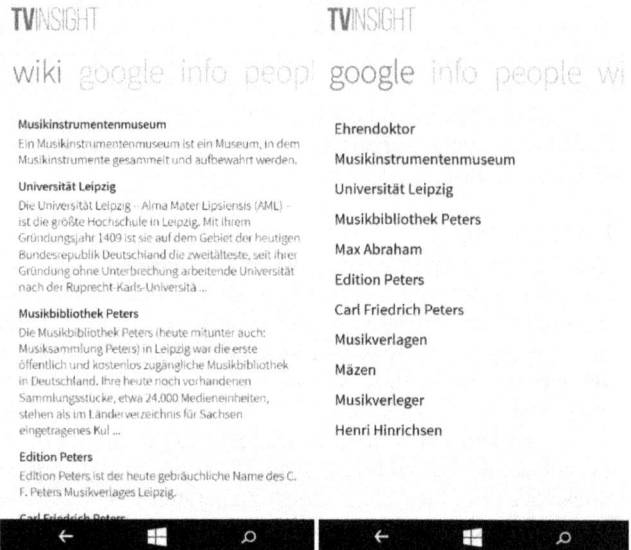

Figure 5. TVInsight shows Wikipedia articles relevant to the current TV topic (left) and extracted keywords to launch a corresponding *Google* search (right).

real-time by the server, content can be pushed out to the app in a timely manner as well.

Scenarios

Here, we want to depict two scenarios how additional content delivered through our second-screen app can be used to augment TV programs and serve educational purposes.

Language Learning

Learning language vocabulary is very much topic-driven. The vocabulary required to go grocery shopping is different from the vocabulary of a geopolitical discussion. An obvious extension of our second-screen app is using the keywords extracted from subtitles of foreign tv shows to compile a word list that reflects the topic of the show and can be used in-situ or post-hoc for studying.

General Knowledge Acquisition

The information need of regular tv consumers is relatively pronounced [8, 5]. Results from our online study also show that users often act on cues provided by the tv program to trigger further searches. The conventional approach is to try to remember, for example, the name of a person in order to start a web search at some point bearing the risk of either forgetting to actually perform the search later on or misspelling the keyword. Previous work showed an increased cognitive load when search tasks were being performed while watching, which lead to missing important information [31]. Our second-screen app based on automated keyword extraction from subtitles allows us to retrieve and display or store important entities for later look-up. While the app proactively triggers web searches and retrieves, for example, relevant Wikipedia articles, contents displayed can be bookmarked for later review while minimizing interruptions in the current TV experience.

SYSTEM EVALUATION

To evaluate the utility of our approach and quantify the effects on consumers' TV experience, we conducted a user study in which we applied our entity linking approach to automatically display relevant contents from Wikipedia in synchronization with the current TV program. We were especially interested in objective as well as subjective effects on program comprehension and the utility of proactive provision of additional content. In contrast to previous works we did not manually select the content stream, but used the actual output of our content generation algorithm applied on an actual TV broadcast. We conducted this user study with the following 4 hypotheses in mind:

- *H1*: Using TVInsight leads to better comprehension of the current program's contents based on *objective* assessments.

- *H2*: Using TVInsight leads to better comprehension of the current program's contents based on *subjective* assessments.

- *H3*: Using TVInsight is less distracting than manually searching the web using the Smartphone browser app.

- *H4*: Using TVInsight leads to a better user experience than using the Smartphone browser app for look-ups.

To compare our approach we tested TVInsight against a baseline (no tools available) and the smartphone's browser search capabilities. Participants were asked to watch different documentaries while being able to use the available tools for additional content retrieval.

Method

For this study we employed a repeated-measure design with the tool available for web searches as the independent variable, which resulted in the following 3 conditions:

- A: No tools available (baseline): participants watching a documentary without a secondary device.

- B: Smartphone browser: participants were given a Smartphone with Internet access and asked to use web searches as they saw fit to retrieve additional information.

- C: TVInsight app: participants were given a Smartphone equipped with our prototype and asked to use it as they saw fit.

To avoid learning effects between conditions we counterbalanced the sequence of conditions for each participant. Furthermore, the order of the documentaries, ad breaks and questions were randomized to mitigate the influence of participants' preferences and reduce learning effects.

In each condition participants were asked to watch a documentary. As dependent variables we measured comprehension in the shape of multiple-choice questionnaires about the documentary content and applied a recall test up to a week after the study. Comprehension questions were designed with hindsight to testing literal (recalling what has been explicitly stated in the text) and inferential comprehension (requires readers to understand relationships that are not explicitly stated in the text) [3], whereas each test consisted of 15

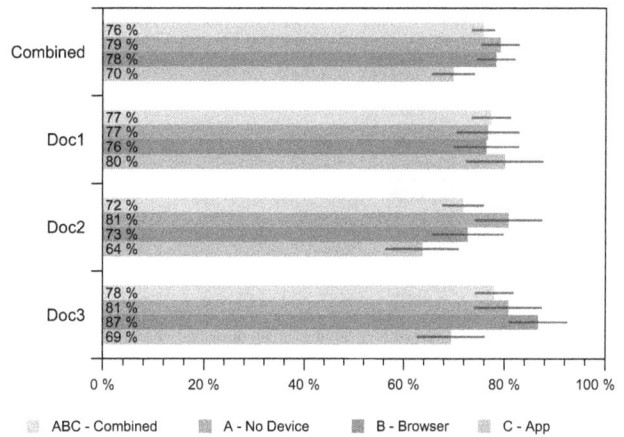

Figure 6. **Percentage of correctly answered comprehension questions, segmented by condition and documentary.**

questions with three levels of difficulty: easy, intermediate, and advanced questions, which we asserted during pilot studies. The recall test consisted of statements which required simple true/false responses. Further, we collected subjective feedback through a questionnaire after each study condition as well as through a semi-structured interview at the end of the study.

Participants

We recruited 30 participants (9 female) with a mean age of 22.5 (SD=4.0) years through university mailing lists and social networks. 93% indicated German to be their first language. 76% of participants reported to at least occasionally watch TV. The total study took about an hour, for which we compensated participants with 10EUR.

Apparatus

During the study all participants were seated in the same room in front of a 22 inch monitor connected to a notebook on which they watched the documentaries, answered the questionnaires and provided subjective feedback. Therefore, we created a proprietary .NET program through which we made sure that the allocation between documentaries, condition, and the viewing sequence was counterbalanced. Questionnaires were directly applied through that same software. For the app and browser condition we handed out a *Microsoft Lumia 640* on which our TVInsight prototype was running as described above. The software further took care of the time synchronization between the played documentary video and delivering the content to the mobile app in real-time to avoid glitches and ensure equally stable conditions for all participants.

Procedure

After participants signed the consent form, we explained the nature of the study and sat them down in front of the screen where we collected basic demographic information through an opening questionnaire. To give an idea of how the comprehension test will look like, three sample questions not related to the following topics were shown. Before each condition we made sure participants could familiarize themselves

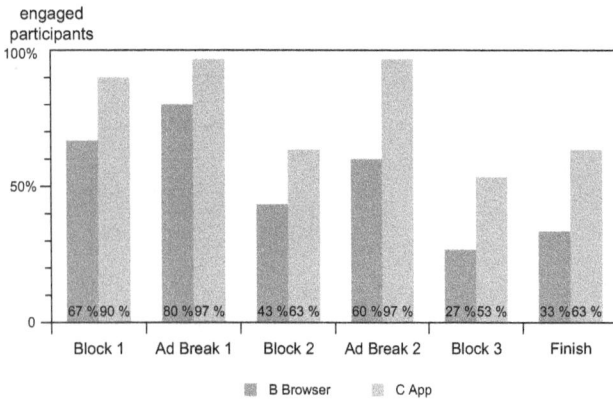

Figure 7. App and browser usage across time including advertisement breaks.

with the tool at hand and were instructed to use the tool as they saw fit during the documentary in order to improve their comprehension score later on. In each condition participants were asked to watch a 10min documentary in which we embedded two commercial breaks, 1min each, in order to simulate a somewhat realistic TV experience. Ad blocks were equally spaced throughout the documentary. The content of the ad breaks had nothing to do with the respective documentary and solely served as a time break for participants to use the second-screen device. The documentaries were in German and included topics about birds of prey, a recent naval accident, and about the history of a publishing house. They all aired on the same TV channel several weeks ago. We made sure that no participant had watched any of them before. At the end of a documentary participants had a 30-second window to finish their current web or app search before the comprehension test started. Comprehension questions were designed solely based on the content of the respective documentaries and before the entity linking algorithm was applied to generate the actual second-screen content. The output of the algorithm was deliberately left untouched to simulate a real-time content extraction setting, thus, some of the articles and search suggestions were evidently irrelevant. The content on the app was synchronized with the viewing experience based on the display time of the respective subtitle lines. We did not allow the use of the app or browser while filling in the comprehension test. After each comprehension test participants were asked to provide a subjective assessment of their comprehension and experience with the tool at hand in form of a 5-point likert scale as depicted in figure 8. After having completed all three condition blocks, we asked participants to provide feedback on the overall experience, what they liked and didn't like about the TVinsight App and for which types of programs they could imagine using it. After 7 to 8 days time we called participants via phone to answer 18 quick questions taken from the pool of comprehension test questions, but this time the questions were transformed into true/false statements.

Results

The selected documentaries contained a mean number of 839 words ($SD = 54$), from which our entity linking algorithm

extracted a total of 67 ($M = 22.3, SD = 2.5$) relevant and 9 ($M = 3, SD = 1$) irrelevant Wikipedia articles, resulting in a 88.2% hit rate.

The Benjamini-Hochberg procedure [16] was applied with a false discovery rate level of 0.05 to account for multiple testing.

Device Usage

Fig.7 shows the usage of both smartphone browser and TVInsight app split in content blocks, ad breaks, and post-documentary searches across all documentaries. TVinsight was used continuously more often than the browser ($\chi^2 = 25.7, p < 0.001$, Pearson's chi-squared test) which is statistically significant. During ad breaks the usage of the TVinsight app is significantly more pronounced than during the documentary ($\chi^2 = 7.1, p < 0.01$, Pearson's chi-squared test), the same holds for using the browser. Participants used TVInsight in 97% of ad breaks whereas only 80% used the browser during the first ad and 60% during the second.

Comprehension Scores

Fig.6 gives a detailed overview of the comprehension scores for each condition and documentary. Using the TVInsight app results in a statistically significant decrease in performance on the comprehension tests compared to no device usage ($t = 3.05, p < 0.003$, paired Student's t test) and to using the browser ($t = 2.57, p < 0.008$, paired Student's t test). Using the browser had no impact on the test scores compared to the baseline. Looking at the results by documentary, participants performed similarly between all three conditions on the first documentary, whereas the scores of the app users drop significantly on the other two conditions.

Subjective Feedback

Fig.8 lists the results of the likert-scale statements with participants' subjective feedback with regard to the tool available (Browser or TVInsight). When using TVInsight participants reported a better subjective comprehension of the program content than when using the smartphone's browser for searches. This difference was statistically significant (Mann-Whitney $U = 679, p < 0.001$). As with regard to ease of use, the app was rated significantly better than using the browser (Mann-Whitney $U = 782, p < 0.001$). Perceived distraction was significantly higher when using TVInsight than when the browser (Mann-Whitney $U = 829, p < 0.001$). When asked at the end of the study which tool (or no tool at all) they preferred for being able to answer the comprehension questions, 40% chose TVInsight and just 7% the browser.

Recall

Most participants left us their phone number with a preferred timeslot for being called for the final recall test a week after the study. We reached 20 out of 30 participants in the end. The percentage of correctly answered questions on the baseline condition dropped from 78% to 73% compared to a slight increase from 64% to 66% on condition C (TVinsight app). However, neither change on the recall scores was statistically significant.

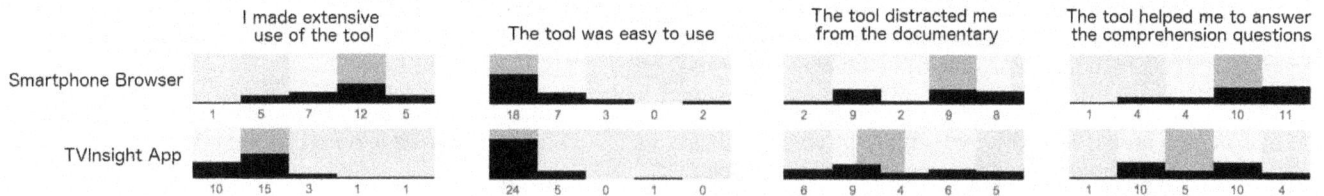

	I made extensive use of the tool	The tool was easy to use	The tool distracted me from the documentary	The tool helped me to answer the comprehension questions

Smartphone Browser

I made extensive use of the tool: 1 5 7 12 5

The tool was easy to use: 18 7 3 0 2

The tool distracted me from the documentary: 2 9 2 9 8

The tool helped me to answer the comprehension questions: 1 4 4 10 11

TVInsight App

I made extensive use of the tool: 10 15 3 1 1

The tool was easy to use: 24 5 0 1 0

The tool distracted me from the documentary: 6 9 4 6 5

The tool helped me to answer the comprehension questions: 1 10 5 10 4

Figure 8. Subjective assessment after each condition in form of 5-scale likert scales with *I totally agree* on the left and *I don't agree* on the right. The orange color depicts the median, yellow the interquatile area.

Qualitative Assessment

Overall, participants agreed that using real-time look-ups contributes to the user experience while watching TV. Especially the mechanism of delivering content right in time when the respective topic or person was mentioned on the program was positively mentioned in the interviews by 9 participants and 6 explicitly stated they liked that the app *"allows for quick results / access"*. The vast majority rated the app content as informative and well fitting, only 7% disagreed. The user interface was described by 12 participants as *"clearly structured"* and *"easy to use"*.

"Inappropriate topics" and "too few people entities" were the most common negative remarks made about the content. As things to improve participants mentioned a stronger integration of contents with regard to the Google search keywords. Instead of routing the user to the external browser application, search results should be directly integrated in the app, similar to the Wikipedia articles. Also, there is room for improvement with regard to personalization, e.g. through dynamic bookmarks or a customizable entity menu.

As to which types of programs participants could imagine TVInsight to be especially useful, documentaries were mentioned 21 times, quiz shows or news 8 times respectively, sports 4 times, and movies and entertainment 3 times. Rather inappropriate TV formats would be movies (mentioned 15 times), entertainment shows (3) or TV series (2).

DISCUSSION

Due to the size of our data corpus and our extended entity linking approach, articles extracted from Wikipedia were highly relevant as the hit rate of more than 88% confirmed. Also, participants overwhelmingly stated that articles were a good fit for the documentaries. The real-time aspect of proactively showing additional content with the current program was further well received, which created an overall positive TV experience when using TVInsight. Also, the content in the documentary turned out to be more relevant in order to answer the comprehension questions. As compared to traditional web searches with the smartphone browser, our second-screen app scored higher both in objective usage measure, but also in subjective ratings.

However, the extent of how to use the available tools was up to participants in order to self-select an optimal strategy for multitasking. This lead to an imbalance between browser and app usage with our app ending up being much more frequently used. Some participants barely used the browser for web searches which is why there are few measured differences between the use of no tools and the browser. One reason for rejecting the browser may be the fact that search keywords need to be formulated by the user whereas TVInsight continuously presents new keywords along with the current program. Hence, extended usage of TVInsight also took effect in the comprehension scores, which is why we need to reject our first hypothesis (*H1*). The objective comprehension scores therefore confirm the distracting nature of second-screen applications.

TVInsight was perceived as more distracting than the browser. However, this does not allow us to fully reject *H3*, especially due to the relative imbalance between app and browser usage. When there is no need to actively type and search for keywords, more time is spent in browsing available contents. Furthermore, users were not alerted to new second-screen content, it just appeared. Neate *et al.* [24] found that users would like to be actively notified of new content, preferably with an auditory icon or visual indicator on the TV itself. However, both methods are not feasible for independent second-screen apps with automatically generated content. The extensive usage may also be due to some novelty effect, which causes the app to be more appealing than the actual documentary. Long-term studies in real-world scenarios will be able to give more insights into the nature of distraction.

Since there was a tendency of increasing subjective comprehension of the TV content through our TVInsight app, we were able to confirm *H2*. This is certainly a reason why many participants found the app being helpful for completing the comprehension test. The well received app usability and the positive feedback regarding the real-time feature of proactively pushing additional content to the second-screen, benefited the overall user experience, which allows us to confirm *H4*; the content relevance and the notion of real-time delivery of additional content leads to a better user experience than using the smartphone browser for look-ups.

We performed the study on documentaries since they are a natural fit to observe learning effects from an educational standpoint. It should be noted, however, that our content extraction algorithm was not specifically optimized for documentaries. Rather, the training set was sourced from a variety of different program genres. Hence, it is reasonable to assume that the participants' ratings and opinions towards the displayed information generalizes to other types of programs.

The perceived distraction varied greatly which suggests that the capacity to multitask strongly depend on the individual user. Hence, users should be in control of adjusting information density and focus.

While many participants criticized irrelevant content, there was hardly any comment about missing topics. This indicates that precision is more important than recall when evaluating content retrieval algorithms for second screen use cases.

We were not able to detect any statistically significant differences between conditions with regard to the recall scores, but users of TVInsight tended to perform equally well in the direct comprehension tests and the recall test a week later. Participants using the browser or no tool at all, on the other hand, tended to perform worse in the recall than in the comprehension test. Further studies will need to be conducted to assess the long-term utility of TVInsight, especially when equipped with bookmarking features, where users could save or even share content as they watch it. We are further in the process of developing TVInsight with another focus on integrating audio fingerprinting for automatic channel recognition. This feature will be vital before further studies in the large can be conducted by releasing TVInsight on mobile app stores.

CONCLUSION

Second-screen apps have become increasingly popular in recent years. Instead of requiring users to install numerous different apps tailored to each of their favorite TV shows, we proposed a context-sensitive second-screen app that creates additional content automatically by linking existing resources and pushing that content to the user in real-time when it is most relevant. We therefore described an entity linking algorithm that extracts keywords from live subtitles and uses Wikipedia to provide additional program information. Having built a rich database with data from 30 TV stations over the course of 4 months, we were able to extract highly relevant content. The utility of the prototype was confirmed in a comprehensive user study where we investigated its effect on user experience and content comprehension. The resulting insights can be used by app developers to create second-screen apps that take advantage of existing content resources, and bear the potential to keep user distraction at a minimum by proactively providing content in a context-sensitive way. By constantly expanding the number of TV stations recorded by our server we are planning on refining our subtitle corpus in order to improve the entity linking and therefore the relevancy of the provided contents. Further resources can be linked, such as social network chatter, historical archives, current news articles, or product databases in order to provide users with a holistic second-screen experience.

ACKNOWLEDGMENTS

We thank the participants of our study. We further acknowledge the funding through the Future and Emerging Technologies (FET) programme within the 7th Framework Programme for Research of the European Commission, under FET grant number: 612933 (RECALL).

REFERENCES

1. ETS 300 706. 1997. Enhanced Teletext specification. (1997).

2. James Allan. 1995. *Automatic hypertext construction.* Technical Report. Cornell University.

3. Deni Basaraba, Paul Yovanoff, Julie Alonzo, and Gerald Tindal. 2013. Examining the structure of reading comprehension: do literal, inferential, and evaluative comprehension truly exist? *Reading and Writing* 26, 3 (2013), 349–379.

4. S Adam Brasel and James Gips. 2014. Enhancing television advertising: same-language subtitles can improve brand recall, verbal memory, and behavioral intent. *Journal of the Academy of Marketing Science* 42, 3 (2014), 322–336.

5. Katrin Busemann and Florian Tippelt. 2014. Second Screen: Parallelnutzung von Fernsehen und Internet. *Media Perspektiven* 7 (2014), 408–416.

6. Carlos Castillo, Gianmarco De Francisci Morales, and Ajay Shekhawat. 2013. Online Matching of Web Content to Closed Captions in IntoNow. In *Proceedings of the 36th International ACM SIGIR Conference on Research and Development in Information Retrieval (SIGIR '13).* ACM, New York, NY, USA, 1115–1116. DOI:http://dx.doi.org/10.1145/2484028.2484204

7. Yu-Ling Chuang, Chia-Wei Liao, Wen-Shiuan Chen, Wen-Tsung Chang, Shao-Hua Cheng, Yi-Chong Zeng, and Kai-Hsuan Chan. 2013. Use second screen to enhance TV viewing experiences. In *Cross-Cultural Design. Methods, Practice, and Case Studies.* Springer, 366–374.

8. The Nielsen Company. 2014. The Digital Consumer. *Online Resource.* (2014), 1–28.

9. Leon Cruickshank, Emmanuel Tsekleves, Roger Whitham, Annette Hill, and Kaoruko Kondo. 2007. Making interactive TV easier to use: Interface design for a second screen approach. *The Design Journal* 10, 3 (2007), 41–53.

10. Andras Csomai and Rada Mihalcea. 2008. Linking documents to encyclopedic knowledge. *Intelligent Systems, IEEE* 23, 5 (2008), 34–41.

11. Norberto Fernandez Garcia, Jesús Arias Fisteus, and Luis Sanchez Fernandez. 2014. Comparative evaluation of link-based approaches for candidate ranking in link-to-wikipedia systems. *Journal of Artificial Intelligence Research* (2014), 733–773.

12. Alexandre Fleury, Jakob Schou Pedersen, Mai Baunstrup, and Lars Bo Larsen. 2012. Interactive TV: Interaction and Control in Second-screen TV Consumption. In *10th European Interactive TV Conference.* 104–107.

13. David Geerts, Rinze Leenheer, Dirk De Grooff, Joost Negenman, and Susanne Heijstraten. 2014. In Front of

and Behind the Second Screen: Viewer and Producer Perspectives on a Companion App. In *Proceedings of the 2014 ACM International Conference on Interactive Experiences for TV and Online Video (TVX '14)*. ACM, New York, NY, USA, 95–102. DOI: http://dx.doi.org/10.1145/2602299.2602312

14. Google. 2012. The New Multi-screen World:Understanding Cross-platform Consumer Behavior. (2012).

15. Abdolmajid Hayati and Firooz Mohmedi. 2011. The effect of films with and without subtitles on listening comprehension of EFL learners. *British Journal of Educational Technology* 42, 1 (2011), 181–192.

16. Yosef Hochberg and Yoav Benjamini. 1995. Controlling the False Discovery Rate : a Practical and Powerful Approach to Multiple Testing. *Journal of the Royal Statistical Society. Series B (Methodological)* 57, 1 (1995), 289–300.

17. Christian Holz, Frank Bentley, Karen Church, and Mitesh Patel. 2015. "I'M Just on My Phone and They'Re Watching TV": Quantifying Mobile Device Use While Watching Television. In *Proceedings of the ACM International Conference on Interactive Experiences for TV and Online Video (TVX '15)*. ACM, New York, NY, USA, 93–102. DOI: http://dx.doi.org/10.1145/2745197.2745210

18. Niels Janssen and Horacio A Barber. 2012. Phrase frequency effects in language production. *PLoS ONE7* (2012).

19. Emmanuel Keuleers, Marc Brysbaert, and Boris New. 2010. SUBTLEX-NL: A new measure for Dutch word frequency based on film subtitles. *Behavior research methods* 42, 3 (2010), 643–650.

20. Geza Kovacs. 2013. Smart Subtitles for Language Learning. In *CHI '13 Extended Abstracts on Human Factors in Computing Systems (CHI EA '13)*. ACM, New York, NY, USA, 2719–2724. DOI: http://dx.doi.org/10.1145/2468356.2479499

21. Christos Makris, Yannis Plegas, and Evangelos Theodoridis. 2013. Improved Text Annotation with Wikipedia Entities. In *Proceedings of the 28th Annual ACM Symposium on Applied Computing (SAC '13)*. ACM, New York, NY, USA, 288–295. DOI: http://dx.doi.org/10.1145/2480362.2480425

22. Holger Mitterer and James M McQueen. 2009. Foreign subtitles help but native-language subtitles harm foreign speech perception. *PloS one* 4, 11 (2009), e7785.

23. Abhishek Nandakumar and Janet Murray. 2014. Companion Apps for Long Arc TV Series: Supporting New Viewers in Complex Storyworlds with Tightly Synchronized Context-sensitive Annotations. In *Proceedings of the 2014 ACM International Conference on Interactive Experiences for TV and Online Video (TVX '14)*. ACM, New York, NY, USA, 3–10. DOI: http://dx.doi.org/10.1145/2602299.2602317

24. Timothy Neate, Matt Jones, Michael Evans, and R Bbc. 2015. Mediating Attention for Second Screen Companion Content. In *Proceedings of the 33rd Annual ACM Conference on Human Factors in Computing Systems (CHI '15)*. ACM, New York, NY, USA, 3103–3106. DOI: http://dx.doi.org/10.1145/2702123.2702278

25. Boris New, Marc Brysbaert, Jean Veronis, and Christophe Pallier. 2007. The use of film subtitles to estimate word frequencies. *Applied Psycholinguistics* 28, 04 (2007), 661–677.

26. Daan Odijk, Edgar Meij, and Maarten de Rijke. 2013. Feeding the Second Screen: Semantic Linking Based on Subtitles. In *Proceedings of the 10th Conference on Open Research Areas in Information Retrieval (OAIR '13)*. Le Centre de Hautes Etudes Internationales D'Iinformatique Documentaire, Paris, France, France, 9–16. http://dl.acm.org/citation.cfm?id=2491748.2491751

27. José Luis Redondoio Garcia, Laurens De Vocht, Raphael Troncy, Erik Mannens, and Rik Van de Walle. 2014. Describing and Contextualizing Events in TV News Show. In *Proceedings of the 23rd International Conference on World Wide Web (WWW '14 Companion)*. ACM, New York, NY, USA, 759–764. DOI:http://dx.doi.org/10.1145/2567948.2579326

28. Scott Robertson, Cathleen Wharton, Catherine Ashworth, and Marita Franzke. 1996. Dual Device User Interface Design: PDAs and Interactive Television. In *Proceedings of the SIGCHI Conference on Human Factors in Computing Systems (CHI '96)*. ACM, New York, NY, USA, 79–86. DOI: http://dx.doi.org/10.1145/238386.238408

29. Wei Shen, Jianyong Wang, and Jiawei Han. 2015. Entity linking with a knowledge base: Issues, techniques, and solutions. *Knowledge and Data Engineering, IEEE Transactions on* 27, 2 (2015), 443–460.

30. Aaron Smith and Jan Lauren Boyles. 2012. The rise of the connected viewer. *Pew Internet & American Life Project* (2012).

31. Anna Van Cauwenberge, Gabi Schaap, and Rob Van Roy. 2014. TV no longer commands our full attention: Effects of second-screen viewing and task relevance on cognitive load and learning from news. *Computers in Human Behavior* 38 (2014), 100–109.

GameBridge: Converging Toward a Transmedia Storytelling Experience through Gameplay

Rachel Miles[1], Arielle Cason[2], Larry Chan[2], Jing Li[3], Ryan McDonnell[1], Janet Murray[1], Zixuan Wang[1]

Digital Media[1]
Georgia Institute of Technology
Atlanta, Georgia, USA

Human Computer Interaction[2]
Georgia Institute of Technology
Atlanta, Georgia, USA

China Central Television[3]
State Administration of Press, Publication, Radio, Film and Television, Beijing, China

rachelmiles@gatech.edu, ariellecason@gmail.com, larrychan@gatech.edu, lieli1@qq.com, rpmcd@gatech.edu, jmurray@gatech.edu, wangzixuan@gatech.edu

ABSTRACT
Transmedia storytelling enables a narrative to traverse various media platforms in order to create a richer storyworld. To achieve this goal, our group envisioned a product called *GameBridge*, which builds upon the concept of transmedia storytelling by implementing a cross-platform narrative. For our prototype, we decided to take the television show *Game of Thrones* and the corresponding book series, *A Song of Ice and Fire*, to create a game using content from both media to form our own storyline. By using both the television show and the book series, *GameBridge* creates a convergence point between the two media and allows the interactor to have agency of the story through gameplay. In the future, this model could be recreated with any storyworld that is told through various media, including movies.

Author Keywords
Expressive interaction; interactive narrative; television; genre fiction; dramatic agency.

ACM Classification Keywords
H.5.2. Information interfaces and presentation: User Interfaces—*input devices* and *strategies, interaction styles*; K.8 [Personal Computing]: *Games*.

INTRODUCTION AND BACKGROUND
Long-form narrative television shows such as *Game of Thrones*, cause viewers to feel eagerness and anticipation while waiting for the network to release new episodes. Jason Mittel discusses the spectrum of closure that modern television shows invoke. Some abrupt endings are extra-textually motivated (the network pulls the plug on the show),

while others involve careful strategizing of the writers [8]. However an ending may occur, it entices viewers to learn more about the show.

Learning more about the show may include discussing theories on Twitter, exploring a show's wiki, or talking to friends — the developing digital world gives interactors a plethora of opportunities to delve into a story. Moreover, through the variety of media available, there is not just one place to consume a story. With the breadth of resources available on the Internet, "fans now expect to see not just repetition of the familiar story elements, but an elaboration with additional information" [11]. To satisfy this expectation, we developed a model to provide the viewers a chance for further immersion into the storyworld that we have dubbed *GameBridge*. This is accomplished by providing cumulative comprehension through interactive narrative in conjunction with a television series.

GameBridge builds upon the concept of transmedia storytelling by implementing a cross-platform narrative. According to Henry Jenkins, "transmedia storytelling expands what can be known about a particular fictional world while dispersing that information" [5] (Figure 1). Currently, the entertainment industry *adapts* story information across different media. For instance, movies are often based on books, video games, or true stories; however, the majority of these cases are adaptations, rather than a different way aspect of the story and a dispersion of information. For instance, *Lord of the Rings* adapts J.R.R. Tolkien's acclaimed book series, but the core story remains the same and information is not dispersed.

If narratives in media were to explain each other, we would call that relationship "reciprocal explanation." *GameBridge* explores the design considerations associated with implementing reciprocal explanation. For our prototype, we decided to take the television show *Game of Thrones* and the corresponding book series, *A Song of Ice and Fire*, to create a

Permission to make digital or hard copies of all or part of this work for personal or classroom use is granted without fee provided that copies are not made or distributed for profit or commercial advantage and that copies bear this notice and the full citation on the first page. Copyrights for components of this work owned by others than ACM must be honored. Abstracting with credit is permitted. To copy otherwise, or republish, to post on servers or to redistribute to lists, requires prior specific permission and/or a fee. Request permissions from permissions@acm.org.

TVX 2016, June 22–24, 2016, Chicago, IL, USA.
© 2016 ACM ISBN 978-1-4503-4067-0/16/06...$15.00.
http://dx.doi.org/10.1145/2932206.2932209

game using content from both media to form our own storyline.

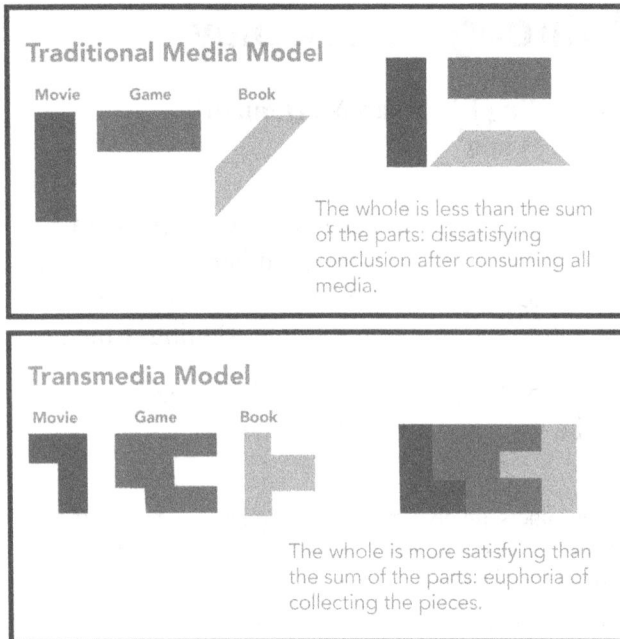

Figure 1: Adapted from *Transmedia Storyteller*

GameBridge differs from other transmedia storytelling examples in that the game is inter-episodic, a game episode is released after each television show episode. As opposed to *Castle*, *X-Files*, and *Community*, which all continued the story across media, *GameBridge* has a separate narrative that does not interfere with the show or books, but still connects back to the main story. In other words, the narratives of both the television show and the game evolve in tandem as opposed to after one medium has ended or as brand extension. Contrastingly, the TellTale *Game of Thrones* game episodes are released on an independent time schedule to the television show. Other franchises, such as *The Hunger Games*, combines transmedia with marketing to generate excitement for fans. *The Hunger Games* marketing campaign generated advertisements and web campaigns containing characters and imagery from the series. On the other hand, the movie is an adaptation of the book series, not telling a different aspect of the storyworld.

By using both the television show and the book series, *GameBridge* creates a convergence point between the two media and allows the interactor to have narrative control of the storyworld in order to increase the phenomena of reciprocal explanation and improved comprehension.

Because the show and the books diverge in later seasons, we built our game around an event in both season two and book two. The goal of the game is to create emotional connections to minor characters with little on-screen development in order to foster deeper empathy. In this way, the game is for fans "not content with just passing through and commenting on the story." Instead, fans can "move into the storyworld and play a more active role in the plot" [9].

As Janet Murray states, "like the language in film and TV, the language of video games is now transparent to us and can be employed to enter more deeply and empathetically into a wider range of human experience" [12]. Increasingly, the convergence of digital television with websites, social media, and games has taught viewers to become accustomed to playing games. As a cultural practice, games afford players a different experience than that of film and television, exemplified by "the pleasure we find in synchronizing our behavior with one another" [3].

In this project, our game is an alternate method of storytelling to make players interact with the story, rather than observe it onscreen or in print. The game can be played several times and gives players opportunities to make their own decisions and explore possibilities of the story. When players participate in the game, they have dramatic agency in the story, which they could not experience when watching or reading the series. In this way, the interactors have the freedom to create a personalized story within the framework *GameBridge* creates.

RELATED WORK

After we identified our key goal of creating an interactive narrative that supplements existing narrative, we researched other digital artifacts that accomplish similar goals. We looked at Pottermore, *Blood and Laurels*, and two games by TellTale Games. Although Pottermore and *Blood and Laurels* both contain useful features, we learned the most from TellTale Games.

Telltale Games rose to popularity with *The Walking Dead*, a game that mimics the style of the original comic book series with the dramatic storytelling elements from the television show. The game combines "choose-your-own adventure" with a cinematic experience—the player has a limited time to make a choice as she watches the action unfold. Based on the decisions, minor changes happen in the game that affect the outcome of the interactor's experience. Interactors of the game call the decision-making process "the illusion of choice - as in what we're doing or saying really doesn't matter because it all nets out relatively the same." But other reviews counter that point, saying that the game "is like a coloring book: we each have the same black and white sketch, but it's up to us to fill it in as we see fit" [7].

TellTale Games also created a *Game of Thrones* companion game, which we researched closely and used as the overall inspiration for our prototype. In the game, the player experiences the world through the eyes of various members of House Forrester, a family briefly mentioned in the book series and not referenced in the show.

Figure 2: *TellTale's Game of Thrones* – Left to right: Margaery Tyrell, Cersei Lannister, Mira Forrester, and Sera Flowers

TellTale's *Game of Thrones* creates a cinematic quality experience that heightens excitement and immersion into the show, in much the same was as *The Walking Dead* game does. However, TellTale's *Game of Thrones* does not forge deeper connections with interactors to established characters on the show. While this works for this game, our concept involves the creation of the storyline for the show and game in tandem.

For instance, if the protagonist of the game interacts with a main character from the series, it is to further the interests of House Forrester, not to learn about the character. For instance, one of the family members is Mira Forrester, a handmaiden to Margaery Tyrell. Throughout the game, Mira interacts with Margaery, Cersei Lannister, and Tyrion Lannister, all important and major characters in the show (Figure 2). Mira must plead with Margaery to intercede with Joffrey, her betrothed, on her family's behalf. In turn, Mira makes deals with the Lannisters to protect her family. These interactions do not significantly build deeper characterization of these characters. Instead, the interactions enhance the storyline for House Forrester. Contrastingly, a main goal of our prototype is increasing emotional connections with the existing characters in the series.

TellTale's *Game of Thrones* enables the player to play the "game of thrones," or in other words, try to survive in the cutthroat world in which the story takes place. In this manner, the game accomplishes the transmedia component of immersively experiencing the storyworld. However, in *GameBridge* the choices the interactor makes affect the outcome of the minor characters rather than invented characters. In TellTale's *Game of Thrones*, the interactor is given the illusion of agency because the choices they make do not actually affect whether a character in the game survives. The decisions in TellTale's *Game of Thrones* only affect minor gameplay elements.

Each of the artifacts we researched informed the way in which we designed our game. From the criticism that *Blood & Laurels* lacked visual appeal, we decided to go with the visual novel style for games, which contains the "choose your own adventure" conventions, but involves visually appealing artwork. We learned from the clunky interface of the original Pottermore site that a steep learning curve affects overall enjoyment and satisfaction. Through the TellTale Games, we saw how decision-making heightens involvement and anticipation; however, we also saw that users were not as satisfied having the "illusion of choice." Therefore, we decided to build a prototype taking the feedback for other artifacts and creating something unique—a game where the player interacts with the characters in the show, but has true agency over her or his storyline.

SCENARIO AND GAME DEVELOPMENT

We invented a hypothetical media scenario for *Game of Thrones* to demonstrate the implementation of reciprocal explanation when writers coordinate narratives across media. In our hypothetical scenario, the stories for the television series and for a video game had been written together and had built upon events from the books.

Figure 3: Brienne removes her helmet for the first time, revealing her identity as a woman.

After much consideration, we decided to focus our prototype around an event in season two of *Game of Thrones* because the show and the books had not diverged at this point in the narrative. The gameplay occurs between two episodes of the show, making it the perfect example of our concept. We focused on the relationship between Brienne of Tarth and Renly Baratheon. Brienne of Tarth is an unusual character within the series. She is described as an abnormally tall, fairly unattractive woman who has decided to don armor and fight, rather than assume the role of a lady. Meanwhile, Renly Baratheon recently declared himself king and is fighting to gain the Iron Throne, which would mean that he is king of the whole realm. The complication arises because there are four other self-declared kings fighting for the throne as well.

The show introduces Brienne to the viewers after she has bested Loras—the Lord Commander of Renly's Kingsguard—in a tournament. Brienne shocks the tournament's onlookers when she removes her helmet and reveals herself as a woman (Figure 3). Renly offers Brienne a boon, or asks that she makes a victor's request and he will grant it. She surprises everyone by asking to be part of his kingsguard, or his knightly bodyguards. There is a collective gasp in the crowd, but after a moment of deliberation Renly announces, "Done!" and Brienne joins his kingsguard.

There are a few scenes in the same episode where the viewer can spot Brienne in the background fulfilling her role as a member of the kingsguard. In the following episode, Renly's brother, Stannis, appears behind Renly, in the form of a shadowy apparition, and literally stabs him in the back. Brienne's heart-wrenching grief at Renly's murder may cause confusion to a viewer who has not read the books because she had only been introduced briefly in the show and seems to not know Renly very well. When, in fact, they knew each other previously.

Our game takes place before the episode in which Brienne is introduced. The interactor explores Renly's camp as Mirelda, a spy for Baelish, who is a master of deception and secrecy. Mirelda does not exist in the show or in the books, so we have complete control over her character development. Through Mirelda's interactions with other characters in the camp, she learns the backstory of Brienne and Renly's relationship. After the interactor has played the game, the interactor understands Brienne's character and why she is so upset when Renly dies—because they knew each other from before.

The game introduces Brienne in a way that allows the interactor to make an immediate connection to her when she appears on the show, but does not reveal future plot points. In other words, while learning her backstory is a goal of the game, the story centers around the interactor gathering information and exploring the war camp, thus heightening overall immersion.

In the ideal narrative development, the game and the show would be strategically written in order to introduce a character to create the best, overall comprehension.

PROTOTYPE

A primary focus of *GameBridge* is to explore the potential of interactive narrative to provide continuous additive rewards throughout a television season, reinforcing the transmedia concept of the "whole is more satisfying than the sum of its parts" (Figure 1). Neil Young's concept of "additive comprehension" represents a key design objective in that knowledge of the story universe becomes richer through consuming related media. In this case, watching the show and playing the game creates a richer narrative experience [6].

We decided to use a visual novel format (Figure 4), which gives us the ability to give an interactor agency, but also allows us to clearly define the scenario that the interactor experiences. The visual novel is a dialogue driven form of interactive narrative that enables players to determine the narrative by choosing from a selection of predefined choices (Figure 5). We used the application TyranoBuilder Visual Studio to create our prototype.

Although we decided to use the visual novel format for our prototype, other interactive formats could also be used to satisfy the goal of creating this convergence point.

Figure 4: Introductory scene in our prototype where Baelish assigns the mission to the interactor.

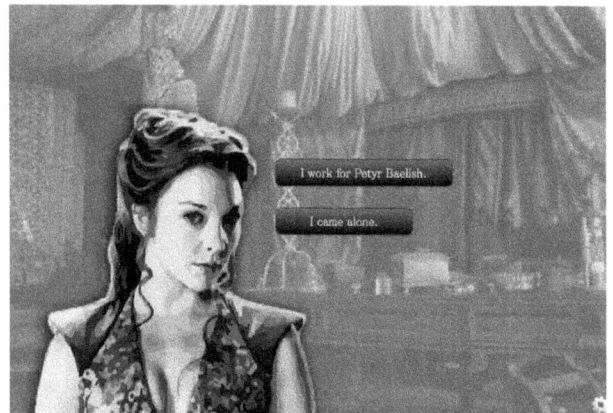

Figure 5: Player has dialogue choices to determine the future of the character.

For example, the player might simply be presented with options for wagering on the outcome of the melee tournament where Brienne defeats Loras. This interaction could be designed to demonstrate specifically that defeating Loras is highly unlikely and a viewer could be led to a higher appreciation for the magnitude of Brienne's martial accomplishment.

We chose to build upon the experience of additive comprehension primarily by focusing on the relationship between two characters, Renly and Brienne. In the moment they are introduced in the series, these characters appear to be strangers to each other. However, in the book series and in an episode that aired three seasons later, the interactor learns about a past relationship between the two characters where Renly showed kindness to Brienne in a moment of great humiliation. This single event produces additive comprehension by illuminating the initial introduction of Brienne as well as providing insight into her character for the rest of the series. Revealing this event, before the characters are introduced, adds novel material for interpreting the motivations of multiple characters in two pivotal scenes: when Renly and Brienne are reunited and when he is killed while in her protection.

Additionally, the *Game of Thrones* storyworld has many complex plotlines so discovering the characters through an alternative viewpoint allows for a rich expansion of the narrative. Using *Game of Thrones* as a test case provides a rich area of exploration of this topic due to the unique morality exhibited in the show, mainly its lack of interest in keeping popular characters alive. This is exemplified by a quote from the character Cersei Lannister, "in the game of thrones, you either live or you die" (Season 1, Episode 7). Following the morality of the show decreases the chance that players will feel disconnected from the storyworld.

In 1998, Janet Murray "offered the term 'hyperserial' to describe the kind of storytelling that I [she] expected to be fostered by the movement of television to digital delivery and the advent of the web" [11]. Thus, as she predicted, "in a well-conceived hyperserial, all the minor characters would be potential protagonists of their own stories, thus providing alternate threads within the enlarged story web" [9]. *GameBridge* takes a step in that direction where the minor characters have alternate threads in our prototype that increase comprehension for the story web.

TESTING
Planning

In order to understand how to carry out our vision, we needed to test both of these goals by conducting a preliminary usability test of the early prototype, which would provide us with a formative evaluation of the prototype.

We decided on a within-subject test because we knew our sample size would be under 10 users. Because of this small pool, we did not have the luxury of assuming that person-to-person variations in rankings or opinion would "wash out" toward some average; for instance, one user could give the game terrible reviews and another could give great reviews. However, the average scoring of two user perspectives was not the key goal in our usability testing. We were looking for overall comprehension of the *Game of Thrones* storyworld. Specifically, we were interested in comparing how one person's review of the *Game of Thrones* franchise changes based on playing our game.

We decided that, because *Game of Thrones* has so many evolving plot points, we needed a "refresher course" for our users before playing our game. To accomplish this, we used a video that reviewed the major plot points going on in the episodes immediately surrounding our prototype. Since our game was meant to be played after season 2, episode 2, we showed users a highlight reel of relevant scenes during the user testing. This method also allowed us to test with users who were not fans of *Game of Thrones*.

To test an increase in emotional investment, we decided on a qualitative ranking evaluation using the Positive and Negative Affect Schedule (PANAS) method. This method asks users to rank how strongly they feel certain emotions like "interested" or "distressed." Users completed the PANAS test twice, once before playing our game and once again after. To test usability, we used the System Usability Scale (SUS) which asks to rank their agreement with 10 statements such as, "I found this system unnecessarily complex." In order to test both comprehension and the intangible connections our users made between the prototype and the *Game of Thrones* universe, we used qualitative questions throughout the study; some coming up organically during gameplay and others planned as summary questions for post-gameplay.

Usability Testing

The same testing protocol was used for every participant, but each participant had a different moderator who was part of the *GameBridge* prototype development team. Moderators attempted to very closely rely on the testing script to increase validity between subjects. Some of the tests were completed in person, with the moderator and participant sitting side by side and viewing the game, while others were conducted remotely, with the moderator sharing the video and game URL with the participant and watching the participant's screen through screen sharing software.

While most of the tests allowed for strictly following a script, the usability test specifically allowed moderators the freedom to deviate. This was the biggest flaw in our user testing, as each moderator had a different style. Some explicitly requested a lot of user feedback, while other moderators allowed the user to decide when they'd give feedback, which could be very sparse at times.

Another variation in data between moderators had to do with language. Two of our moderators and two of our participants were not native English speakers, which led to a few misunderstandings of the script's questions, as well as some misunderstandings of the answers users gave. On the whole, though, this multi-linguistic testing style was valuable in that it also allowed different cultural viewpoints to be represented in the findings.

Results

After analyzing the results of our tests, we feel that we had a useful variety of users test our game (Figure 6). Because of this, we were able to learn much through user testing and modify our prototype based off of the feedback.

Age	Gamer?	Fan?
19	Yes	Yes, seasons 1-4
20	Yes	Yes, seasons 1-5
22	No	No
23	No	No
27	No	Yes, seasons 1-5 and books 1-3
36	No	Yes, seasons 1-4

Figure 6: The breakdown of our users in age, whether or not they consider themselves a gamer, and whether they consider themselves a fan of the show.

Due to our modifications based off of the feedback through usability testing, the prototype that we tested has a few major differences between the final version of our prototype. In the prototype that we tested, the game took place between the episode in which Brienne was introduced and the episode where Renly dies. Additionally, Mirelda was a concubine rather than a spy to Baelish. Moreover, our some of our visuals were high fidelity and others were low fidelity, which led to some confusion among users who were surprised by the differences.

PANAS: Positive and Negative Affect Measures

The PANAS test revealed the users' positive affect, or emotional experience, increased after playing our game, and their negative affect decreased (Figure 7).

	PANAS Average	Game Before	Game After
Positive Affect	29.7	20.83333333	23
Negative Affect	14.8	15.5	11.11666667

Figure 7: Based on our findings, emotional connection increased after playing the game and apathetic reactions decreased.

This finding is very valuable in that it confirms our hypothesis that this game will help users feel more emotionally invested in the *Game of Thrones* universe, due to the marked increase in positive affect after playing the game and the decrease after playing the game.

SUS: System Usability Scale

Our average	67.5
SUS average	68

Figure 8: Usability was just under the average, showing that we needed to improve our prototype.

Based on the SUS results, we scored just below the SUS average (Figure 8). This was to be expected, though, as our testing prototype was still transitioning from low fidelity to high fidelity. We expected to continue iterating based on the usability test's feedback.

Qualitative Feedback Summary

The feedback our users provided outside of the quantitative rankings was very valuable. Their overall impressions, their moments of confusion, and their questions were all revealing. The most common feedback we found includes:

1. No clear call to action on the opening screen. Users weren't sure where to click to "get started."

2. Questions about the character: Users wanted more information about who they were playing as in the

game world. These questions included, "Am I someone from the clip?" and "Who am I here?"

3. Sexuality: Users were taken aback at the overt sexuality in the game. This included the fact that their character was a "concubine," or a prostitute, as well as the sexualized dialogue between characters.

4. Transitions and scenes: Users could become confused about where they were in the game, who they were talking to, and what their mission was. Subtlety in any form was easy to miss in this format and users' memory wasn't reliable for either details or larger plot points unless overt explanations were provided.

5. Fidelity: Users expected the images, both characters and background images, to be a higher fidelity and quality. They made assumptions about characters' importance based on fidelity that the designers didn't anticipate.

6. 3/6 users said they were more likely to watch Game of Thrones after playing our game than they had said before playing our game. The other 3 said they were very likely before and still very likely after. No users were less likely to watch the show after playing our game.

7. 4/6 said they would play a game like this, while 2/6 said they would not.

DESIGN CONCLUSIONS

Based on the usability testing, we modified our prototype to address the concerns the users expressed. We updated the art style to create a more cohesive and visually pleasing design throughout the gameplay. In order to maximize additive comprehension, we shifted the episode placement to be before Brienne was introduced, to create an emotional impact not only when Brienne is revealed, but also when she is heartbroken at Renly's death.

Based upon the user feedback of discomfort while playing as a concubine, we changed the dialogue options to allow the player to decide to merely be a spy or also utilize the option of exercising power through the character's sexuality. The latter option often happens in the storyworld. Because the society of *Game of Thrones* is so patriarchal, women find outlets for power in varied ways. Sometimes through their sexuality and also other means. It provides the opportunity for a larger discussion of sexuality as a whole.

Through our researching and findings, we have formulated several design strategies for future work. Games should be:

- Realized between episodes and reveal additional story depth.
- A brief engagement with dramatic agency – not too lengthy.

- Parallel action, referencing the main story, but does not disrupt continuity.
- Reinforcing immersion with the main plot, but not competing with it.

These design strategies should inform future iterations of the *GameBridge* project in order to create a more comprehensive, transmedia experience.

FUTURE WORK

While the prototype provides players with a single narrative thread, a final version of *GameBridge* will interweave narrative threads to create a rich, expansive landscape that reflects a more "novelistic canvas" [4]. Through that experience, the interactor would enjoy the participatory affordance of the digital medium: the ability to determine experience by selecting certain story elements and skipping the rest [10].

Future of iterations of the game could provide the interactor with the option of additional characters to play through diverging storylines as well as multiple dialogue options that affect the overall storyline. By utilizing another platform for gameplay, the visuals in the game could provide players with cues of what to do along with bringing the characters in the game to life through the expressive nature that a detailed cinematic-style game affords.

In the process of creating the prototype, we discovered the requirements and restrictions involved in creating an interactive complement to an existing narrative. Although using an existing series allowed us to focus on design, we had to treat the narrative of the television show as a canonical text. Therefore, we had to be careful to avoid violating existing character depictions. To more accurately test design constraints in the future, an interactive narrative of this nature should be designed as an integral part of the canon from the story's inception.

In the future, this model could be recreated with any storyworld that is told through various media, including movies. An ideal transmedia scenario of *GameBridge* would involve the story developers designing a comprehensive storyworld that spreads across various media: novels, television episodes, movies, and games. The games would create a convergence point between various in order create a richer experience through dramatic agency.

All in all, "when the medium itself melts into transparency, we will be lost in the make believe and care only about the story" [9]. When this happens, then we know that we have achieved our goal.

ACKNOWLEDGMENTS

We thank Janet Murray, Pedro Silva, Mariam Nazripour, and the rest of our fellow classmates in the Experimental Television Lab at Georgia Tech for their help in developing our idea and prototype.

REFERENCES

1. Bruner, J. S. Acts of Meaning. Harvard University Press, 1990.

2. Herman, D. Story logic: Problems and possibilities of narrative. University of Nebraska Press, 2004.

3. Jenkins, H. Inventing the Digital Medium: An Interview with Janet Murray (Part One), on *Confessions of an Aca-Fan: The Official Weblog of Henry Jenkins.* (August 1, 2011).
http://henryjenkins.org/2012/02/an_interview_with_janet_murray.html

4. Jenkins, H. Transmedia 202: Further Reflections, on *Confessions of an Aca-Fan: The Official Weblog of Henry Jenkins.* (August 1, 2011).
http://henryjenkins.org/2011/08/defining_transmedia_further_re.html

5. Jenkins, H. Transmedia Storytelling 101: Further Reflections, on *Confessions of an Aca-Fan: The Official Weblog of Henry Jenkins.* (March 22, 2007).
http://henryjenkins.org/2011/08/defining_transmedia_further_re.html

6. Jenkins, H. Convergence culture: Where old and new media collide. NYU press, 2006.

7. Miller, G. The Walking Dead: The Game Review, on IGN. (Dec 12, 2012)
http://www.ign.com/articles/2012/12/12/the-walking-dead-the-game-review

8. Mittel, J. Complex TV: The Poetics of Contemporary Television Storytelling. NYU Press, 2015.

9. Murray, J.H. Hamlet on the Holodeck: The Future of Narrative in Cyberspace. Free Press, 1997.

10. Murray, J.H. Inventing the Medium: Principles of Interaction Design as a Cultural Practice. MIT Press, 2011.

11. Murray, J.H. Transcending Transmedia: Emerging Story Telling Structures for the Emerging Convergence Platforms. (July 4, 2012).

12. Murray, J.H. Future of Storytelling/Dramatic Agency on *Inventing the Medium.* (September 22, 2015).
http://inventingthemedium.com/2015/09/22/future-of-storytelling-dramatic-agency/

13. Turner, M. The literary mind: The origins of thought and language. (1998).

Practical UX Research Methodologies

Sarah E. Garcia

UEGroup

1165 Lincoln Avenue, Suite 221

San Jose, CA 95125 USA

sarah@uegroup.com

Permission to make digital or hard copies of part or all of this work for personal or classroom use is granted without fee provided that copies are not made or distributed for profit or commercial advantage and that copies bear this notice and the full citation on the first page. Copyrights for third-party components of this work must be honored. For all other uses, contact the Owner/Author.

Copyright is held by the owner/author(s).

TVX'16, June 22-24, 2016, Chicago, IL, USA

ACM 978-1-4503-4067-0/16/06.

http://dx.doi.org/10.1145/2932206.2932417

Abstract

Half-Day course on the practical research methods used to understand the changing technology climate within television and online media. Experts from UEGroup, a Silicon Valley research and design company, will lead an interactive discussion and give practical suggestions for developing methodologies including: Ethnography, Out of Box Experiences, and Usability Testing.

Author Keywords

User Experience; Research Methodologies; UX; Media Studies; Ethnography; Out of Box Experience; OOBE; Usability Testing; Benchmark Studies; Interactive

ACM Classification Keywords

Measurement; Human Factors; Algorithms; Verification

Overview of Research Methods

A brief lecture on the different research methods used for understanding the changing technology landscape across all industries, with an emphasis on television and online media.

Key Takeaways:

- Brief overview of the main research methods available (Expert Review, Focus Groups, Ethnography, Out of Box Experience Research, Usability Testing, Benchmark Testing, Quantitative Studies, Customer Experience Studies, Personas)

- Learn how to apply the right methodologies to answer the right questions.

Ethnography

General overview on how to create ethnographic research plans aimed at observing actual users in their technology saturated lives, focusing on environments where media is most often consumed. Tips will be given for structuring ethnographic visits to allow for useful discussion and observations. Attendees will learn how to make use of diaries and other interceptive methods to augment the ethnographic visits.

Key Takeaways:

- Brief overview of different ethnographic approaches and how to approach a plan for conducting ethnographic research.

- Techniques for ensuring getting the most out of ethnographic visits

- Understanding how to extend the learning past the initial visit (follow-up diary studies, interviews, interceptive data gathering, and keeping the participants engaged).

Out of Box Experiences

Learning how to create OOBE testing plans that lead to an understanding of branding messages, set-up process, pain points, the overall initial experience, and understanding how expectations are met. Product focus will include streaming media devices as well as traditional set top box experiences. Qualitative, as well as, quantitative recording methods will be discussed.

Key Takeaways:

- Brief overview of definition of an OOBE, and a discussion on the different ways of running an OOBE

- Understanding what elements to record and include in an OOBE study (expectations, branding messages, time on task, observations, areas of confusion or delight, attention to instructions, etc.).

- Learning how to creating a realistic environment in the lab.

Usability Testing

Learning how to prepare testing plans that produce an understanding of the usability of media interfaces across multiple devices. Attendees will learn how to structure a testing plan that can be leveraged across multiple device platforms.

Key Takeaways:

- Brief overview of types of usability testing and ways to incorporate a variety of devices.

- Understanding what metrics are available for recording and the tradeoffs in user testing for each (first impressions, observations, errors, time on task, number of steps, moderator help, success, frustrations and delights, ratings).

- Learning how to put together a benchmark study that compares multiple brands, devices and versions. Attendees will learn how to consider the main objective of the study and write a testing plan that allows for a fair comparison across brands and devices.

- Learning how to creating a realistic environment in the lab, and techniques for moderating a fruitful session, and keeping the participant engaged and comfortable.

Course Presenter:

Sarah Garcia is UEGroup's Senior Lead Researcher with a background in market and user experience research. Sarah's experience with UX research is extensive, ranging from consultancy work with Disney Interactive Media and a large-scale benchmark study with DirecTV to groundbreaking medical research for companies such as Boston Scientific and Stryker. Sarah is experienced with on screen and device usability, developing innovative testing methodologies and training while mentoring other UEGroup staff for the past 10 years.

About UEGroup

UEGroup is a User Experience and Design company in Silicon Valley that has established long term relationships with leaders in the entertainment and digital media field, medical, consumer electronics, gaming and handheld industries.

Incorporating Kids and Teens into UX Research

Sarah E. Garcia
UEGroup
1165 Lincoln Avenue, Suite 221
San Jose, CA 95125 USA
sarah@uegroup.com

Permission to make digital or hard copies of part or all of this work for personal or classroom use is granted without fee provided that copies are not made or distributed for profit or commercial advantage and that copies bear this notice and the full citation on the first page. Copyrights for third-party components of this work must be honored. For all other uses, contact the Owner/Author.
Copyright is held by the owner/author(s).

TVX 2016, June 22–24, 2016, Chicago, IL, USA
ACM 978-1-4503-4067-0/16/06.
http://dx.doi.org/10.1145/2932206.2932418

Abstract

Half day course on the unique needs of television and media UX research with kids and teens. When we think of UX participants, we typically think of adults, but there is a growing generation of kids and teens who are bypassing their parents in their tech savviness and making their own decisions regarding television and media purchases. For companies thinking ahead to new technologies or wanting to target this demographic, it makes sense to include the insight of their young audience who will soon question, "why wouldn't I do it that way?"

Kids testing and UX research can be fun and insightful, but poses a unique set of challenges. In this session, we'll learn which methodologies work best for kids and some practical tools for making the most out of our time with them.

Author Keywords

User Experience; Research Methodologies; UX; Media Studies; Ethnography; Out of Box Experience; OOBE; Usability Testing; Children's Testing; Kid's Testing; Interactive

ACM Classification Keywords

Measurement; Human Factors; Algorithms; Verification

Course Presenter:

Sarah Garcia is UEGroup's Senior Lead Researcher with a background in market and user experience research. Sarah's experience with UX research is extensive, ranging from consultancy work with Disney Interactive Media and a large-scale benchmark study with DirecTV to groundbreaking medical research for companies such as Boston Scientific and Stryker. Sarah is experienced with on screen and device usability, developing innovative testing methodologies and training while mentoring other UEGroup staff for the past 10 years.

About UEGroup

UEGroup is a User Experience and Design company in Silicon Valley that has established long term relationships with leaders in the entertainment and digital media field, medical, consumer electronics, gaming and handheld industries.

Overview

A brief overview on why kids and teens should be incorporated into television and media user research, as well as a brief overview of the types of research suitable for children.

Key Takeaways:

- Understanding why it is important to include kids and teens into user research

- Brief overview of the main research methods suitable for child/teen inclusion (Focus Groups, Ethnography, Out of Box Experience Research, Usability Testing, Quantitative Studies, Customer Experience Studies, Personas)

Age Appropriate Research Methods

General overview of the cognitive ability of children and teens, and how that corresponds to different research methods. A more detailed discussion regarding each stage of cognitive development and what types of questions are appropriate and effective.

Key Takeaways:

- Understanding the differences of cognitive abilities in children and teens

- Understanding which research methods are most appropriate and effective for each level of cognitive ability

- Examples of different research methods used with kids and the specific issues associated with them

Interactive Activity:

- Activity to determine the type of research to apply to specific scenarios for specific age groups

Recruiting Children and Teens

A discussion on the special considerations that is necessary for recruiting teens and children for a study, as well as practical tips for how to recruit, where to recruit, who to recruit and what safety measures must be in place when recruiting kids and teens.

Key Takeaways:

- Understanding the specific issues that are associated with recruiting teens and children; including legal and scheduling issues

- Practical guidance on best practices related to recruiting, scheduling and recording sessions with children and teens

Setting the Scene

Learning how to create the right space for different research methods, while keeping the special needs of kids and teens in mind.

Key Takeaways:

- Understanding how to think about creating a space that allows for child participants to feel comfortable giving useful feedback

- Understanding how to minimize distractions of the cameras and products you are testing

Session Structure & Tools for Feedback

A discussion on how to structure research sessions with kids and teens as well as an overview of different metrics that are particularly useful with kids and teens.

Key Takeaways:

- Understanding how to structure a session, including appropriate time, metrics and other ideas for getting kids to open up during a research session

Interactive Activity:

- Examples will be shown of research methods being used with children which will allow for a discussion on what works well and what doesn't work well with kids and teens

Soft Skills

A discussion on the special set of soft skills that are required for interacting with children and teens during research.

Key Takeaways:

- Understanding communication methods especially suitable for relating to kids and teens during research

- Practical techniques for asking questions and probing for more feedback, as well as suggestions for activities appropriate to children.

Interactive Television Experience in Convergent Environment: Models, Reception and Business

Valdecir Becker

UFPB - Federal University of Paraíba

João Pessoa, Paraíba, Brazil

Permission to make digital or hard copies of part or all of this work for personal or classroom use is granted without fee provided that copies are not made or distributed for profit or commercial advantage and that copies bear this notice and the full citation on the first page. Copyrights for third-party components of this work must be honored. For all other uses, contact the Owner/Author.

Copyright is held by the owner/author(s).

TVX 2016, June 22–24, 2016, Chicago, IL, USA

ACM 978-1-4503-4067-0/16/06.

http://dx.doi.org/10.1145/2932206.2932419

Abstract

This course will discuss the interactivity on television, which has evolved considerably in recent years. After the walled garden model, widely discussed in this congress some year ago, models based on applications and connected TVs are emerging, with two consequences: effective participation of viewers in programming, especially live, and deprogramming schedule in pay TV systems. Planning the content for this scenario happens to be the biggest challenge of the current television. Finally, the course will explore possible paths for the future of interactivity, such as immersion in videos through spatial and temporal zoom with synchronization of things.

Author Keywords

Interactive Television; convergence; audience reception; future applications.

ACM Classification Keywords

H.5.1 Multimedia Information Systems: Video (e.g., tape, disk, DVI). H.5.3 Group and Organization Interfaces. H.m MISCELLANEOUS.

Introduction

Interactive TV has evolved considerably in recent years. New forms of interactivity have emerged, bringing the viewer into the television programming. In simple terms, it is possible to analyze and define interactivity in terms of three approaches: referring to technologies that support interactivity and have evolved to improve information exchange; relating to content exchanged between the medium and the user; and considering the end user as a client of the system, which should, therefore, be adapted to user needs. The latter view seems to better suit the current stage of television, without ignoring that digital technology still expands the range of possibilities in communication and messaging between user and television system. Thus, a holistic approach to the subject, which maintains the catalytic role of digital technologies to improve the exchange and access to information by the user, is needed, because technological changes are quickly reflected in the perception of value that the user has about the content.

However, other authors argue that television has always been interactive, since the audience was engaged in attending and dialoguing with the television programs. What have changed over the decades are the technological resources, which have improved this participation and have made the real dialogue with programs possible.

In this course, we will start from this premise, for a more complete analysis, which aggregates all technologies that can be used to interact. So, we consider interactivity to bringing close together content producer and the audience, through the enhancement of audiovisual resources, to improve dialogue and exchange of information between sender and receiver. One expected result is an increased supply of content, with improvement in the quality of the viewing experience and greater power to the viewer.

From this conceptual and theoretical framework, we can note that the concern with the participation of the viewer has played a central role in the development of TV, whether from the perspective of the media, or from the point of view of its product, which is the programming. On one hand, technologies restrict or facilitate participation; on the other, programs call and invite viewers to interact.

Historically, we have entered a third generation of interactivity. The first generation started with television, and is still present today. This phase is called here the Analog Model. In view of the limitations of analog TV, digital TV has proposed a new model, called Walled Garden, which had its heyday in Europe in the mid-2000s.

With the spread of connected devices and easy installation of applications, the third generation of interactivity was started in the late 2000, treated here as Connected Model. The starting point was the interactivity-based on applications (both social networks as applications dedicated to specific programs). This model is also composed by connected TVs, which use the TV as a communication platform without necessarily being organized in channel. Allied to connected TVs, pay TV providers offer automatic recording of programming, allowing a new stage of interactivity: the deprogramming of television, which increases the power of the viewers, by organizing their own program schedule.

breaks comes to play a secondary role. In this course, these aspects will be discussed in detail.

Course Structure:

1st part: concepts and history (30 min):

We introduce the concepts needed to follow the course, especially those related to the concept of interactivity, viewer participation and the dialogue inherent to the television audience. This section will also discuss the motivations of interactivity and forms of participation in analog and digital TV. We will emphasize the importance and the limitations of the walled garden model, which predominates in digital TV.

2nd part: Interactivity state of the art (60 min):

This part will discuss the current forms of interactivity, their uses and limitations. From interactivity by applications, connected TVs and automatic recordings, impacts in television content and audience behavior will be analyzed. The options of managing one´s own program schedule change the concept of television based on ongoing and planned flow.

3rd part: Future iTV applications (45 min):

In this section we analyze the creative potential of interactivity evolution. Based on researches on immersion in the video, with spatial and temporal zoom, and synchronization of things, we will discuss future scenarios for interactivity, with impacts on audiovisual narratives.

4th part: strategies for content planning (45 min):

The use of applications, connected TVs and automatic recordings have developed differently around the world, with different impacts on market and business. In US markets, applications are stronger; in Europe, automatic recordings have developed well; in Latin America there is a large supply of content on connected TVs.

One should consider that Brazil is still trying to implement a hybrid model that mixes Walled Garden with Connected Model. With the proximity of switch-off, there is a large investment by the Brazilian government in the development of e-government applications. It is expected to make free distribution of 15 million set top boxes. Everyone will have those applications embedded.

Finally, the course will discuss the future of interactivity, listing scientific and market challenges. The next steps of interactivity tend to be related to immersion in video, both spatially and temporally, with synchronization of things, allowing interactivity in all forms. Spatial zoom in videos with very high resolutions and temporal zoom with very high frame rates represent the threshold of current research. In addition, the synchronization of things, such as tactile sensations, smells and tastes, is bringing new narrative to the experience.

From the market point of view, interactivity is allowing a TV without schedule and also direct connection between real-time audiences with the production of live programs. The contents must be consistent with these resources, allowing, in live programs, dialogue and in recorded programs, the binge watching. New business models are emerging, where advertising in commercial

Finally, this section will address requirements for high quality content creation in this convergent scenario in which television is inserted. For this purpose, strategies to engage the audience will be discussed for live content, which require real-time dialogue, and recorded content, which seeks binge watching.

Potential target audience

This course is aimed at researchers and practitioners working in television, developing interactivity applications and user interfaces, and at those designing home entertainment experience. A mix of participants from research and industry is ideal. No previous knowledge is required.

References

1. Abreu, J., Almeida, P., & Teles, B. 2014. TV discovery & enjoy: a new approach to help users finding the right TV program to watch. In Proceedings of the 2014 ACM international conference on Interactive experiences for TV and online video - TVX '14 (pp. 63–70). New York, New York, USA: ACM Press.

2. Abreu, J., Almeida, P., Teles, B., & Reis, M. 2013. Viewer behaviors and practices in the (new) television environment. In Proceedings of the 11th european conference on Interactive TV and video - EuroITV '13 (p. 5). New York, New York, USA: ACM Press.

3. Becker, B. V., Gambaro, D., Crisnir, A., & Coutinho, S. 2015. Migration of Television Audience to Digital Media : Impacts on TV Schedule and Journalism. Athens Journal of Mass Media and Communications, 1(4), 275–288.

4. Chu, Jean Ho, et al. 2015. Universal Threshold Object: Designing Haptic Interaction for Televised Interactive Narratives. Proceedings of the Ninth International Conference on Tangible, Embedded, and Embodied Interaction. ACM.

5. Joseph Straubhaar , Robert LaRose, and Lucinda Davenport. 2013. Media now: Understanding media, culture, and technology. Cengage Learning.

6. Konstantinos Chorianopoulos. 2004. Virtual television channels: conceptual model, user interface design and affective usability evaluation. A thesis submitted for the degree of Doctor of Philosophy Department of Management Science and Technology. Athens University of Economics and Business. Athens.

7. Kristyn Gorton. 2009. Media audiences: television, meaning and emotion. Edinburgh: Edinburgh University Press.

8. Henry Jenkins. 2008. Convergence Culture: Where Old and New Media Collide. NY: NYU Press.

9. Iris Jennes and Wendy Van den Broeck. 2014. Digital TV innovations: industry and user perspective. info, Vol. 16 Iss 6 pp. 48 - 59

10. Marianna Obrist, et al. 2015. Online video and interactive TV experiences. interactions 22.5 (2015): 32-37.

11. Nancy Paterson. 2012. Walled gardens: the new shape of the public internet, Proceedings of the 2012 iConference, p.97-104, Canada

12. Nicola Matteucci. 2013. Standards, IPR and digital TV convergence: theories and empirical evidence. Munich Personal RePEc Archive.

13. R. Malhotra. 2013. Hybrid broadcast broadband TV: The way forward for connected TVs, IEEE Consum. Electron. Mag., vol. 2, no. 3, pp. 10–16, Jul. 2013

14. Raymond Williams. 1974. Television: Technology and Cultural Form. London: Fontana.

15. Stan J Liebowitz and Alejandro Zentner. 2015. The Internet as a Celestial TiVo. Journal of Cultural Economics · (December 2015)

Course Presenter:
Valdecir Becker is a journalist, Master of Engineering and Knowledge Management (2006, Federal University of Santa Catarina) and Doctor of Science (Electrical Engineering, 2011, University of São Paulo). He is Professor at Science Computer Center and Postgraduate Program in Journalism at the Federal University of Paraíba (Brazil), and works with research and interactivity development since 1999. He has actively participated in Brazilian digital television patronization, especially with middleware Ginga definitions. Over the years, he has participated in several projects related to Digital interactive TV, studying new formats of convergent and multi-platform content and the impact of digital technologies in content and business models. He has written books and papers about digital TV, interactivity, HCI, audience and reception studies.

Region-of-Interest-Based Subtitle Placement Using Eye-Tracking Data of Multiple Viewers

Wataru Akahori
Waseda University
Tokyo, Japan
akahori@akane.waseda.jp

Tatsunori Hirai
Komazawa University
Tokyo, Japan
thirai@komazawa-u.ac.jp

Shunya Kawamura
Waseda University
Tokyo, Japan
s.kawamura@ruri.waseda.jp

Shigeo Morishima
Waseda Research Institute for
Science and Engineering
Tokyo, Japan
shigeo@waseda.jp

Permission to make digital or hard copies of part or all of this work for personal or classroom use is granted without fee provided that copies are not made or distributed for profit or commercial advantage and that copies bear this notice and the full citation on the first page. Copyrights for third-party components of this work must be honored. For all other uses, contact the Owner/Author. Copyright is held by the owner/author(s).
TVX'16, June 22–24, 2016, Chicago, IL, USA
ACM 978-1-4503-4067-0/16/06.
http://dx.doi.org/10.1145/2932206.2933558

Abstract

We present a subtitle-placement method that reduces viewer's eye movement without interfering with the target region of interest (ROI) in a video scene. Subtitles help viewers understand foreign-language videos. However, subtitles tend to attract viewers' line of sight, which cause viewers to lose focus on the video content. To address this problem, previous studies have attempted to improve viewer experiences by dynamically shifting subtitle positions. Nevertheless, in their user studies, some participants felt that the visual appearance of such subtitles was unnatural and caused them fatigue. We propose a method that places subtitles below the ROI, which is calculated by eye-tracking data from multiple viewers. Two experiments were conducted to evaluate viewer impression and compare line of sight for videos with subtitles placed by the proposed and previous methods.

Author Keywords

Dynamic Subtitles; User Experience; Accessibility; Eye-Tracking; Region of Interest

ACM Classification Keywords

C.4 [Performance of Systems]: Design studies; H.1.2 [Models and Principles]: User/Machine Systems—*Human factors*; H.5.1 [Information Interfaces and Presentation (e.g., HCI)]: Multimedia Information Systems

Introduction

While viewing subtitled foreign-language videos, viewer line of sight is drawn to the subtitles to gain a better understanding of the story. Consequently, viewers overlook some visual content when subtitles are placed away from the region of interest (ROI). To address this problem, the effect of varying subtitle position has been experimentally tested [1, 2]. Brown et al. [2] stated that the gaze patterns of people who are watching a movie with dynamic subtitles are closer to those of people who are watching a movie without subtitles. However, a qualitative index for effective placement of subtitles was insufficiently evident; therefore, the position of manually placed subtitles subjectively depends on the editor's judgment.

There are two main approaches in automatic placement of dynamic subtitles. First, is placing subtitles near the active speaker's face [3, 4]. Hong et al. [3] identified the active speaker from multiple characters and placed the subtitles around the speaker's face. Consequently, the problem that hearing-impaired viewers could not recognize the active speaker was solved. Nevertheless, the subtitles sometimes interfere with the important region because the region is only defined by the speaker's face features. Second, is to place subtitles based on viewer gaze position. Katti et al. [5] proposed an interactive subtitle-placement method that uses eye-tracking data and a saliency map. They focused on spatial gaze position to predict real-time individual ROI acquired with an eye-tracker. Although their method places subtitles in real-time, there is a problem that the remaining subtitles placed on the screen can overlap with an important region when the region temporally changes while displaying the subtitles.

Previous studies have found that eye-tracking data contains semantic information that is useful for estimating

an important region of a video [6, 7]. Sawada et al. [6] proposed an automatic comic generation method and calculated the informative region from video using eye-tracking data. Following this method, we use eye-tracking data to bind the most common viewing area. By not restricting the area of focus, we overcome the problem of subtitles interfering with important images, i.e., subtitles are positioned relative to the line of sight. Moreover, we consider viewers' efforts by always placing subtitles at the lower part of the ROI and help viewers to easily anticipate the upcoming subtitle.

Subtitle Placement Method

To reduce eye movement when watching a video with subtitles, we attempt to position subtitles near the line of sight. First, in order to acquire sufficient eye tracking data, viewers watch a video without subtitles (Fig. 1a). Then, the ROI for the majority of viewers is estimated using the mean and standard deviation of the eye tracking data (Fig. 1b). Finally, subtitles are placed under the estimated ROI (Fig. 1c).

Estimating the ROI

To maintain quality, subtitles should not overlap the ROI. Furthermore, individual viewers' ROIs must be considered. Thus, the ROIs in a video without subtitles are determined using eye-tracking data obtained from multiple viewers. By positioning subtitles outside but close to the ROI, the visual appearance becomes natural and viewers can effectively focus on the ROI.

The rectangular ROI is calculated by the mean and standard deviation of the eye tracking data for a given scene. Katti et al. [5] revealed that subtitles which move dynamically according to the changes in the ROI negatively impact viewer comprehension. Hence, we place subtitles at the calculated position for a period of time.

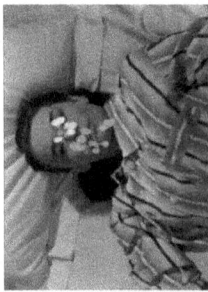

(a) Input Video with Eye Tracking Data

(b) Region-of-Interest Estimation

(c) Subtitle Placement

Figure 1: Eye tracking data is used to determine a viewer's ROI (red rectangle) and position subtitles at the lower part of the estimated region.

bottom-center of the screen, which is the same as traditional subtitle placement methods.

Experiments

Data selection and setup

To acquire eye-tracking data while watching videos without subtitles, we prepared nine video clips with approximately 90 seconds long each as described in Table 1.

Movie Name	Language	ID	The number of subtitles
"Roman Holiday"	English	C1	14
		C2	26
		C3	29
		C4	20
"The Bicycle Thief"	Italian	C5	14
		C6	27
		C7	25
"Pépé le Moko"	French	C8	25
		C9	35

Table 1: Video clips used for experiments.

Six native Japanese speakers (five males and one female), who had basic knowledge of English and little knowledge of Italian and French, were recruited from the university community. They were aged between 22 and 24 years old ($\bar{x} = 23.3$, $\sigma = 0.82$). An EMR-9 was used to measure eye-tracking data. The EMR-9 is a cap-type eye mark recorder that records line-of-sight data (VGA) at 60 Hz. The participants and the (calibrated) eye tracker were positioned 2.0 m from the display. The participants

The ROI is computed from the gaze position $x_i(t) = (x_i^1(t), x_i^2(t))$, $i = 1, 2, ..., N$, where N is the number of participants. With the N eye-gaze dataset for the scene, the mean value $\boldsymbol{\mu} = (\mu^1, \mu^2)$ and the standard deviation $\boldsymbol{\sigma} = (\sigma^1, \sigma^2)$ are computed as follows:

$$\mu^k = \frac{1}{N} \sum_{i=1}^{N} \sum_{t=t_s}^{t_e} x_i^k(t), \tag{1}$$

$$\sigma^k = \sqrt{\frac{1}{N} \sum_{i=1}^{N} \sum_{t=t_s}^{t_e} (x_i^k(t) - \mu^k)^2}, \tag{2}$$

where $k \in \{1, 2\}$ represents 2 dimensions of x and y axis, and t_s and t_e are the time wherein the subtitles appear and disappear, respectively. The ROI is defined as a rectangular region within $\mu \pm 2\sigma$. This region contains approximately 95% of the eye-gaze patterns for a scene, assuming that the patterns follow a normal distribution.

Subtitle placement

Subtitles are placed on the basis of the estimated ROI to expand the viewer's scene. Hong et al. [3] reported that frequently changing subtitle position made videos appear unnatural. Thus, we place subtitles according to a certain rule such that viewers can anticipate the position of subtitles. Subtitles are then placed on the top, bottom, left, and right part of the ROI. However, there may be insufficient space to place subtitles on the left or right part of the ROI because subtitles are horizontally written. Although subtitles can be placed on the top part of the ROI, there are many cases wherein subtitles are placed at the bottom of the screen [8]. Therefore, in consideration of viewer experience, we place subtitles at the bottom part of the ROI. For instance, when the ROI is estimated to be the entire screen, the subtitles are placed at the watched the video clips in a sitting posture. The original size was 640 pixels wide by 480 pixels high. The movies were played on a 41" display with sound on, and with black letterboxing to maintain the original aspect ratio of the videos.

By using the eye-tracking data, we placed subtitles based on the proposed method. To evaluate the effectiveness of the proposed method, two different types of subtitles were prepared, as described in Table 2.

Subtitles type	Description
Static Subtitles (SS)	Traditional static subtitles at the bottom of screen
Dynamic Subtitles (DS)	Combine [Hong et al. 2010]'s subtitle placement with manual adjustment

Table 2: Subtitle placement types.

All subtitles were in Japanese. For Dynamic Subtitles (DS), we combined the method with manual adjustment. For the automatic scheme by Hong et al. [3], there are some cases whereby the speaker is not accurately identified. Therefore, speaker identification was visually determined, and the mouth position was used to determine a region that included the speaker's face. There were several cases wherein the speaker was not facing the camera; then, we also identified him/her with the speaker. Note that when the speaker did not appear on the screen, the subtitles were placed at the bottom-center. In some cases, the subtitles overlapped the speaker's face region when the speaker moved or the subtitles included many words. As stated by Hong et al. [3], adjusting subtitle

location manually is effective for improving users' impressions. Therefore, we manually adjusted the position so that the subtitles did not interfere with the speaker's face.

Eye tracking data analysis

We evaluated the percentage of recorded gaze data that was within the ROI calculated by the proposed method for videos with subtitles. We compared SS and the proposed method in this paper. In addition, six native Japanese speakers (six males, aged between 22 and 24), who have basic knowledge of English and little knowledge about Italian and French, were recruited from the university community. After they were shown nine clips in one subtitles type, they were shown nine clips in the other subtitles type. A short break was taken between sets. The measurement conditions were the same as those for measuring eye tracking data without subtitles. The percentage of gaze data was calculated as the number of frames for which gaze data were included inside the ROI to the total number of frames wherein subtitles appear.

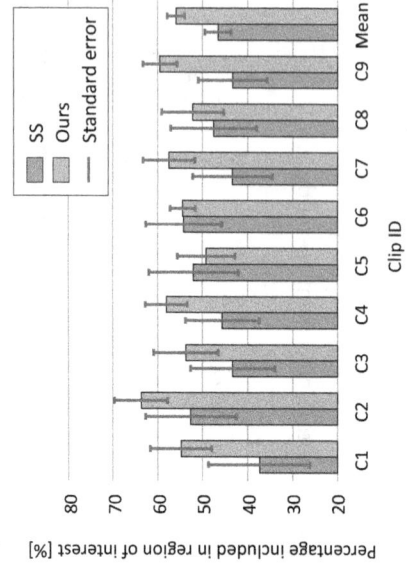

Figure 2: The mean percentage included in ROI for each clip and the mean percentage of all clips.

Figure 2 shows the percentage for nine clips and the mean percentage. As observed, the time required to watch the ROI of videos with the proposed method are more than that with SS. Thus, the result shows that the proposed method allows viewers to watch the important region for longer periods of time than the traditional static one.

User study

We conducted a user study to evaluate how the proposed method affects viewer experience. We recruited 251 native Japanese speakers through an online crowdsourcing service. The participants were paid after the experiments to maintain their motivation. They were shown nine pairs of clips with different types of subtitles, i.e., the proposed method and two comparative methods (SS and DS). They watched 18 clips in total. These two methods—SS and DS—were used as comparative methods, and we prepared two versions of nine pairs wherein the comparative methods differed. 106 of them watched one version and 145 of them watched the other one. Every time they watched one pairs of clips, we asked them the three questions as follows.

Q1. Which subtitle-placement method comfortably enabled you to follow both the subtitles and video content?

Q2. Which subtitles felt most natural from a visual appearance perspective?

Q3. Which subtitle placement method matched your expectation?

The participants scored them from 1 (comparative method) to 5 (proposed method) by comparing the clips with each subtitles in the three aspects.

Figure 3 shows the viewer experience results. The baseline is 3.00, and higher scores indicate that proposed method

is better than the comparative method. The results show that the participants tend to prefer SS over the proposed method. Several factors can be considered for such a preference. In a user study, Brown et al. [2] stated that some participants placed importance on the familiarity of traditional subtitles, and others felt uncomfortable when subtitles frequently changed. Thus, it is important for viewers to be used to dynamic subtitles. It is also effective to introduce a temporal constraint on subtitle position. The results also show that most participants prefer the proposed method to DS. These results indicate that the proposed method can maintain a natural visual appearance and reduce the viewers' effort of searching for subtitles more effectively than other dynamic subtitle methods.

Conclusions and Future Work

We presented a dynamic subtitle placement method that is based on multiple-viewer ROI. Subtitles are placed in the lower part of the ROI determined using eye-tracking data. Our experimental results show that viewers can focus on the ROI in videos without subtitles when they watch our results in more time than traditional ones. Furthermore, a user study has shown that most participants prefer the proposed method to previous dynamic subtitle methods.

We would like to add a temporal constraint for the placing of subtitles because viewers feel uncomfortable when the position frequently changes. We would also like to improve readability by considering the background and determining effective subtitle colors and fonts.

Acknowledgements

We thank T. Fukusato, T. Fuji, and T. Kato (Waseda University, Japan) for their advisory. This work was supported in part by CREST, JST.

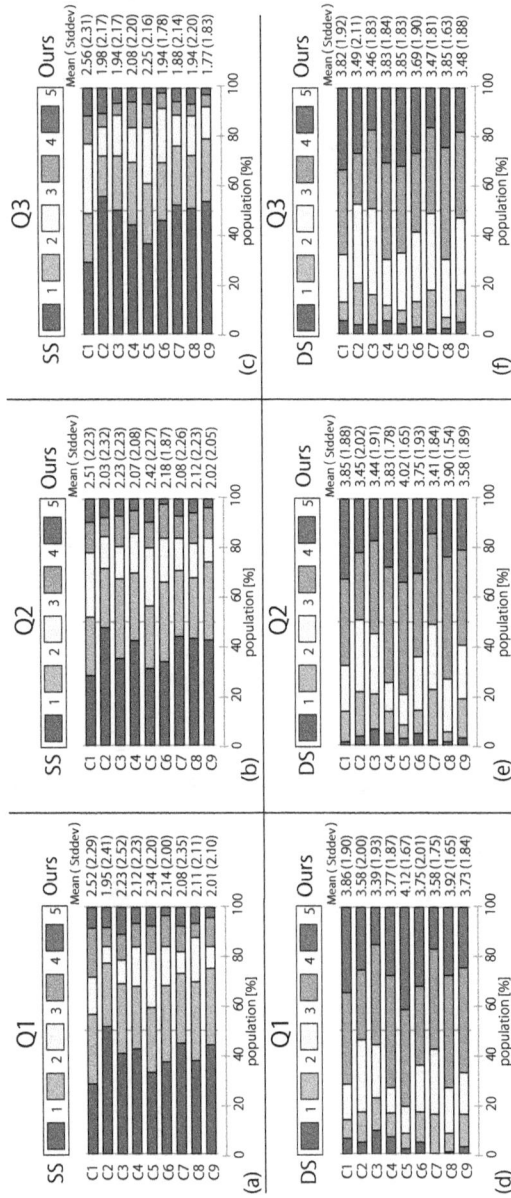

Figure 3: User answers to questions Q1–3. (a), (b), and (c) answer to Q1–3, respectively (SS vs. Ours); (d), (e), and (f) answer to Q1–3, respectively (DS vs. Ours.)

Q1 (SS) — Ours Mean (Stddev):
C1 2.52 (2.29); C2 1.95 (2.41); C3 2.23 (2.52); C4 2.12 (2.23); C5 2.34 (2.20); C6 2.14 (2.00); C7 2.08 (2.35); C8 2.11 (2.11); C9 2.01 (2.10)

Q2 (SS) — Ours Mean (Stddev):
C1 2.51 (2.23); C2 2.03 (2.23); C3 2.23 (2.23); C4 2.07 (2.08); C5 2.42 (2.27); C6 2.18 (1.87); C7 2.08 (2.26); C8 2.12 (2.23); C9 2.02 (2.05)

Q3 (SS) — Ours Mean (Stddev):
C1 2.56 (2.31); C2 1.98 (2.17); C3 1.94 (2.17); C4 2.08 (2.20); C5 2.25 (2.16); C6 1.94 (1.78); C7 1.88 (2.14); C8 1.94 (2.20); C9 1.77 (1.83)

Q1 (DS) — Ours Mean (Stddev):
C1 3.86 (1.90); C2 3.58 (2.00); C3 3.39 (1.93); C4 3.77 (1.87); C5 4.12 (1.67); C6 3.75 (2.01); C7 3.58 (1.75); C8 3.92 (1.65); C9 3.73 (1.84)

Q2 (DS) — Ours Mean (Stddev):
C1 3.85 (1.88); C2 3.45 (2.02); C3 3.44 (1.91); C4 3.83 (1.78); C5 4.02 (1.65); C6 3.75 (1.93); C7 3.41 (1.84); C8 3.90 (1.54); C9 3.58 (1.89)

Q3 (DS) — Ours Mean (Stddev):
C1 3.82 (1.92); C2 3.49 (2.11); C3 3.46 (1.83); C4 3.83 (1.84); C5 3.85 (1.83); C6 3.69 (1.90); C7 3.47 (1.81); C8 3.85 (1.63); C9 3.48 (1.88)

References

[1] Brooks, M., and Armstrong, M. Enhancing subtitles. In *Proceedings of the International Conference on Interactive Experiences for TV and Online Video*, ACM (2014), 27–28.

[2] Brown, A., Jones, R., Crabb, M., Sandford, J., Brooks, M., Armstrong, M., and Jay, C. Dynamic subtitles: the user experience. In *Proceedings of the International Conference on Interactive Experiences for TV and Online Video*, ACM (2015), 103–112.

[3] Hong, R., Wang, M., Yuan, X. T., Xu, M., Yan, S., and Chua, T. S. Video accessibility enhancement for hearing-impaired users. *ACM Transactions on Multimedia Computing, Communications, and Applications (TOMM)* 7, 1 (2011), 1–19.

[4] Hu, Y., Kautz, J., Yu, Y., and Wang, W. Speaker-Following Video Subtitles. *ACM Transactions on Multimedia Computing, Communications, and Applications (TOMM)* 11, 2 (2015), 1–17.

[5] Katti, H., Rajagopal, A. K., Kankanhalli, M., and Kalpathi, R. Online estimation of evolving human visual interest. *ACM Transactions on Multimedia Computing, Communications, and Applications (TOMM)* 11, 1 (2014), 1–21.

[6] Sawada, T., Toyoura, M., and Mao, X. Film comic generation with eye tracking. *Lecture Notes in Computer Science 7732*, Springer (2013), 467–478.

[7] Jain, E., Sheikh, Y., Shamir, A., and Hodgins, J. Gaze-Driven Video Re-Editing. *ACM Transactions on Graphics (TOG)* 34, 2 (2015), 1–12.

[8] Karamitroglou, F. A proposed set of subtitling standards in Europe. *Translation Journal 2*, 2 (1998), 1–15.

Semi-Automatic Camera and Switcher Control for Live Broadcast

Jeff Daemen
Jens Herder
Cornelius Koch
Philipp Ladwig
Roman Wiche
Kai Wilgen
Hochschule Düsseldorf,
University of Applied Sciences
Faculty of Media
Münsterstraße 156,
40476 Düsseldorf, Germany
vsvr.medien.hs-duesseldorf.de
herder@hs-duesseldorf.de

Example video material is online available:
http://vsvr.medien.hs-duesseldorf.de/productions/rob2015/

Permission to make digital or hard copies of part or all of this work for personal or
classroom use is granted without fee provided that copies are not made or distributed
for profit or commercial advantage and that copies bear this notice and the full citation
on the first page. Copyrights for third-party components of this work must be honored.
For all other uses, contact the Owner/Author. Copyright is held by the owner/author(s).
TVX'16, June 22-24, 2016, Chicago, IL, USA
ACM 978-1-4503-4067-0/16/06.
http://dx.doi.org/10.1145/2932206.2933559

Abstract

Live video broadcasting requires a multitude of professional expertise to enable multi-camera productions. Robotic systems allow the automation of common and repeated tracking shots. However, predefined camera shots do not allow quick adjustments when required due to unpredictable events. We introduce a modular automated robotic camera control and video switch system, based on fundamental cinematographic rules. The actors' positions are provided by a markerless tracking system. In addition, sound levels of actors' lavalier microphones are used to analyse the current scene. An expert system determines appropriate camera angles and decides when to switch from one camera to another. A test production was conducted to observe the developed prototype in a live broadcast scenario and served as a video-demonstration for an evaluation.

Author Keywords

automated robotic camera system; actor tracking; switcher control; scene analysis; film rules; automated shot control;

ACM Classification Keywords

H.5.1. [Information Interfaces and Presentation (e.g. HCI)]: Artificial, augmented, and virtual realities

Introduction

Live broadcasting requires many operators to control numerous pieces of equipment, e.g. switching between different video signals or operating cameras. Cameras can be controlled manually or if robotic systems are present, they can be moved along predefined paths. If more than one camera is used in a dialog scene, the position and the field of view of each camera have to be chosen in a way, that the final camera images accomplish a good image structure and that they allow a proper transition. For this purpose, filmmakers have developed a set of rules and conventions [4].

We developed a system, which uses rules to determine the optimal camera settings and shot transitions, using the position of the host and the guest, acquired by a markerless motion capturing system. A height adjustable and rotatable robotic camera system, moving on tracks (Egripment Generic Track System), is controlled using the determined parameters.

The Virtual Cinematographer [4], an implementation of a real-time camera controller for automatic cinematography in the domain of virtual reality games and interactive fiction is an inspiration for our implementation. A more complex type of a virtual cinematographer is presented in [5]. The approach is inspired by the distinct role and key functions of each member in a filmmaking team, such as director, camera operator, and editor. An automated computation of appropriate viewpoints in complex 3D scenes is presented in [3]. The approach defines camera agents which are either in a scouting mode, searching for relevant events to convey, or in a tracking mode following one or more unfolding events. A more recent approach to autonomous virtual camera control is described by Gaddam et al. [2]. Chen et al. [1] gives a broad overview of existing autonomous cam-

era systems. An early approach for automatic systems in a TV studio was conducted by Pinhanez and Bobick [8]. They built multiple intelligent robotic cameras reacting to verbal requests by a director. Furthermore Tsuda et al. [9] describe an intelligent robot camera system to broadcast television programs with network-connected cameras. Okuda et al. [7] extended on the approach of connected cameras and added an automatic generation of shooting rules.

System Layout

To achieve the proposed features we have developed the system layout, which is outlined in Figure 3 and consists of the following core components. OpenStage[1], a markerless motion capturing system by Organic Motion, is used to track the actor positions, which are essential for the determination of the optimal camera angle. We use two tracked cameras, one manually controlled, which is attached to a camera arm and one computer-controlled robotic system. For each camera one chroma keyer and one real-time render engine are needed to respectively separate the actors from the consistent coloured background and to create the virtual graphics (background signal). The chroma keyer uses this signal to depict selected areas of the background signal on top of the foreground (camera image). A dedicated computer works as camera controller which steers the robotic camera. The operator for the jib-arm has a tablet attached to the camera. This tablet runs an app, signaling the operator to set a specific camera perspective requested by the expert system. Additionally, the request gets played back as an acoustic command on the operators headphones. However, the operator does not have to follow the recommendation of the expert system.

The markerless motion capturing system determines the position and orientation of each joint of multiple actors and

Figure 1: Augmented reality on robotic camera, showing the degrees of freedom as well as the constraints; dolly track of 4,04 m; lift column 1,57-2,11 cm; field of view 9°-96°

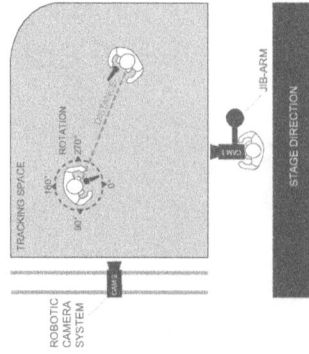

Figure 2: Simplified top view perspective of our virtual studio setup; actors' orientation and voice level as well as time are used to determine a camera cut; the jib-arm has a 120 cm radius and is tracked

[1]http://www.organicmotion.com/mocap-for-animation/

sition, tilt, pan and zoom parameters for the virtual camera of the proposed shot. The focus of the robotic camera was automatically adjusted based on actor distance.

The video switcher bridge gives a signal to the switcher to change the output to the other camera. When a specific command is received by the render engine, the calculated parameters of the virtual camera are send over OSC to the computer, running the camera controller software, which then gives the needed commands to move the robotic camera to the received position. The camera controller translates the absolute data from the render engine into relative commands for the robotic camera, such as direction and speed. One constraint is that the robotic camera (see Figure 1) needs a specific time to reach the end-position, more specifically the position of the computed virtual camera before a camera switch can be executed.

Camera Control Algorithm

The control engine manages the parameters of a virtual camera such as position, field of view and focus distance. This data will be transmitted to the camera controller and represents the reference position. The error deviation between the virtual camera position and the current state of the robotic camera can be used, to control the robotic camera. This control mechanism can be designed as a proportion-only controller and is depicted in Figure 4. Low control gains produce smooth movements which can be used to compensate person tracking errors, but the system will be unable to follow dynamic object trajectories. High control gains produce faster accelerations and allows the system to follow fast moving objects. Very high control gains lead to an overshooting of the destination and end in oscillation.

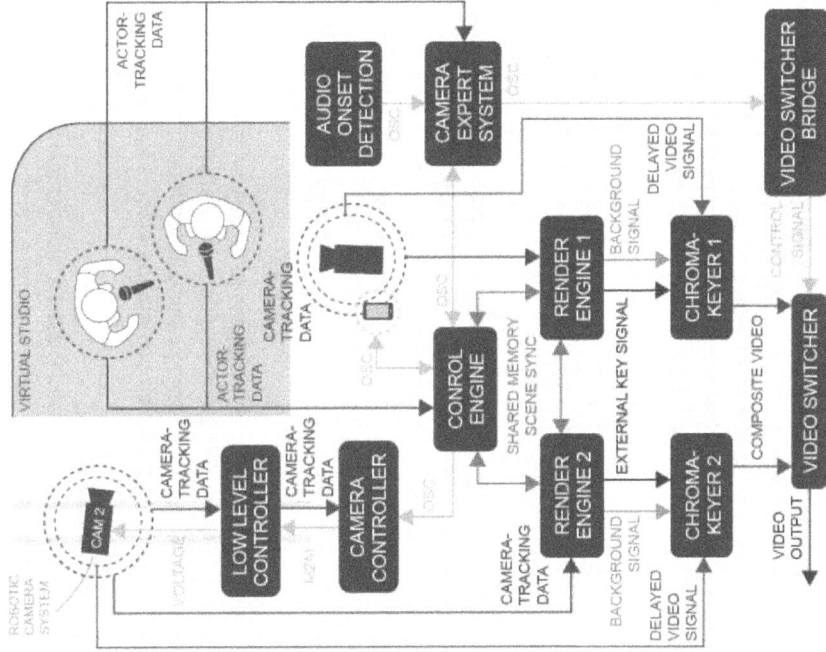

Figure 3: Virtual studio layout

transmits the information to the first render engine. This data is used to display the movements of the actors as small avatars on a virtual table in front of the scene and can also be processed by a script within the render engine. By using the sacrum joints' position (base of the spine) of each actor, for every frame, an algorithm determines the best po-

Scene Analysis

The actors wear lavalier microphones with a wireless transmitter. An audio module measures the volume and verifies if it exceeds a defined threshold and sends a message to the expert system. This threshold is determined in tests before the live broadcast and can be adjusted at runtime. The message contains the person's identifier (A or B), as well as the probability of current speaking. Microphone levels as an indicator for scene situations was already successfully used by Okuda et al. [7]. Besides the audio information, we take actors' positions and rotations into consideration.

The sacrum joint is used to determine the position and rotation of the actors. The positional data is used to measure the distance between two actors, which is another indicator for the current scene format.

The rotation is converted into angle values in relation to the stage direction (see Figure 2). As our robotic camera and jib-arm are restricted to a specified range, e.g. in the area of approximately 45 to 135 degrees for the robotic camera, upper and lower bounds of angle values for the cameras are defined. This way we detect which camera the actor is facing.

Overall our scene analysis provides the following parameters for our expert system: Position and distance between both actors, probability of speaking for both actors, and rotation to determine which camera the actor is facing.

Expert System

As He et al. [4] successfully used a hierarchical finite state machine to model appropriate camera perspectives for relating scene idioms, we chose to take a similar implementation to represent the knowledge of our expert system.

We chose the Unity3D Game Engine[2] as our development environment for the expert system because it provides Mecanim, an integrated visual programming tool for state machines (see Figure 5). The modeling of the state machine can be adjusted to fit only general film rules, but it can also be constructed in a more linear way, if the director has a clear sequence of camera shots in mind.

Besides the codified film rules as a state machine and the parameters from the scene analysis, the expert system adds two more information to its knowledge. First, it saves the duration since the last cut between the cameras. In addition, the expert system knows which camera is currently active. For example, we added similar rules as described by Liu et al. [6], avoiding jump cuts and having minimum and maximum durations between cuts. The maximum duration helps to avoid excessive durations for individual shots, also keeping the viewers attention. It also enables the listening actor in the dialog to get shown, if one actor is talking for a long time. The minimum duration allows the jib-arm operator and robotic camera to prepare a requested camera perspective.

The expert system performs the following routine to control the cameras and the switcher. First, the expert system considers the next suitable camera perspectives by examining the transitions to the next possible states. These are then checked within the low level camera module. Depending on the necessary position for a camera perspective, a certain camera module might not be possible to set, as the robotic camera is restricted to a rail and can only apply positions in a specified range. Thus the low level module answers with a confidence between 0 and 1 to a requested camera module. The expert system uses this confidence and combines it with additional preferences, manually set by the director

---

[2]https://unity3d.com

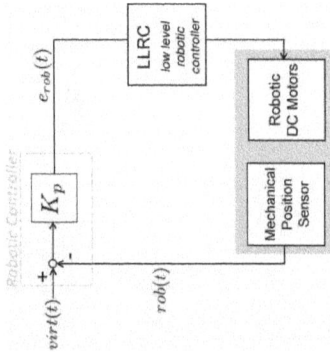

Figure 4: Block diagram of the closed control loop with the error deviation:
$$e_{rob}(t) = K_p \left(virt(t) - rob(t) \right)$$

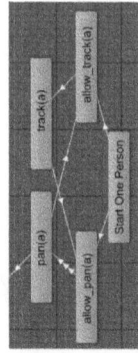

Figure 5: Extract from the Mecanim hierarchical state machine; A cut between the cameras happens when the camera had enough time to prepare the shot or the actor has faced the camera;
Allow_pan(a)/allow_track(a) are temporary states and pan(a)/track(a) the executing states.

Low-level camera modules

pan(Actor1) camera pan following specified actor

track(Actor1) track movement following specified actor, no panning

apex(Actor1,Actor2) apex/master shot showing both actors

ext(Actor1,Actor2) external shot, over the shoulder of one actor facing the second

int(Actor1,Actor2) internal shot, near-frontal view on first specified actor

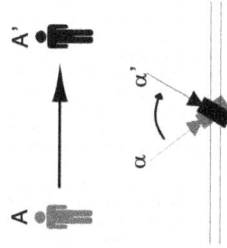

Figure 6: Pan-setting: camera has a fixed position and its direction follows the actors movement

for this perspective. The importance for this preference can be adjusted to put different emphases on manual or automatic control. This way, the most suitable camera shot gets selected and prepared.

As the camera has to prepare the next shot before transitioning, the system does not cut immediately between the cameras. Initially it goes into a temporary state and only transitions between the cameras when specific conditions are met (see Figure 5). After the camera transition, the described routine is repeated and the expert system runs through the state machine, depending on automatic confidences, manual preferences for individual camera perspectives and the provided scene parameters. The expert system communicates with the switcher to cut to the robotic camera or the jib-arm respectively.

Implemented Shot Types and Calculation

The following shot types have been implemented in the shot control application so far. These include two shot types fit for a single person in the scene in addition to three shot types fit for a two person scene: Pan camera - Follow actor by panning (Figure 6), Track camera - Follow actor by moving on the track (Figure 7), Apex camera / Master shot, External camera / Over the shoulder Shot (Figure 8), Internal Camera - Close up,

Test Production and Evaluation

For the evaluation we analyzed the production recordings[3] and made statistics about the applied shot types and shot lengths. We interviewed five experts using a questionnaire about the correct use of the film rules. Following the triangle principle a dialog scene with two moving players was shot. In this setup one robotic camera and one manual camera on a jib-arm is used. Due to the absence of a third camera

for the apex of the triangle, one of the two cameras takes care of it in those situations the position of the line of interest admits it. Analyzing the shot lengths of this production, we calculated an average shot length of 7.7 seconds with 4 seconds for the shortest shot up to 13 seconds for the longest shot.

The evaluation reveals following aspects: Concerning the editing and the composition, the results of this production received middle to poor grades. The main points of criticism are that cuts happen to late. Because the cuts in this implementation are based on the actor's rotation or the time, the cut takes place after the movement. This contradicts the technique of invisible cuts, whereby the viewer is fully aware of the cut. Furthermore, the actor framed by the camera is positioned overly in the middle, which results in too much headroom. In this context the participants suggest to consult the golden ratio for the division of the screen space. Also the camera movements are criticized. Following the answers the camera robotic reacts too sensitive, since even small movements of the player result in camera movements, which leads to disturbances.

The participants recommend the use of an automatic system for simple setups used in newscasts. Concerning the complexity of other shows such as game shows would be beyond the scope of a fully automatic system. In this case they recommend the use of semi-automatic systems.

Conclusion and Future Work

Our approach enables cost-effective TV studio productions by reducing the number of operators. Regarding future developments, an implementation of additional rules would be a major enhancement. The framing of certain shots should consider also shot type, framing rules, virtual and real objects which are involved by the actors. The inherent

---

[3]http://vsvr.medien.hs-duesseldorf.de/productions/rob2015/

problem that cuts are executed too late could be tackled by introducing video delays so that more time is available for the decision and execution. Alternatively that part could be handed to an operator or a more scripted flow implementation with voice recognition.

Acknowledgments

Vizrt Austria GmbH supported this project by providing the viz engine studio render software. Thanks belong to A. Müller for keeping the studio equipment running and elaborating the light setup. Andrea Gerhard acted as host in the example video. Following team members took part in the two productions: U. Braas, J. Burga, M. Friedrich, T. Geldner, J. Jochheim, A. Jussen, M. Kascholke, D. Kirchhof, O. Köse, D. Meyer, M. Tiator, F. Barnjak, M. Heilemann, N. Petau, M. Säger, and M. Urbaniak.

REFERENCES

1. Jianhui Chen and Peter Carr. 2014. Autonomous Camera Systems: A Survey. In *Workshops at the Twenty-Eighth AAAI Conference on Artificial Intelligence*. 18–22.

2. Vamsidhar Reddy Gaddam, Ragnhild Eg, Ragnar Langseth, Carsten Griwodz, and Pål Halvorsen. 2015. The Cameraman Operating My Virtual Camera is Artificial: Can the Machine Be As Good As a Human? *ACM Trans. Multimedia Comput. Commun. Appl.* 11, 4 (2015), 1–20.

3. Quentin Galvane, Marc Christie, Rémi Ronfard, Chen-Kim Lim, and Marie-Paule Cani. 2013. Steering Behaviors for Autonomous Cameras. In *Proceedings of Motion on Games (MIG '13)*. ACM, New York, NY, USA, Article 71, 10 pages.

4. Li-wei He, Michael F. Cohen, and David H. Salesin. 1996. The Virtual Cinematographer: A Paradigm for Automatic Real-Time Camera Control and Directing. In *SIGGRAPH 96 Conference Proceedings*, Holly Rushmeier (Ed.). ACM SIGGRAPH, Addison-Wesley, 217–224. New Orleans, Louisiana, 4-9 August 1996.

5. Tsai-Yen Li and Xiang-Yan Xiao. 2005. An Interactive Camera Planning System for Automatic Cinematographer. In *Multimedia Modelling Conference, 2005. MMM 2005. Proceedings of the 11th International*. 310–315.

6. Qiong Liu, Yong Rui, Anoop Gupta, and J. J. Cadiz. 2001. Automating Camera Management for Lecture Room Environments. In *Proceedings of the SIGCHI Conference on Human Factors in Computing Systems (CHI '01)*. ACM, 442–449.

7. Makoto Okuda, Takao , Kazutoshi Mutou, Hitoshi Yanagisawa, and Seiki Inoue. 2008. Method of shot determination in a robot camera cooperative shooting system. *Proc. SPIE* 6820 (2008).

8. Claudio Pinhanez and Aaron F. Bobick. 1995. Intelligent Studios: Using Computer Vision to Control TV Cameras. In *IJCAI Workshop on Entertainment and AI/Alife*.

9. Takao Tsuda, Yuri Hayakeyama, Shinichi Yoshimura, and Daiichiro Kato. 2003. Automatic program production using network-connected robot cameras. In *2003 IEEE/RSJ International Conference on Intelligent Robots and Systems (IROS)*, Vol. 1. 260–265.

Figure 7: Track-setting: cameras direction is static, it keeps the actor in view by copying their x-axis movement

Figure 8: Ext-setting: over the shoulder shot facing one actor while keeping the other in the image

Multi-Platform Application Toolkit

Miggi Zwicklbauer
Fraunhofer FOKUS
Berlin, 10589, Germany
miggi.zwicklbauer
@fokus.fraunhofer.de

Matthew Broadbent
Lancaster University
Lancaster, LA1 4WA, UK
m.broadbent@lancaster.ac.uk

Jean-Claude Dufourd
Telecom ParisTech
Paris, 75634 , France
jean-claude.dufourd
@telecom-paristech.fr

Christian Fuhrhop
Fraunhofer FOKUS
Berlin, 10589, Germany
christian.fuhrhop@fokus.fraunhofer.de

Stefano Miccoli
Fincons
Milano, 20123, Italy
stefano.miccoli@finconsgroup.com

Fabian Schiller
Institut für Rundfunktechnik
Munich, 80939, Germany
schiller@irt.de

Ville Tuominen
Leadin
Tampere, 33180, Finland
ville.tuominen@leadin.fi

Permission to make digital or hard copies of part or all of this work for personal or classroom use is granted without fee provided that copies are not made or distributed for profit or commercial advantage and that copies bear this notice and the full citation on the first page. Copyrights for third-party components of this work must be honored. For all other uses, contact the Owner/Author.
Copyright is held by the owner/author(s).

TVX'16, June 22-24, 2016, Chicago, IL, USA
ACM 978-1-4503-4067-0/16/06.
http://dx.doi.org/10.1145/2932206.2933560

Abstract

This paper presents the current status of the Multi-Platform Application Toolkit, an extensible platform for the simple creation of interactive multi-media applications for connected TVs.

Developing applications from scratch requires considerable resources. For this reason, they are often considered too costly for use alongside short-run programming or in response to spontaneous real-world events. The situation is exacerbated when multiple target platforms are considered, such as HbbTV and Open Web. MPAT addresses this using an approach based on WordPress, aiming to make application development affordable and sustainable. It also creates a new eco-system for content creators, theme and plug-in developers. With MPAT, media companies can semi-automatically author their own set of customised applications. These are then populated with content by the editorial staff, or by linking MPAT to existing content management solutions.

Author Keywords

CMS; HbbTV; Multi-Platform; TV program-related content; Social Media; Multi-screen

ACM Classification Keywords

H5.2 Graphical user interfaces, Screen design, User interface management systems

Introduction

To date, over 20 countries have launched HbbTV services while others have announced future support. This makes it the de facto standard in the European connected TV market. HbbTV plays a major role in media convergence. However, development of applications is still not sufficiently convenient due to market fragmentation, both in devices and revisions of the standard. The lack of widely adopted solutions increases time and cost of delivery.

MPAT aims to fill the gap between quality and the need for cost-effective solutions. Designed for broadcasters and creative agencies alike, it is built on top of the most widely used content management system: WordPress. It utilizes the existing WordPress interface to quickly create web applications with HbbTV specific features, while also maintaining a high level of quality.

The latest version of the HbbTV specification directly supports second screen discovery and timed text markup language. Yet content providers should not need to be aware of these technical details in order to use these features. The toolkit will provide an abstraction layer from the underlying hardware, whether this involves different HbbTV versions or other, web based, connected TV platforms. MPAT will provide a wide set of components and strict rules for third-party plugins to ensure backward compatibility.

By the end of the development, MPAT will also provide tools to automate the management of media assets and the deployment of applications to speed up delivery processes.

Related Work

There is a wealth of Document Engineering techniques for web application authoring, but the reality is that web sites are often designed with commercial authoring tools. Recently, many frameworks have emerged to ease the burden of web application creation. Blogging frameworks like WordPress have been of increasing importance for the creation of simple web sites.

In the web domain, content creators, especially those creating small websites, are most likely to use WordPress. Even though the specific numbers depend on the market segment, it has the largest market share by a wide margin. According to Wappalyzer, 68% of web sites use WordPress [1], with Joomla coming second with 11%. The main advantage for the content creator are the availability of tried and tested, but customizable, templates of professional quality. It is also complimented with a wide range of plug-ins for specific, often used, functions. In most cases a WordPress user does not need to pay specific attention to making their web pages responsive, as it can be assumed that the template will be designed to cover device adaptation.

The Multi-Platform Application Toolkit has its predecessor in the HbbTV Application Toolkit (HAT) editor created in the FI-CONTENT 2 project. HAT [2] embodied the same underlying concepts of providing a simple to use tool for content creators and developers of programme-accompanying content. Unlike MPAT, the system provided its own proprietary web interface and was specifically aimed at the creation of primary screen HbbTV 1.0 applications. HAT was limited by a small set of GUI templates that could be filled with text, images, audio and video content via a responsive HTML5 user interface for desktop and mobile devices alike. A REST-API to the content model of the HAT editor allowed its integration into the existing production environment of content creators and thus supports the alignment of HbbTV apps to established workflows.

An alternative approach to allow the creation of programme-accompanying content is the TV Application Layer (TAL) created by the BBC, which provides a set of JavaScript libraries, which abstract the device capabilities (Connected TVs, set-top boxes, games consoles, Blu-ray players) from the application and acts as a compatibility layer. TAL does not address how the applications themselves are created [3].

Toolkit Created Applications

So far, three applications built with HAT were on air in 2014 and 2015 at the German broadcasters Rundfunk Berlin-Brandenburg (RBB), KiKa and einsfestival [4].

Over the weekend of 8-9 November 2014, Rundfunk Berlin-Brandenburg broadcast a 25-hour long programme to mark the 25th anniversary of the fall of the Berlin Wall. Using the HbbTV Application Toolkit (HAT) technology developed by Fraunhofer FOKUS and IRT, the broadcaster incorporated a live social media feed in the programme. HbbTV-Viewers equipped with HbbTV-enabled TV sets could access this additional content in order to interact with on-screen messaging and photos. Users were able to contribute content via social networks and/or RBB website, and RBB editors acted as moderators of the resulting blog.

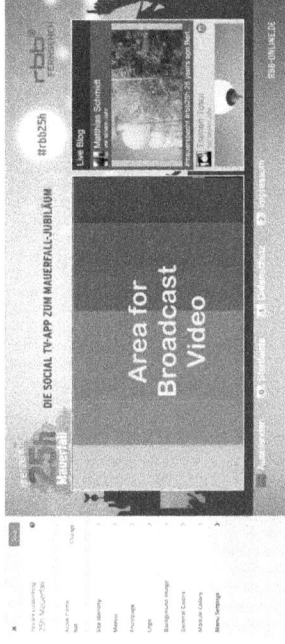

Figure 1: "Mauerfall" application in editor view

The second HAT generated application was the "Verknallt & Abgedreht" app in February 2015. The show was broadcast over 20 episodes. During its initial airing, the app was available in the live feed. The application was available over DVB-T and DVB-S, and had more than 16.500 app interactions made by users.

Figure 2: HbbTV Application Toolkit generated app - Sandmänchen

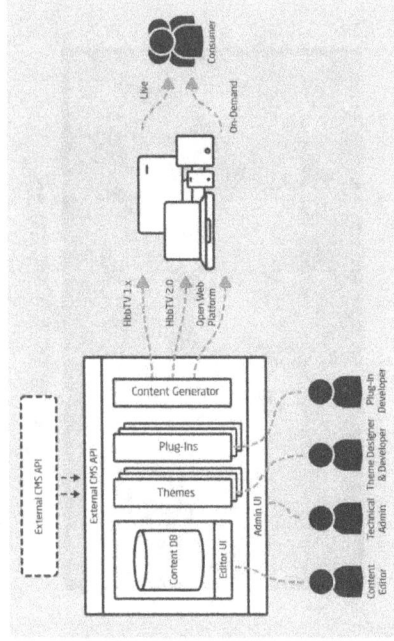

Figure 3: MPAT Core Functionality and Roles

The third, and still on air, application generated by the HbbTV Application Toolkit is the "Sandmännchen" app. The "Sandmännchen" is a popular daily German children's TV show on RBB, KiKa and MDR. The daily "Sandmännchen" is a short, self-contained video of about 10 minutes. The application shows today's episode, alongside four older episodes, in a carousel. The application utilizes the same API as the mobile application of the "Sandmännchen".

Concept

While HAT supported a small number of basic modules (image gallery, video, gallery, social media feed), MPAT builds upon this with an enhanced set of modules. This includes novel functionality that is not available in current applications. MPAT will also provide a fixed set of guidelines for the creation of future modules.

MPAT will also provide an evolution of the simple and accessible authoring interface pioneered in HAT. This will be extensively designed, and suitable for all types of content creators. As well as catering for rapid development, it should also create high quality applications, suitable for widespread distribution and use. To compliment this, MPAT will also provide a set of design guidelines and *golden rules* for developers to follow.

The applications created through MPAT should also allow for a seamless transition between live TV and on-demand consumption. The accompanying user experience should always adapt to the context.

MPAT goes beyond the functionality of HAT by supporting role definition and allocation. These align with the existing work flows used by broadcasters and other content producers. In many cases, the current work flows have strictly defined responsibilities of the participating individuals. A designer is only responsible for the look of the application, but may not add or change content. An editor may add content, but not change the basic layout of a page.

However, the rigid definition of some of these roles is not in place in all organisations, and thus a flexible approach is required. WordPress allows the creation and definition of roles, which MPAT will build upon.

Architecture

The MPAT system architecture is presented in Figure 4. There are three primary parts in this architecture:

1. the WordPress subsystem, which is detailed below;

2. the backend software is responsible for responding to dynamic requests from TVs and second screens;

3. the content server is responsible for serving media in all forms to TV and second screens;

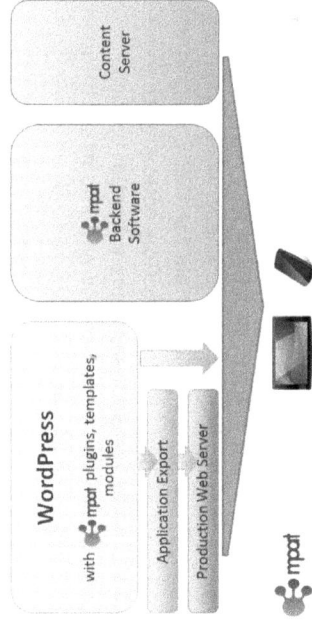

Figure 4: MPAT system overview

As our broadcasting partners often have web servers already in place in their production environment, they have expressed the requirement that WordPress should not be mandatory for the provision of the created application to the end users. As a result, we have added an export of WordPress content to web applications. This can then be served by existing web servers and content distribution networks.

The MPAT system is extensible. The MPAT project will provide a core of open source and free WordPress modules, templates and widgets. A set of APIs will be available to extend the MPAT core with your own plugins, as well as with commercial plugins from any vendor.

It will also be possible to integrate external tools into the MPAT system, such as tools like media editors and encoders are already used by broadcasters; online social media integration services, such as Scribble; and new tools like timed metadata editors, which allow for the specific placement of MPAT applications within media content. This includes points of interests in the broadcast stream to provide, for example, follow-up URLs or of interactive advertisements.

Use Cases

MPAT is a solution to build rich content centric social experiences. Finding the right balance between content producer needs, enabling technologies and consumer value is critical for media companies. MPAT encapsulates the interactions between content producers, broadcasters and the audience. Multiple roles are included in building the actual experience.

During the MPAT project, a number of use cases will be identified, implemented and piloted in more detail. The design phase is heavily driven by a user-centric approach, with use cases determined by user insight gained from previous studies and workshops with focus groups.

A number of unique use cases were proposed by the project partners themselves. These were collected through a variety of mechanisms, including engagement with internal project teams responsible for content creation and presentation, and interviews with external organizations that have no experience with creating applications for television. Previous research activities within partner organizations were also proposed and for some use cases, there was already existing business rationale.

139

provide a platform that grants content creators access to tested building blocks. These need to be sufficiently powerful as to allow creators to produce quality applications. They also need to be sufficiently generic as to allow them to be used over a wide range of applications.

Acknowledgements

This work is supported by the Collaborative Project Multi-Platform Application Toolkit (www.mpat.eu) funded by the European Commission through the Horizon 2020 Programme (H2020-ICT-2015, call ICT-19-2015) under grant agreement n° 687921. These contents are the sole responsibility of the MPAT Partnership and can under no circumstances be regarded as reflecting the position of the EU or the Programme's management structures.

The partners in the project are Fraunhofer FOKUS (DE), Institut fuer Rundfunktechnik (DE), rbb (DE), Mediaset (IT), Fincons (IT), Leadin (FI), University of Lancaster (UK), ParisTech (FR)

References

1. Open Source CMS, webpage, Retrieved May, 5th, 2016 from http://www.opensourcecms.com/general/cms-marketshare.php

2. HbbTV Application Toolkit, webpage, Retrieved April, 6, 2016 from http://lab.mediafi.org/discover-hbbtvapplicationtoolkit-overview.html

3. TV Application Layer, webpage. Retrieved April, 6, 2016 from http://lab.mediafi.org/discover-tvapplicationlayer-overview.html

4. C. Ziegler, M. Zwicklbauer, M. Gordon - HbbTV Application Toolkit - HAT, Industrial Paper at TVX 2015

Prioritization of use cases was achieved through a ranking mechanism, with each project partner declaring the set of use cases that they deemed to be most important. Given that the project consortium is diverse, with broadcasters, universities and research organizations all included, the resulting outcome could be consider relatively representative. In fact, those use cases chosen for inclusion in the project had almost unanimous agreement between partners. By focusing on actual consumer experience, a joint framework can be formed which incorporates business needs, technical possibilities and consumer value.

Moving Forward and Future Work

Progress continues on developing MPAT, with effort now placed in implementing the functionality described previously. Furthermore, graphical user interface designs are also being created. These will be used in further focus groups to ascertain feedback early in the project development lifecycle. Consequently, changes will be made in response to any potential usability concerns or improvements deemed important through the conduction of this testing.

Finding the focus and common vision between diverse partners (designers, programmers, content creators and broadcasters) involved in the project is essential for both productive work and ensuring wider applicability.

Conclusion

The Multi-Platform Application Toolkit as a connected TV platform provides many technical possibilities. Its goal is to create a baseline for rapid content development and distribution. The challenge is to

Automated News Generation for TV Program Ratings

Soomin Kim
Human-Computer Interaction &
Design Lab.
Seoul National University
soominkim@snu.ac.kr

JongHwan Oh
Human-Computer Interaction &
Design Lab.
Seoul National University
whee0501@snu.ac.kr

Joonhwan Lee
Human-Computer Interaction &
Design Lab.
Seoul National University
joonhwan@snu.ac.kr

Permission to make digital or hard copies of part or all of this work
for personal or classroom use is granted without fee provided that
copies are not made or distributed for profit or commercial
advantage and that copies bear this notice and the full citation on the
first page. Copyrights for third-party components of this work must
be honored. For all other uses, contact the Owner/Author.
Copyright is held by the owner/author(s).
TVX'16, June 22-24, 2016, Chicago, IL, USA
ACM 978-1-4503-4067-0/16/06.
http://dx.doi.org/10.1145/2932206.2933561

Abstract

Automated journalism, automatically generating stories
based on algorithms, has received considerable critical attention in diverse fields. However, automated journalism
has not addressed the TV industry in much detail. This research aims to create a system to automatically generate
news about TV ratings. The framework will involve under-
going the processes of data gathering, identifying important events by predefined algorithms, generating a story in
narrative format, and publishing the output. The algorithm
that determines the structure of the stories is defined by
analyzing existing news about TV ratings that reflects key
variables. Although the output of the research is limited to
one type of news template, further attempts could expand
to various formats.

Author Keywords

Automated News; Automated Journalism; Computational
Journalism; Natural Language Generation

ACM Classification Keywords

K.4.3 [Computers and Society]: Organizational Impacts; J.4
[Social and Behavioral Science]: Sociology; H.3.5 [Online
Information Services]: Web-based services

Introduction

In January 2015, an article titled "Apple Tops Street 1Q Forecast" was released [1]. It was a piece of ordinary finance news published by the Associated Press (AP), written by an algorithm developed by Automated Insights [2]. Subsequently, the convergence of journalism and computational science led to the advent of the emerging field of "computational journalism." Computational journalism can be defined as an area where "computation advances journalism by drawing on innovations in topic detection, video analysis, personalization, aggregation, visualization, and sensemaking" when stories including news and reports are "discovered, presented, aggregated, monetized and archived [3]." In the realm of computational journalism, "automatic journalism," also referred to as "algorithmic journalism [6]," specifically refers to the field where algorithms are used to automatically generate news stories [2].

Automated journalism is often applied in the areas of weather [8], finance [3], and sports [1], where the underlying data are accurate and reliable. This is because automated journalism requires high-quality data that is structured and accurate [2]. Despite the growing number of applications of automated narratives in various domains, no attempts have been made that applied to the television industry.

This paper suggests a methodology of automatically generated news about TV ratings to increase efficiency by automating repetitive tasks. The framework goes through the processes of data gathering, identifying key events by a predefined algorithm, generating a story, and publishing.

---

[1] http://finance.yahoo.com/news/apple-tops-street-1q-forecasts-213944804.html

[2] https://automatedinsights.com/

[3] https://blog.ap.org/announcements/automated-earnings-stories-multiply, http://www.forbes.com/sites/narrativescience

The algorithm that determines the structure of the story is defined by analyzing existing news of TV ratings reflecting key variables. Furthermore, not only TV ratings but also diverse data such as online streaming viewers, social opinions, and online clip views could be the topic of automated news in the television industry.

Related Work

Automated journalism

Automated journalism is the process of automatically generating stories with predefined algorithms [2]. An algorithm refers to a "well-defined computational procedure that takes some value, or set of values as input and produces some value, or set of values as output [5]." Algorithms include the process of input, throughput (processing), and output. Therefore, algorithms are designed to logically process the data for a meaningful output. This also applies to algorithm-based automated journalism. To produce news stories automatically, we need high-quality data (input) and reliably designed algorithms (throughput) to create relevant news stories in narrative form (output). The typical companies providing automated journalism solutions are Automated Insights [4] and Narrative Science [5]. Their solutions are not limited to news or journalism areas. They also cover financial services, business reports [6], etc. However, far too little attention has been paid to the television industry.

TV ratings

In the television industry, one of the most important indexes is TV ratings, which determine the popularity of TV programs and charges for advertisement. Among TV ratings, the demographic of viewers in the age range of 18 to 49 is crucial because of their buying habits [9]. Representative

---

[4] https://automatedinsights.com/

[5] https://www.narrativescience.com/

[6] https://automatedinsights.com/solutions/

TV ratings include the ratings points, share, and total viewers among adults 18-49 [7].

Even though ratings points/share is the major evaluation criterion for the value of TV programs, the diffusion of digital media has weakened its impact. Because of the widespread use of digital media, the watching pattern of TV programs has changed. According to Ericsson [4], 86 percent of smartphone users watch video content on their phones. Applying the new trend of media use, "social rating [8]" is suggested as the new measure of audience engagement. It measures both activities (authors, tweets) and reach (unique audience, impressions) on Twitter. The research restricted the object of analysis to traditional TV ratings, after which the social data could be included as part of the input data if the data processing method was well defined.

System Overview

Framework

Primarily, natural language generation is explained within the framework of algorithmic selection along the Input-Transform-Outcome (ITO) model [6]. Based on the natural language generation process [7], the framework of auto-mated news generation of TV program ratings has been subdivided into five stages: 1) collecting data, 2) identifying interesting events, 3) prioritizing insights, 4) generating the narrative, and 5) publishing the story (Figure 1).

- Collecting data: The first step is data collecting and cleaning. Data could be obtained from databases, files, logs, system interfaces, etc. The original source of the raw data requires a processing procedure, which includes merging, subsetting, and transforming to be ready for the next level. After gathering data, a procedure for identifying useful information (struc-tured data) is needed for the intended output. Data is accessible through APIs or databases.

- Identifying interesting events: This is the stage that identifies the input-output relationship with a specific algorithm. Predetermined rules are applied to the algorithm to choose and process data for meaningful outcomes.

- Prioritizing insights: In this stage, meaningful vari-ables and events are selected. For Nielson televi-sion ratings, "ratings points/share" and "total viewers" could be the variables. In this case, fluctuation (up-ward/downward) and ranking (of broadcast networks or programs) of those indexes are important events. In addition to traditional ratings, with the widespread use of digital media, social media indexes such as "Nielsen Twitter TV Ratings [9]," a new method to as-sess TV programs' influence, could be included as a significant factor. After important events in the data are defined, the algorithm categorizes and identi-fies those events by importance. This is the process of creating the mood of the stories, which would be specified afterward.

- Generating the narrative: Based on the algorithm, the news narrative is generated by predefined structures and specific sentences.

- Publishing the story: Finally, the completed story is uploaded and published. In this stage, the story could be uploaded either automatically or after examination.

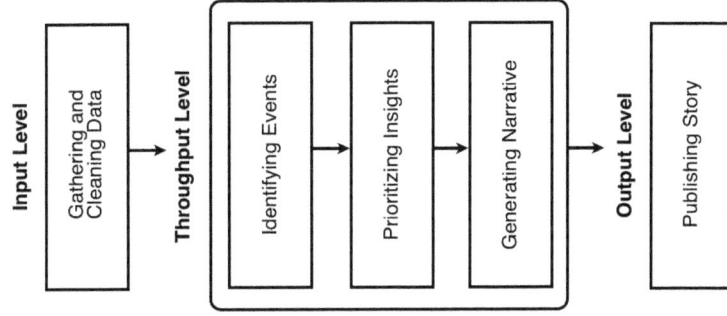

Figure 1: Framework of Automated Journalism

Input Level

Gathering and Cleaning Data

Throughput Level

Identifying Events

Prioritizing Insights

Generating Narrative

Output Level

Publishing Story

---

[7]Rating: Estimated percentage of the universe of TV households (or other specified group) tuned to a program in the average minute. Ratings are expressed as a percent. Share is the percentage of television sets in use that are tuned to the program.

[8]http://www.nielsensocial.com/

[9]http://www.nielsensocial.com/product/nielsen-twitter-tv-ratings/

143

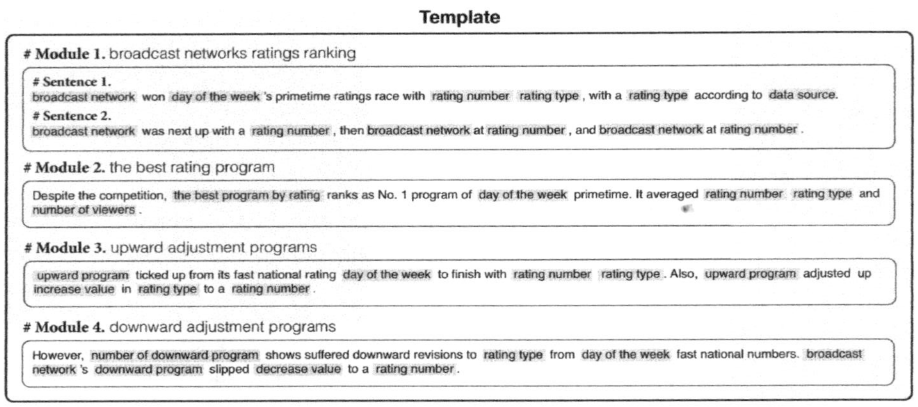

Template

Module 1. broadcast networks ratings ranking

Sentence 1.
broadcast network won day of the week 's primetime ratings race with rating number rating type according to data source.
Sentence 2.
broadcast network was next up with a rating number , then broadcast network at rating number , and broadcast network at rating number .

Module 2. the best rating program

Despite the competition, the best program by rating ranks as No. 1 program of day of the week primetime. It averaged rating number rating type and number of viewers .

Module 3. upward adjustment programs

upward program ticked up from its fast national rating day of the week to finish with rating number rating type. Also, upward program adjusted up increase value in rating type to a rating number.

Module 4. downward adjustment programs

However, number of downward program shows suffered downward revisions to rating type from day of the week fast national numbers. broadcast network 's downward program slipped decrease value to a rating number.

Figure 2: Example of News Article Structure

News Article Structure

The structure of news has several variables, defined below (Figure 2). Figure 2 illustrates the relationship between four variables.

- Template: A template is the whole structure of the news story. Based on selected events through the process of prioritizing insights, the algorithm chooses one from the predefined set of templates. In this example, only one template—one type of news article—is suggested. Nevertheless, it would expand to various templates, each of them containing a different point of view.
- Module: A module is the building block of the template. Each of the modules contains critical issues, such as the daily ranking of broadcast networks, the best rating program, etc. Some modules could be ruled out if they are not so significant to the situation.

A module is composed of sentences that are predefined by the developer.

- Sentence: Sentences compose the module. It is the unit of the module that actualizes the main topics into natural language.
- Data: Data are the initial input of the overall process of automated journalism. By assembling, cleaning, and analyzing data, the whole narrative is completed.

Discussion & Conclusion

We have suggested a way of automating the generation process of news in the TV industry. By automating processes such as data gathering, data analysis, writing stories and reports, and publishing, the speed and accuracy of the working process could be increased [2]. The suggested framework and news article structure would be the foundation for further research on TV news generation in the future.

There are several points that might be improved in future research. Above all, by implementing a working prototype, more experiments that could evaluate the results may be developed in order to identify the different qualities of the articles generated by the algorithm and those written by human journalists.

In addition, the type of news article template could be further expanded by analyzing significant data in the TV industry. Not only TV ratings but also public opinions about TV programs could serve as a form of report by analyzing social data. More comprehensive research on news format and data processing may be used to develop automated journalism in the TV industry.

Acknowledgments

This work was supported by the CPRC program of MSIP/IITP. (IITP-2015-H8201-15-1004)

This study was financially supported in part by the Institute of Communication Research, Seoul National University.

REFERENCES

1. Nicholas D Allen, John R Templon, Patrick Summerhays McNally, Larry Birnbaum, and Kristian J Hammond. 2010. StatsMonkey: A Data-Driven Sports Narrative Writer.. In *AAAI Fall Symposium: Computational Models of Narrative.*

2. Tow Center. 2016. Guide to Automated Journalism. (7 January 2016). Retrieved from http://towcenter.org/research/guide-to-automated-journalism/.

3. Sarah Cohen, James T Hamilton, and Fred Turner. 2011. Computational journalism. *Commun. ACM* 54, 10 (2011), 66–71.

4. Ericsson ConsumerLab. 2015. TV and Media, 2015. (September 2015). Retrieved from http://www.ericsson.com/res/docs/2015/consumerlab/ ericsson-consumerlab-tv-media-2015.pdf.

5. Thomas H Cormen. 2009. *Introduction to algorithms.* MIT press.

6. Konstantin Nicholas Dörr. 2015. Mapping the field of Algorithmic Journalism. *Digital Journalism* (2015), 1–23.

7. Ehud Reiter, Robert Dale, and Zhiwei Feng. 2000. *Building natural language generation systems.* Vol. 33. MIT Press.

8. Ehud Reiter, Somayajulu Sripada, Jim Hunter, Jin Yu, and Ian Davy. 2005. Choosing words in computer-generated weather forecasts. *Artificial Intelligence* 167, 1 (2005), 137–169.

9. Michael Storey. 2009. The TV column: Not in 18–49 age group? TV execs write you off. *Arkansas Online* 23 (2009).

A System Designed to Collect Users' TV-Watching Data Using a Smart TV, Smartphones, and Smart Watches

Jehwan Seo
Core Tech Lab, VD Division
Samsung Electronics
jehwan.seo@samsung.com

Hyunchul Lim
Human Centered Computing Lab
Seoul National University
hyunchul@snu.ac.kr

Changhoon Oh
Human Centered Computing Lab
Seoul National University
yurial@snu.ac.kr

Hyun-kyu Yun
Core Tech Lab, VD Division
Samsung Electronics
hyunkyu.yun@samsung.com

Bongwon Suh
Human Centered Computing Lab
Seoul National University
bongwon@snu.ac.kr

Joongseek Lee
User Experience Lab
Seoul National University
joonlee8@snu.ac.kr

Permission to make digital or hard copies of part or all of this work for personal or classroom use is granted without fee provided that copies are not made or distributed for profit or commercial advantage and that copies bear this notice and the full citation on the first page. Copyrights for third-party components of this work must be honored. For all other uses, contact the Owner/Author.
Copyright is held by the owner/author(s).

TVX'16, June 22-24, 2016, Chicago, IL, USA
ACM 978-1-4503-4067-0/16/06.
http://dx.doi.org/10.1145/2932206.2933562

Abstract

In this study, we suggest an enhanced smart TV logging system composed of a smart TV, smartphone, and smart watch. It can be used to research the audience's complicated and segmented behaviors while watching TV. We designed a prototype of the system, which can not only detect whether viewers are located in the TV-viewing area but also measure their movements and activities by analyzing beacon signals and sensor data from the smart watch. We conducted a technical evaluation to verify its fidelity and measure its performance, and a user study identified what factors affect the users' level of engagement with the TV content. The experiment results showed that the system accurately detected and measured users' location and engagement levels while watching TV. We found that smartphone usage while watching TV is important in understanding users' TV-viewing behavior.

Authors Keywords

TV-watching behavior; beacon; smart TV; smart watch; TV rating; machine learning.

ACM Classification Keywords

H.5.m. Information interfaces and presentation (e.g., HCI), miscellaneous

Introduction and Related Work

TV-viewing behaviors are not simple. Viewers do many other activities after turning on the TV, including moving around the house, using a smartphone, and doing chores, which may distract viewers from watching TV [2, 9]. Hence, advertisers and TV networks want to know not only if the TV is turned on but also if viewers are paying close attention to TV programs. Understanding the viewers' TV-watching context could help to measure their engagement level. Recognizing a viewer's engagement level could benefit both viewers and TV-rating firms: viewers could receive a personalized service, while TV-rating firms could build enhanced business models by using viewers' engagement level.

To address the issue, we suggested the smart TV logging system [9] that utilized a beacon and smartphones to investigate the viewer's TV-watching behavior. However, the system has a number of limitations: (1) viewers do not necessarily carry their smartphone with them all the time, (2) the system does not capture viewers' activities not involving digital devices (e.g., house chores), and (3) multiple beacons incur the high cost of installation and maintenance.

In order to address these issues, we propose an enhanced smart TV logging system by adding smart watches with a beacon to the previous system. Using smart watches has many benefits. First, TV viewers can wear a smart watch all the time, which can help avoid data loss. Second, the inertial sensors embedded in smart watches can track the motion of viewers and infer their activities [3, 4] while they watch TV. Lastly, our system uses a few beacons for detecting viewers' location because it requires only one beacon per a viewer.

To verify the feasibility of our system, we installed a prototype in two types of apartments and conducted experiments, consisting of a technical evaluation and user study. The results of the technical evaluation show that (1) both beacon signals and inertial sensors from the smart watches can accurately detect whether viewers are in front of TV, and (2) they provide information to infer viewers' activities while watching TV. Moreover, through the user study, we found that the TV-viewing engagement level could be measured based on the system logs.

System Design

We designed an enhanced smart TV logging system that comprises smart watches with a beacon, smartphones, and a smart TV with a beacon collector (Figure 1). Our goal is to collect viewers' TV-watching data from the system for understanding their TV-viewing behavior. To attain this goal, we used the RSSI (Received signal strength indiccation) [8], accelerometer, and gyroscope data from smart watches to keep track of users' activities and then detect whether users are located in TV-watching zone. Along with these users' information, smartphone app-usage data were employed to figure out what users actually did while watching TV.

Figure 1: The research prototype system comprises a smart watch with a beacon, a smartphone, and a smart TV with a beacon collector.

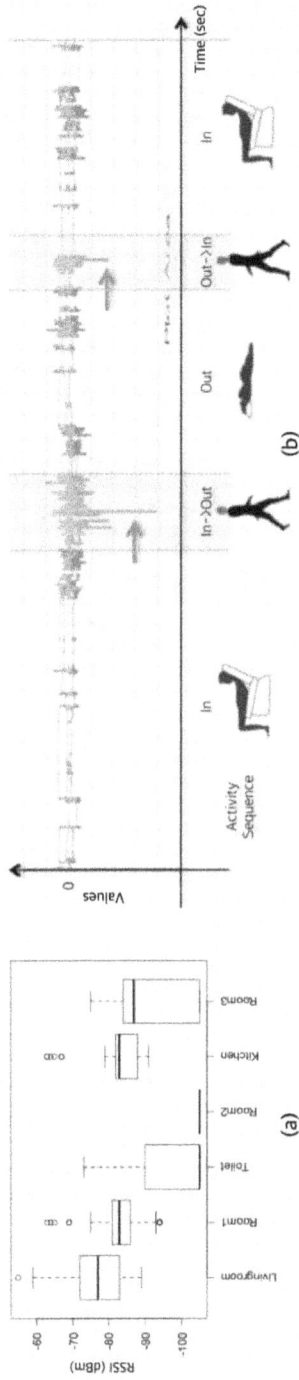

Figure 3: (a) Box plot of RSSI from a smart watch when a participant moves around the house. (b) The six values from an accelerometer and a gyroscope show typical patterns when a person moves from one place to another.

Technical Evaluation

In the first part of the evaluation, we conducted a technical evaluation of the prototype. We estimated how the system accurately finds the user's location and how much it has been enhanced according to the each system component.

Method

We recruited two households for the experiments and installed the prototype in these two houses. Both houses were typical Korean apartments. One is an 80-m^2 apartment with three bedrooms, one bathroom, a living room, and a kitchen. The other is a 159-m^2 house with four bedrooms, two bathrooms, a living room, and a kitchen. Two family members from each household took part in the experiment, and we gathered data from a total of four participants (two males and two females aged between 29 and 38). Participants wore a smart watch with a beacon on the left or right wrist. A beacon collector was installed in front of the TV. This setup allowed us to receive the beacon's signal from the smart watch and then identify if viewers were in

To assess the effectiveness of data metioned above as features for detecting viewers' location, we performed a pilot study with two participants who we asked to move around a house while wearing a smart watch. We collected the data at 100 Hz from a beacon (Gimbal) and a smart watch (Samsung Galaxy Gear Live). As shown in Figure 3, when participants moved from one place to another, (a) there are differences in RSSI values among locations in a house. Also, (b) the accelerometer and gyroscope values had typical patterns when participants were moving or staying in the places. From our initial insights, we select RSSI and sensors' values to detect whether viewers are located in a certain area as Zone A, the user's TV-watching zone (Figure 2).

In order to determine if a person is not watching TV when he or she is located in Zone A, we collected smartphone usage logs using the App Usage Tracker [1]. We analyzed the usage logs and the activitiy logs to identify the relationship among smartphone use, viewer's activitiy and TV viewing.

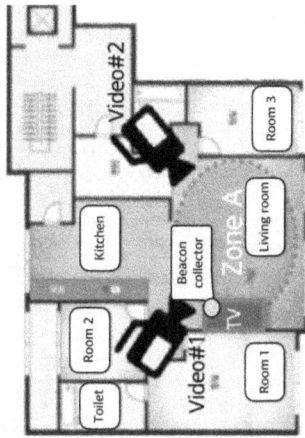

Figure 2: We assumed that the TV with the beacon collector is located in the living room (called Zone A), where the person usually watches TV. For the user study, we recorded the TV screen and viewers with two cameras.

Lastly, since RSSI values fluctuate considerably due to environmental factors such as reflections and wall damping [5], we used the majority-voting technique to improve the accuracy of the system. The result shows that the accuracy of using RSSI values alone increased from 91.16% to 94.00.%, and the accuracy of using beacon and sensor values combined increased from 93.95% to 96.58%.

Result 2. Per-User Classifiers vs. Per-Location Classifiers

Inspired by Harrison et al. [7], we evaluated our system in three different conditions: ten-fold cross validation using all data, per-user classifiers, and general classifiers.

	System Accuracy (%)			
	BO	BO (MV)	BO+SV	BO+SV (MV)
10-fold cross validation	91.16%	94.00%	93.95%	96.58%
Per-user classifiers	90.90% (1.97%)	94.00% (1.17%)	94.20% (0.79%)	96.80% (0.72%)
Per-location classifiers	90.04% (1.62%)	94.36% (1.48%)	94.67% (0.11%)	97.11% (0.77%)

Table 1: Accuracy (SD in parentheses) of our system: ten-fold cross validation with all data, per-user classifiers, and per-location classifiers. BO = beacon data only; SV = beacon and sensor values combined; MV = majority-voting technique used in the data.

Ten-Fold Cross Validation with All Data: We ran a conventional ten-fold cross validation using all data from the four participants. As shown in Table 1, the 10-

Zone A (Figure 2). We simultaneously collected three types of data: (1) we recorded the TV screen and viewers' TV-viewing activities with two video cameras (Figure 2); (2) we collected beacon signal logs and sensor values from the smart watches at 100 Hz; and (3) we gathered smartphone usage logs with the App Usage Tracker application on the participants' smartphones. Each experiment lasted about two hours.

After the experiment, we analyzed the beacon signal logs and measured how the signals detected if viewers were in the TV-watching zone using machine-learning approaches, such as random forest, logistic regression, and multilayer perceptron.

Result 1. The Effect of Sensor Values, Window Size and Majority-Voting Method

First, we examined the effect of the window size because it could affect the performance of classifiers [6]. We examined five types of window sizes: 5, 11, 21, 41, and 61 seconds. We used RSSI and sensor values combined to validate the performance of random forest, logistic regression, and multilayer perceptron. The results (Figure 4) show that accuracy improves until the 11-second window. The random forest approach performed better than the other two classifier methods. Thus, we decided to use the random forest technique with the window size of 11 for the following evaluation.

Next, we investigated the effect of the sensor values from the smart watches. We compared the accuracy of RSSI values alone with the accuracy of RSSI and sensor values combined. As shown in Figure 5, using both beacon data and sensor values achieved high accuracy of 96.58% with small standard deviation.

Figure 4: The accuracy of RSSI and sensor values combined with different size of window and classifiers (ten-fold cross validation).

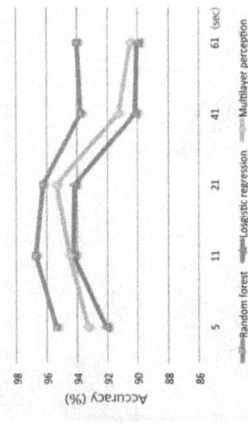

Figure 5: The accuracy of RSSI values alone vs. The accuracy of RSSI and sensor values combined.

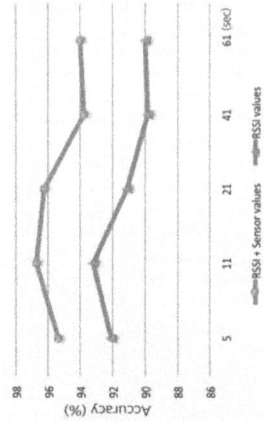

151

fold cross validation showed high accuracy of over 96% when using combined beacon and sensor values and majority-voting technique. This result gives us a basic evaluation where the users' data is known a priori, and we can train and adjust a model to a particular group of users. Two further evaluations and analyses examined our techniques in more realistic situations.

Per-User Classifiers: It is important to understand how the features perform at a per-user level [7]. We divided the data between the participants and conducted a ten-fold cross validation for each participant's data. The features are not related to specific users (see Table 1; there is a small standard deviation).

Per-Location Classifiers: The experiment locations had different dimensions. Therefore, we performed an analysis to find out if spatial dimensions affect our system and if we can use it as a general model regardless of house size. Table 1 shows that house size does not affect system accuracy.

User Study

Participants completed a survey to identify in detail what actually happens while they watch TV. In other words, we aimed to identify users' level of engagement and whether they focused on TV content, even when the system log showed they were in front of the TV.

Methodology

To measure the users' engagement level with TV content, we provided the participants with a simple survey about the TV content and conducted a post hoc interview. The survey consisted of video clips and questions asking whether they remember the content. We extracted the video clips from the content the

participants had watched and edited them into one-minute units. We randomly showed the clips to the participants and asked them to choose an answer from three options: (1) 'watched', (2) 'don't know', and (3) 'didn't watch.' We collected a total of 90 responses from the participants. After the survey we interviewed the participants about what they thought of the system and what factors could affect their TV-watching level of engagement.

Result

From 90 answers, the number of 'watched' was 63, the number of 'don't know' was 6, and the number of 'didn't watch' was 22 (Table 2). The result shows that the participants watched the TV more than half of the time. However, even if the participants were located in front of the TV, they sometimes lost concentration and did other things.

We classified each response according to the system log information, such as users' location. As shown in Table 3, among the responses that were classified in Zone A (69), 62 responses were the cases where the participants actually watched the content. However, in the remaining seven cases (10.1%), they didn't concentrate on the TV even if they were in front of the TV. To investigate what factors affected their distraction, we checked the users' smartphone app usage from the system logs and their behavior video data. In four out of seven cases, the participants showed various non-TV-watching behaviors, such as doing the laundry or talking to other people. In the other three cases, the participants used their smartphones and did not concentrate on the TV content. Using a web browser, they sometimes checked portal sites and read news articles. One participant

Response	Count
Watched	62
Don't know	6
Didn't watch	22
Total	90

Table 2: Video clip survey responses

	Video Clip Survey	
	Watched	Didn't Watch
TV Watching Zone In/Out (times)	In: 62 Out: 0	In: 7 Out: 15
Smartphone Use (times)	8	5

Table 3: Video clip survey results classified by TV watching zone in/out and smartphone usage.

looked at old pictures in his Gallery folder for more than three minutes. Noting the importance of the smartphone, we also checked smartphone usage in the cases where users answered that they watched the video clips. We identified eight cases, and users often browsed messengers apps or Facebook, or they sometimes searched the Internet for information related to the TV content they were watching. These results show that it is important to integrate users' smartphone usage in order to comprehensively understand viewers' TV-watching behavior and measure their level of engagement with TV content.

We briefly present the result of the post hoc interview, which might be helpful to understand the participants' thoughts about the experiments and their engagement with the TV screen. P01 said, "Remember the first 30 seconds, but I do not remember the rest!" Because we had split the video clips into one-minute units, users could not entirely remember the content if they had moved or been distracted when watching the unedited TV content during the experiment. Results from the technical evaluation logs support these explanations. The participants frequently moved in and out of Zone A during the experiment (62 times). Meanwhile, the interview let us discover the effect of smartphone usage on the viewers' TV immersion. We asked P02 to describe the video content played when he was using his smartphone, and he said, "This scene looks as though I haven't been paying much attention." Lastly, the issue about the boundary of TV-watching Zone A was also raised. P03 said, "I was not in the living room, but I was watching once in a while in the room while doing my chores." This was possible because the door of the room was open, and the participant could watch TV without entering the living room. In the experiment, we made the TV-watching zone a fixed area, such as the living room. However, depending on the TV's location or the layout of the rooms, the boundary of the TV-watching zone could be enlarged into marginal areas.

Conclusions and Future Work

In this study, we proposed a system that can be used to accurately measure and analyze the diverse and subdivided patterns of users' TV-watching behavior. Above all, by integrating users' smart watches into the system, we could overcome the disadvantages of previous user location tracking systems. In order to evaluate our system's feasibility, we installed prototypes and conducted a technical evaluation and user study. The result of the experiment showed that the accuracy and reliability of the proposed system were significantly acceptable. Moreover, from the results of the user study, we could find out users' behaviors while watching TV and what factors affect their level of engagement with the TV content.

Although we obtained statistically significant results from the technical evaluation of the proposed system, we could not gather enough data to analyze users' TV-watching patterns. Obtaining clearer data and training the model will lead to more accurate study results. In future work, we plan to conduct a large-scale user study to overcome this drawback and to introduce various sensor technologies in the system design. In addition, a pattern recognition method could be used to monitor the TV-watching behavior of users in Zone A. Information about viewers' smartphone application usage while watching TV, their search queries, and their application usage time could be used to calculate the specific level TV viewers' immersion.

References

1. App Usage Tracker
   https://play.google.com/store/apps/details?id=com
   .agrvaibhav.AppUsageTracking&hl=ko

2. Abreu, Jorge, et al. "Viewer behaviors and practices
   in the (new) Television Environment." In Proc. on
   Interactive TV and video. ACM, 2013

3. Bieber, Gerald, Marian Haescher, and Matthias
   Vahl. "Sensor requirements for activity recognition
   on smart watches." *Proceedings of the 6th
   International Conference on PErvasive Technologies
   Related to Assistive Environments.* ACM, 2013.

4. Case, Meredith A., et al. "Accuracy of smartphone
   applications and wearable devices for tracking
   physical activity data." *Jama* 313.6 (2015): 625-
   626.

5. Feldmann, S., Kyamakya, K., Zapater, A., & Lue, Z.
   (2003, June). An Indoor Bluetooth-Based
   Positioning System: Concept, Implementation and
   Experimental Evaluation. In *International
   Conference on Wireless Networks* (pp. 109-113).

6. Fujinami, Kaori, and Satoshi Kouchi. "Recognizing a
   Mobile Phone's Storing Position as a Context of a
   Device and a User." *Mobile and ubiquitous
   systems: computing, networking, and services.*
   Springer Berlin Heidelberg, 2012. 76-88.

7. Harrison, Chris, Julia Schwarz, and Scott E.
   Hudson. "TapSense: enhancing finger interaction
   on touch surfaces." Proceedings of the 24th annual
   ACM symposium on User interface software and
   technology. ACM, 2011.

8. RSSI, Wikipedia
   https://en.wikipedia.org/wiki/Received_signal_stre
   ngth_indication

9. Seo, J., Kim, D., Suh, B., & Lee, J. (2015, April).
   Design of a Smart TV Logging System Using
   Beacons and Smartphones. In Proceedings of the
   33rd Annual ACM Conference Extended Abstracts
   on Human Factors in Computing Systems (pp.
   2157-2162). ACM.

Towards Biometric Assessment of Audience Affect

Jacob L. Wieland
DR[1]
jlwieland@gmail.com

Lotte I. Jørgensen
AAU[2]
lija12@Student.aau.dk

Lars B. Larsen
AAU[2]
lbl@es.aau.dk

Anne Mette K. Jessen
AAU[2]
amkj11@Student.aau.dk

Jeanette K. Laursen
AAU[2]
jelaur12@Student.aau.dk

Charlotte T. Jensen
AAU[2]
ctje12@Student.aau.dk

1) DR Media Research, The Danish Broadcasting Corporation, Copenhagen Denmark
2) Aalborg University, Aalborg Denmark

Permission to make digital or hard copies of part or all of this work for personal or classroom use is granted without fee provided that copies are not made or distributed for profit or commercial advantage and that copies bear this notice and the full citation on the first page. Copyrights for third-party components of this work must be honored. For all other uses, contact the Owner/Author.
Copyright is held by the owner/author(s).

TVX'16, June 22-24, 2016, Chicago, IL, USA
ACM 978-1-4503-4067-0/16/06.
http://dx.doi.org/10.1145/2932206.2933563

Abstract

This paper investigates how reliable affective responses can be obtained using objective biometric measures for media audience research. We use Galvanic Skin Response (GSR) to detect sixteen respondents' arousal levels and as an objective measure to show how self-reporting disrupts the experience of respondents watching video content. The subjective experiences from nine subjects were captured by self-reporting via the widely used SAM pictogram scale every three minutes. We found that interruptions induced by the self-reporting events cause them to consistently exhibit arousal peaks. Our post test measures show a negative effect on the subjects' overall experience of the video and their empathy and identification with the main characters compared to the remaining subjects. We observed a 30 second return period from abnormal arousal levels after the self-reporting interruptions.

Author Keywords

Audience Research; Galvanic Skin Response; Biometrics; Self-reporting; SAM; Affect Response; Emotions.

ACM Classification Keywords

H.1.2 User/Machine Systems, Human factors, *Human information processing.* H.5.1. Information interfaces and presentation (e.g. HCI), Multimedia Information Systems, *Evaluation/methodology, Video.*

Introduction

Digital mass media audience research broadly deals with audience reactions, opinions, preferences, etc., towards media contents and formats. Thus, it is a multi disciplinary and very diverse field applying a plethora of methods with different goals and from different viewpoints. Among these, test screenings have at least two equally important purposes within applied audience research:: To assess the potential appeal for the intended audience and to help those creatively responsible (script writers, directors, etc.) to determine if their creative visions are reflected in the audience reactions. In the present work we will focus on the emotional impact on audiences when exposed to video in test screening scenarios using biometric measures.

We set out investigate how objective GSR measures of human emotional expressions can be reliably obtained and aggregated from individual persons. In addition, we use the GSR data to show the disruptive effect of self-reporting. The overall context of the study is defined by a setup developed jointly by the Nordic broadcasting corporations and used for a number of years [1]. It has been applied in various forms, e.g. using mentometers and other tools to collect participants' emotional responses. Very briefly described, the present approach at DR[1] applies GSR recordings at video screenings. GSR captures the respondents' emotional arousal (or engagement). The screening is followed by a cued-recall session [4], where the high-arousal scenes are reviewed and respondents are asked to recall and identify their emotional state during the screening using Rolls emotions diagram [22]. Some well-known issues are associated with this [18]. The respondents' recall of the experienced emotions might be faulty and low-intensity emotions can be hard to recall at a later time or may be

overshadowed due to the *peak-end rule* [30]. The method corresponds to what Rosenberg and Ekman denote *cued review* in [23].

An alternative approach would be to interrupt the respondents at pre-set intervals during the screening session and ask them to self-report their emotional state at that instant, e.g. using the SAM scale [15] or a mentometer app installed on their iPad. Indeed, this approach is common and has also been applied at DR. The drawback is the risk that such interruptions can disrupt the experience and hence bias the emotional response of the respondents negatively.

The following section discusses how human affect can be modelled and measured using either self-reporting (subjective) or biometric (objective) methods. The experimental setup is described in the subsequent section. The final sections present the results, a discussion and the conclusions.

Measuring Human Affect

Emotions are perceived and cognitively interpreted by the brain, but are closely linked to the physical reactions of the body, such as heart rate, perspiration, facial expressions, etc. [9]. Early researchers such as James-Lange argued that we experience emotions by detecting and interpreting our bodily reactions [6], while more recent theories view this as a more complex and mixed cognitive-physiological interplay [6], [28].

The Core Affect model

A widely used model for description of emotional experience is the *Core Affect Model* see e.g. [24]. Russell defines core affect as "A neurophysiological state that is consciously accessible as a simple, non reflective feeling

---

Human Affect and Emotions

Human Affect and Emotions have been studied for millennia. Ancient Chinese and Greek scholars were the first to put forward theories. Modern time research started with Charles Darwin, William James and Carl Lange in the late nineteenth century [9].

In 2001 Plutchick counted more than 90 different theories and models of human emotions formulated during the 20th century [20].

Affect and Emotion

Affect and Emotion are often used interchangeably and some researchers do not distinguish them in practical use. Plutchik defines emotion as *"the person's overall feeling that can be influenced by (among others) context, past experience, recent experiences, personality, affect, and the net cognitive interpretation of these influences"* [21]. In contrast, Bentley et al defines affect as *"a short term, discrete, conscious subjective feeling that may have an influence upon a person's overall emotion"* [4], supported by e.g. [29].

that is an integral blend of hedonic (pleasure–displeasure) and arousal (sleepy–activated) values" [27]. However, a person is not able to make this "split" of his/her experienced core affect and express emotions directly in terms of the two axes of the core affect [27]. In this paper will use the core affect model and refer to the two axes as *Valence and Arousal.*

Self reporting emotions
Different methods for self-reporting have been proposed. Rolls emotions diagram [22], the Affect Grid [25] based on the core affects and the Self Assessment Manikin (SAM) shown in the sidebar, [15] are well-known examples. The SAM dimensions for pleasure (valence) and arousal are shown in Figure 1. Depending on the experimental design, self-reporting methods may be used either during or after the stimulus. Both designs may cause problems as discussed in the previous section.

Biometric measures
Biometrics encompasses measures such as facial expressions, skin conductance (GSR), heart rate, brain activity (EEG), respiratory changes or pupil dilation. Some, like EEG and respiration are quite intrusive and time-consuming to capture and analyse. Although yielding high-quality results, EEG requires the respondent to have 10-20 electrodes attached to the scalp and go through a lengthy calibration process. Heart rate and pupil dilation are more easily accessible, but can be hard to interpret, because other factors, such as cognitive load or light intensity can cause similar reactions. In contrast, GSR data is relatively easy to obtain and analyse. Furthermore, GSR only requires two electrodes to detect, usually fixated on the index and middle finger of the respondent [2],[3],[11].

As demonstrated by [16] GSR is linearly correlated with arousal, but does not capture the valence dimension. The valence can be obtained using detection of facial expressions, e.g. based on Action Units described by Ekman [8] using the Facial Action Coding System (FACS).

Method

Based on these considerations, we will investigate if and how GSR can reliably be used to estimate respondents' affective arousal response to video stimulus. We will furthermore use the GSR data to obtain an objective measure of the disruptive effects of self-reporting. As GSR can only generate information about the arousal dimension, we will use the SAM scale for self-reporting the valence during the stimulus.

Experimental setup
We let 16 test participants watch the Academy Award winning short-film *Helium* [33] for a duration of approximately 20 minutes. Meanwhile GSR was measured continuously to estimate the degree of arousal. They watched the movie individually on a computer monitor. The facilitator was present, but sat behind a screen to minimize any influence on the respondents. The subjective experiences from nine of the subjects (the intervention group) were captured by self-reporting via the SAM scale displayed on the monitor every three minutes. The movie was paused during the interruption. The remaining seven subjects formed a control group and watched the movie without interruptions. Thus, the experiment has a between-subject design. The GSR data is gathered for both intervention and control groups and used to estimate periods and scenes stimulating high arousal responses (denoted phasic peaks). The respondents controlled the

---

SAM. In 1985 Lang proposed a pictogram-based self-reporting scale called the "Self Assessment Mannequin" or SAM [15]. It comprises three scales for valence, arousal, and dominance. The arousal and valence pictograms are shown below. It has been widely used since.

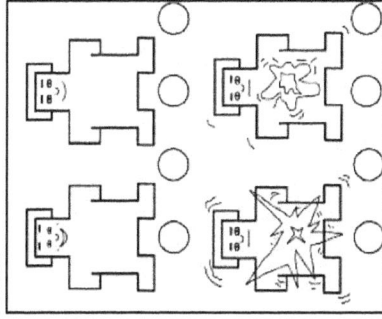

Figure 1. The first points of the SAM scale for self-reporting pleasure (valence) and arousal. Reproduced from [15]

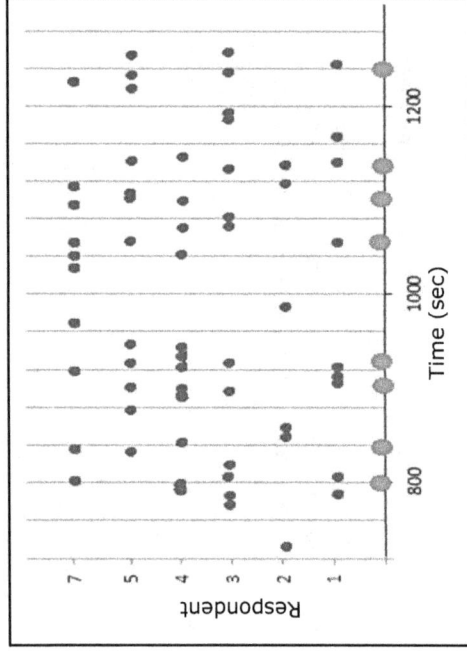

Figure 2. Arousal peaks for the control group from 750 seconds and onwards. A purple dot denotes an individual peak and the orange dots indicates where 3-5 respondents peaked in the same 10 sec interval.

Figure 3 in the sidebar shows the raw GSR data from the 9 respondents in the intervention group. An analysis of the data reveals that all intervention group members indeed peak at all interruptions and these peaks are also the most dominant.

To further investigate the effect, the average *recovery time* is calculated (31.5 seconds). The result is shown in Figure 4 the sidebar in the following page. Inspecting the remaining peaks for the intervention group, we found only a limited agreement with the control group. At the 10 second threshold described above only one co-occurring event was identified. Increasing the threshold to 15 secs, we found only four of eight events co-occurring with the control group.

duration of the interruptions, which were typically less than ten seconds. The overall experience and attitude towards the video content of the intervention and control groups were collected post-test using the "Movie Evaluation Measure" (MEM) scale described in [14] and scales designed to capture the empathy and identification with the characters in the movie [5], [13].

Results

The GSR data was captured using the Shimmer3 sensor [32] and recorded through the iMotions Biometric Research Platform [10]. Approximately 23 minutes of data sampled at 104 Hz were recorded for each person. The data analysis was carried out via the Ledalab Matlab Toolbox [2], [3] and focused on peak detection of the phasic driver. A peak denotes a high arousal event and the 15 highest peaks from each test person were extracted and used in the analysis.

Results of the GSR peak detection

The peaks detected from the control group were aggregated and resulted in the identification of eight common high-arousal emotional events during the movie. We define a high arousal event when at least half of the respondents peak within the same 10 sec interval. This is shown in Figure 2 below.

All events took place in the second half of *Helium* and were found to match scenes in the film, where a high emotional response could be anticipated. These events were then compared to the intervention group.

The figure shows an example of the **raw GSR data** from the intervention group. The vertical lines indicate the self-reporting events. These are spaced 180 seconds apart. The horizontal gridlines are the conductance levels and are spaced 2 micro Siemens apart. The disruptive effect of the self-reporting events is easily seen as all respondents peak at the vertical lines. Note the large individual differences between the individual respondents (coloured curves).

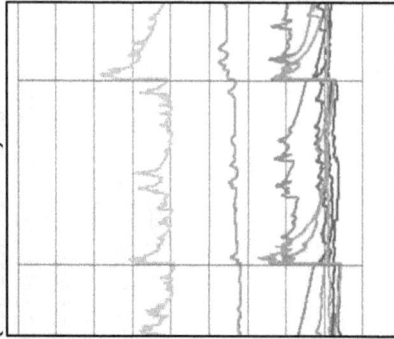

Figure 3. Excerpt from the raw GSR response for the intervention group.

The Recovery time is defined as the time it takes for the GSR intensity to return to the level it was before a peak event. The boxplot shows shows the recovery time for the interruption peaks for the intervention group. The median is 30.1 sec and the quartiles (24.5 and 35.6 secs) are quite close indicating a high agreement between respondents.

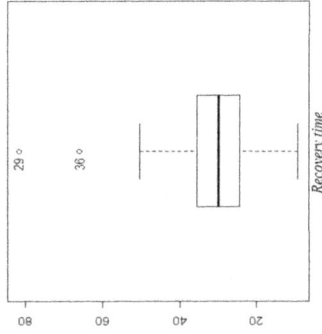

Figure 4. A boxplot of the intervention group's recovery time

Attitudes towards the movie and characters

As mentioned in the previous section we carried out a post-test investigation of the respondents' attitudes towards *Helium*. The purpose was to discover any differences between the control and intervention groups' experiences. We used scales developed by [5], [13], [14]. The scales have been individually validated, but not in combination and not in the present context. We carried out a Cronbach's Alpha (CA) test to verify the overall internal reliability. [17] recommends a CA value not less than 0.75 and preferably above 0.80. The combined post-test questionnaire showed a CA of 0.80 after minor adjustments. The corrected item-total correlation (r) should be 0.4 or higher [17], which is also the case here (r=0.4).

We defined two subcategories when analysing the questionnaire data; "*Assessment of Helium*" (cat1) and "*Empathy and Identification with Characters*" (cat2). The questionnaire statements were then analysed according to these. A two-tailed unpaired T-test (equal variances) was carried out for the two categories. These showed a difference between the control and intervention group for both categories. For cat1 we found a strong tendency (t = -2.09, p = 0,055) and for cat2 a significant difference (t = -2,21, p = 0,043) at a significance level of 0.05. In both cases the intervention group expressed a less positive attitude.

Respondents' comments

An exit interview showed that a majority of the intervention group accepted the interruptions and expressed a positive attitude towards them. Some would even accept more interruptions. However, a few voiced their irritation, but all tolerated the interruptions "*due to the experimental context*".

Discussion

This section discusses the implications of the findings presented in the previous section.

Detecting emotion events by GSR peaks

The respondents' GSR data varied considerably, both the intensity and the number of peaks as can be seen in Figures 2 and 3. This is to be expected, as there can be a factor 10 in difference of the intensity across different persons [11]. However, the peak detection algorithms are based on the fluctuations (the phasic driver) and robust to this [2],[3],[11]. Likewise, it has been shown that the emotional experience can vary considerable for different persons experiencing the same media [12]. This could be a problem and call for a within-subject experimental design. However, we judge the present design is able to reliably show the effects of the disruptions caused by the self-reporting scheme. The high agreement between respondents' *recovery time* shown in Figure 4 is an indication of this. Overall, we accept the GSR data as a reliable indicator for detecting high arousal events.

Assessment of respondents' subjective attitudes

Attitudes were collected post-test via validated questionnaires. Results showed the intervention group expressed a less positive attitude both towards the movie in general and regarding the empathy and identification they experienced with the characters. We found statistical evidence for this, despite the small sample. During the exit interview a majority of the intervention group respondents expressed a positive attitude towards the interruptions. This is a paradoxical result and can probably be ascribed to pleasing effects. However, the finding emphasises the negative consequences of the disruptions: Even though respondents apparently did not mind the interruptions, they still expressed less empathy with the movie characters. Therefore, we accept the finding that interruptions indeed have an overall effect and cause a less positive experience.

Self-reporting

Our focus was not on the method chosen for the self-reporting task nor on the results. Only the intervention group self-reported their emotions, so no comparisons can be made. Rather, the goal was to investigate the *act* of self-reporting. Therefore, we did not analyse the results captured by the SAM scale any further. However, the choice of the SAM scale can be questioned as other more recent self-reporting methods, such as CAAT may be less intrusive [7]. Care should therefore be taken in the choice of scale, whether it is applied during or retrospective to the screening.

Choice of Helium

Helium was chosen due to its cinematic qualities (it was the 2014 Academy Award winner for short films) and its relative short duration. Furthermore, we expected a high degree of identification and empathy towards *Helium's* main characters. This was important, as we used these parameters to gauge the experience. Material from a movie database specifically designed for emotion elicitation may have been used instead [31]. It has the advantage of containing carefully selected clips, already proven to stimulate specific emotions. However, this would lead to showing several clips without a coherent narrative and thus lower the ecological validity. Furthermore, all respondents were native Danish speakers and we preferred a Danish language stimulus to avoid any biases.

Conclusion

Even though the study only includes a limited number of participants, we conclude that interruptions induced by the self-reporting approach have a negative effect on respondents. This is supported by the biometric data showing identical high arousal events for all intervention group members, as well as the subjective responses gathered after the experiment. In addition, we found consistent evidence of a 30 second recovery time after interruptions, indicating that disruptive effects are persistent over a prolonged period of time.

We were able to identify common events with high emotional response from the GSR data across the control group, which indicates this indeed is a reliable measure for automated detection of objective emotional responses to media. As GSR recordings is a cost-effective and low-intrusive measure, we recommend using this for future automated detection of emotional events for audience research of media. This could be investigated in a larger follow-up study, for example in combination with automatic detection of facial expressions.

What's Next? This work should be seen as a step towards the ultimate goal of developing objective, cost-effective and non-intrusive measures for affective media research. Ultimately such a scheme may be used remotely.

As such, GSR has proven to be a promising candidate for finding high intensity scenes through arousal detection. Future steps could be to further automate GSR analysis and aggregate data from several respondents in real time for direct feedback to facilitators and other stakeholders. This should be done in a large-scale experiment. As a next step automated facial expression analysis could be integrated and used in a similar manner for affective valence. Thus, inline self-reporting could in time become redundant.

Acknowledgements

We wish to thank DR (the Danish Broadcasting Corporation) and Aalborg University for financial support of the work presented here. We are also grateful to our respondents, who donated their time and efforts to the experiment. Finally, we thank the support staff at iMotions for their quick and valuable help.

References

1. Backman, E., Snell, S., Muller, J., Lindhé, T., Sterner, M., Braathen, L., Andresen, S., Heiselberg, L. and Wieland, J. L. (2010) Emotionelt fokus for kvalitativ metode: Optimering og effektivisering af kvalitative metoder til analyse af respondenters emotioner i forbindelse med evaluering af tv-indhold. Technical report, YLE, SVT, NRK, DR.

2. Benedek, M. (2010). Analysis of eda data using ledalab. "http://www.ledalab.de/download/Analysis of EDA data using Ledalab.pdf"

3. Benedek, M. and Kaernbach, C. (2010). A continuous measure of phasic electrodermal activity. Journal of neuroscience methods, 190(1):80_91.

4. Bentley, T., Johnston L., Baggo, K. (2005). Evaluation using Cued-Recall Debrief to Elicit Information about a User's Affective Experiences. OzCHI 2005 proceedings.

5. Boerner, S., Jobst, J. (2013) Enjoying theater: The role of visitor's response to the performance. Psychology of Aesthetics, Creativity, and the Arts, Vol 7(4), pp391-408

6. Cacioppo, J. T., Berntson, G. G., Larsen, J. T., Poehlmann, K. M., and Ito, T. A. (2000). The psychophysiology of emotion. Handbook of emotions, 2:180_191.

7. Cardoso, B., Santos, O., & Romão, T. (2015). On Sounder Ground: CAAT, a Viable Widget for Affective Reaction Assessment. In Proc. 28th Annual ACM Symposium on User Interface Software & Technology (pp. 501-510). ACM.

8. Ekman, P., Friesen, W. V., and Hager, J. C. (1978). Facial action coding system: a investigator's guide. CA: Consulting Psychologists Press.

9. Healy, J. (2015) Physiological Sensing of Emotion. The Oxford Handbook of Affective Computing edited by Calvo, D'Mello and Kappas. Oxford University Press. 206-216

10. iMotions (2016). iMotions Biometric Research platform http://imotionsglobal.com/ (visited April 2016)

11. iMotions (2015). What is GSR? The Definite Guide. WWW link visited January 2016. https://help.imotions.com/attachments/token/IM6WR HbQ9HakX1Gf6RT1ssoqJ/?name=iMotions_Guide_GS R_2015.pdf

12. Jantzen, C. and Vetner, M. (2008). Underholdning, emotioner og personlighed: Et mediepsykologisk perspektiv på underholdningspræferencer. MedieKultur.

13. Kaufman, G. F., & Libby, L. K. (2012, March 26). Changing Beliefs and Behavior Through Experience-Taking. Journal of Personality and Social Psychology

14. Knobloch-Westerwick, S., Gong, Y., Hagner, H., and Kerbeykian, L. (2013). Movie evaluation measure [psyctests database record]

15. Lang, P. J. (1985). The Cognitive Psychophysiology of Emotion: Anxiety and the Anxiety Disorders. Hillsdale, N.J. Lawrence Erlbaum.

16. Lang, P.J. (1995). The Emotion Probe: Studies of motivation and attention. American Psychologist, 50(5), 372-385

17. Lounsbury, J. W., Gibson, L. W., and Saudargas, R. A. (2006). Scale development. Psychology Research Handbook: A Guide for Graduate Students and Research Assistants, 2nd ed. Sage, Thousand Oaks, CA, pages 125_146.

18. Lyle, J. (2003). Stimulated Recall: a report on its use in naturalistic research. British Educational Research Journal, Vol. 29, No. 6.

19. Plutchik, R. (1980). A general psycho evolutionary theory of emotion. Emotion: Theory, research, and

experience Vol. 1: Theories of emotion, pp. 3-33. New York: Academic.

20. Plutchik, R. (2001). The Nature of Emotions. American Scientist, Vol. 89, pp. 344-350

21. Plutchik, R. (2003). Emotions and Life: perspective form psychology, biology and evolution. American Psychological Association.

22. Rolls, Edmund T. (2000). The Brain and Emotion. Oxford University Press.

23. Rosenberg, E. L. and Ekman, P. (1994). Coherence between expressive and experiential systems in emotion. Cognition & Emotion, 8(3):201_229.

24. Russell, J. A. (1980). A circumplex model of affect. Journal of personality and social psychology, 39(6):1161.

25. Russell, J. A., Weiss, A., & Mendelsohn, G. A. (1989). Affect grid: a single-item scale of pleasure and arousal. Journal of personality and social psychology, 57(3), 493.

26. Russell, J. A. (1997). How shall an emotion be called? Circumplex model of personality and emotions.

27. Russell, J. A. and Barrett, L. F. (1999). Core affect, prototypical emotional episodes, and other things personality and social psychology, 76(5):805.

28. Russell, J. A. and Mehrabian, A. (1977). Evidence for a three-factor theory of emotions. Journal of research in Personality, 11(3).

29. Russell, J. A. (2003) Core Affect and the Psychological Construction of Emotion Psychological Vol. 110, No. 1, 145–172

30. Schachter, S. and Singer, J. (1962). Cognitive, social, and physiological determinants of emotional state. Psychological review, 69(5):379.

31. Schaefer, A., Nils, F., Sanchez, X., & Philippot, P. (2010). Assessing the effectiveness of a large database of emotion-eliciting films: A new tool for emotion researchers. Cognition and Emotion, 24(7), 1153-1172

32. Shimmer (2014b). Shimmer3 gsr+ unit. http://www.shimmersensing.com/shop/ shimmer3-wireless-gsr-sensor.

33. Walter, A. (2014). Shortfilm Helium. Imdb Entry: http://www.imdb.com/title/tt3346410/ The full movie can be viewed on youtube: https://www.youtube.com/watch?v=mQQr1i-o9to (links visited April 2016)

REFLEX:
Face Micro-Expression Recognition System for TV Content Curation

Paula Falco

IIT Institute of Design
Chicago, IL 60654, USA
paulafalco@gmail.com

Christina Noonan

IIT Institute of Design
Chicago, IL 60654, USA
noonan.christina@gmail.com

Ge Cao

IIT Institute of Design
Chicago, IL 60654, USA
caoge09@gmail.com

Permission to make digital or hard copies of part or all of this work
for personal or classroom use is granted without fee provided that
copies are not made or distributed for profit or commercial
advantage and that copies bear this notice and the full citation on the
first page. Copyrights for third-party components of this work must
be honored. For all other uses, contact the Owner/Author.
Copyright is held by the owner/author(s).
TVX'16, June 22-24, 2016, Chicago, IL, USA
ACM 978-1-4503-4067-0/16/06.
http://dx.doi.org/10.1145/2932206.2932427.

Abstract

REFLEX is a service that reads and translates emotions
through facial micro-expressions using a recognition
system and an integrated content curating service.
Using a camera attached to the user's television,
REFLEX can recommend content based on these micro-
expressions to help improve the user's current mood.
(Ex. If the user is feeling sad, comedic content would
be recommended by the service) The system is
connected to several content providers accessible to
the user within a unified interface. The camera will
persistently track the user's expressions throughout the
content viewing experience; therefore enhancing the
data used to track such emotions.

Author Keywords

Reflex; micro-expression; feeling; camera recognition;
second-screen; TV content curation.

ACM Classification Keywords

H.0: GENERAL; H.1.1 Systems and Information Theory; H.1.2 User/Machine Systems; H.3.5 Online Information Services; H.5.1 Multimedia Information Systems; H.5.2 User Interfaces

Introduction

REFLEX is a service that reads and translates emotions through facial micro-expressions using a recognition system and a unified integrated curating service. The micro-expressions are captured by a cellphone camera or small camera that can be attached to the television. REFLEX understands and recommends what type of TV content would be best for the user to watch, helping the user shift from the current feeling state to a new feeling state. When capturing the micro-expression, the algorithm in the system will do the analysis of what content needs to be displayed on the user's content menu, helping them change their current state of mood. (Image 1) The whole system is integrated, granting the user access to several provider accounts into one interface. The camera will keep tracking the user's facial expressions while they watch the TV content as well, mapping and enhancing the data bank. Based on these records, REFLEX can make better choices for the user in the future, providing better recommendations and a more personalized experience. For the first concept, we used the ten most popular genres and matched them with emotions. (Image 2) For example, some people may experience happiness when they watch horror movies, REFLEX will keep that in record. The next time when REFLEX thinks this user wants to experience that feeling of happiness again, it may recommend them to watch a horror movie.

Research

According to Nielsen's report[1], nearly 60% of media consumers watch TV and use the Internet simultaneously. How to take advantage of this behavior and create an interaction that is seamless to the user was the main point of the research. Participants

included in the primary research study consisted of 16 individuals from different groups: Single; Single with Roommate; Married; Lives with children; and Lives with parents. From some of the interviewed subjects, we found that a second screen is supposed to help users engage with a primary screen instead of distracting their attention from it (visual distribution). The interaction should be redesigned. Also, most second screens are just synchronizing content with the TV screen. Instead of showing the exact same content on the phone, what if we used the second screen to communicate people's feelings with TV content? We feel that there is a great potential in this area. The main findings/insights were:

• Adults that live alone usually watch video on a TV or computer.

• Users leave the TV on to keep themselves company. - Users choose a certain type of content based on events (parties, dinners, background), and their interests.

• Easy access technologies for cognitive search on mood panel and other features are welcome.

• Users need to search through multiple streaming service platforms to find the perfect entertainment. There is an overlap of content among these services, and the ranking and preferences are not connected.

Data Synthesis

To understand our future users, we created a 2x2 framework, where we could easily distribute them and create personas. (Image 3) The four axes were named as Novice, Guru, Group, and Self. The Novice cluster refers to users that don't watch TV or movie content regularly, and can be considered a blank canvas. The Novice user is to be the opposite from the Guru user. The Guru user watches TV or movies regularly, not to mention their own curation methods and rituals. The other axes are people that watch TV with friends/family, or alone.

facial recognition, where the main user's face would be recognized, and then expression recognition would feed the system with information. The user is now set to start using the product.

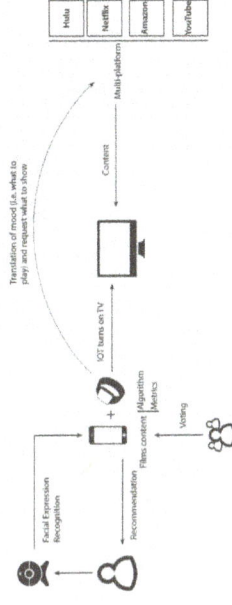

Figure 1: REFLEX System Flow.

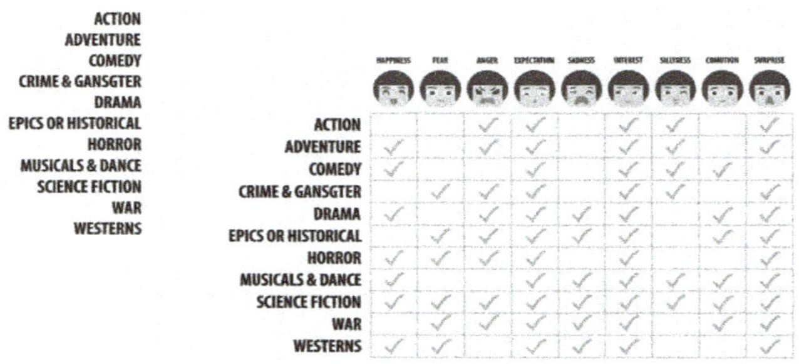

Figure 2: Default Internal Rating System.

Personas Scenarios

The methodology of analysis used was the 5 E's: Entice, Enter, Engage, Exit and Extend. The persona chosen to complete the user journey concept was Josh. (Image 3) Josh represents 45% of our market target and it's important to develop a story around his routine. (Image 4) Entice: Tired, not happy about coming back to an empty house - used to a busy and loud fraternity **and would like** background noise. Josh is also depressed because he didn't have time to exercise. Enter: Upon arriving home, the REFLEX camera reads his face expressions, and turns on automatically at the beginning of the next comedy show. The device has learned how to cheer up its owner. Engage: Josh prepares dinner and spends the rest of the night doing homework, but enjoys cheesy jokes of the shows, too. It helps him feel like there's more activity in his home, so he's not so alone. Exit: Josh's REFLEX knows he loved the show and wants more of that night on weekdays. Extend: REFLEX learns over time how to understand its user, introducing new shows and movies.

Blueprint (Image 5)

A service blueprint was developed to match target user's needs. The distribution of data was helpful to gain an understanding when the interactions would occur more often and with which section of the product.

Digital Prototype (Image 6-14)

Two types of prototypes were developed, one for the TV2 and another for the cellphone. A first time user will be able to create an account and add all TV content providers accounts to it. The system will pair all duplicates and match rankings and lists; whish is how the system understands the user's preferences in genres and specific movies. The second step would be

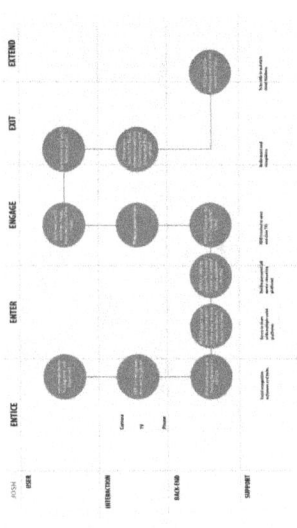

Figure 5: Blue Print

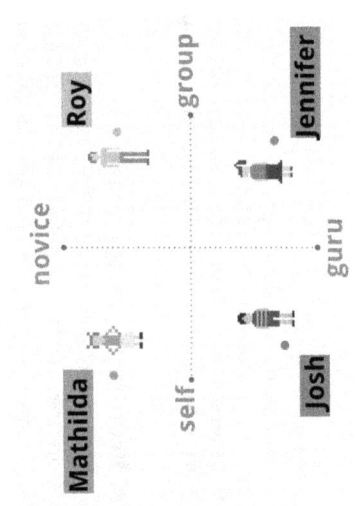

Figure 6: Splash Screen

Figure 7: Landing Screen

Figure 3: Data Syntesis: Personas

Figure 4: Persona Scenario: Josh

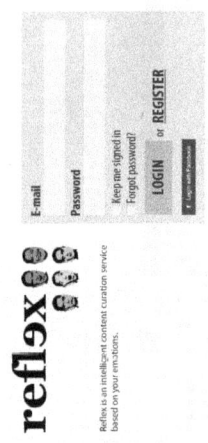

Figure 8: Login Screen

Figure 9a: Account Setup

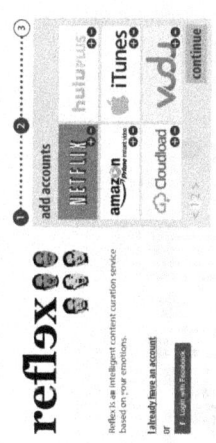

Figure 9b: Account Setup

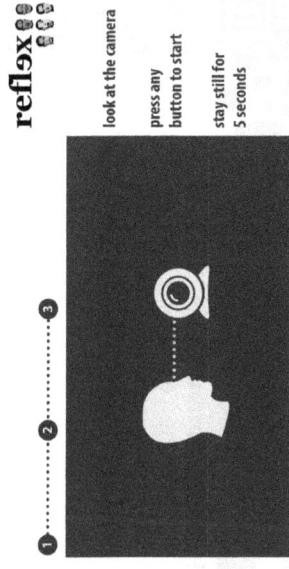

Figure 10a: Face Recognition

Figure 10b: Face Recognition

Figure 11a: Expression Recognition

Figure 13: Movie Stream

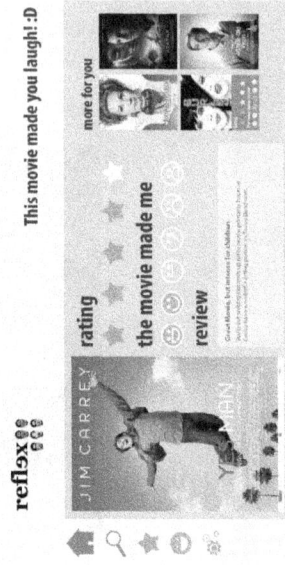

Figure 14: Rating System

Conclusion

The interaction between users and devices continues to evolve over time. We are not expected to watch TV as our grandparents once did, however, we do expect at the same level, a mix of fantasy and facts that digital devices have been providing to us. Millennials are more often finding themselves so connected to a device, that the necessity of one to understand their feelings is eminent. We believe REFLEX is a jump to that connection.

Acknowledgments

We thank all the volunteers, interviewees, professors and teammates, who wrote and provided helpful comments on previous versions of this document.

References

1. NIELSEN Reports. Retrieved February 7, 2016 from http://www.nielsen.com/us/en/insights/reports.html
2. TV Prototype. Retrieved February 7, 2016 from http://tinyurl.com/ReflexTV
3. Cellphone Prototype. Retrieved February 7, 2016 from http://tinyurl.com/ReflexPHONE

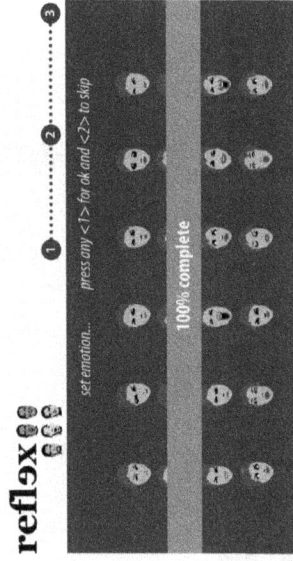

Figure 11b: Expression Recognition

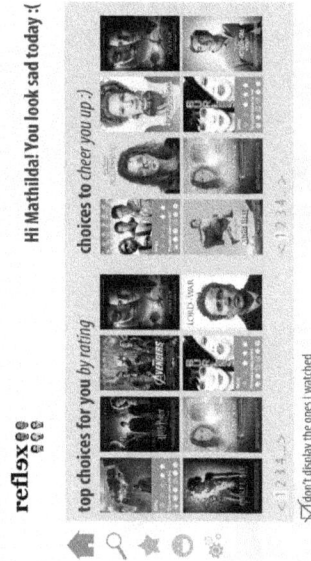

Figure 12: Home Page

4. BRS Labs: Behavior Recognition Without Human Intervention. Retrieved February 7, 2016 from http://www.brslabs.com/
5. Animetrics: Facial Recognition & Identity Solution. Retrieved February 7, 2016 from http://animetrics.com/technology/frapplications.html/

6. Fogg, B. J. Persuasive Technology: Using Computers to Change What We Think and Do. Amsterdam: Morgan Kaufmann, 2003. Print.

Towards Media for Wellbeing

Carla Bernardino
LaSIGE, Faculdade de Ciências
Universidade de Lisboa
1749-016 Lisboa, Portugal
carlasofb@gmail.com

Hugo Alexandre Ferreira
Instituto de Biofísica e Engenharia
Biomédica, Faculdade de Ciências,
Universidade de Lisboa
1749-016 Lisboa, Portugal
hhferreira@fc.ul.pt

Teresa Chambel
LaSIGE, Faculdade de Ciências
Universidade de Lisboa
1749-016 Lisboa, Portugal
tc@di.fc.ul.pt

Permission to make digital or hard copies of part or all of this work for personal or classroom use is granted without fee provided that copies are not made or distributed for profit or commercial advantage and that copies bear this notice and the full citation on the first page. Copyrights for third-party components of this work must be honored. For all other uses, contact the Owner/Author. Copyright is held by the owner/author(s). TVX'16, June 22-24, 2016, Chicago, IL, USA ACM 978-1-4503-4067-0/16/06. http://dx.doi.org/10.1145/2932206.2933565

Abstract

Media has the potential to generate attitudes and emotions and influence our state of mind, our health, happiness and sense of wellbeing, and it is becoming pervasive in our lives. This paper explores the potential of advances in neuroscience and informatics to support people in becoming more aware of and in regulating their emotional states and sense of wellbeing, which is aligned with the aims and scope of positive computing. It presents main motivation and concepts, a preliminary user survey to learn about the relation of people with media, in this context, and Media4Wellbeing, an interactive media application being designed and developed to access, explore and visualize media based on their impact on emotional states and sense of wellbeing, using physiological sensors.

Author Keywords

Affective Computing; Positive Computing; Emotions; Wellbeing; Health; Consciousness, Awareness; Interactive Media Access; Video, Audio, Music; Visualization; Physiological Sensors.

ACM Classification Keywords

H.1.2. User/Machine Systems: Human factors; H.5.1. Information Interfaces and Presentation (e.g. HCI): Multimedia Information Systems – video, audio; H.5.2. (e.g. HCI): User Interfaces – graphical user interfaces, input devices and strategies, user-centered design.

Introduction

Nowadays, there are many types of media widely available. Technological developments and the ubiquity of the internet made it easier and more common to access, and even to create and share, different types of information, like text, pictures, music and video. Media, and especially video and audio, has the potential to generate attitudes and emotions and influence our state of mind. Emotions permeate people's daily lives, influencing the way we think and act, our health, our happiness and our sense of wellbeing [5].

The current advances in neuroscience and informatics hold the potential to support people in becoming more aware of and in regulating their emotional states and sense of wellbeing, which is aligned with the aims and scope of positive computing [3]. Calvo and Peters [3] proposed this concept to inform the design and development of technology to support psychological wellbeing and human potential. In fact, digital technology has become ubiquitous, having an unprecedented major impact in how we live, with the capacity to increase stress and suffering, but also the potential to improve the wellbeing of individuals, society, and the planet. The latter is part of a larger emerging public concern for how our digital experience is impacting our emotions, our quality of life, and our happiness, reflecting a broader renaissance of focus on humanistic values in different disciplines. Neuroscientists have been studying the physiology of healthy minds and the role of empathy, mindfulness and meditation, supporting a growing attention to emotional intelligence and positive psychology [18] to improve wellbeing. Technology has the potential to play a significant part in these multidisciplinary efforts to support wellbeing and human flourishing.

This paper explores this potential, presenting: main motivation and concepts concerning emotional impact, wellbeing and physiological signals and sensors; a preliminary user survey to learn about the relation of people with media, their perceived influence on emotional states and wellbeing, and previous experience and expectation for supporting technologies; and Media4Wellbeing, an interactive media application that is being designed and developed to access, explore and visualize media based on their impact on emotional states and sense of wellbeing, using physiological sensors for biofeedback. This work involves a multidisciplinary cooperation of computer science and biomedicine in our Faculty and the Universal Values Museum in Portugal. The museum aims to promote these values, through culture, education, technology, R&D and entertainment. Media and technology to raise people's awareness about human values, emotional reactions and wellbeing aligns with these goals in the context of a museum and beyond, in daily life.

Models of Emotion and Wellbeing

There are two main classes or models of emotion: 1) The Dimensional Model [16] defines a spatial circumplex with two dimensions: arousal (intensity) and valence (polarity); 2) The Categorical Model defines emotions as discrete states. Ekman [8] identified 6 basic categorical emotions based on facial expressions recognized across cultures: anger, disgust, fear, joy, sadness and surprise. There is a correspondence of categorical emotions in Russel's circumplex (e.g. positive valence and high arousal as happiness, with low arousal as calmness): Fig.1. A third dimension can be considered: dominance, which transla-tes the subjective feeling of control. These are actually the 3 dimensions considered in the subjective Self-Assessment Manikin scale (SAM) [10,19]. Plutchick [13] used both categorical and

Rationale for the Media4WellBeing Emotional Model

Criteria: 1) emotional richness; 2) cover positive emotions associated with media and wellbeing; and 3) be simple enough to enable an automatic identification of emotions.

Chosen set: the 6 basic emotions of Ekman; appreciation (or admiration) and interest, completing 8 Plutchick's (Plut.) emotions; and the other two intensities in Plut's model associated with happiness (the only positive in Ekman's): ecstasy and serenity; enthusiasm/ inspiration/motivation to match users' choices in [5]; contentment, serenity and boredom (both also in Plut's) and sleepiness, to guarantee good coverage of Russel's dimensional model [16,20] (>= 2 per quadrant), to ease the identification of categorical emotions based on arousal and valence (which detection can be supported by sensors or self reports using SAM [19]).

dimensional models and defined a 3D model (polarity, similarity, intensity) with 8 primary emotions: 6 like in Ekman's, plus: anticipation/ interest, and trust/admiration, represented around the center, in colors, with the intensity as the vertical dimension (in 3 levels).

Positive emotions are among wellbeing factors, others include engagement and meaning (the 3 dimensions of positive psychology [18,5], later extended with relationships and achievement). Other factors refer to self-awareness, mindfulness, empathy, and compassion [3]. One of the challenges in this type of approach refers to how wellbeing and emotions can be measured. Social sciences and medicine have been addressing this since the last decades and recent technological advances in computing have been contributing to the field [3].

The Role of Physiological Signals and Sensors

In most studies, emotional assessment corresponds to identifying the user's arousal and valence (or pleasure) that vary in a continuum [16]. Different electrophysiological signals have been used, related both to the central and the peripheral nervous systems, the latter comprising the somatic and the autonomous nervous systems. It is then possible to assess both emotions for which the user is, or is not, consciously aware of.

Electroencephalographic (EEG) signals, that translate the electrical activity of the brain (part of the central nervous system along with the spinal cord), and their frequency components (delta, theta, alpha, beta and gamma) have been associated with arousal, valence and dominance [14]. EEG signals have also been shown to assess attentive and meditative states [1].

Electrocardiography (ECG) measures electrical activity of the heart (the autonomous nervous system). Heart rate (HR) and its variability (HRV) can translate a state of relaxation and a state of anxiety/stress. The electrodermal activity (EDA), aka galvanic skin response (GSR), like ECG is a widely used signal in emotion recognition. It translates skin conductance, related with skin sweat, under control of the autonomous nervous system, allowing to assess stress and conflicting situations, but is dependent on external factors such as temperature. Other signals that have been used for emotion detection include: Electromyography (EMG), both for conscious and unconscious cognitive processes, used to detect facial expression, and anxious or arousal states; Electro-oculography (EOG), used to monitor eye movements, to detect anxiety, and withdrawal [4]; and Electroglottography (EGG) measuring the electrical flow across the larynx, to depict emotional content of speech.

These signals have been used individually, but multimodal approaches have shown improved accuracies in emotion detection [9].

Related Work

In [5,12] we made a literature review concerning models and representations of emotions, the emotional classification of movie content (through content analysis) and their impact on viewers (through physiological measures), video access and visualization, and eliciting and visualizing emotions. In summary, some related work exists in these different perspectives, but not so much allowing to access movies and videos based on emotions. In our own work, in iFelt, we classified and accessed videos based on the emotions felt by the user while watching them, using three biosensors (respiration, heart rate, and galvanic skin response) to detect five of the basic emotions (all but surprise) of Ekman's, and represented them with Plutchick's color model in the movie spaces and timelines in the interface. In Movie Clouds [6], we presented an interactive web application that adopts the tag cloud paradigm (for the power, flexibi-

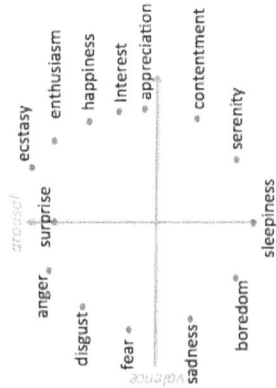

Figure 1: Emotional model in Media4WellBeing

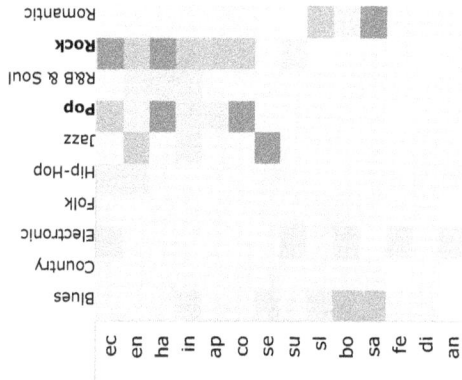

Table 1: emotions (Tab.2) vs **music** genres in the survey: from dark to light (freq>=50%, 40%, 25%, 0%)

lity, engagement and fun usually associated with clouds) and allows to access, explore and watch movies through the information conveyed in their contents, mainly audio, and subtitles, where most semantics is conveyed, and with a focus on emotions expressed in the subtitles, detected as the mood of the music, and felt by the user. In our previous application [7], electrocardiographic signals were used to modulate the videogaming experience: the more anxious the user was (higher HR) the more challenging the game would become.

In addition we summarize here works from other authors that have been addressing technological support for emotions and wellbeing. Several use virtual reality (VR) and sensors to influence the experience, and often involve games [7,9,14]. [1,2] address mindfulness and meditation. The group of Picard on affective computing has extensively used sensors and cameras, to help deal with such factors as stress, sleep, attention, associated with wellbeing e.g. [17], but usually not with media. Exceptions include facial expression analysis to detect users' reactions (liking) to video ads [11]. Video and music are among the media most used to improve emotional states. In [6] we present work related with accessing music based on mood, as a consumer. Rothera [15] explored the perspective of the creator, through Flutter, an experimental app that uses music to help those experiencing the loss of a loved one, by expressing themselves in a safe, positive environment.

User Survey

This section presents the objectives, method and results of a user survey conducted to learn about: 1) the relation of people with media, concerning their habits, attitudes, awareness and preferences; 2) how these relate to their pursuit of emotional states and wellbeing; and 3) their previous experience and expectations concerning applications that provide emotional feedback or use physiological sensors.

Method and Results

The survey was based on an online questionnaire distributed to students, professors, and staff in several faculties of the University of Lisbon. It had seven sections mostly based on closed questions with the opportunity to specify 'other' options and to provide additional comments. We present a summary of the results of first 37 participants, focusing only on the aspects that more closely inform this work in progress. Section 1:Demographic Information: Participants age:21-56 (mean:29.4; std:10.3), 68% Fem 24% from informatics, 16% biology, 16% languages, and others from areas like chemistry, math, psychology and art. 19% completed high school, 5% had a professional course, 32% BSc, 30% MSc, and 14% PhD degrees.

Section 2:Media: Music, followed by videos/movies, and by images/photographs, were the media they perceived to access more often to alter their wellbeing. Their motivation to use media: to feel more relaxed (86.5% agree or totally agree); feel well (78.3%); more motivated (70.2%); work better (62.1%); be informed (59.4%); feel more creative (51.3%); deal with difficult situations (48.6%); influence others positively (43.2%); improve myself as a person (37.8); feel better with myself (35.1%); and learn to know myself (29.7%).

Section 3:Music: 62.1% often or always turn to music to alter their emotional state (21.6% do it sometimes). 70.3% mentioned they take into account their emotional state when selecting a music. Table 2 presents the genres they more often associate with each emotion, and the genres perceived to be listened to more often (pop and rock) are associated with most positive emotions. And they associated ecstasy/excitement, enthusiasm/inspiration/motivation, joy/happiness, and interest with

1.(ec)stasy/excitement;
2.(en)thusiasm/inspiration/motivation;
3.(ha)ppiness/joy;
4.(in)terest; 5.(ap)preciation;
6.(co)ntentment/satisfaction;
7.(se)renity;
8.(su)rprise; 9.(sl)eepiness;
10.(bo)redom; 11.(sa)dness;
12.(fe)ar; 13.(di)sgust; 14.(an)ger.

Table 2: List of emotions in Media4WelBeing, with synonyms, ordered by valence (+-) and arousal (+--+)

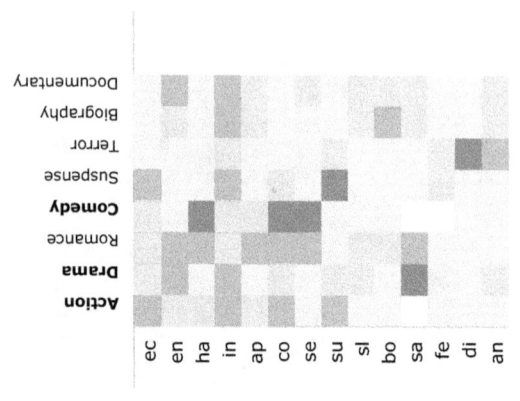

	Action	Drama	Romance	Comedy	Suspense	Terror	Biography	Documentary
ec								
en								
ha								
in								
ap								
co								
se								
su								
sl								
bo								
sa								
fe								
di								
an								

Table 3:emotions (Tab.2) vs movie genres in the survey: from dark to light (freq>=50%, 40%, 25%, 0%)

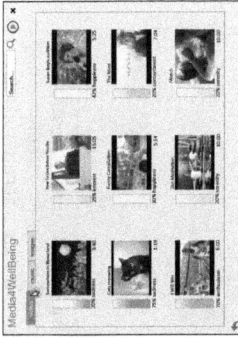

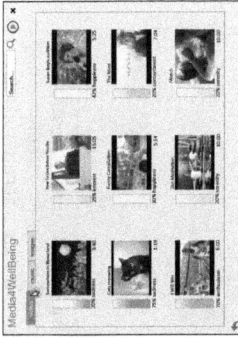

Figure 2: videos (music or images) with dominant emotion in colored sidebar. User selects to watch.

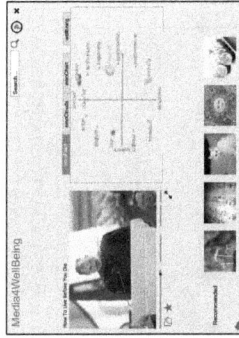

Figure 3a:emoPaint: emotions painted as colored dots in circumplex while watching the video. Current emotion highlighted in circumplex & timeline. Painting synchronized & as index to video (e.g. to moments I felt serene).

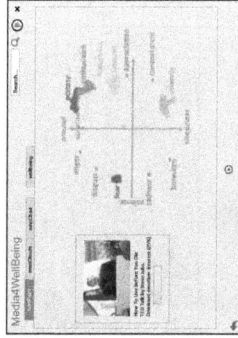

Figure 3b:emoPaint: final painting accessed afterwards, as summary of emotional experience: static or animation of emotional evolution.

3 of their favourite musics. Section 4:Videos: Movies (54% often and always) and music videos (22%) are the most visualized videos. Other options were: talks, motivating clips and short films. 13.5% often or always turn to video to alter their emotional state (40.5% do it sometimes). 48.6% take into account their emotional state when selecting a movie. Table 3 presents the genres they more often associated with each emotion, and the genres perceived to be watched more often (comedy, action and drama) are associated with most positive emotions, with the exception of sadness, also associated with drama, along with enthusiasm/inspiration/motivation and interest. Emotions associated with 3 of their favourite movies were the same as for music (above), i.e. high-arousal positive emotions.

Section 5:Activities of wellbeing: more often: sports (24% often or always, 30% sometimes), and meditation (11% often, 5% sometimes). Other options were yoga and massages. The most used media for sports were music and videos; and music for meditation. Section 6: Media and wellbeing. They were asked to name 3 examples of media use: 1) where they experienced commotion; 2) that contributed to their engagement, their sense of value, purpose or meaning; and 3) that were impactful to them, contributing to their wellbeing, in life. The associated emotions were enthusiasm/inspiration/ motivation, and sadness (in commotion), and the most selected factors for wellbeing were: positive emotions, engagement, meaning in life, self-awareness, empathy and mindfulness (conscious presence).

Section 7:Technology and wellbeing. Not many applications were reported as previously used to choose and access media to provide wellbeing (open questions). Exceptions related with exercise and yoga. Only one application with biosensors was mentioned to have been used, to monitor exercise and running. Positive aspects:

the biometric information; negative: being commercialized and security. Anyway, 51.3% found it (very) interesting that a media access application would take into account emotional states and wellbeing. The top desired ways of having the emotional state and wellbeing information displayed were colored graphics (46%) and text (16%). Most participants not having an opinion. The use of physiological sensors was perceived as (very) interesting by 43.2%, to help having better measurements, self-awareness, and a scientific basis.

Media4WellBeing

It is an interactive media application being designed and developed to access, explore and visualize media based on their impact on emotional states & sense of wellbeing. We are taking the results of the survey into account, and experimenting different interactive features and sensors.

Emotional Model

In previous work on emotional impact of movies [5,12], we adopted Ekman's model of emotions, because it was a well accepted model covering the emotions recognized across cultures, was richer than the bi-dimensional model on its own (valence and arousal) as adopted by most related work, and had a fairly small number of emotions to still make feasible some automation in recognition. However, in a user study [5], we realized that in movies there is a tendency in preference towards positive emotions like fun, feeling good, happiness, and mostly, imagining, dreaming, inspiration and motivation, aligned with the goals of positive psychology, to lead a happy life [18]: through positive emotions, engagement and meaning; results confirmed and extended in the recent survey reported here. The rationale for the Media4WellBeing emotional model is summarized in the sidebar of page 2, presented in Fig.1 around Russel's circumplex, and listed in order in Table.2.

Conclusion and Perspectives

This paper addressed the potential of using computational and physiological technology to support accessing media based on their impact on emotions and wellbeing. The user survey allowed to learn about the relation of people with media, and provided more evidence to confirm that media is accessed to change emotional states, preferred media include mainly music and videos and are associated with positive emotions in a range going beyond basic emotions like Ekman's (confirming [5]). Participants did not have much experience with applications providing emotional feedback or using physiological sensors, but were open to such technology and shared a couple of expectations or intended features in line with our suggestions. Based on these results and our previous work [5,12,7], Media4Wellbeing is being designed and developed to access, explore and visualize media based on their impact on emotional states & sense of wellbeing.

Future work includes: 1) further developments in automatic recognition of emotional states and sense of wellbeing and refinement of the models adopted to represent them, to provide effective detection and adequate alignment with emotions and states that the user identifies, which is often a rich model [5]; 2) refine, evaluate and extend the interactive features designed for Media4Wellbeing, in order to provide useful and interesting means for accessing, exploring and visualizing media that can impact users emotions and wellbeing and help them raise their self awareness and regulation; and 3) further explore areas of application that can benefit from this technology, including those of the Universal Values Museum and in everyday life.

Acknowledgements

This work is partially supported by FCT through LaSIGE Multiannual Funding, and by FCT and MCE Portugal (PIDDAC) under the grant UID/BIO/00645/2013.

Self-Awareness and Physiological Sensors

We are adopting physiological sensors, mainly for EEG, ECG and GSR signals. Main emotions are associated with levels of valence and arousal, and focus/concentration and meditative states to brain frequencies. These will allow to provide feedback to the users and catalog media. As a complement and to help refine the automatic detection, users will be able to provide self assessments, based on categorical emotions, or levels of arousal and valence, through e.g. SAM [19].

Interactive Media Access Based on Emotions & Wellbeing

Users are able to access media. In a first phase we are focusing mainly in short videos, including inspirational clips and music clips, and ambient images, music or videos to help create the atmosphere for meditation. As an extension to previous work on iFelt [5,12] and Movie Clouds [6], we are using colors and tag clouds to represent emotions felt along time when experiencing media, and as overviews of aggregate information summarizing the experience. Colors have a mapping with emotions, and tag clouds represent their semantics and frequency, and thus, their impact. Emotions can be represented in the circumplex for increased awareness about the essence and proximity of emotions. Emotional feedback can be provided while users are experiencing media (for instant feedback) synchronized with the media (if video or audio), or afterwards (for a more immersive media experience clear of additional info that could distract and influence the natural impact) as an overview or summary: in a static image or an animation of the emotional experience. The overviews can be used to represent media by the emotional experience or impact, and be used to index them. Figs.2-6 illustrate some examples. The emotional information will also allow to enrich recommendations, but not a central component in our approach.

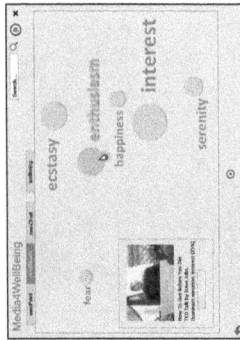

Figure 4: emoCloud: tag cloud of the emotional experience. Info about the video on the left.

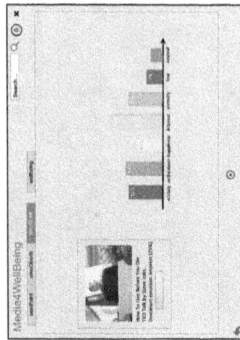

Figure 5: emoChart: emotions presented in colored charts.

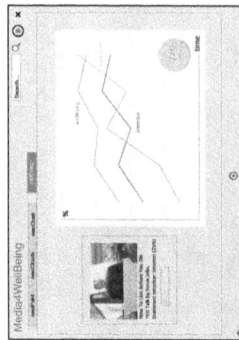

Figure 6: wellbeing, attention & meditative states: graphic along time and final aggregated values. May help identifying media that help reaching intended states. Will tend to be simpler and more subtle, when accessing the media, aligned with context of use.

References

[1] Ahani, A., Wahbeh, H., Nezamfar, H., Miller, M., Erdogmus, D. and Oken, B. 2014. Quantitative change of EEG and respiration signals during mindfulness meditation. *Journal of Neuroengineering and Rehabilitation*, 11(1), p.1.

[2] Amores, J., Benavides,X., and Maes, P. 2016. PsychicVR: Increasing mindfulness by using Virtual Reality and Brain Computer Interfaces. *CHI 2016*.

[3] Calvo, R., and Peters, D. 2014. *Positive Computing: Technology for Wellbeing and Human Potential*, MIT Press.

[4] Calvo, R. and D'Mello, S., 2010. Affect detection: An interdisciplinary review of models, methods, and their applications. *Affective Computing, IEEE Transactions on*, 1(1), 18-37.

[5] Chambel, T., Oliveira, E., and Martins, P. 2011. Being Happy, Healthy and Whole Watching Movies that Affect our Emotions. In *Proceedings of ACII 2011*, 4th Int. Conf. on Affective Computing and Intelligent Interaction, Springer. 35-45.

[6] Chambel, T., Langlois, T., Martins, P., Gil, N., Silva, N., and Duarte, E. 2013. Content-Based Search Overviews and Exploratory Browsing of Movies with MovieClouds. *Int. Journal of Advanced Media and Communication*, InderScience, 5(1): 58-79.

[7] Chec, A., Olczak, D., Fernandes, T. and Ferreira, H. A. 2015. Physiological computing gaming: Use of electrocardiogram as an input for video gaming. In *Proc. of the Int. Conf. on Physiological Computing Systems (PhyCS)*,157-163.

[8] Ekman, P. 1992. Are there basic emotions? *Psychological Review*, 99(3):550-553.

[9] Kim, J., Bee, N., Wagner, J. and André, E. 2004. Emote to win: Affective interactions with a computer game agent. *GI Jahrestagung*, 1, 159-164.

[10] Lang, P. J. 1980. Behavioral treatment and bio-behavioral assessment: computer applications. In

[11] McDuff D., Kaliouby R., Demirdjian, D., and Picard R.W. 2013. Predicting Online Media Effectiveness Based on Smile Responses Gathered Over the Internet. *The 10th IEEE Int. Conf. on Automatic Face and Gesture Recognition*, Shanghai, China.

[12] Oliveira, E., Martins, P., and Chambel, T. 2013. Accessing Movies Based on Emotional Impact. *ACM/Springer Multimedia Systems Journal*, ISSN: 0942-4962, 19(6), Nov. 559-576.

[13] Plutchik, R. 1980. *Emotion: A psychoevolutionary synthesis*. Harper & Row New York.

[14] Reuderink, B., Mühl, C. and Poel, M. 2013. Valence, arousal and dominance in the EEG during game play. *International journal of Autonomous and Adaptive Communications Systems*, 6(1), 45-62.

[15] Rothera, A. 2015. *Flutter*. Retrieved Apr 17, 2016 from: http://www.alexrothera.com/flutter

[16] Russell J. 1980. A circumflex model of affect. *Journal of Personality and Social Psychology*, 39:1161–1178.

[17] Sano, A. 2015. *Measuring College Students' Sleep, Stress, Mental Health and Wellbeing with Wearable Sensors and Mobile Phones*. MIT PhD Thesis, Oct.

[18] Seligman, M., and Csikszentmihalyi, M. 2000. Positive Psychology: An Introduction. *American Psychologist*, 55 (1): 5-14.

[19] The PXLab Self-Assessment-Manikin Scales. Retrieved Apr 17, 2016 from: http://irtel.uni-mannheim.de/pxlab/demos/index_SAM.html

[20] Wolf. G. 2009. Measuring Mood – Current Research and New Ideas. In Quantified Self, Retrieved Apr 17, 2016 from: http://quantifiedself.com/2009/02/measuring-mood-current-resea/

J. B. Sidowski, J. H. Johnson, & T. A. Williams (Eds.), *Technology in mental health care delivery systems*. 119-137. Norwood, NJ: Ablex.

4th International Workshop on Interactive Content Consumption (WSICC'16)

Britta Meixner
FX Palo Alto Laboratory, Inc., Palo Alto, CA, USA,
meixner@fxpal.com

Werner Bailer
JOANNEUM RESEARCH, Graz, Austria,
werner.bailer@joanneum.at

Maarten Wijnants
Hasselt University - tUL - iMinds, Diepenbeek, Belgium,
maarten.wijnants@uhasselt.be

Rene Kaiser
JOANNEUM RESEARCH, Graz, Austria,
rene.kaiser@joanneum.at

Joscha Jäger
Merz Akademie, Stuttgart, Germany,
joscha.jaeger@merz-akademie.de

Rik Bauwens
Vlaamse Radio- en Televisieomroeporganisatie (VRT), Brussels, Belgium,
rik.bauwens@vrt.be

Frank Bentley
Yahoo, Sunnyvale, CA, USA,
fbentley@yahoo-inc.com

Permission to make digital or hard copies of part or all of this work for personal or classroom use is granted without fee provided that copies are not made or distributed for profit or commercial advantage and that copies bear this notice and the full citation on the first page. Copyrights for third-party components of this work must be honored. For all other uses, contact the owner/author(s).

Copyright is held by the author/owner(s).
TVX'16, Jun 22-24, 2016, Chicago, IL, USA
ACM 978-1-4503-4067-0/16/06
http://dx.doi.org/10.1145/2932206.2932424

Abstract

WSICC has established itself as a truly interactive workshop at EuroITV'13, TVX'14, and TVX'15 with three successful editions. The fourth edition of the WSICC workshop aims to bring together researchers and practitioners working on novel approaches for interactive multimedia content consumption. New technologies, devices, media formats, and consumption paradigms are emerging that allow for new types of interactivity. Examples include multi-panoramic video and object-based audio, increasingly available in live scenarios with content feeds from a multitude of sources. All these recent advances have an impact on different aspects related to interactive content consumption, which the workshop categorizes into Enabling Technologies, Content, User Experience, and User Interaction. The resources from past editions of the workshop are available on the http://wsicc.net website.

Author Keywords

workshop; multimedia; content consumption; interaction; HCI; user experience;

ACM Classification Keywords

H.5 [Information Interfaces and Presentation]: [Multimedia Information Systems]

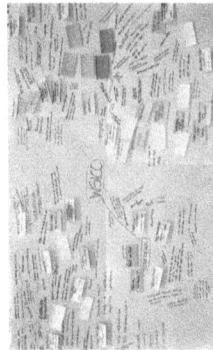

Figure 1: Mindmap result of WSICC'13.

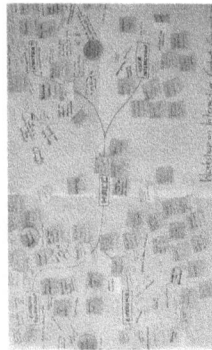

Figure 2: Mindmap result of WSICC'14.

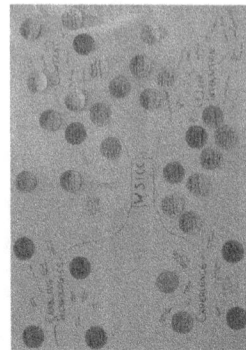

Figure 3: Mindmap result of WSICC'15. Available in better resolution on the website. All mindmaps are currently being digitized by the organization team to be further analyzed for scientific publication of the workshop results.

Workshop Aims and Scope

WSICC's objective is to provide a highly interactive discussion forum that allows capturing a comprehensive view on the research area it addresses. During the workshop, an overview on new content interaction concepts, research activities, and future challenges in this area is concluded and documented. An interdisciplinary view on the topic is compiled by contributions from technical research, conceptual work, user-centric studies, industry developments, as well as experimental showcases. In other words, the workshop aims to examine and evaluate new forms of content interaction by discussing the field along three axes:

- **Recent technological advances** that enable new forms of audiovisual content interaction;
- **User-centric studies** that evaluate new types of audiovisual content interaction, especially in the realm of societal trends and media consumption paradigm shifts;
- **Studies from industry** considering and evaluating user needs and the impact of advances in this area.

As another way to look at the workshop's scope, as also done in previous workshop editions, the research landscape was characterized along four dimensions (see Figures 1–3): Enabling Technologies, Content, User Experience, and User Interaction. The following taxonomy defines the workshop's scope by examples:

Enabling Technologies: This dimension searches for technology and tools for consumption and authoring of interactive content, especially:

- Techniques for content adaptation, rendering, and converting for a wide variety of devices and delivery channels;

- Approaches for interactive personalization and recommendation (e.g., Virtual Director approaches);
- Research on interactive and adaptive content delivery (e.g., MPEG-DASH);
- Studies on immersive devices, such as VR goggles, wearables, and cyber-physical systems;
- Novel approaches in content production technology (object-based or format-agnostic);
- Novel media coding technologies that inspire interactivity (e.g., H.265/HEVC tiling);
- Tools to infuse interactivity in passive content;
- Approaches for media synchronization and orchestration.

User Experience: The user experience dimension explores research on quality of user experience (QoE) theory and evaluations, the impact and effects of interaction on perceived quality, the role of the audience, and the role of social context. It investigates the effect of increased interactivity and user engagement, empowerment, but also overload and distraction, e.g.:

- Studies and foundations from the social sciences;
- Evaluation of user needs regarding personalized content consumption;
- Research on collaborative and community-based multimedia consumption and creation;
- Exploration of immersive audiovisual content;
- Approaches for inclusion and improved accessibility (e.g., automatic content enhancement for special needs).

Beyond these four areas, the workshop welcomes discussion on best practices, future challenges, and research road-mapping in the area of interactive content consumption.

Workshop Format

WSICC has developed an interactive workshop format to stimulate both networking and knowledge transfer among the participants. The full day workshop is an active forum to discuss research challenges, methodologies, and results in a field that maintains relevance in an ever-changing landscape of new device types, content forms, and growing technical infrastructure. Both media consumption needs and habits are constantly evolving.

More than half the time is reserved for discussion. The chairs aim at establishing an informal atmosphere, inspired by the basic principles of the Barcamp format[1]. In an active moderating role, they make sure the workshop's underlying questions are discussed, answered as far as possible, and documented. Nevertheless they allow some flexibility in order to meet the interest of the audience spontaneously, as appropriate.

Both organizers and participants collect inputs on large flip charts along multiple question dimensions throughout the day. During the workshop, the audience is encouraged to contribute, and especially to comment existing inputs (*I'd love to collaborate on this!... This has already been solved in my project!*). The outcome of the workshop is summarized on a poster for presentation at the main conference, based on the inputs accumulated on the flip charts. A publication summarizing the workshop results is submitted to http://ceur-ws.org/. Further, the WSICC

---

[1]See http://en.wikipedia.org/wiki/BarCamp (accessed 03/25/16)

User Interaction: This dimension analyzes novel interaction approaches, concepts, and paradigms. Thereby, interactivity might be interpreted both as computer mediated communication as well as human computer interaction. Interest lies in:

- Research on natural interaction techniques;
- Experiments on multi-modal interaction and social signal processing, especially gesture control and speech recognition;
- Studies on social interaction during content consumption and mobile content consumption;
- Methods of feedback for user control, including visual, acoustic, and tactile interaction;
- Studies on lean-forward interaction trends and joint interaction of larger groups;
- Studies on the balance between active (lean-forward) and passive (lean-backward) content consumption.

Content: The content dimension researches new types and forms of interactive content, such as:

- Content from gaming or the mobile, AR and VR domains;
- Live and recorded materials;
- Data representation formats for interactive content;
- Adaptable content and content of variable length;
- High-quality and ultra-high definition content;
- Content captured by novel types of sensors (e.g., 3D, panoramic, or 360° video).

Figure 4: Fishbowl discussion at WSICC'13.

Figure 5: Fishbowl discussion at WSICC'14.

Figure 6: Fishbowl discussion at WSICC'15.

regarded an essential part of the workshop as they allow discussion upon hands-on experience. This session shall establish an understanding of everybody's work, focus, and interest;

- Three research paper based *talks*: In line with the informal atmosphere, questions are allowed during the talks;
- Two sessions in *fishbowl* discussion format, focusing on aspects raised during WSICC. In a nutshell, there is a limited number of active seats. If you want to say something, you have to take an empty active seat or wait for one to become available. This format of a dynamically changing working panel has empirically proven to work well for discussions among experts on concrete questions. Attendants of previous WSICC editions readily understood the fishbowl approach and were able to quickly adopt its methodology (see Figures 4-6);
- *Concluding session* where the group revisits the knowledge and insights that have been collected throughout the day; conclusions are summarized and a best paper award is given to one contribution regardless of its type.

Organizing Committee

The bios of the organizational team can be found below. The team represents the workshop's target audience in the areas of technical research, social sciences research, and industry. Team members complement each other well and are dedicated to contribute to the research community by conducting their respective activities. The team continues to stimulate discussions within the community, using social media platforms.

organization team givs a short overview of inputs from previous editions (mind maps) and from the MTAP Special Issue *Interactive Media: Technology and Experience* to process the results of the last years for the scientific community.

Some of the results from previous editions are accessible via the workshop website[2] which already contains the 2014 proceedings[3], a link to the 2015 proceedings published on CEUR-WS.org[4] (2013's were part of the adjunct EuroITV proceedings[5]), and visual impressions[6,7,8].

WSICC'16 consists of the following sessions:

- *Welcome*, introduction to the workshop format, and presentation of workshop aims;
- Interactive *participant introduction* in Barcamp style (name, affiliation, role, 3 keywords/hashtags);
- *Invited keynote* about emerging research related to one or more of the focus areas of the workshop, as an input to the interactive sessions (see Figures 7-9);
- A *guided tour* session to kick-start the poster/demo session, each contribution is introduced via a short 5 minute pitch in front of the poster or demo;
- The *poster and demo session*: Posters are based on short paper contributions; technical demos are

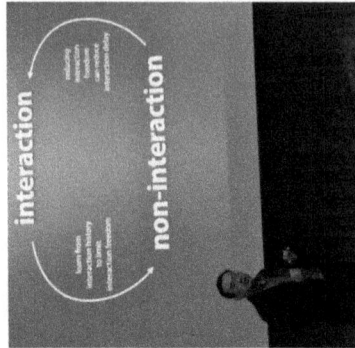

Figure 7: WSICC'13 keynote by Wei Tsang Ooi.

Figure 8: WSICC'14 keynote by Marian F. Ursu.

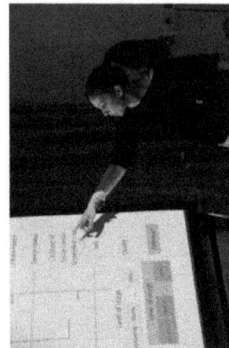

Figure 9: WSICC'15 keynote by Judith Redi.

---

[2] http://wsicc.net/ (accessed 03/25/16)
[3] http://wsicc.net/2014/Proceedings-WSICC-2014.pdf (accessed 03/25/16)
[4] http://ceur-ws.org/Vol-1516/ (accessed 03/25/16)
[5] https://sites.google.com/a/euro-itv.org/2013/program/proceedings (accessed 03/25/16)
[6] https://www.flickr.com/photos/49520289@N04/sets/72157634457839167/ (accessed 03/25/16)
[7] https://www.flickr.com/photos/49520289@N04/sets/72157645061214918/ (accessed 03/25/16)
[8] https://www.flickr.com/photos/49520289@N04/albums/72157651953922744 (accessed 03/25/16)

Figure 10: Group photo at WSICC'13.

Figure 11: Group photo at WSICC'14.

Figure 12: Group photo at WSICC'15.

Britta Meixner[9] is a researcher at FX Palo Alto Laboratory. She received her PhD degree in computer science at the University of Passau, in 2014 (Title of the thesis: "Annotated Interactive Non-linear Video Software Suite, Download and Cache Management"). Britta is a reviewer for the MTAP Journal (Springer), an associate chair for TVX2015 and TVX2016, and was a (co-)organizer of WSICC at TVX2014 and TVX2015. She is an awardee of the ARD/ZDF Förderpreis "Frauen + Medientechnologie" 2015 (2015 Award "Women + Media Technology', granted by Germany's public broadcasters ARD and ZDF) and received a Honorable Mention recognition from the ACM SIGMM in the 2015 SIGMM Outstanding PhD Thesis Award.

Werner Bailer[10] is a key researcher of the audiovisual media group at the DIGITAL – Institute of Information and Communication Technologies at JOANNEUM RESEARCH in Graz, Austria. He received a degree in Media Technology and Design in 2002 for his diploma thesis on motion estimation and segmentation for film/video standards conversion. His research interests include digital film restoration, audiovisual content analysis and retrieval, as well as multimedia metadata. He is contributing to multimedia standardization activities in the W3C, MPEG and EBU/AMWA FIMS.

Maarten Wijnants[11] is a post-doctoral researcher affiliated with iMinds, a research institute founded by the Flemish Government in Belgium. He received his PhD in computer science at the Expertise Centre for Digital Media, the ICT research institute of Hasselt University, in 2010. The title of his PhD dissertation is "Service Quality Improvement and User Experience Optimization by Introducing Intelligence in the Network". Maarten is currently participating in the EU FP7 ICoSOLE project, where he is involved in the work package dealing with playout and (adaptive) delivery. His research interests include multimedia networking, network bandwidth brokering, QoS, QoE, Web-based technologies and HTTP adaptive streaming. Maarten has been a TPC member for the two most recent editions of the international WEBIST conference.

Rene Kaiser is a key researcher for JOANNEUM RESEARCH and has been involved in a number of European projects dealing with automation of content production such as NM2, APOSDLE, FascinatE, TA2 and Vconect. His research focus is on *Virtual Director* software, on automating the selection/editing of live video streams by executing cinematographic behavior models in real-time. Rene is a PhD student at TU Graz and head of the Knowledge Management Forum Graz. He has co-organized every WSICC edition since 2013. Rene also organized the Interactive and Immersive Entertainment and Communication Special Session at MMM'12. He is part of a group hosting the annual PhD cooperation workshop at the i-KNOW conference, active member and E-Letter chair of IEEE STCSN, and co-organizer of the Barcamp Graz, a yearly 3-day *unconference* which is an interactive and open discussion format.

Joscha Jäger[12] is a researcher at Merz Akademie Stuttgart and interface designer at yovisto GmbH in Potsdam, Germany. His research covers Web-based

[9]https://www.linkedin.com/in/britta-meixner-35892545 (accessed 03/25/16)
[10]https://www.linkedin.com/in/wbailer (accessed 03/25/16)
[11]https://www.researchgate.net/profile/Maarten_Wijnants2 (accessed 03/25/16)

[12]https://de.linkedin.com/in/joschajaeger (accessed 03/25/16)

hypervideo technology, time-based interaction, and semantic video search interfaces. Joscha has a strong focus on film as information architecture, collaborative editing systems for non-linear film, and user-driven annotation systems. He is interested in finding new ways of distributed interaction with open video technologies and interfaces on the web. He co-organized WSICC at TVX2014 and TVX2015.

Rik Bauwens[13] attended Hogeschool Gent and obtained his MSc in Applied Engineering (Computer Science) in 2011. Thereafter, he studied English and music, whilst developing web applications for third parties. In 2012, he co-founded an e-learning project, followed by the development of a health care web application. He was responsible for R&D, design and database/server management. Rik is passionate about innovation in web technologies and new media. In 2014, he joined VRT Research & Innovation.

Frank Bentley[14] is a Principal Researcher at Yahoo in Sunnyvale, CA where he focuses on systems that use content to inspire communication as well as leads user research for the Search organization. Frank was the program chair for ACM TVX in 2015 as well as teaches Mobile HCI classes at MIT, on EdX, and at Stanford. He has built and studied a wide variety of mobile video applications as well as studied how people interact with mobile devices and online services while watching television.

Acknowledgements
The workshop is supported by the European Commission under the contract FP7-610370, "ICoSOLE – Immersive Coverage of Spatially Outspread Live Events". We also want to thank Santosh Basapur for his input to the workshop and his help during the review process.

---

[13]https://be.linkedin.com/in/rik-bauwens-8068123a (accessed 03/25/16)
[14]https://www.linkedin.com/in/frankbentley (accessed 03/25/16)

Design Methods for Persuasive Media Experiences

Tom MacTavish
Santosh Basapur
Illinois Institute of Technology
Institute of Design
Chicago, IL 60654, USA
[tomm, Basapur]@id.iit.edu

Permission to make digital or hard copies of part or all of this work for personal or classroom use is granted without fee provided that copies are not made or distributed for profit or commercial advantage and that copies bear this notice and the full citation on the first page. Copyrights for third-party components of this work must be honored. For all other uses, contact the Owner/Author.
Copyright is held by the owner/author(s).
TVX'16, June 22-24, 2016, Chicago, IL, USA
ACM 978-1-4503-4067-0/16/06.
http://dx.doi.org/10.1145/2932206.2932427

Abstract

Many theories and models have been generated from the fields of informatics, medicine, psychology, and sociology on the topic of persuasion to describe aspects of human behavior, human/computer interaction, and information systems involved in supporting behavior change. But, what specific methods should we select to design specific user experiences, especially for iTV experiences? In this workshop, we will seek and share perspectives on how to create user experiences for iTV and other media by building on BJ Fogg's initial description of a general user research and design method [1], draw from Harri Oinas-Kukkonen's Persuasive Systems Design model [2], and explore pragmatic approaches for creating user experiences design knowledge for aspects of iTV and Online Media.

Author Keywords

Persuasive design; behavior chang; iTV user experience design; iTV UX design; Media Experiences; Interactive Design Strategies.

ACM Classification Keywords

H.5.4. Information interfaces and presentation (e.g., HCI): K.8.0 Personal Computing: Serious Games

Introduction

This First International Workshop on "User Experience Design Methods for Persuasive ITV Experiences" provides a forum for sharing and evaluating advances in user experience research and design methods. The persuasive user experiences could be to create engaging media experiences to enable Healthy Living, Medication Adherence, Senior living etc. This workshop will be shaped by a clear focus on health and well-ness in home context and design methods relevant to media experience design prac-tices to persuade people in adoption and sustenance of wellness technology on inter-active media devices and platforms. We suggest that future workshops in this series should focus on other contexts such as Media Experiences for Environmental Sustain-ability and Green Living etc.

Motivation

Substantial investigations and new knowledge have been published in many fields associated with persuasive technology such as human/computer interaction, informatics, medicine, psychology, and sociology. While each discovery is useful in its own domain, we seek to move from the theory and models of separate disciplines toward integrated methods and techniques that can be used to design engaging user experiences. In this workshop, we seek to capture and clarify design methods for creating specific behavior change experiences. There are precedents from the field of persuasive technology that we would like to build on to create a more complete foundation for persuasive user experience design. Early work by BJ Fogg sought to offer pragmatic advice on designing for behavior change by identifying a modest target based on existing successes in behavior change [1].

Sunny Consolvo sought to clarify design strategies and their connection to theory [3]. Ahtinen, Aino et al proposed design approaches related to social features [4]. Shyam Sundar et al offered a more specific approach by exploring connections between Self Determination Theory and interaction design attributes [5]. From the field of multimedia learning, the work of Richard E. Mayer explores participant engagement and the need for cognitive learning [6]. Also, Dan Lockton, provides a pragmatic tool for supporting education about persua-sive techniques. His "Design with Intent" toolkit card deck was released in 2010 and will be further described in this forthcoming book on the same topic [7]. And, Susan Michie has captured the perspective of the Society of Behavioral Medicine in creating a behavior change technique taxonomy [8]. From a user experience design perspective, we see a need for more clear process of using methods and tools to elicit user involvement in articulating more effective embodiments and experiences to support behavior change.

Research on the interactive narratives and content that pulls people into the user experience is quite well explored in ITV space and its challenges are well documented by researchers at BBC and other fine institutes (9,10,11, and 12). But not many have written guidelines and/or design methodologies on how we might create experiences for people that will persuade them, through narratives and interactions, to change behaviors especially related to life style and wellness.

Workshop Plan

While workshop participants must be registered for the ACM TVX (2016) conference, they are not required to submit a paper. Those who are writing papers are re-quested to make submissions either as position papers (2-4 pages), research-in-progress papers (2-6 pages), or full research papers (6-12 pages) in the SIGCHI paper template format. The papers will be reviewed by the workshop organizers and selected according to their significance as well as their potential to inspire discussions. Page limits do not include references or bibliographic listings. The papers do not need to be anonymous and should be submitted to the organizers at Basapur@id.iit.edu or tomm@id.iit.edu

Format and schedule

1. 09:00 – 9:30 am -- Introductions and Overview of UX design methods
2. 09:30 – 10:00am -- Paper presentations
3. 10:00 – 10:15am -- Break
4. 10:15 – 11:00am -- Paper presentations
5. 11:00 – 12:00pm – Methods and Taxonomy workshop
6. 12:00 – 12:30pm -- Reflections, accomplishments and potential directions.

Expected Outcomes

a. A catalogue of methods, models, and techniques
b. A taxonomy discussion for media experiences for persuasion

c. An updated taxonomy of behavior change in the healthcare context
d. Identification of research areas that are newly described, need further exploration, or need re-evaluation.

Potential Technical Committee

a. Tom MacTavish, Assistant Professor, Illinois Institute of Technology - Institute of Design, Chicago, IL, USA
b. Santosh Basapur, Lecturer, Illinois Institute of Technology - Institute of Design, Chicago, IL, USA
c. Paula Falco, UX Architect Salesforce Inc
d. Christina Noonan, UX Design, Moment Design Consulting Inc.
e. Anijo Mathew, IIT Institute of Design
f. Pete Wendel User Experience lead, Walgreens
g. Etc

References

1) Fogg, BJ, "Creating Persuasive Technologies: An Eight-Step Design Pro-cess," Persuasive'09, April 26-29, Claremont, California, USA.

2) Oinas-Kukkonen, Harri and Harjumaa, Marja, "Persuasive Systems De-sign: Key Issues, Process Model, and System Features," Communications of the Association for Information Systems, March 2009, Volume 28, Article 28. Available at: http://aisel.aisnet.org/cais/vol24/iss1/28

3) Consolvo, Sunny; McDonald, David; Landay, James, "Theory-Driven De-sign Strategies for Technologies that Support Behavior Change in Everyday Life," CHI 2009, April 4–9, 2009, Boston, Massachusetts, USA.

Technique Taxonomy (v1) of 93 Hierarchically Clustered Techniques: Building an International Consensus for the Reporting of Behavior Change Interventions," http://ann. behav. med.

DOI 10.1007/s12160-013-9486-6, The Society of Behavioral Medicine, 2013

9) Marian F Ursu, Maureen Thomas, Ian Kegel, et al. 2008. Interactive TV Narratives: Opportunities, Progress, and Challenges. *ACM Trans. Multimedia Comput. Commun. Appl.* 4, 4: 25:1–25:39. http://doi.org/10.1145/1412196.1412198

10) R Michael Young and Mark Riedl. 2003. *Towards an architecture for intelligent control of narrative in interactive virtual worlds.* ACM, New York, New York, USA. http://doi.org/10.1145/604045.604108

11) Hartmut Koenitz. 2015. Design Approaches for Interactive Digital Narrative. In *Interactive Storytelling.* Springer International Publishing, Cham, 50–57. http://doi.org/10.1007/978-3-319-27036-4_5

4) Ahtinen, Aino; Isomursu, Minna; Mukhtar, Muzayun, "Designing Social Features for Mobile and Ubiquitous Wellness Applications," International Conference on Mobile and Ubiquitous Multimedia (MUM09), November 22-25, 2009 Cambridge, UK.

5) S. Shyam Sundar; Bellur, Saraswathi; and Jia, Haiyan, "Motivational Technologies: A Theoretical Framework for Designing Preventive Health Applications," Proceedings of the 7th International Conference, Persuasive 2012, Linkoping, Sweden, June 2012

6) Mayer, Richard E.; Heiser, Julie; Lonn, Steve, "Cognitive Constraints on Multimedia Learning: When Presenting More Material Results in Less Understanding," Journal of Educational Psychology, 2001, Vol. 93, No. 1, 187-198

7) Dan Lockton, http://designwithintent.co.uk 2015

8) Michie, Susan; Richardson, Michelle; Johnston, Marie; Abraham, Charles; Francis, Jill; Hardeman, Wendy; Eccles, Martin; Cane, James; Wood, Caroline, "The Behavior Change

Design Strategies for Interactive Digital Narratives

Hartmut Koenitz

University of Georgia
Athens, GA 30602, USA
hkoenitz@uga.edu

Author Keywords

Interactive Digital Narrative; Authoring; Narrative Design; Interactive Design Strategies.

Permission to make digital or hard copies of part or all of this work for personal or classroom use is granted without fee provided that copies are not made or distributed for profit or commercial advantage and that copies bear this notice and the full citation on the first page. Copyrights for third-party components of this work must be honored. For all other uses, contact the Owner/Author.

Copyright is held by the owner/author(s).

TVX 2016, June 22–24, 2016, Chicago, IL, USA
ACM 978-1-4503-4067-0/16/06.
http://dx.doi.org/10.1145/2932206.2932428

Abstract

Creating interactive digital narrative (IDN) experiences means to overcome a tradition dominated by conventions for non-interactive, static and pre-fixed narrative. Instead of "interactivizing" legacy structures, a more productive avenue is in the focus on specific design strategies for IDN. These approaches do afford a a different view towards the resulting manifestations – both form and context –, but also include a perspective on the changed role of the author.

ACM Classification Keywords

H.5.4. Information interfaces and presentation (e.g., HCI): Hypertext/Hypermedia; K.8.0 Personal Computing: Games

Introduction

Interactive digital narrative (IDN) poses a challenge for scholars and creative professionals alike. During the Narratology vs. Ludology debate in the early 2000s, game scholars not only rejected narratology as a framework to understand interactive works but also declared narrative as fundamentally incompatible with interactivity [8]. While Juul modified his extreme position shortly after, he and several other "ludologists" [1,2,7,9] continued to describe the relationship as problematic. Indeed, even proponents of IDN like Janet Murray [16,17] and Chris Crawford [5] view this new form of narrative expression as a challenge to potential creators. Murray understands digital media as unknown territory, as a medium that is being invented and necessities novel design approaches. She champions an iterative progression towards the future in that the most successful design strategies will shape the new medium and turn into conventions, similar to how early experiments in film have shaped that medium's conventions. Crawford, on the other hand, describes interactive narrative as a challenge that eclipses game design in complexity and expressive potential. He sees the necessity for a breakthrough work, an artistic milestone that clearly communicates the expressive potential, a Citizen Kane of IDN, and favors an Apollo space program-like effort by a an elite group.

In addition to these more generalized approaches, artists like Toni Dove and Emily Short, but also scholars/practitioners like Marc Cavazza [4], Michael Mateas [14], Nick Montfort [15], Michael Young and Mark Riedl [23], Celia Pearce [18], Nicolas Szilas [21] and many others have worked on the creation and understanding of IDN works. At the same time, IDN has been identified as a specific opportunity for online video and iTV [22].

Authorship and Narrative Design

The foci of research so far has been either on more generalized models or on concrete artifacts. From the perspective of prospective authors neither meet their needs for concrete and easily applicable design guidelines, as the former are too abstract while the latter are too specific. Work on the issue of "third-party" authorship beyond the scholar/practitioner is still in an early phase [11,20] and much more research is necessary. A promising avenue in this regard is the 'design as research' approach developed in HCI [3,6,19]

Workshop Plan

In this workshop, the participants are introduced to design approaches observed and refined in several years of teaching interactive narrative [10,13]. Specifically, the attendees will become familiar with the following preliminary design heuristics and apply them in practice:

- Cyberbardic principle
- Initial interest principle
- Continued motivation principle
- Opportunity magnitude principle

On this basis, groups of attendees will develop an interactive narrative. To jumpstart this aspect, a skeleton narrative will be provided. Finally, the workshop will discuss the results and implications for future research and the participants' own practice.

References

1. Espen J Aarseth. 1997. *Cybertext*. JHU Press.
2. Espen J Aarseth. 2012. A Narrative Theory of Games. 1–5. http://doi.org/978-1-4503-1333-9/12/05
3. Philip Agre. 1997. *Computation and Human Experience*. Cambridge University Press.
4. Marc Cavazza, Jean-Luc Lugrin, David Pizzi, and Fred Charles. 2007. *Madame bovary on the holodeck: immersive interactive storytelling.* ACM, New York, New York, USA. http://doi.org/10.1145/1291233.1291387
5. Chris Crawford. 2012. *Chris Crawford on Interactive Storytelling*. New Riders.
6. A Dunne and F Raby. 2001. *Design noir: The*

secret life of electronic objects.

7. M Eskelinen. 2001. The gaming situation. *Game Studies* 1, 1.

8. Jesper Juul. 1999. A clash between game and narrative. *Danish literature.*

9. Jesper Juul. 2001. Games telling stories. *Game Studies* 1, 1.

10. Hartmut Koenitz and Kun-Ju Chen. 2012. Genres, Structures and Strategies in Interactive Digital Narratives – Analyzing a Body of Works Created in ASAPS. In *Interactive Storytelling: 5th International Conference, ICIDS 2012, San Sebastián, Spain, November 12-15, 2012. Proceedings*, David Oyarzun, Federico Peinado, R Michael Young, Ane Elizalde and Gonzalo Méndez (eds.). Springer, Berlin, Heidelberg, 84–95. http://doi.org/10.1007/978-3-642-34851-8_8

11. Hartmut Koenitz and Sandy Louchart. 2015. Towards a Specific Theory of Interactive Digital Narrative. In *Interactive Digital Narrative*, Hartmut Koenitz, Gabriele Ferri, Mads Haahr, Digdem Sezen and Tonguc Ibrahim Sezen (eds.). Routledge, New York, 91–105.

12. Hartmut Koenitz. 2015. Towards a Specific Theory of Interactive Digital Narrative. In *Interactive Digital Narrative*, Hartmut Koenitz, Gabriele Ferri, Mads Haahr, Digdem Sezen and Tonguc Ibrahim Sezen (eds.). Routledge, New York, 91–105.

13. Hartmut Koenitz. 2015. Design Approaches for Interactive Digital Narrative. In *Interactive Storytelling.* Springer International Publishing, Cham, 50–57. http://doi.org/10.1007/978-3-319-27036-4_5

14. M Mateas and A Stern. 2005. Procedural Authorship: a Case-Study of the Interactive Drama Façade.

15. Nick Montfort. 2005. *Twisty Little Passages.* MIT Press.

16. Janet H Murray. 2012. Transcending Transmedia: Emerging Story Telling Structures for the Emerging Convergence Platforms. ACM, 1–6. http://doi.org/10.1145/2325616.2325618

17. Janet Murray. 1998. *Hamlet on the Holodeck: The Future of Narrative in Cyberspace.* The MIT Press, Cambridge.

18. Celia Pearce, Tom Boellstorff, and Bonnie A Nardi. 2011. *Communities of Play.* MIT Press.

19. Phoebe Sengers, Kirsten Boehner, Shay David, and Joseph Kaye. 2005. Reflective Design. ACM, 49–58. http://doi.org/10.1145/1094562.1094569

20. Ulrike Spierling and Nicolas Szilas. 2009. Authoring Issues beyond Tools. In *Interactive Storytelling: Second Joint International Conference on Interactive Digital Storytelling, ICIDS 2009, Guimarães, Portugal, December 9-11, 2009, Proceedings*, Ido Iurgel, Nelson Zagalo and Paolo Petta (eds.). Springer Berlin Heidelberg, Berlin, Heidelberg, 50–61. http://doi.org/10.1007/978-3-642-10643-9_9

21. Nicolas Szilas. 2010. Requirements for Computational Models of Interactive Narrative. 1–7.

22. Marian F Ursu, Maureen Thomas, Ian Kegel, et al. 2008. Interactive TV Narratives: Opportunities, Progress, and Challenges. *ACM Trans. Multimedia Comput. Commun. Appl.* 4, 4: 25:1–25:39. http://doi.org/10.1145/1412196.1412198

23. R Michael Young and Mark Riedl. 2003. *Towards an architecture for intelligent control of narrative in interactive virtual worlds.* ACM, New York, New York, USA. http://doi.org/10.1145/604045.604108

Author Index

Aguilar, Marc 43
Akahori, Wataru 123
Bailer, Werner 179
Basapur, Santosh 185
Bauwens, Rik 179
Becker, Valdecir 119
Bentley, Frank 69, 179
Bernardino, Carla 171
Broadbent, Matthew 135
Cao, Ge 163
Cason, Arielle 105
Cassany, David 43
Chambel, Teresa 171
Chan, Larry 105
Daemen, Jeff 129
de Feijter, Dimph 59
Dingler, Tilman 93
Dufourd, Jean-Claude 135
Falco, Paula 163
Falelakis, Manolis 49
Fernández, Sergi 43
Ferreira, Hugo Alexandre 171
Frantzis, Michael 49
Fuhrhop, Christian 135
Galpin, Adam 77
Garcia, Sarah E. 113, 115
Geelhoed, Erik 49
Glancy, Maxine 77
Hamilton, William A. 31
Hammond, Matt 83
Henze, Niels 13
Herder, Jens 129

Hirai, Tatsunori 123
Hong, Woneui 3
Huang, Derek 31
Inkpen, Kori 31
Jäger, Joscha 179
Jang, Jincheul 3
Jensen, Charlotte T. 155
Jessen, Anne Mette K. 155
Johns, Allie 77
Jørgensen, Lotte I. 155
Kaiser, Rene 49, 179
Kawamura, Shunya 123
Khan, Vassilis-Javed 59
Kim, Soomin 141
Knittel, Johannes 93
Koch, Cornelius 129
Koenitz, Hartmut 189
Ladwig, Philipp 129
Larsen, Lars B. 155
Laursen, Jeanette K. 155
Lee, Joongseek 147
Lee, Joonhwan 141
Lehr, David 25
Li, Jing 105
Lim, Hyunchul 147
MacTavish, Thomas 185
Mayer, Sven 13
McDonnell, Ryan 105
Meixner, Britta 179
Meredith, Joanne 77
Miccoli, Stefano 135
Miles, Rachel 105

Morishima, Shigeo 123
Murray, Janet 69, 105
Noonan, Christina 163
Oh, Changhoon 147
Oh, JongHwan 141
Park, Youkyoung 3
Plaumann, Katrin 25
Ramdhany, Rajiv 83
Rukzio, Enrico 25
Schiller, Fabian 135
Schlieski, Tawny 1
Seo, Jehwan 147
Suh, Bongwon 147
Tang, John C. 31
Tuominen, Ville 135
Ursu, Marian F. 49
van Gisbergen, Marnix 59
Venolia, Gina 31
Ventura Fierro, Rodrigo 13
Vinayagamoorthy, Vinoba 83
Voit, Alexandra 13
Wang, Zixuan 105
Weber, Dominik 13
Wiche, Roman 129
Wieland, Jacob L. 155
Wijnants, Maarten 179
Wilgen, Kai 129
Yi, Mun Yong 3
Yun, Hyun-Kyu 147
Zhao, Dapeng 3
Zillner, Jakob 31
Zwicklbauer, Miggi 135

www.ingramcontent.com/pod-product-compliance
Lightning Source LLC
Chambersburg PA
CBHW081524220326
41598CB00036B/6318